IN/SPECTRE

14

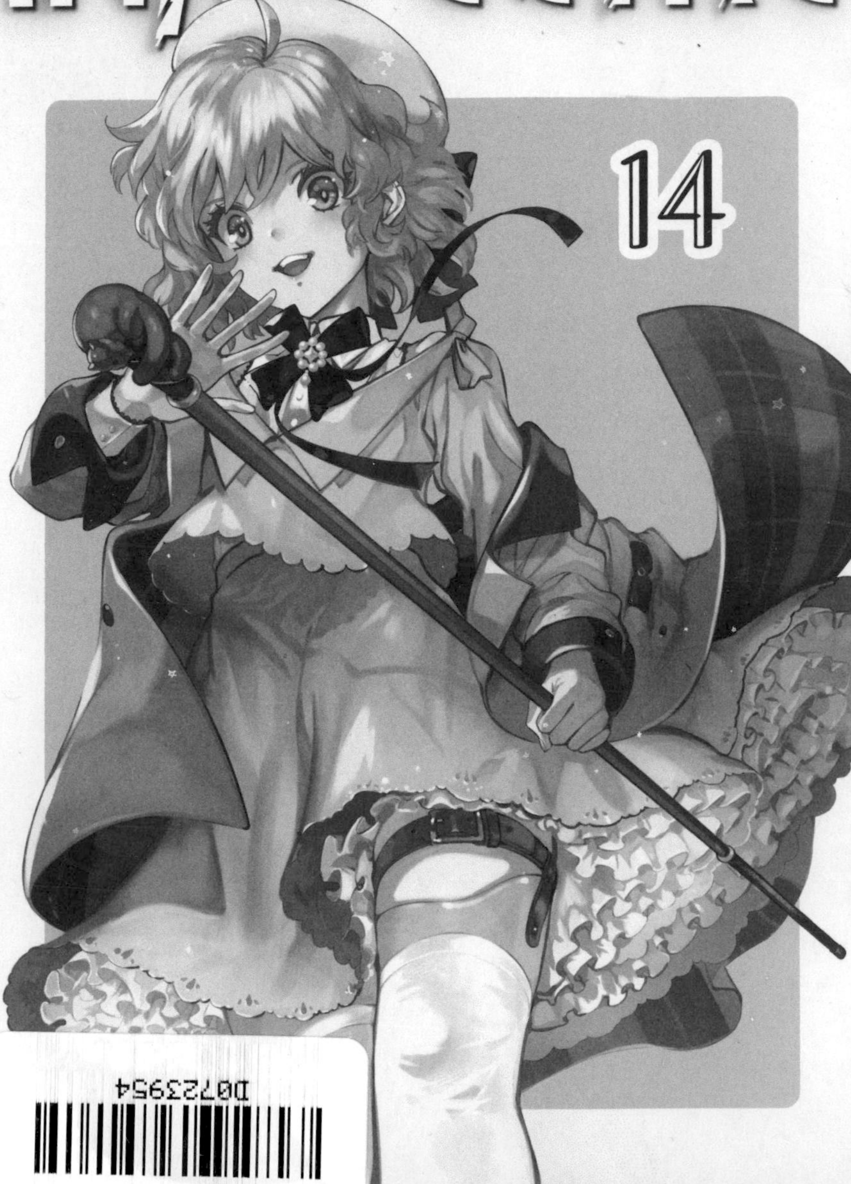

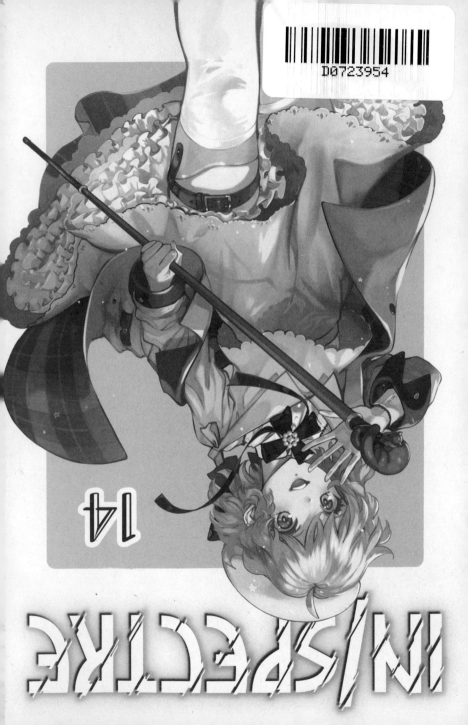

CONTENTS

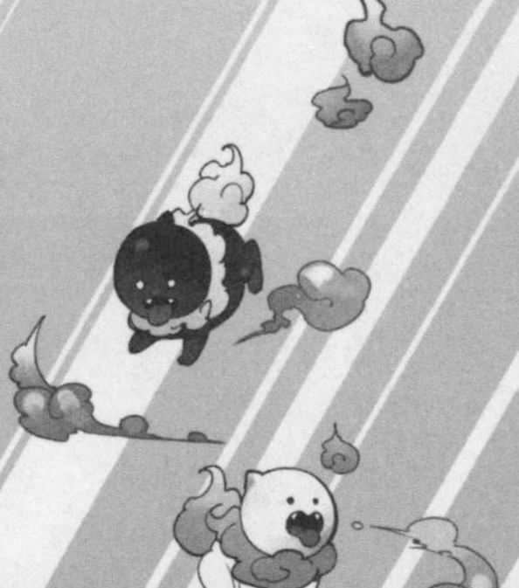

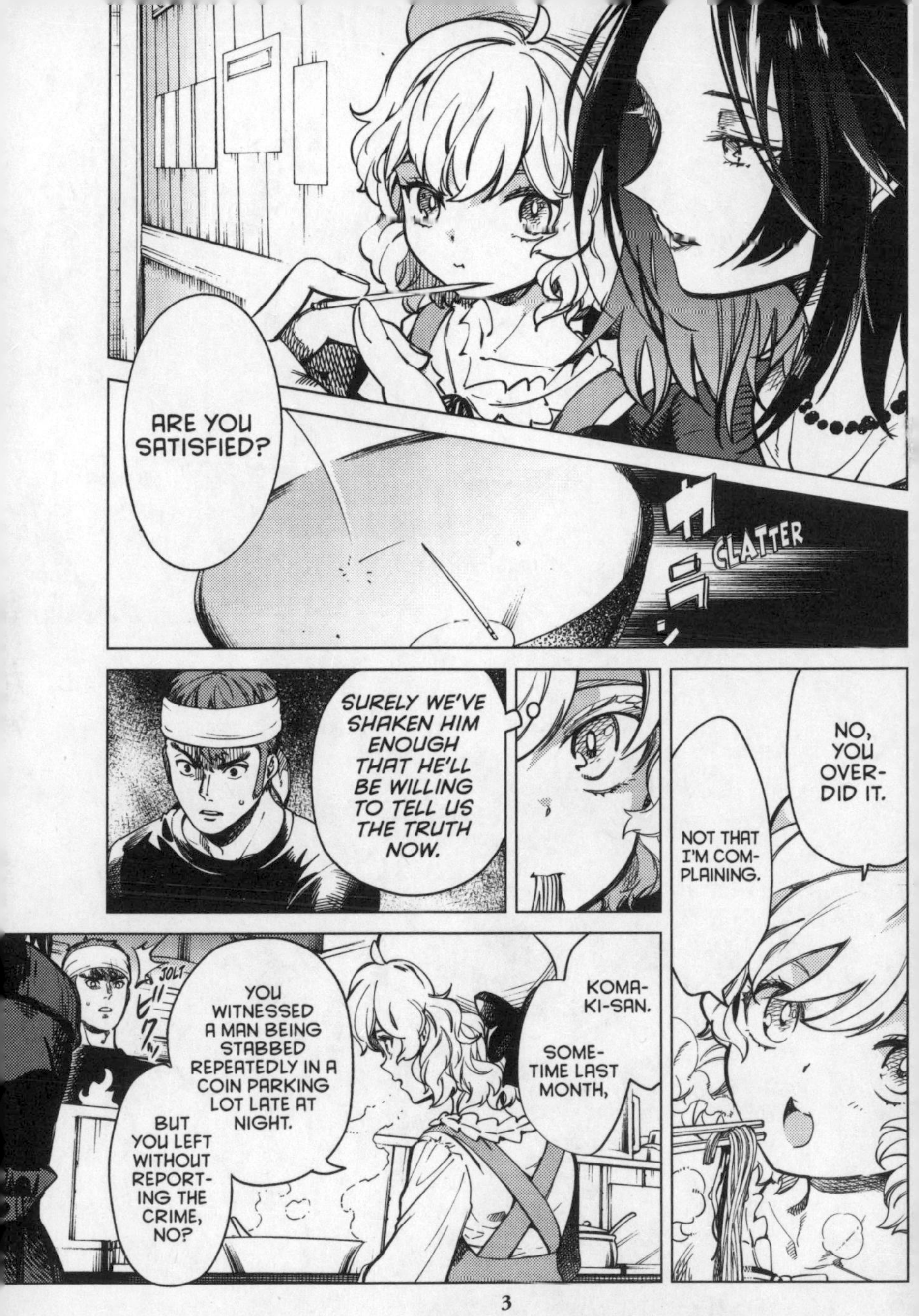
ARE YOU SATISFIED?
CLATTER
NO, YOU OVER-DID IT.
NOT THAT I'M COM-PLAINING.
SURELY WE'VE SHAKEN HIM ENOUGH THAT HE'LL BE WILLING TO TELL US THE TRUTH NOW.
KOMA-KI-SAN.
SOME-TIME LAST MONTH,
YOU WITNESSED A MAN BEING STABBED REPEATEDLY IN A COIN PARKING LOT LATE AT NIGHT.
BUT YOU LEFT WITHOUT REPORT-ING THE CRIME, NO?
JOLT

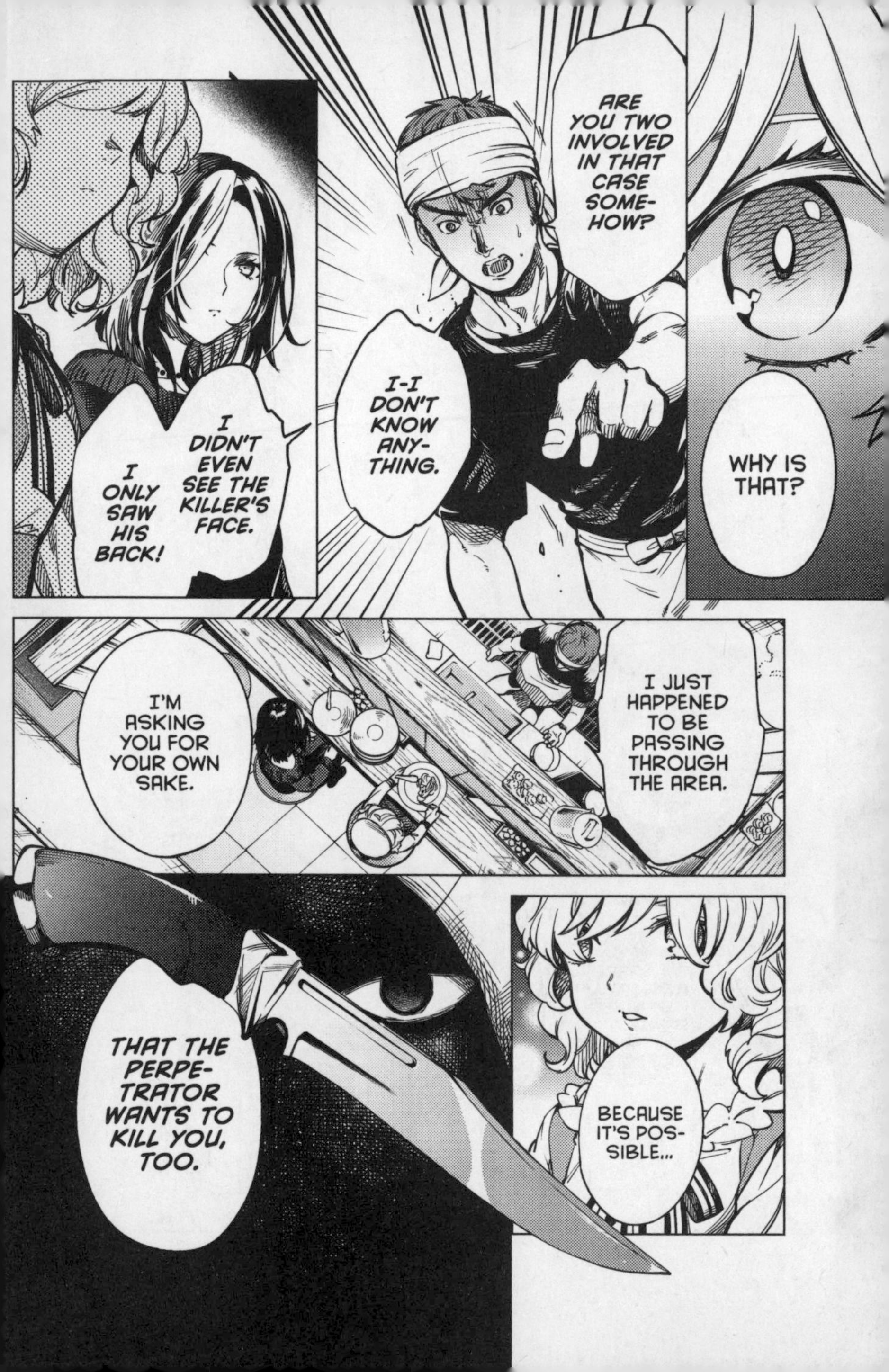
WHY IS THAT?
ARE YOU TWO INVOLVED IN THAT CASE SOME-HOW?
I-I DON'T KNOW ANY-THING.
I DIDN'T EVEN SEE THE KILLER'S FACE.
I ONLY SAW HIS BACK!
I JUST HAPPENED TO BE PASSING THROUGH THE AREA.
I'M ASKING YOU FOR YOUR OWN SAKE.
BECAUSE IT'S POS-SIBLE...
THAT THE PERPE-TRATOR WANTS TO KILL YOU, TOO.

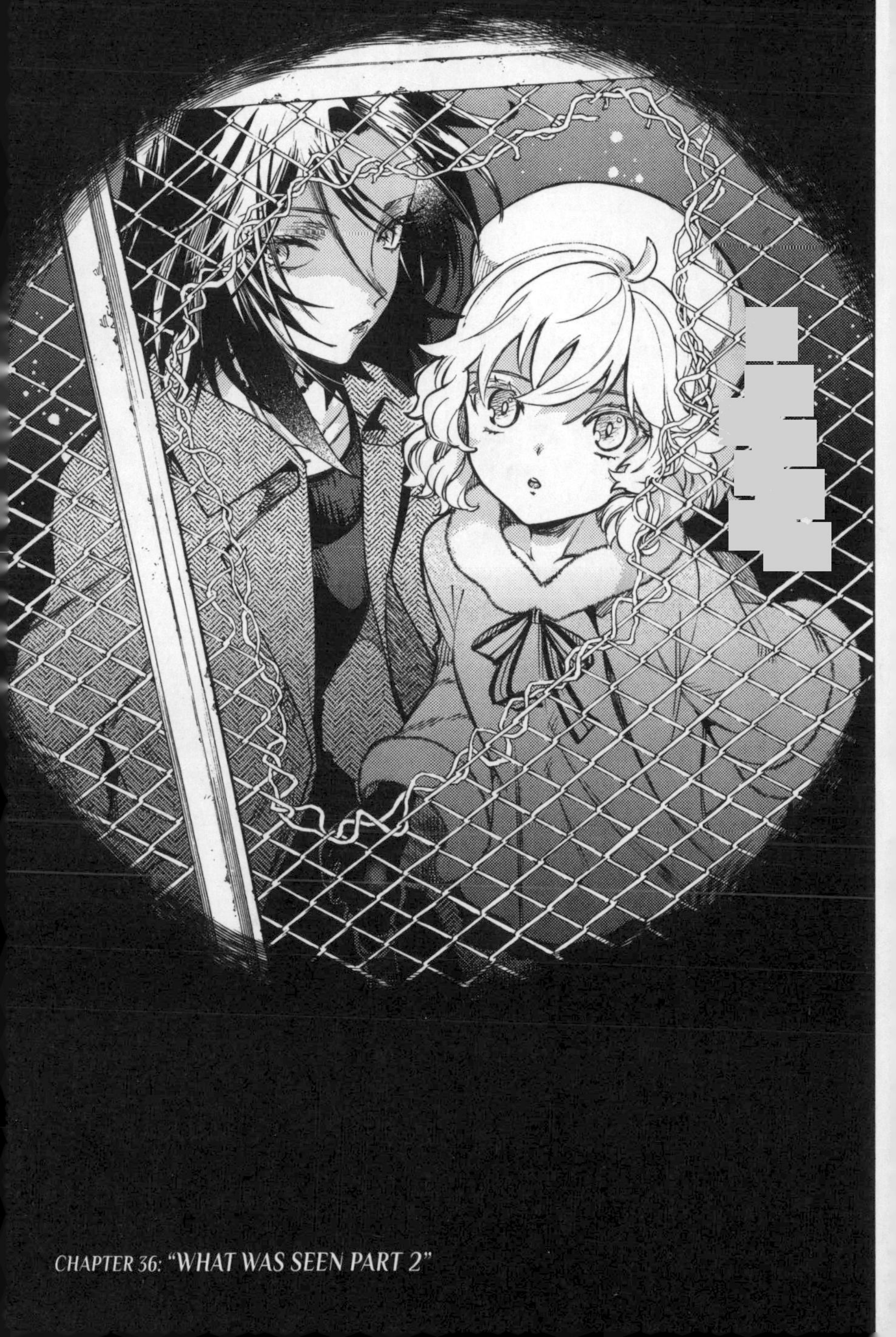

CHAPTER 36: "WHAT WAS SEEN PART 2"

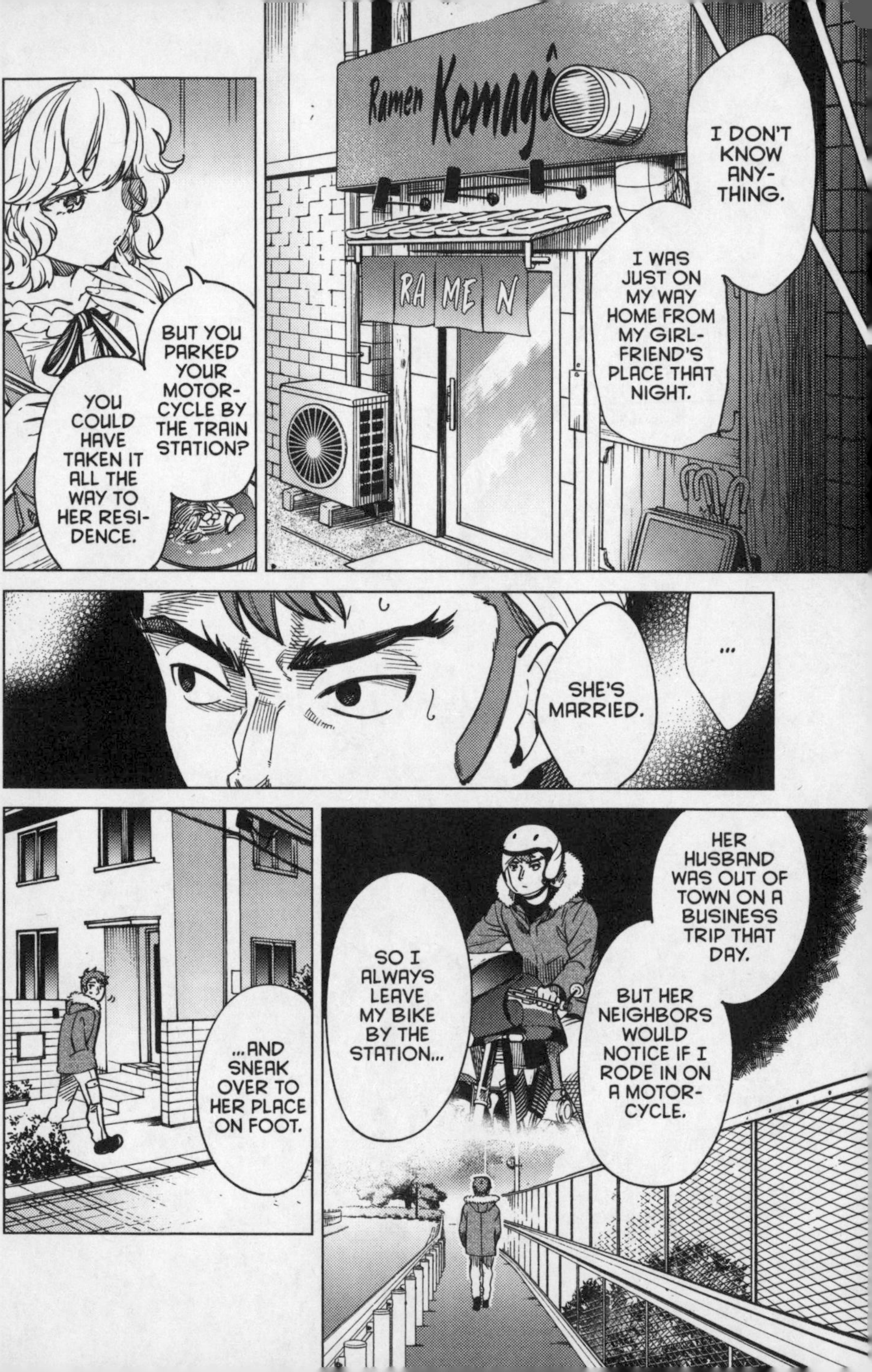
Ramen Komagô
RA ME N
I DON'T KNOW ANY-THING.
I WAS JUST ON MY WAY HOME FROM MY GIRL-FRIEND'S PLACE THAT NIGHT.
BUT YOU PARKED YOUR MOTOR-CYCLE BY THE TRAIN STATION?
YOU COULD HAVE TAKEN IT ALL THE WAY TO HER RESI-DENCE.
...
SHE'S MARRIED.
HER HUSBAND WAS OUT OF TOWN ON A BUSINESS TRIP THAT DAY.
BUT HER NEIGHBORS WOULD NOTICE IF I RODE IN ON A MOTOR-CYCLE.
SO I ALWAYS LEAVE MY BIKE BY THE STATION...
...AND SNEAK OVER TO HER PLACE ON FOOT.

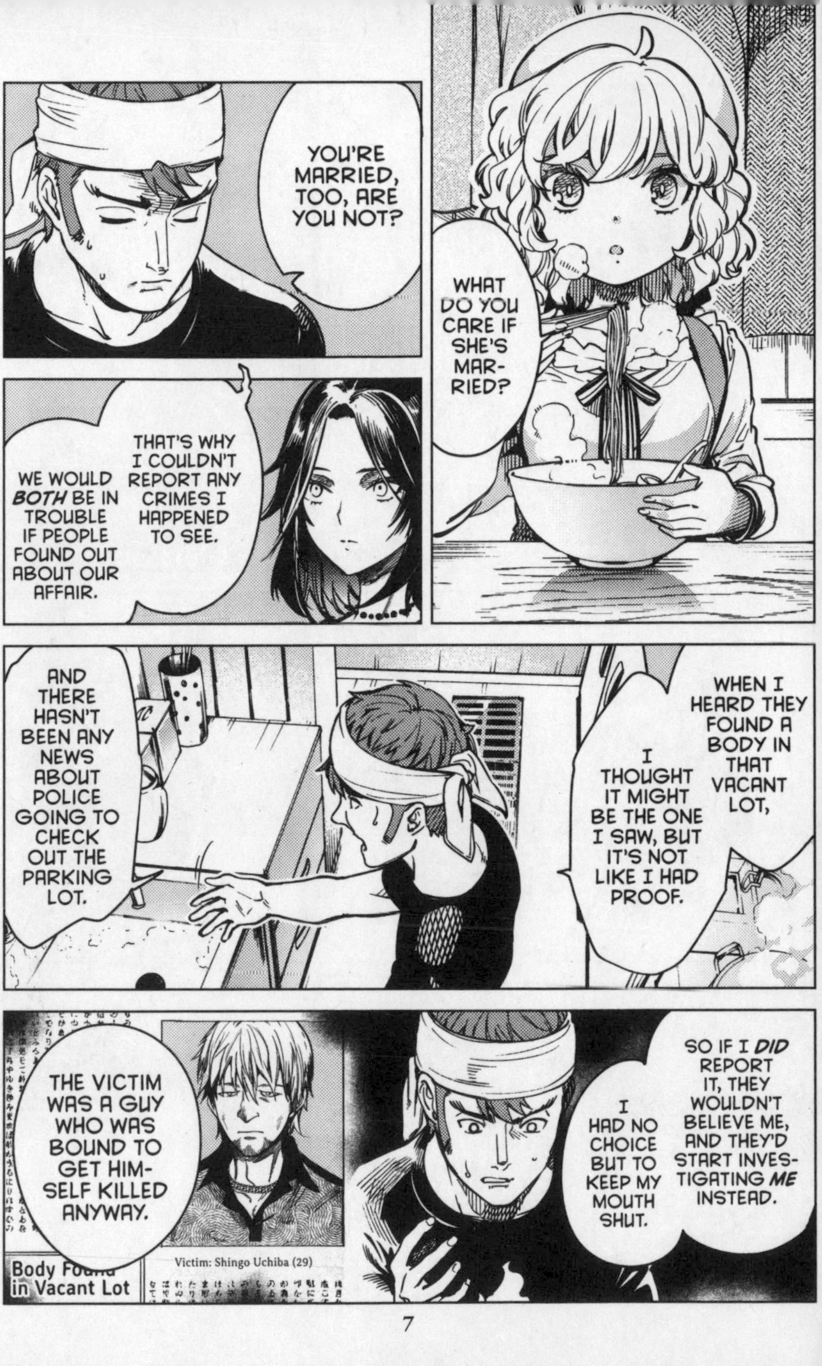
WHAT DO YOU CARE IF SHE'S MAR- RIED?
YOU'RE MARRIED, TOO, ARE YOU NOT?
THAT'S WHY I COULDN'T REPORT ANY CRIMES I HAPPENED TO SEE.
WE WOULD *BOTH* BE IN TROUBLE IF PEOPLE FOUND OUT ABOUT OUR AFFAIR.
WHEN I HEARD THEY FOUND A BODY IN THAT VACANT LOT,
I THOUGHT IT MIGHT BE THE ONE I SAW, BUT IT'S NOT LIKE I HAD PROOF.
AND THERE HASN'T BEEN ANY NEWS ABOUT POLICE GOING TO CHECK OUT THE PARKING LOT.
SO IF I *DID* REPORT IT, THEY WOULDN'T BELIEVE ME, AND THEY'D START INVES- TIGATING *ME* INSTEAD.
I HAD NO CHOICE BUT TO KEEP MY MOUTH SHUT.
THE VICTIM WAS A GUY WHO WAS BOUND TO GET HIM- SELF KILLED ANYWAY.
Victim: Shingo Uchiba (29)
Body Found in Vacant Lot

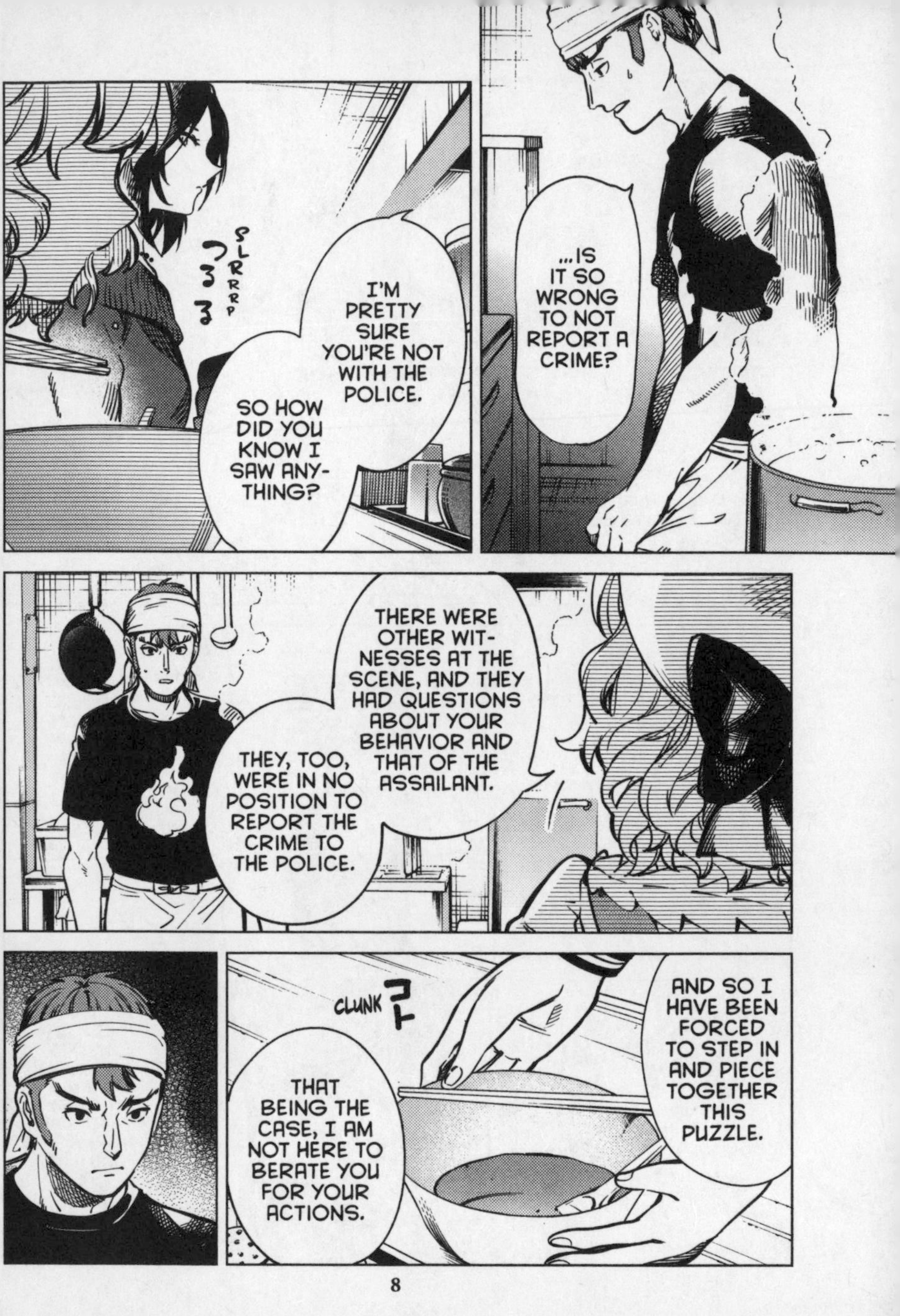
...IS IT SO WRONG TO NOT REPORT A CRIME?
SLRRRP
I'M PRETTY SURE YOU'RE NOT WITH THE POLICE.
SO HOW DID YOU KNOW I SAW ANY-THING?
THERE WERE OTHER WIT-NESSES AT THE SCENE, AND THEY HAD QUESTIONS ABOUT YOUR BEHAVIOR AND THAT OF THE ASSAILANT.
THEY, TOO, WERE IN NO POSITION TO REPORT THE CRIME TO THE POLICE.
AND SO I HAVE BEEN FORCED TO STEP IN AND PIECE TOGETHER THIS PUZZLE.
CLUNK
THAT BEING THE CASE, I AM NOT HERE TO BERATE YOU FOR YOUR ACTIONS.

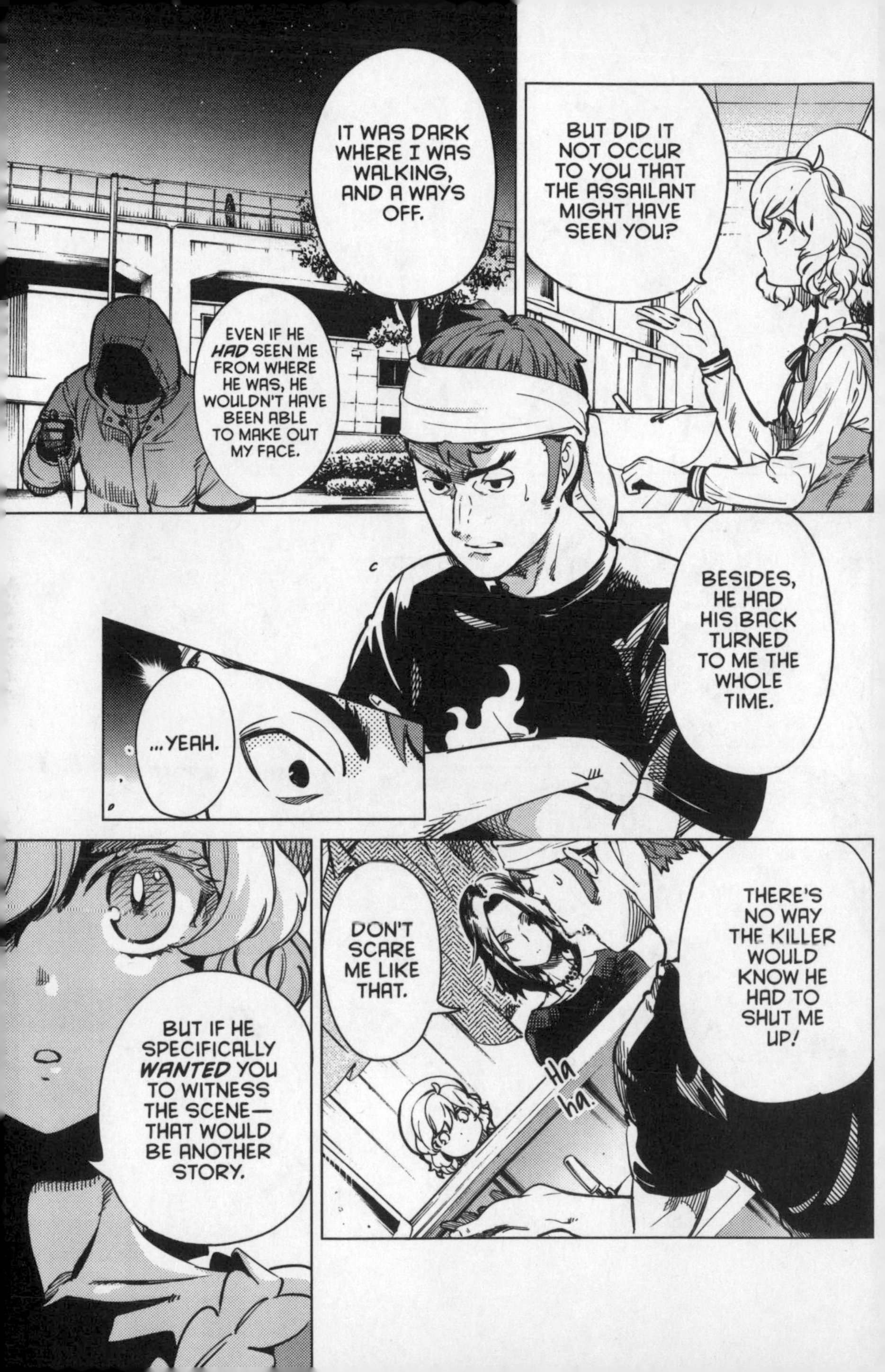
BUT DID IT NOT OCCUR TO YOU THAT THE ASSAILANT MIGHT HAVE SEEN YOU?
IT WAS DARK WHERE I WAS WALKING, AND A WAYS OFF.
EVEN IF HE *HAD* SEEN ME FROM WHERE HE WAS, HE WOULDN'T HAVE BEEN ABLE TO MAKE OUT MY FACE.
BESIDES, HE HAD HIS BACK TURNED TO ME THE WHOLE TIME.
...YEAH.
THERE'S NO WAY THE KILLER WOULD KNOW HE HAD TO SHUT ME UP!
Ha ha.
DON'T SCARE ME LIKE THAT.
BUT IF HE SPECIFICALLY *WANTED* YOU TO WITNESS THE SCENE— THAT WOULD BE ANOTHER STORY.

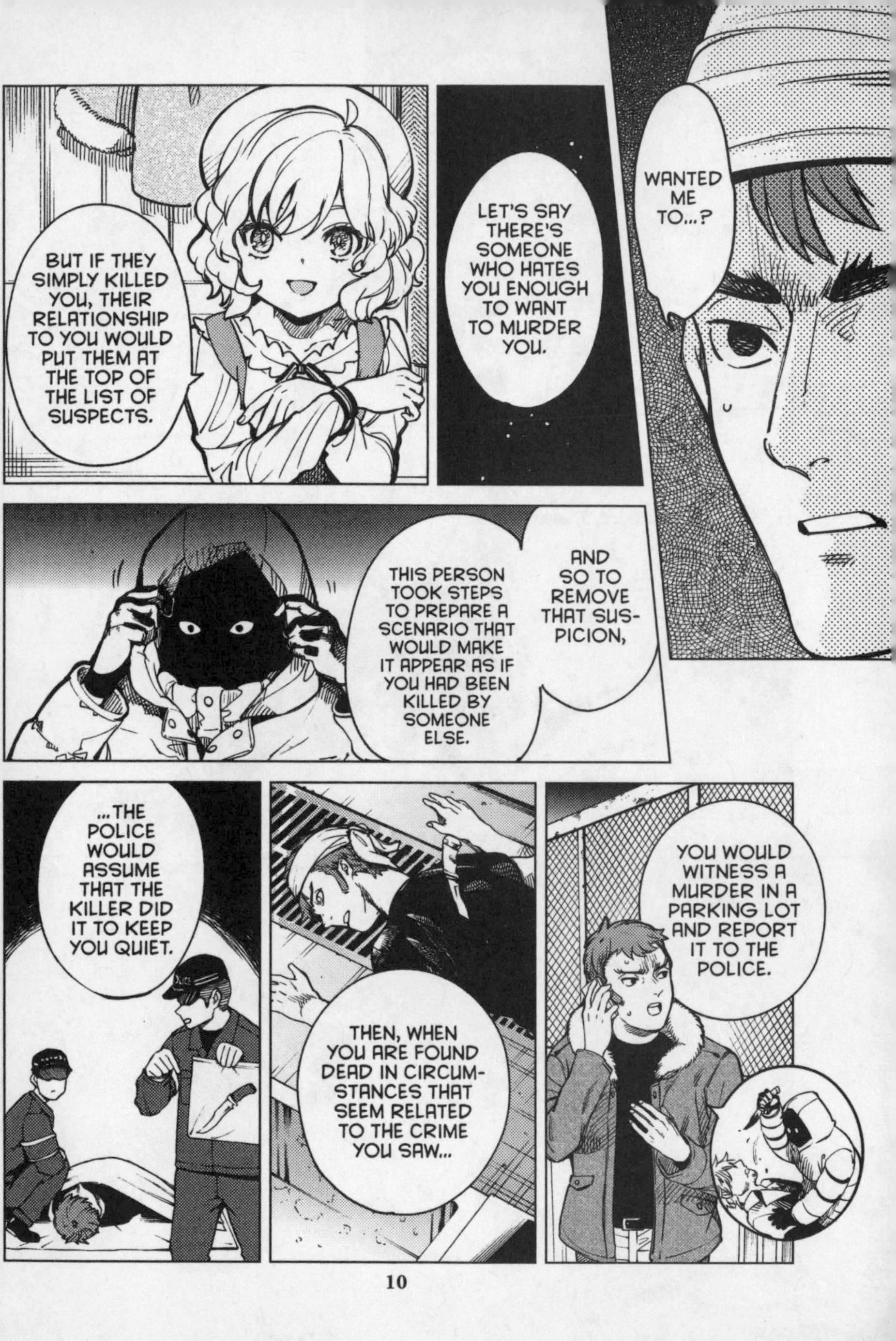
WANTED ME TO...?
LET'S SAY THERE'S SOMEONE WHO HATES YOU ENOUGH TO WANT TO MURDER YOU.
BUT IF THEY SIMPLY KILLED YOU, THEIR RELATIONSHIP TO YOU WOULD PUT THEM AT THE TOP OF THE LIST OF SUSPECTS.
AND SO TO REMOVE THAT SUS-PICION,
THIS PERSON TOOK STEPS TO PREPARE A SCENARIO THAT WOULD MAKE IT APPEAR AS IF YOU HAD BEEN KILLED BY SOMEONE ELSE.
YOU WOULD WITNESS A MURDER IN A PARKING LOT AND REPORT IT TO THE POLICE.
THEN, WHEN YOU ARE FOUND DEAD IN CIRCUM-STANCES THAT SEEM RELATED TO THE CRIME YOU SAW...
...THE POLICE WOULD ASSUME THAT THE KILLER DID IT TO KEEP YOU QUIET.

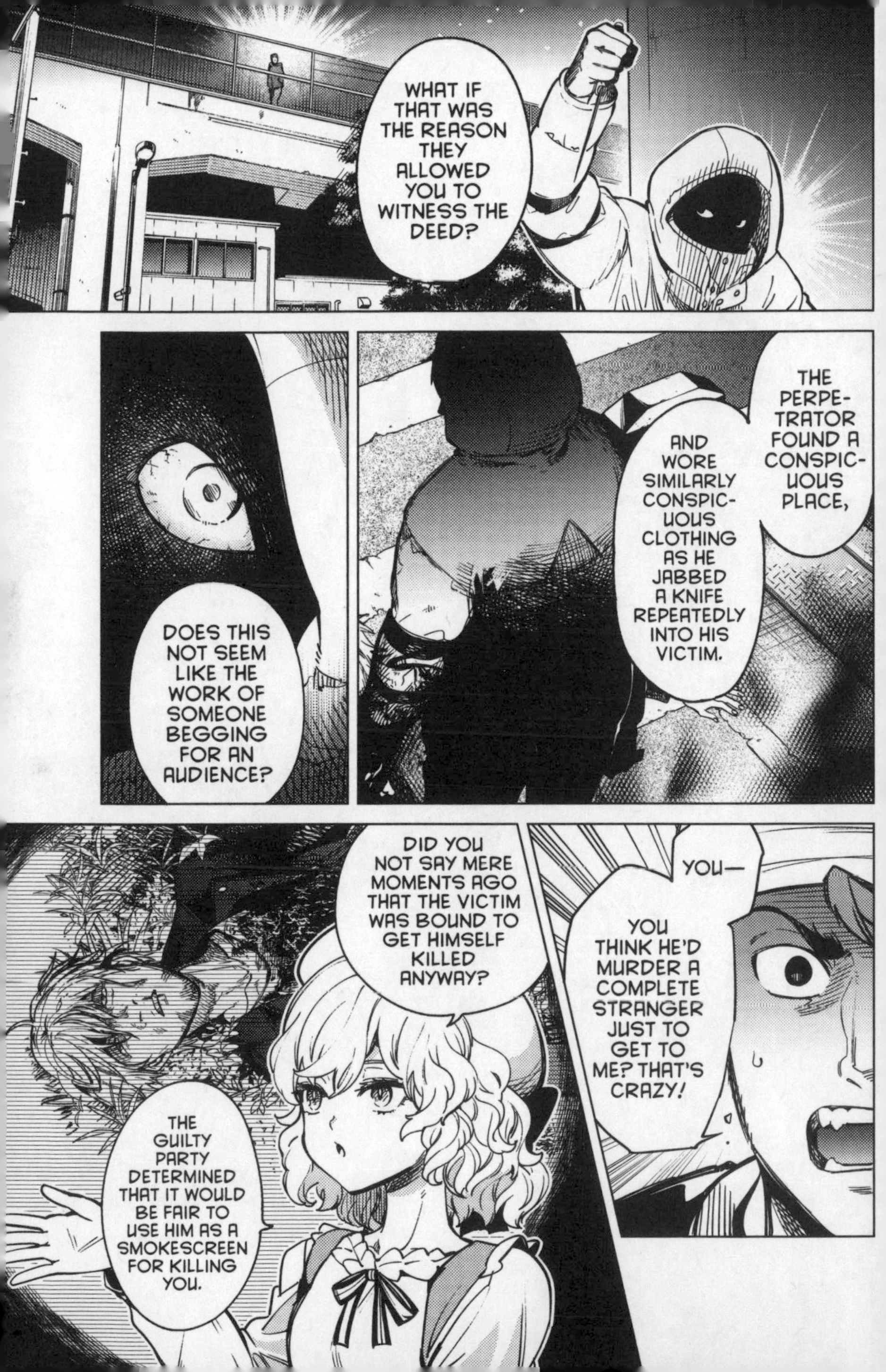
WHAT IF THAT WAS THE REASON THEY ALLOWED YOU TO WITNESS THE DEED?
THE PERPETRATOR FOUND A CONSPICUOUS PLACE,
AND WORE SIMILARLY CONSPICUOUS CLOTHING AS HE JABBED A KNIFE REPEATEDLY INTO HIS VICTIM.
DOES THIS NOT SEEM LIKE THE WORK OF SOMEONE BEGGING FOR AN AUDIENCE?
YOU—
YOU THINK HE'D MURDER A COMPLETE STRANGER JUST TO GET TO ME? THAT'S CRAZY!
DID YOU NOT SAY MERE MOMENTS AGO THAT THE VICTIM WAS BOUND TO GET HIMSELF KILLED ANYWAY?
THE GUILTY PARTY DETERMINED THAT IT WOULD BE FAIR TO USE HIM AS A SMOKESCREEN FOR KILLING YOU.

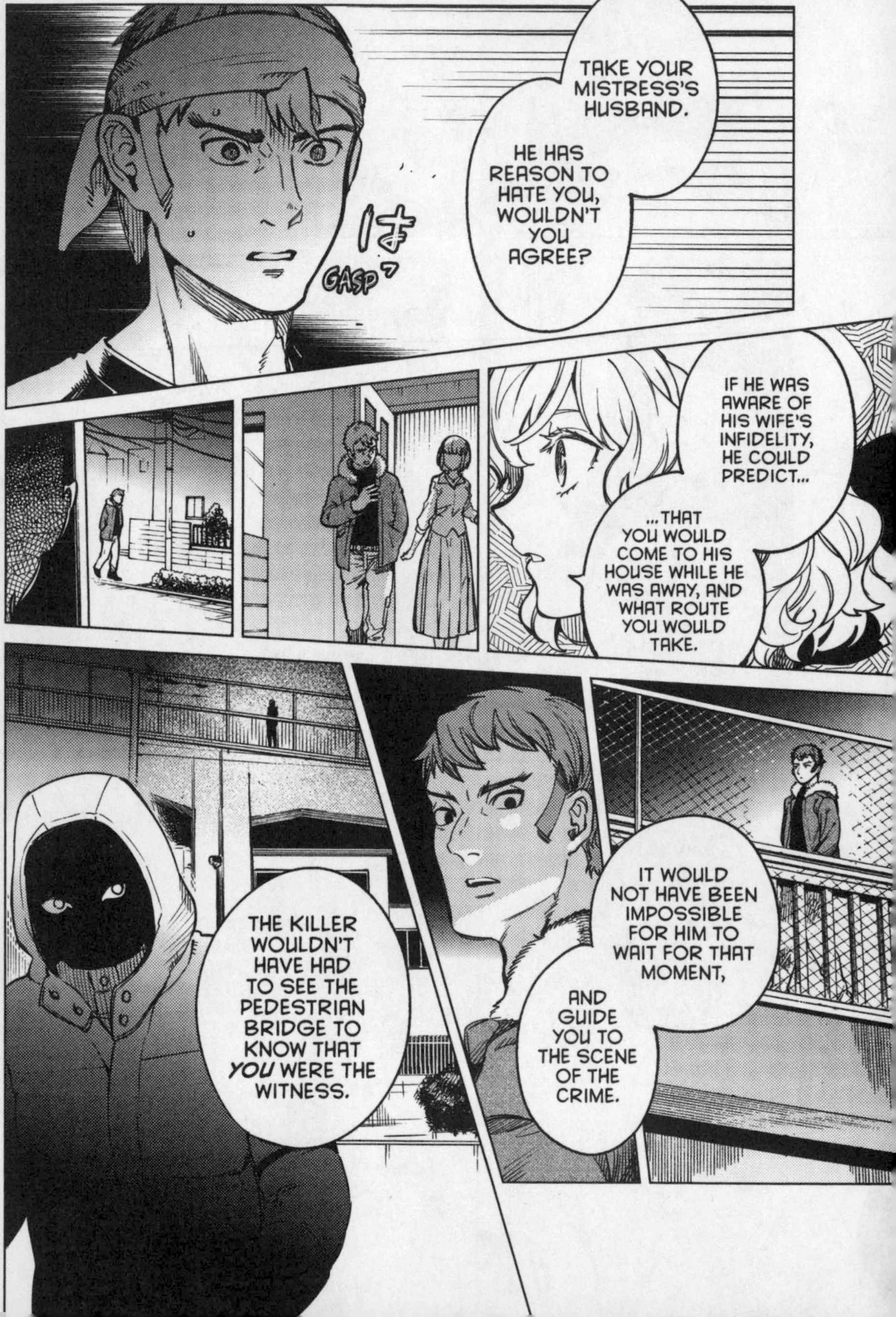
TAKE YOUR MISTRESS'S HUSBAND.
HE HAS REASON TO HATE YOU, WOULDN'T YOU AGREE?
は GASP
IF HE WAS AWARE OF HIS WIFE'S INFIDELITY, HE COULD PREDICT...
...THAT YOU WOULD COME TO HIS HOUSE WHILE HE WAS AWAY, AND WHAT ROUTE YOU WOULD TAKE.
IT WOULD NOT HAVE BEEN IMPOSSIBLE FOR HIM TO WAIT FOR THAT MOMENT,
AND GUIDE YOU TO THE SCENE OF THE CRIME.
THE KILLER WOULDN'T HAVE HAD TO SEE THE PEDESTRIAN BRIDGE TO KNOW THAT *YOU* WERE THE WITNESS.

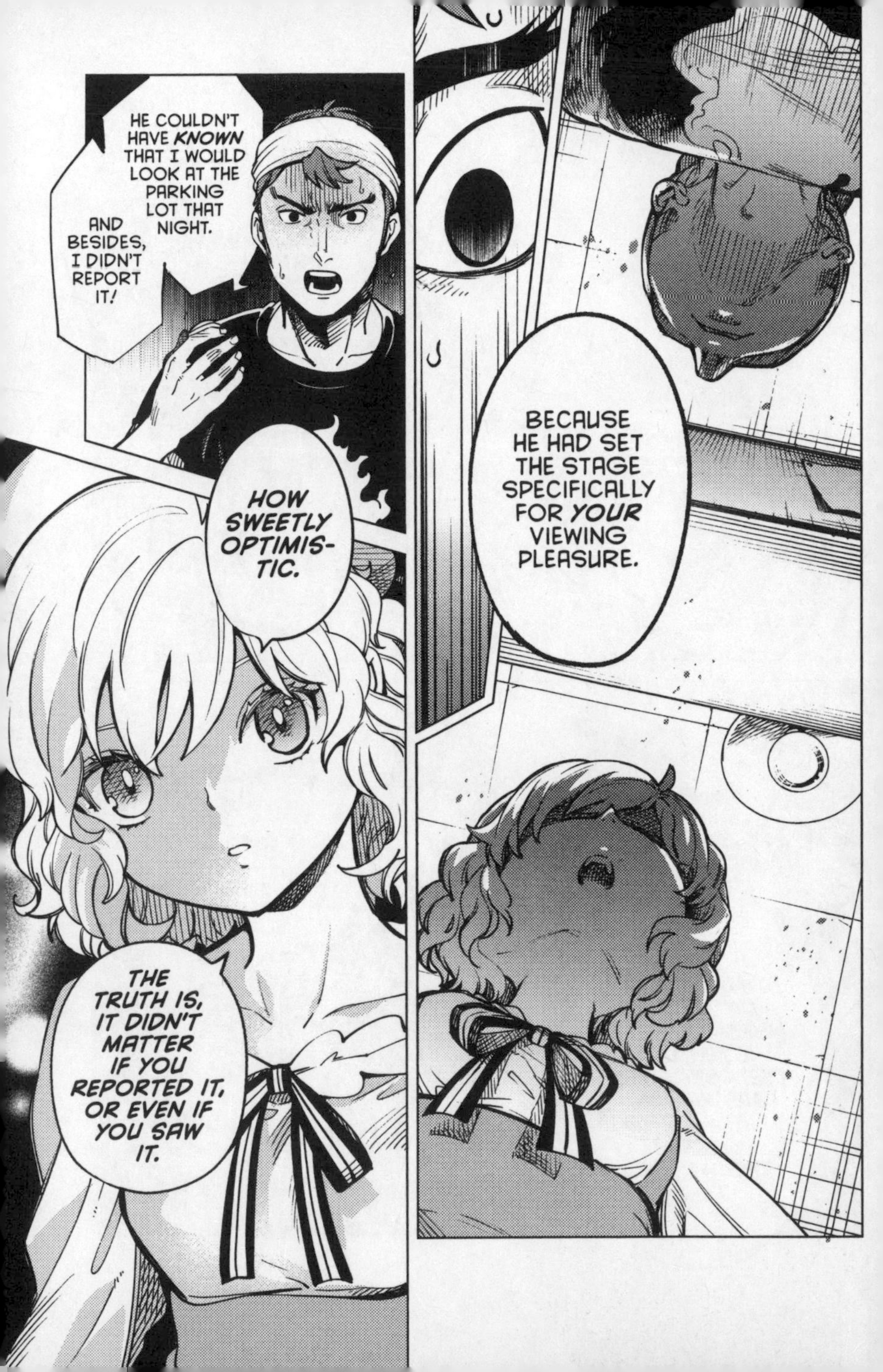
HE COULDN'T HAVE *KNOWN* THAT I WOULD LOOK AT THE PARKING LOT THAT NIGHT.
AND BESIDES, I DIDN'T REPORT IT!
HOW SWEETLY OPTIMIS-TIC.
THE TRUTH IS, IT DIDN'T MATTER IF YOU REPORTED IT, OR EVEN IF YOU SAW IT.
BECAUSE HE HAD SET THE STAGE SPECIFICALLY FOR *YOUR* VIEWING PLEASURE.

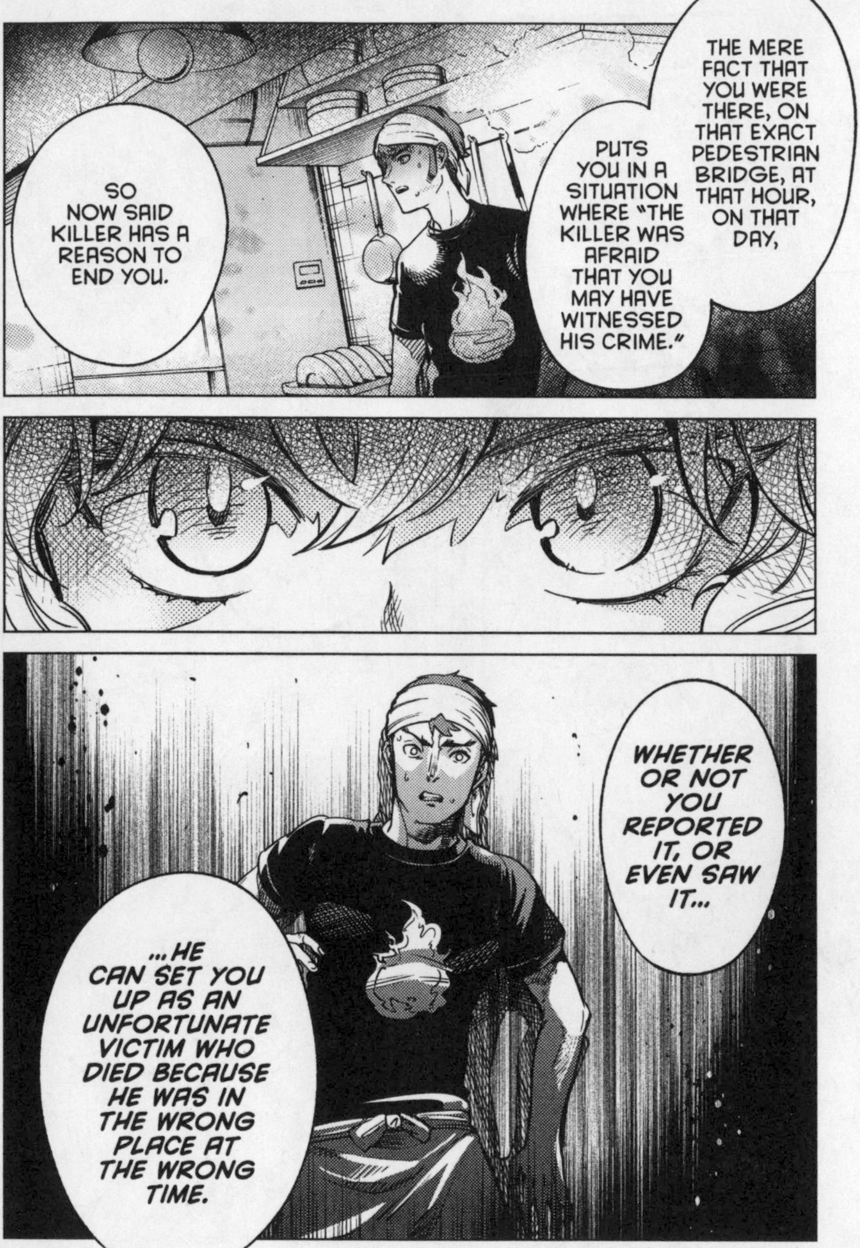
THE MERE FACT THAT YOU WERE THERE, ON THAT EXACT PEDESTRIAN BRIDGE, AT THAT HOUR, ON THAT DAY,
PUTS YOU IN A SITUATION WHERE "THE KILLER WAS AFRAID THAT YOU MAY HAVE WITNESSED HIS CRIME."
SO NOW SAID KILLER HAS A REASON TO END YOU.
WHETHER OR NOT YOU REPORTED IT, OR EVEN SAW IT...
...HE CAN SET YOU UP AS AN UNFORTUNATE VICTIM WHO DIED BECAUSE HE WAS IN THE WRONG PLACE AT THE WRONG TIME.

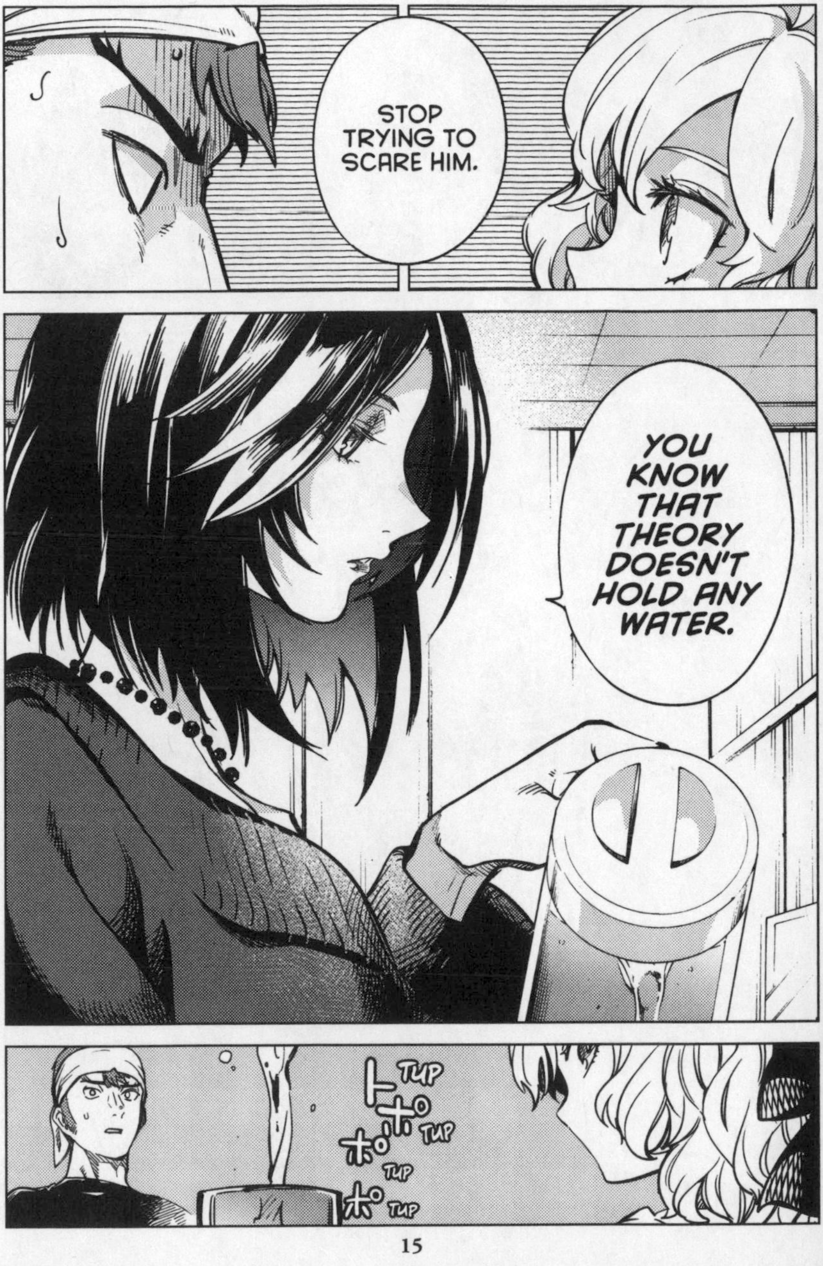
STOP TRYING TO SCARE HIM.
YOU KNOW THAT THEORY DOESN'T HOLD ANY WATER.
トポポポ
TUP TUP TUP TUP

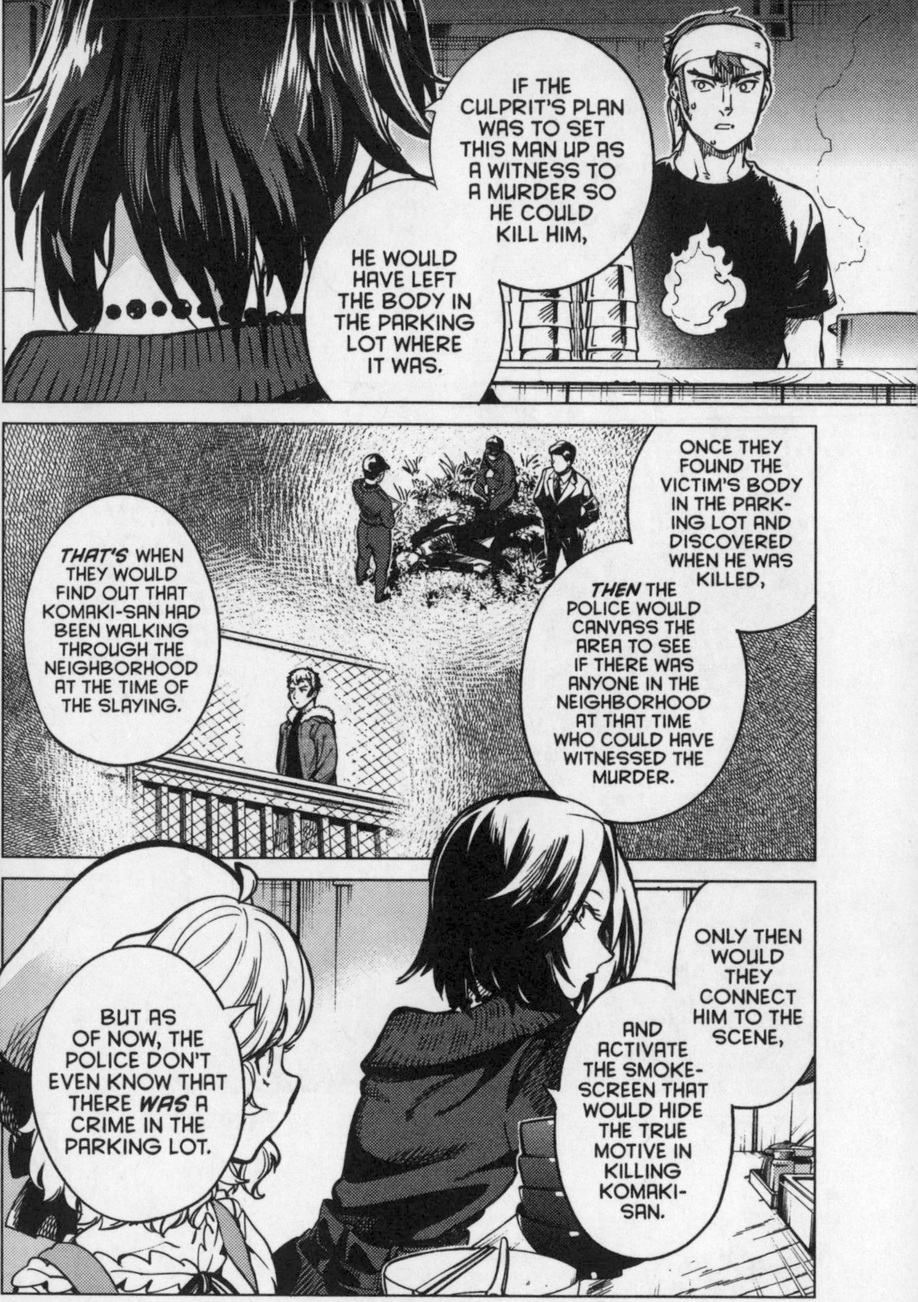
IF THE CULPRIT'S PLAN WAS TO SET THIS MAN UP AS A WITNESS TO A MURDER SO HE COULD KILL HIM,
HE WOULD HAVE LEFT THE BODY IN THE PARKING LOT WHERE IT WAS.
ONCE THEY FOUND THE VICTIM'S BODY IN THE PARKING LOT AND DISCOVERED WHEN HE WAS KILLED,
THEN THE POLICE WOULD CANVASS THE AREA TO SEE IF THERE WAS ANYONE IN THE NEIGHBORHOOD AT THAT TIME WHO COULD HAVE WITNESSED THE MURDER.
THAT'S WHEN THEY WOULD FIND OUT THAT KOMAKI-SAN HAD BEEN WALKING THROUGH THE NEIGHBORHOOD AT THE TIME OF THE SLAYING.
ONLY THEN WOULD THEY CONNECT HIM TO THE SCENE,
AND ACTIVATE THE SMOKE-SCREEN THAT WOULD HIDE THE TRUE MOTIVE IN KILLING KOMAKI-SAN.
BUT AS OF NOW, THE POLICE DON'T EVEN KNOW THAT THERE *WAS* A CRIME IN THE PARKING LOT.

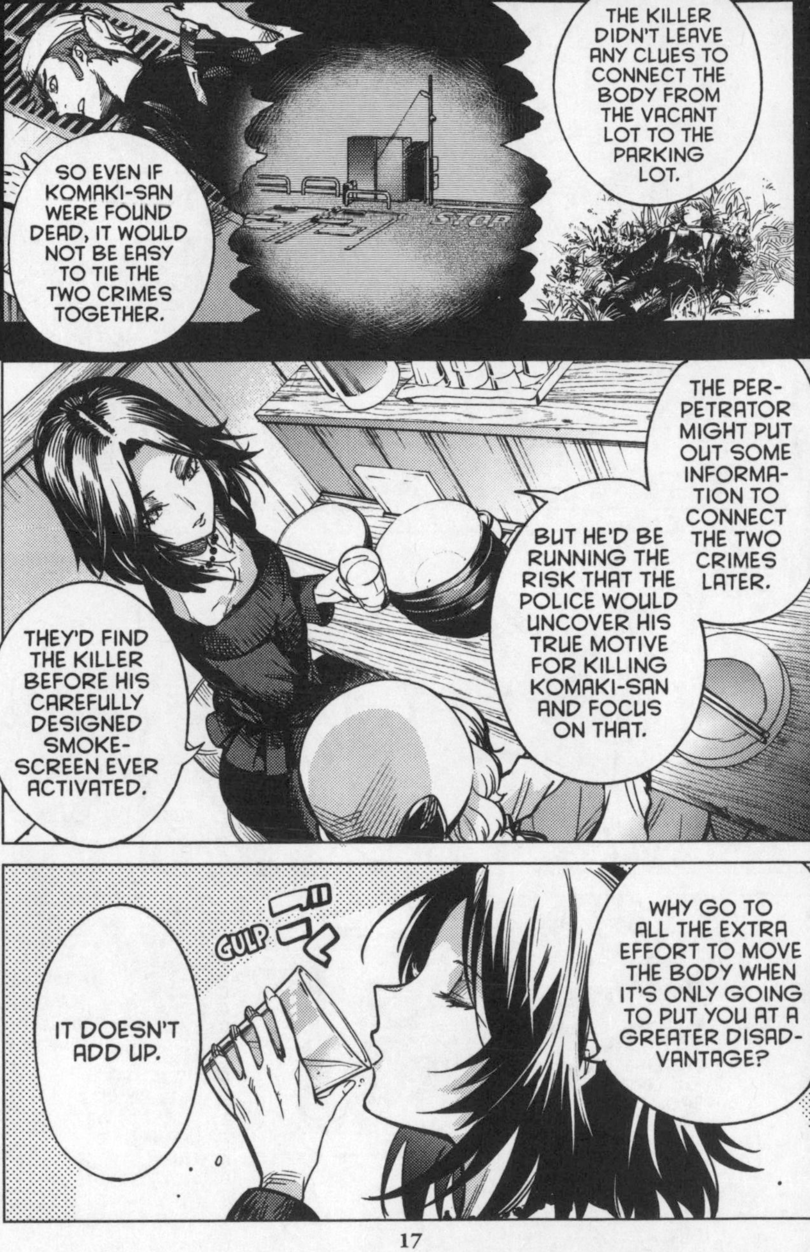
THE KILLER DIDN'T LEAVE ANY CLUES TO CONNECT THE BODY FROM THE VACANT LOT TO THE PARKING LOT.
STOP
SO EVEN IF KOMAKI-SAN WERE FOUND DEAD, IT WOULD NOT BE EASY TO TIE THE TWO CRIMES TOGETHER.
THE PER-PETRATOR MIGHT PUT OUT SOME INFORMA-TION TO CONNECT THE TWO CRIMES LATER.
BUT HE'D BE RUNNING THE RISK THAT THE POLICE WOULD UNCOVER HIS TRUE MOTIVE FOR KILLING KOMAKI-SAN AND FOCUS ON THAT.
THEY'D FIND THE KILLER BEFORE HIS CAREFULLY DESIGNED SMOKE-SCREEN EVER ACTIVATED.
WHY GO TO ALL THE EXTRA EFFORT TO MOVE THE BODY WHEN IT'S ONLY GOING TO PUT YOU AT A GREATER DISAD-VANTAGE?
GULP
IT DOESN'T ADD UP.

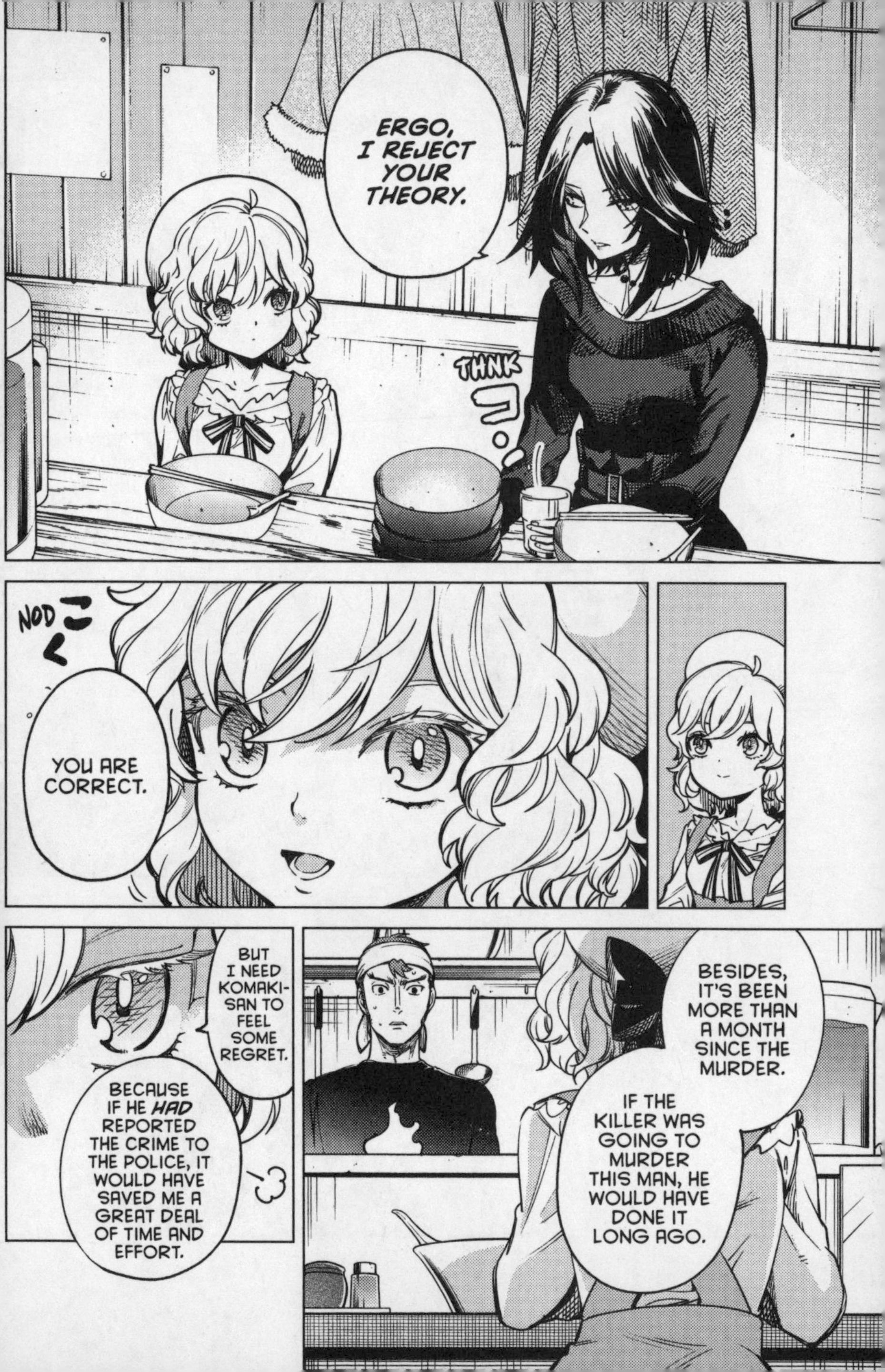
ERGO, I REJECT YOUR THEORY.
THNK
NOD
YOU ARE CORRECT.
BESIDES, IT'S BEEN MORE THAN A MONTH SINCE THE MURDER.
IF THE KILLER WAS GOING TO MURDER THIS MAN, HE WOULD HAVE DONE IT LONG AGO.
BUT I NEED KOMAKI-SAN TO FEEL SOME REGRET.
BECAUSE IF HE *HAD* REPORTED THE CRIME TO THE POLICE, IT WOULD HAVE SAVED ME A GREAT DEAL OF TIME AND EFFORT.

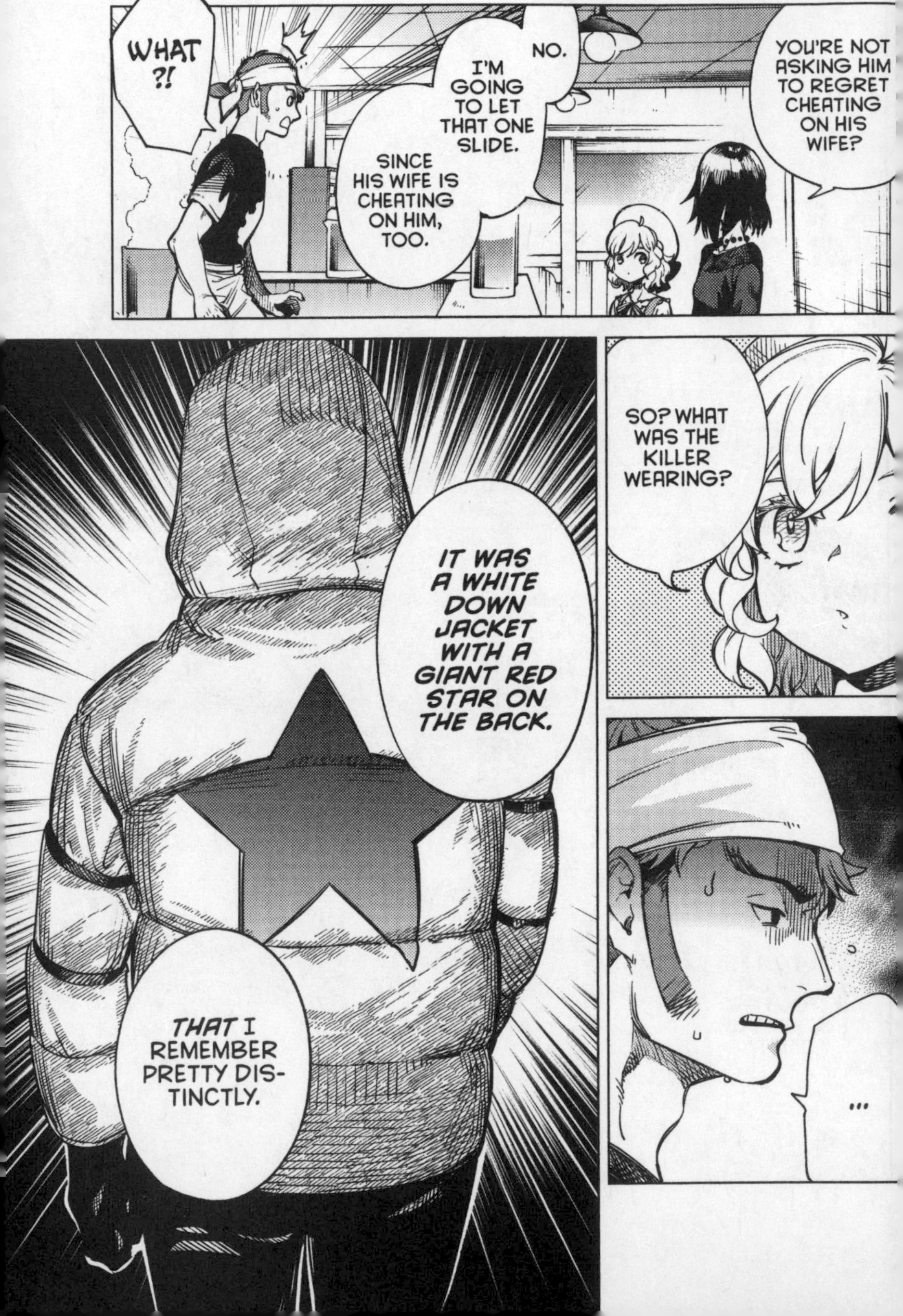
YOU'RE NOT ASKING HIM TO REGRET CHEATING ON HIS WIFE?
NO.
I'M GOING TO LET THAT ONE SLIDE.
SINCE HIS WIFE IS CHEATING ON HIM, TOO.
WHAT ?!
SO? WHAT WAS THE KILLER WEARING?
...
IT WAS A WHITE DOWN JACKET WITH A GIANT RED STAR ON THE BACK.
THAT I REMEMBER PRETTY DIS-TINCTLY.

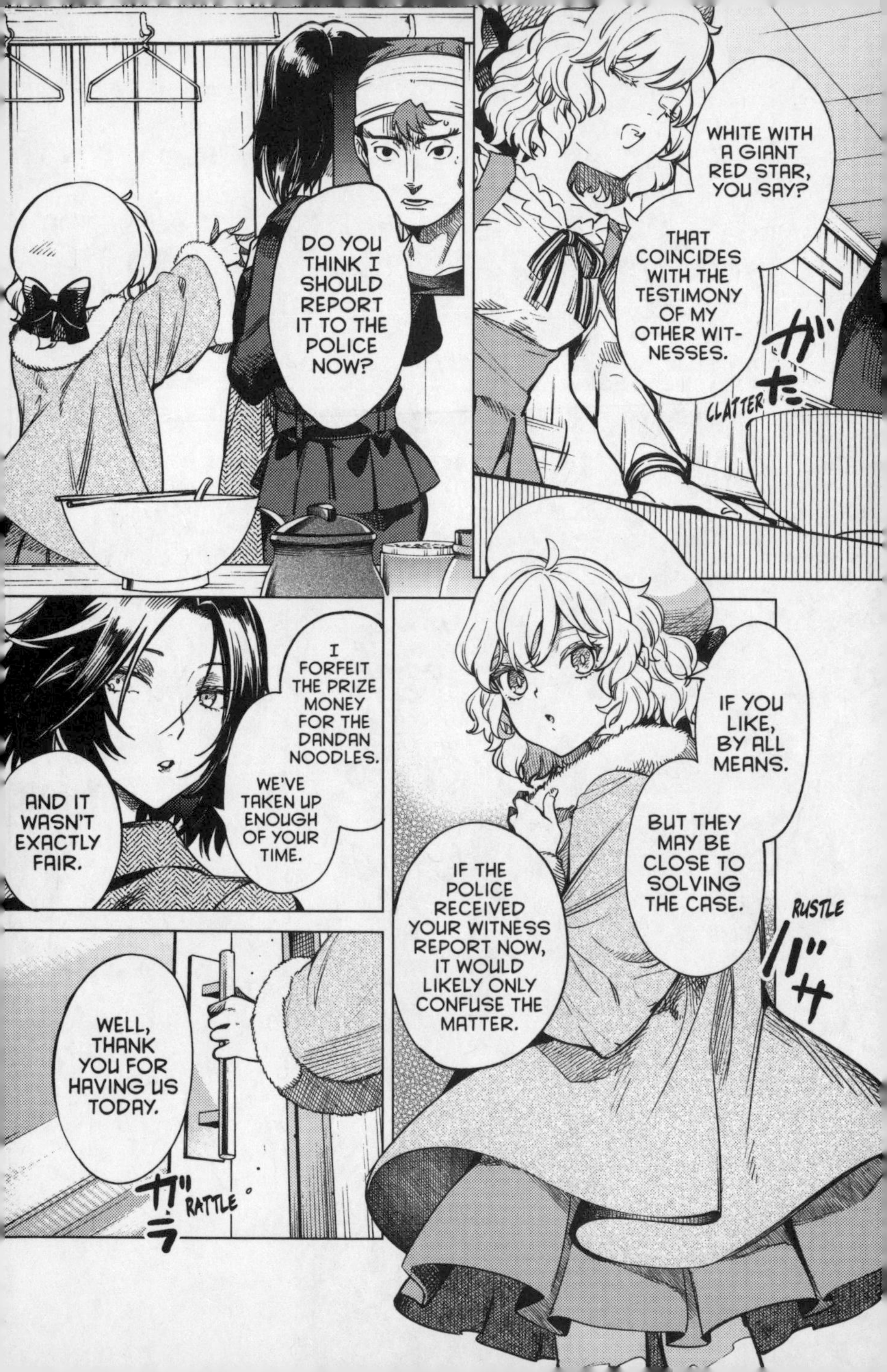
WHITE WITH A GIANT RED STAR, YOU SAY?
THAT COINCIDES WITH THE TESTIMONY OF MY OTHER WIT-NESSES.
ガタ
CLATTER
DO YOU THINK I SHOULD REPORT IT TO THE POLICE NOW?
IF YOU LIKE, BY ALL MEANS.
BUT THEY MAY BE CLOSE TO SOLVING THE CASE.
RUSTLE
バサ
IF THE POLICE RECEIVED YOUR WITNESS REPORT NOW, IT WOULD LIKELY ONLY CONFUSE THE MATTER.
I FORFEIT THE PRIZE MONEY FOR THE DANDAN NOODLES.
WE'VE TAKEN UP ENOUGH OF YOUR TIME.
AND IT WASN'T EXACTLY FAIR.
WELL, THANK YOU FOR HAVING US TODAY.
ガラ
RATTLE

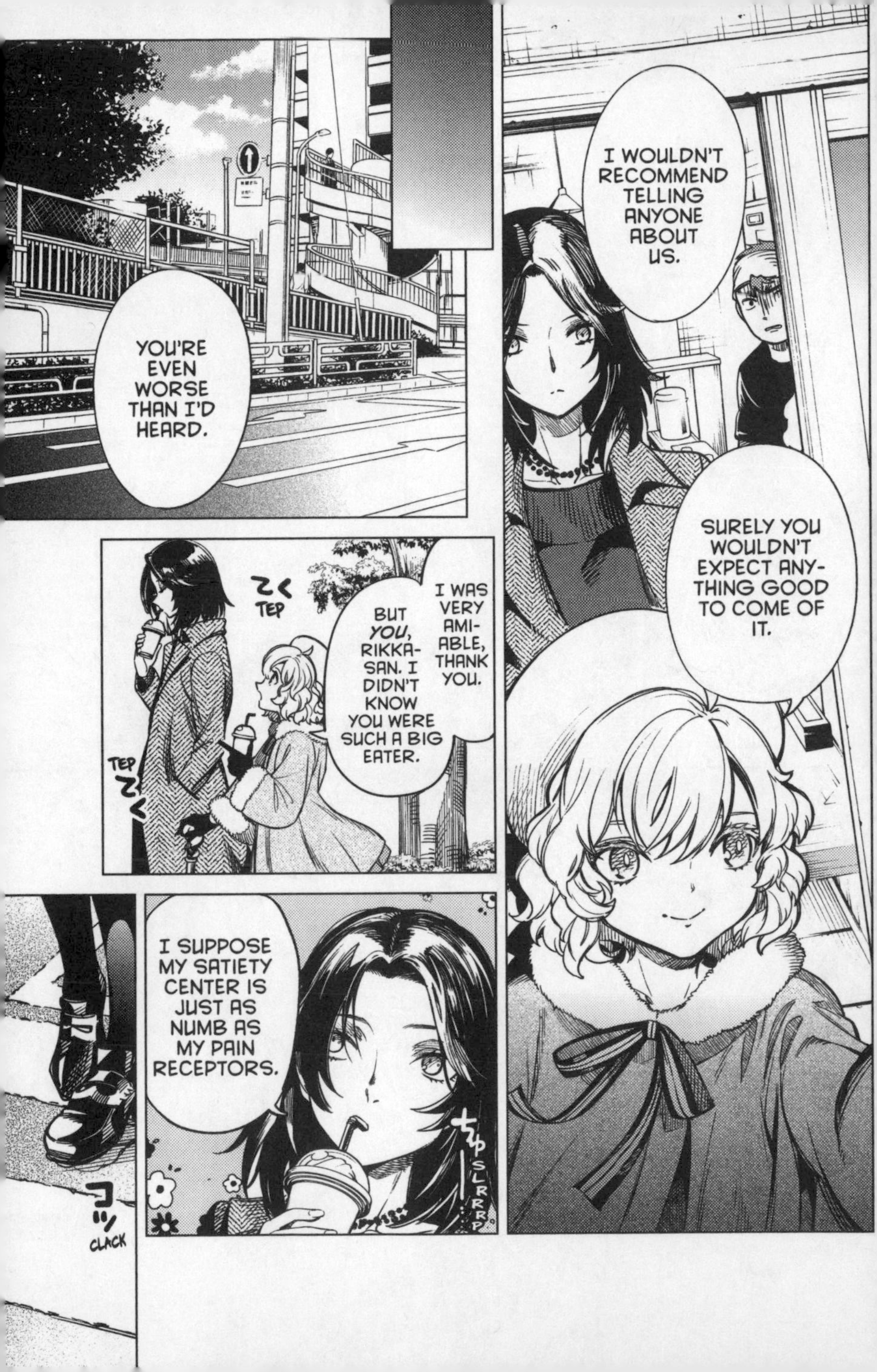
I WOULDN'T RECOMMEND TELLING ANYONE ABOUT US.
SURELY YOU WOULDN'T EXPECT ANY-THING GOOD TO COME OF IT.
YOU'RE EVEN WORSE THAN I'D HEARD.
I WAS VERY AMI-ABLE, THANK YOU.
BUT YOU, RIKKA-SAN. I DIDN'T KNOW YOU WERE SUCH A BIG EATER.
TEP
TEP
I SUPPOSE MY SATIETY CENTER IS JUST AS NUMB AS MY PAIN RECEPTORS.
SLRRRP
CLACK

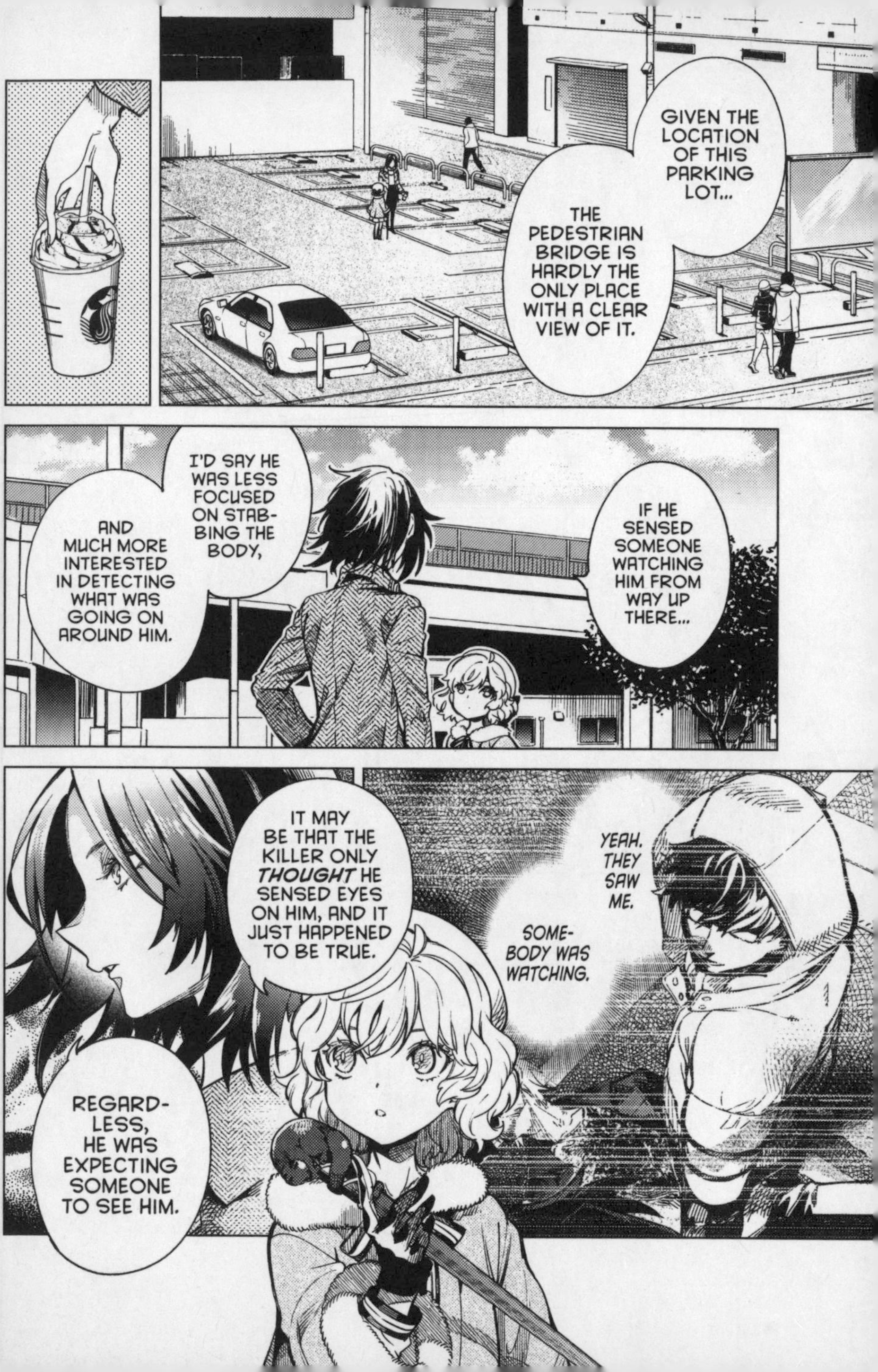
GIVEN THE LOCATION OF THIS PARKING LOT...
THE PEDESTRIAN BRIDGE IS HARDLY THE ONLY PLACE WITH A CLEAR VIEW OF IT.
IF HE SENSED SOMEONE WATCHING HIM FROM WAY UP THERE...
I'D SAY HE WAS LESS FOCUSED ON STAB-BING THE BODY,
AND MUCH MORE INTERESTED IN DETECTING WHAT WAS GOING ON AROUND HIM.
YEAH. THEY SAW ME.
SOME-BODY WAS WATCHING.
IT MAY BE THAT THE KILLER ONLY *THOUGHT* HE SENSED EYES ON HIM, AND IT JUST HAPPENED TO BE TRUE.
REGARD-LESS, HE WAS EXPECTING SOMEONE TO SEE HIM.

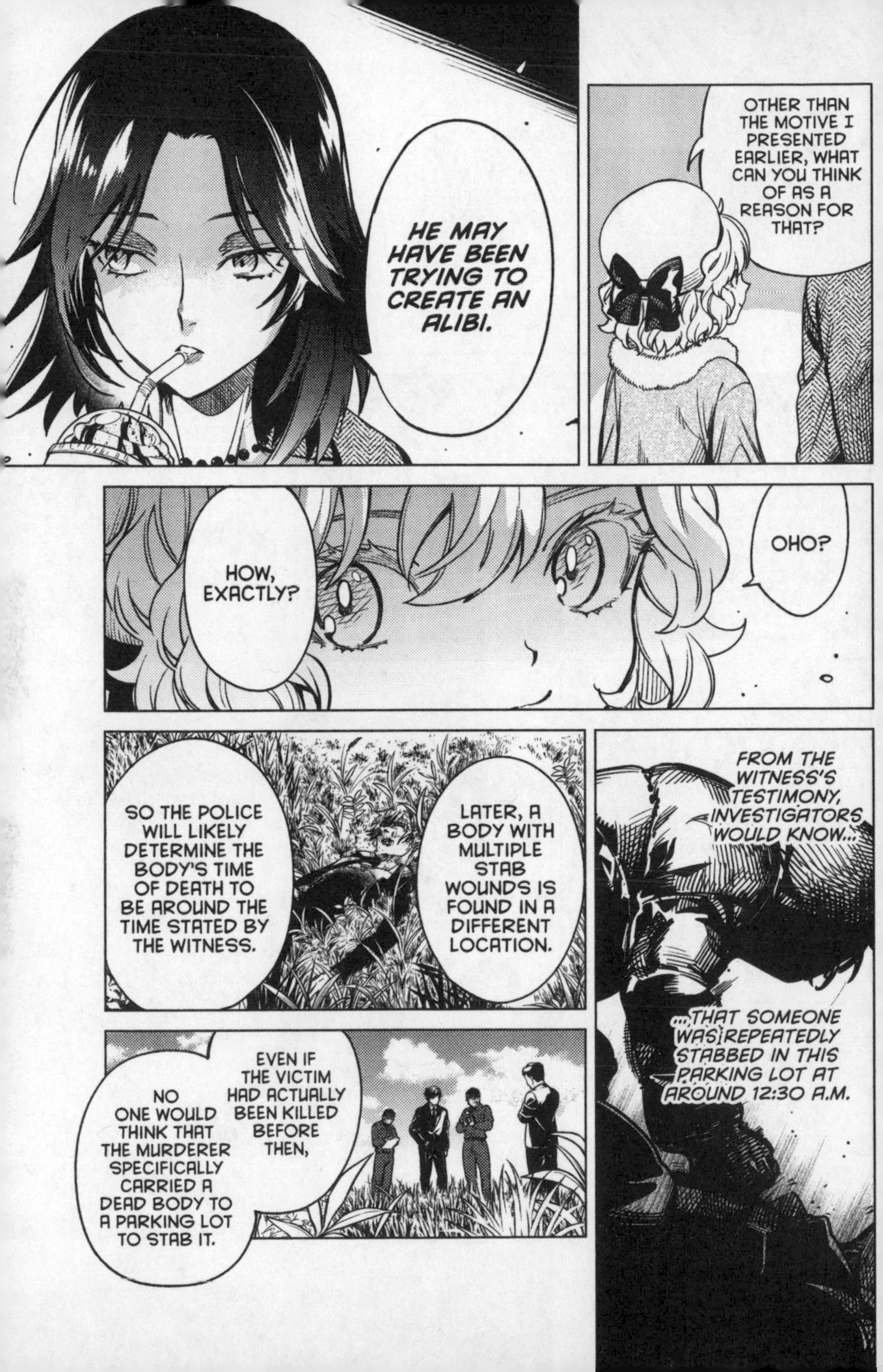
OTHER THAN THE MOTIVE I PRESENTED EARLIER, WHAT CAN YOU THINK OF AS A REASON FOR THAT?
HE MAY HAVE BEEN TRYING TO CREATE AN ALIBI.
OHO?
HOW, EXACTLY?
FROM THE WITNESS'S TESTIMONY, INVESTIGATORS WOULD KNOW...
...THAT SOMEONE WAS REPEATEDLY STABBED IN THIS PARKING LOT AT AROUND 12:30 A.M.
LATER, A BODY WITH MULTIPLE STAB WOUNDS IS FOUND IN A DIFFERENT LOCATION.
SO THE POLICE WILL LIKELY DETERMINE THE BODY'S TIME OF DEATH TO BE AROUND THE TIME STATED BY THE WITNESS.
EVEN IF THE VICTIM HAD ACTUALLY BEEN KILLED BEFORE THEN,
NO ONE WOULD THINK THAT THE MURDERER SPECIFICALLY CARRIED A DEAD BODY TO A PARKING LOT TO STAB IT.

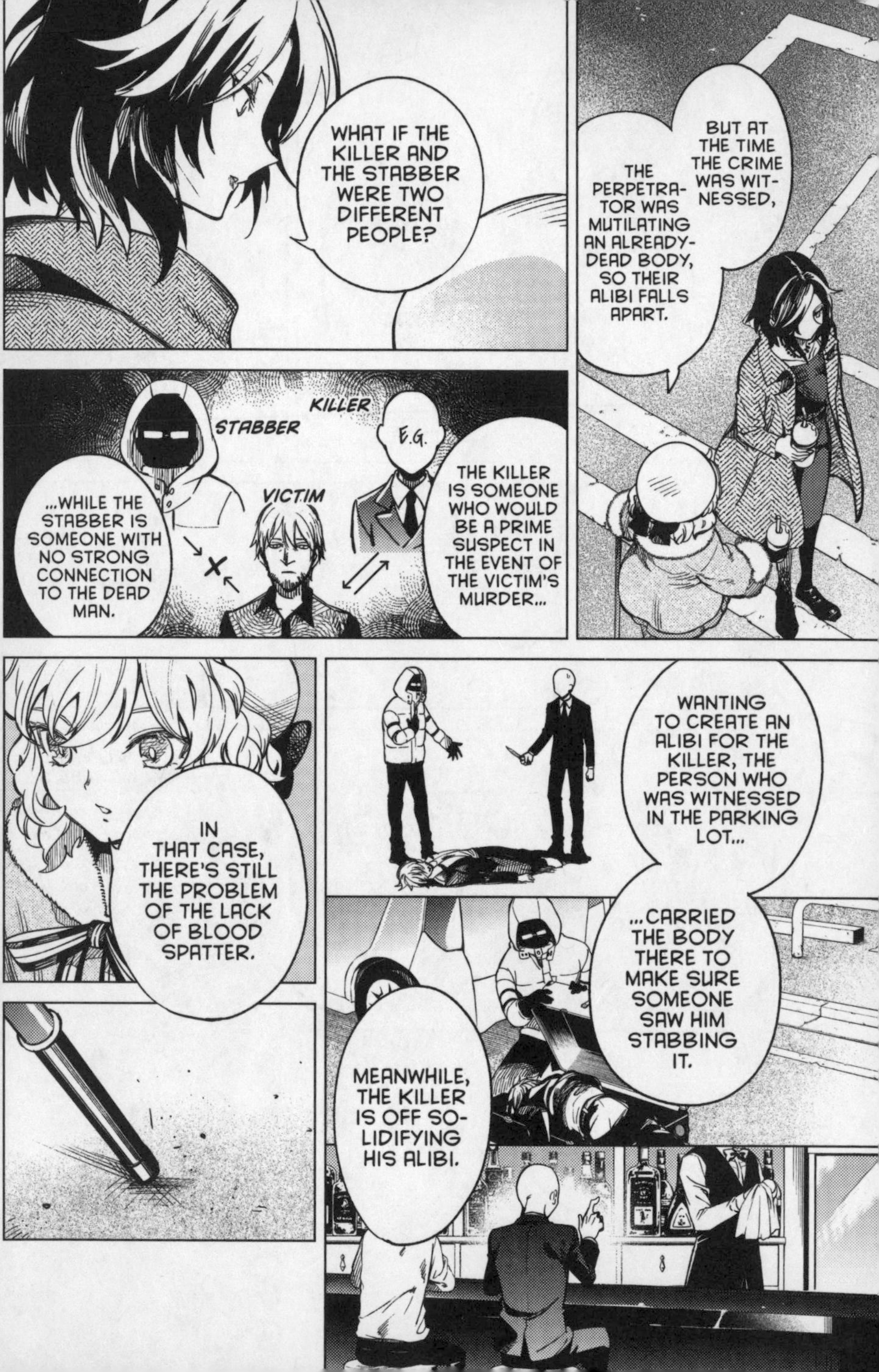
BUT AT THE TIME THE CRIME WAS WIT-NESSED,
THE PERPETRA-TOR WAS MUTILATING AN ALREADY-DEAD BODY, SO THEIR ALIBI FALLS APART.
WHAT IF THE KILLER AND THE STABBER WERE TWO DIFFERENT PEOPLE?
THE KILLER IS SOMEONE WHO WOULD BE A PRIME SUSPECT IN THE EVENT OF THE VICTIM'S MURDER...
KILLER
E.G.
STABBER
VICTIM
...WHILE THE STABBER IS SOMEONE WITH NO STRONG CONNECTION TO THE DEAD MAN.
WANTING TO CREATE AN ALIBI FOR THE KILLER, THE PERSON WHO WAS WITNESSED IN THE PARKING LOT...
...CARRIED THE BODY THERE TO MAKE SURE SOMEONE SAW HIM STABBING IT.
MEANWHILE, THE KILLER IS OFF SO-LIDIFYING HIS ALIBI.
IN THAT CASE, THERE'S STILL THE PROBLEM OF THE LACK OF BLOOD SPATTER.

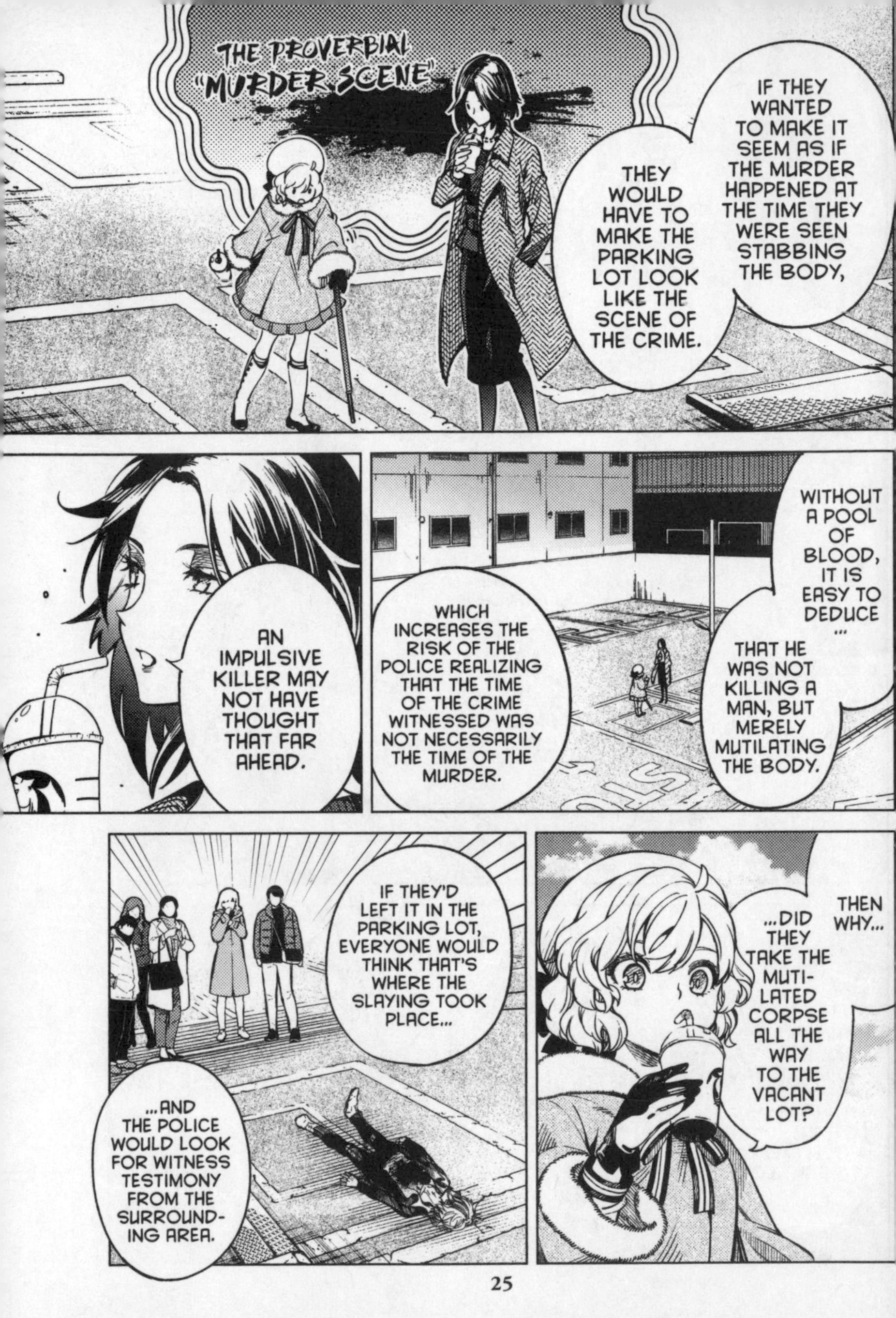
IF THEY WANTED TO MAKE IT SEEM AS IF THE MURDER HAPPENED AT THE TIME THEY WERE SEEN STABBING THE BODY,
THEY WOULD HAVE TO MAKE THE PARKING LOT LOOK LIKE THE SCENE OF THE CRIME.
THE PROVERBIAL "MURDER SCENE"
WITHOUT A POOL OF BLOOD, IT IS EASY TO DEDUCE ...
THAT HE WAS NOT KILLING A MAN, BUT MERELY MUTILATING THE BODY.
WHICH INCREASES THE RISK OF THE POLICE REALIZING THAT THE TIME OF THE CRIME WITNESSED WAS NOT NECESSARILY THE TIME OF THE MURDER.
AN IMPULSIVE KILLER MAY NOT HAVE THOUGHT THAT FAR AHEAD.
THEN WHY...
...DID THEY TAKE THE MUTI-LATED CORPSE ALL THE WAY TO THE VACANT LOT?
IF THEY'D LEFT IT IN THE PARKING LOT, EVERYONE WOULD THINK THAT'S WHERE THE SLAYING TOOK PLACE...
...AND THE POLICE WOULD LOOK FOR WITNESS TESTIMONY FROM THE SURROUND-ING AREA.

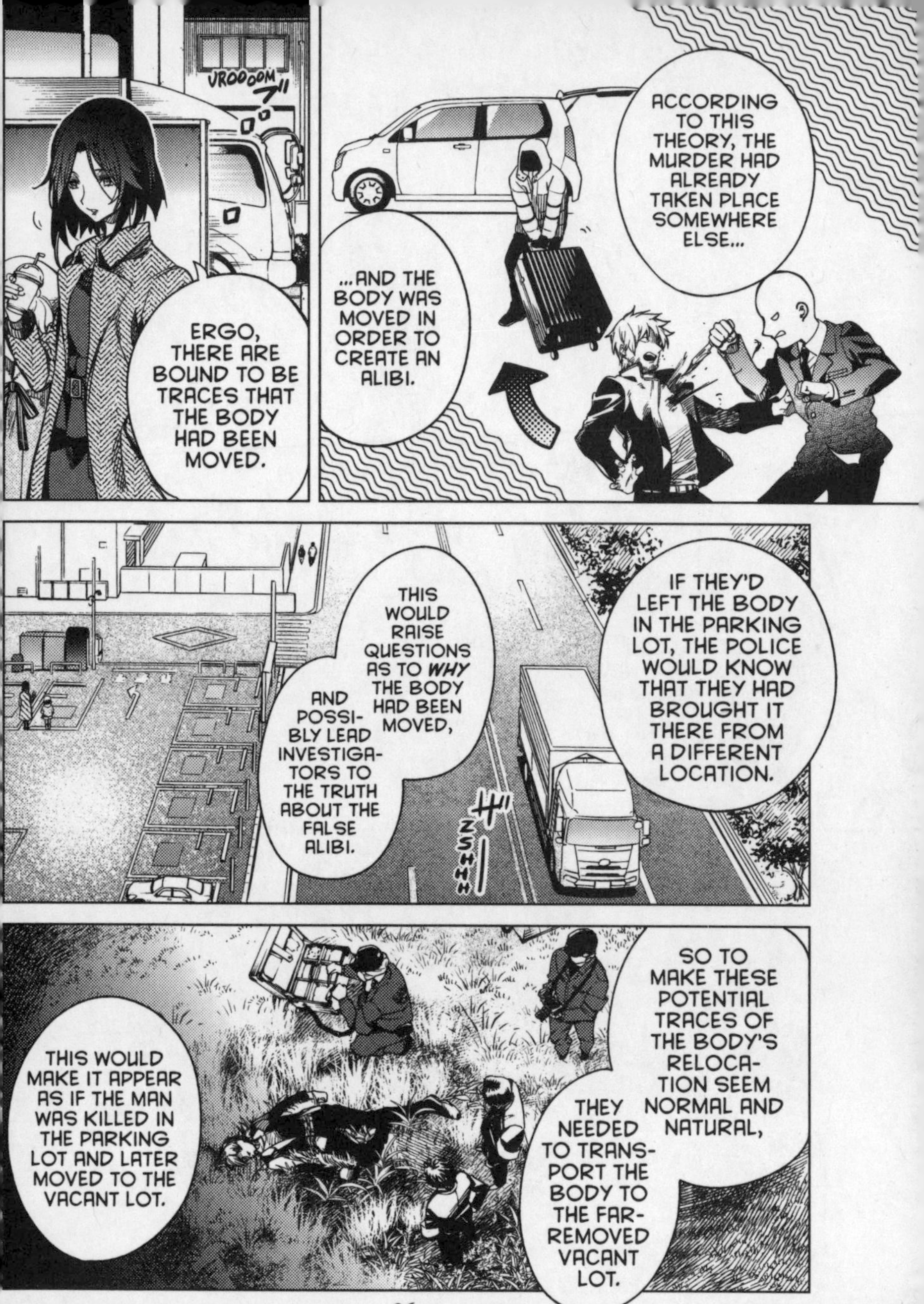
ACCORDING TO THIS THEORY, THE MURDER HAD ALREADY TAKEN PLACE SOMEWHERE ELSE...
...AND THE BODY WAS MOVED IN ORDER TO CREATE AN ALIBI.
VROOOOOM
ERGO, THERE ARE BOUND TO BE TRACES THAT THE BODY HAD BEEN MOVED.
IF THEY'D LEFT THE BODY IN THE PARKING LOT, THE POLICE WOULD KNOW THAT THEY HAD BROUGHT IT THERE FROM A DIFFERENT LOCATION.
ZSHHH
THIS WOULD RAISE QUESTIONS AS TO *WHY* THE BODY HAD BEEN MOVED,
AND POSSI-BLY LEAD INVESTIGA-TORS TO THE TRUTH ABOUT THE FALSE ALIBI.
SO TO MAKE THESE POTENTIAL TRACES OF THE BODY'S RELOCA-TION SEEM NORMAL AND NATURAL,
THEY NEEDED TO TRANS-PORT THE BODY TO THE FAR-REMOVED VACANT LOT.
THIS WOULD MAKE IT APPEAR AS IF THE MAN WAS KILLED IN THE PARKING LOT AND LATER MOVED TO THE VACANT LOT.

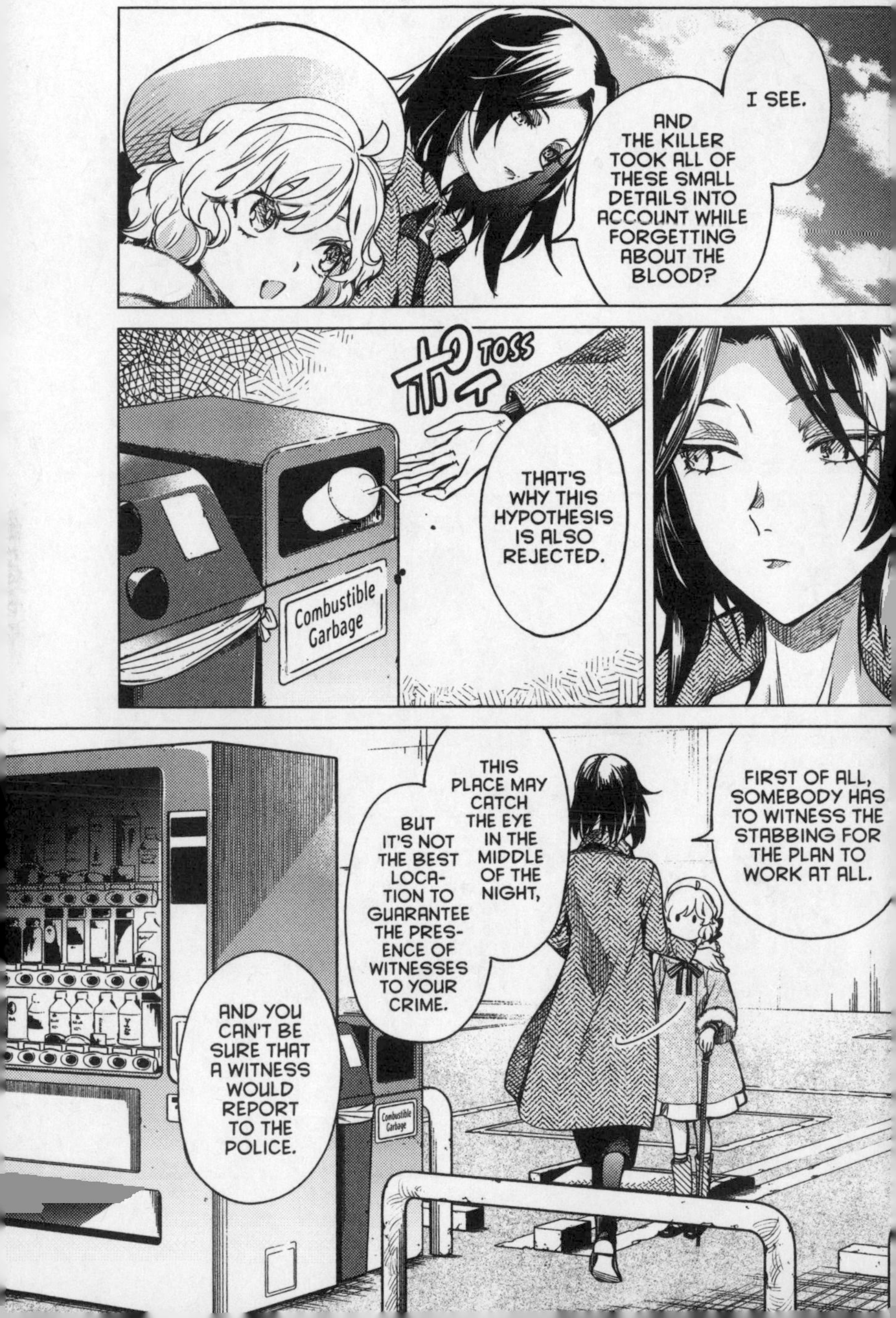
I SEE.
AND THE KILLER TOOK ALL OF THESE SMALL DETAILS INTO ACCOUNT WHILE FORGETTING ABOUT THE BLOOD?
TOSS
THAT'S WHY THIS HYPOTHESIS IS ALSO REJECTED.
Combustible Garbage
FIRST OF ALL, SOMEBODY HAS TO WITNESS THE STABBING FOR THE PLAN TO WORK AT ALL.
THIS PLACE MAY CATCH THE EYE IN THE MIDDLE OF THE NIGHT,
BUT IT'S NOT THE BEST LOCA-TION TO GUARANTEE THE PRES-ENCE OF WITNESSES TO YOUR CRIME.
AND YOU CAN'T BE SURE THAT A WITNESS WOULD REPORT TO THE POLICE.
Combustible Garbage

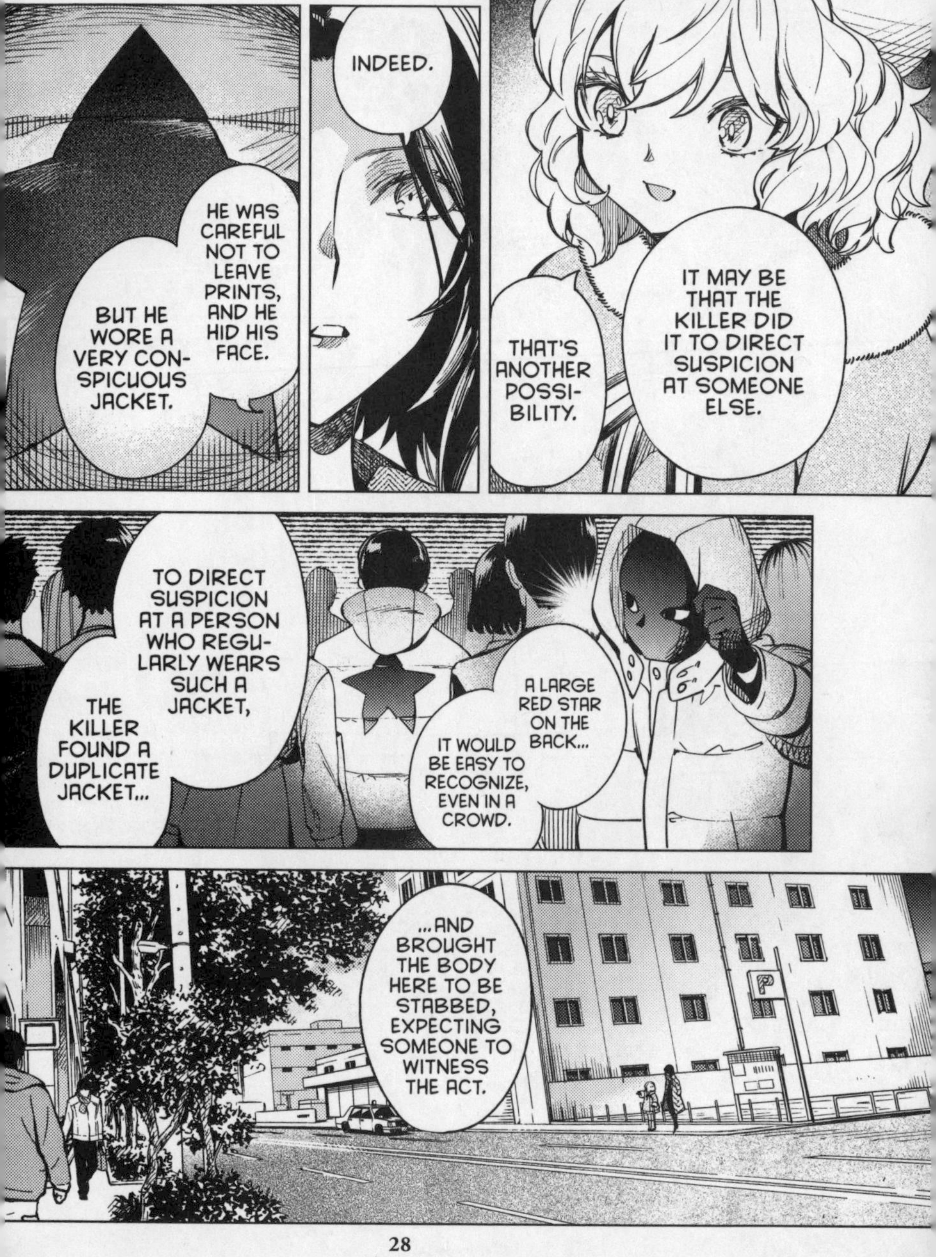
IT MAY BE THAT THE KILLER DID IT TO DIRECT SUSPICION AT SOMEONE ELSE.
THAT'S ANOTHER POSSI- BILITY.
INDEED.
HE WAS CAREFUL NOT TO LEAVE PRINTS, AND HE HID HIS FACE.
BUT HE WORE A VERY CON- SPICUOUS JACKET.
A LARGE RED STAR ON THE BACK...
IT WOULD BE EASY TO RECOGNIZE, EVEN IN A CROWD.
TO DIRECT SUSPICION AT A PERSON WHO REGU- LARLY WEARS SUCH A JACKET,
THE KILLER FOUND A DUPLICATE JACKET...
...AND BROUGHT THE BODY HERE TO BE STABBED, EXPECTING SOMEONE TO WITNESS THE ACT.

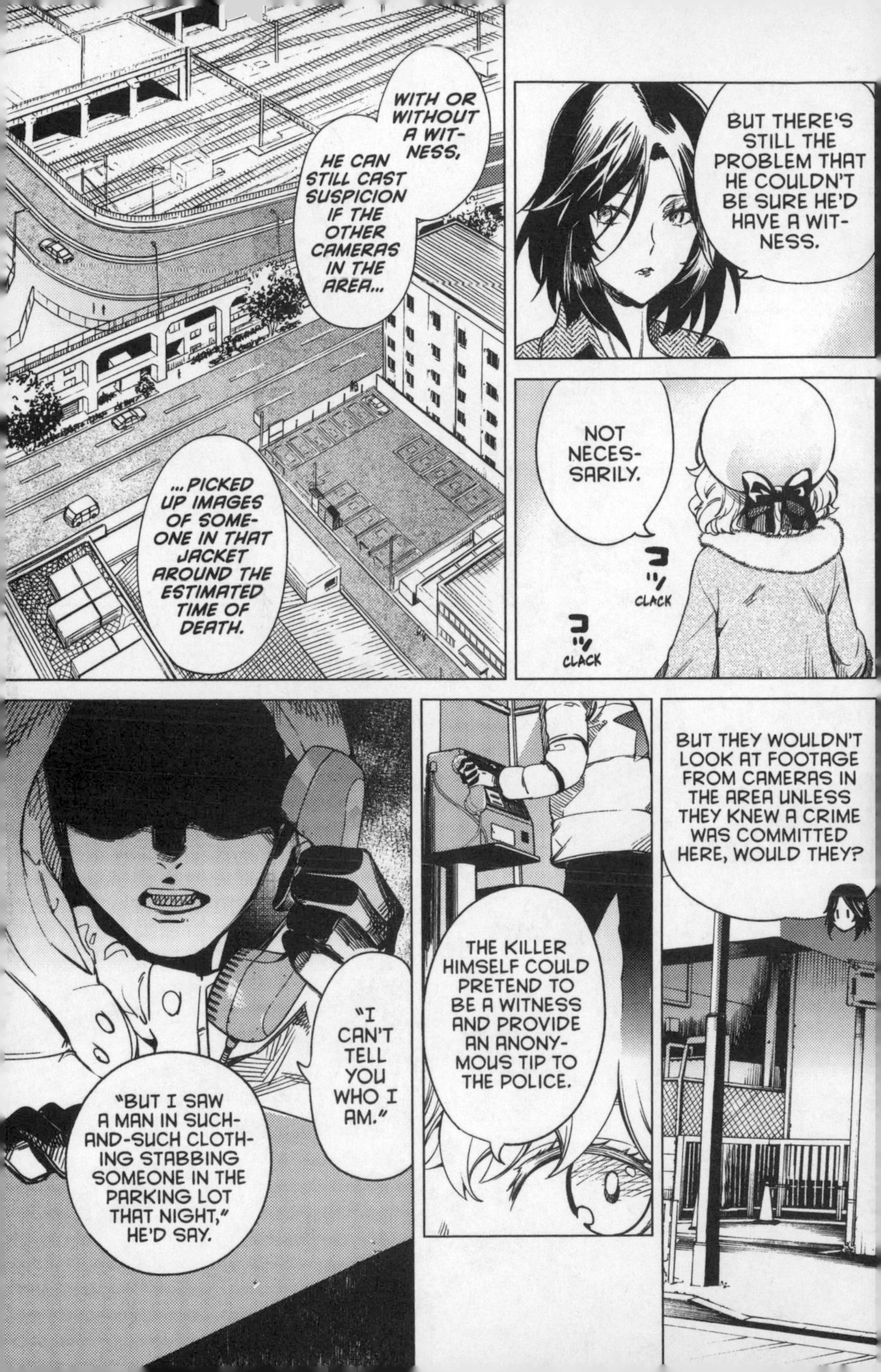
BUT THERE'S STILL THE PROBLEM THAT HE COULDN'T BE SURE HE'D HAVE A WIT-NESS.
NOT NECES-SARILY.
コッ CLACK
コッ CLACK
WITH OR WITHOUT A WIT-NESS,
HE CAN STILL CAST SUSPICION IF THE OTHER CAMERAS IN THE AREA...
...PICKED UP IMAGES OF SOME-ONE IN THAT JACKET AROUND THE ESTIMATED TIME OF DEATH.
BUT THEY WOULDN'T LOOK AT FOOTAGE FROM CAMERAS IN THE AREA UNLESS THEY KNEW A CRIME WAS COMMITTED HERE, WOULD THEY?
THE KILLER HIMSELF COULD PRETEND TO BE A WITNESS AND PROVIDE AN ANONY-MOUS TIP TO THE POLICE.
"I CAN'T TELL YOU WHO I AM."
"BUT I SAW A MAN IN SUCH-AND-SUCH CLOTH-ING STABBING SOMEONE IN THE PARKING LOT THAT NIGHT," HE'D SAY.

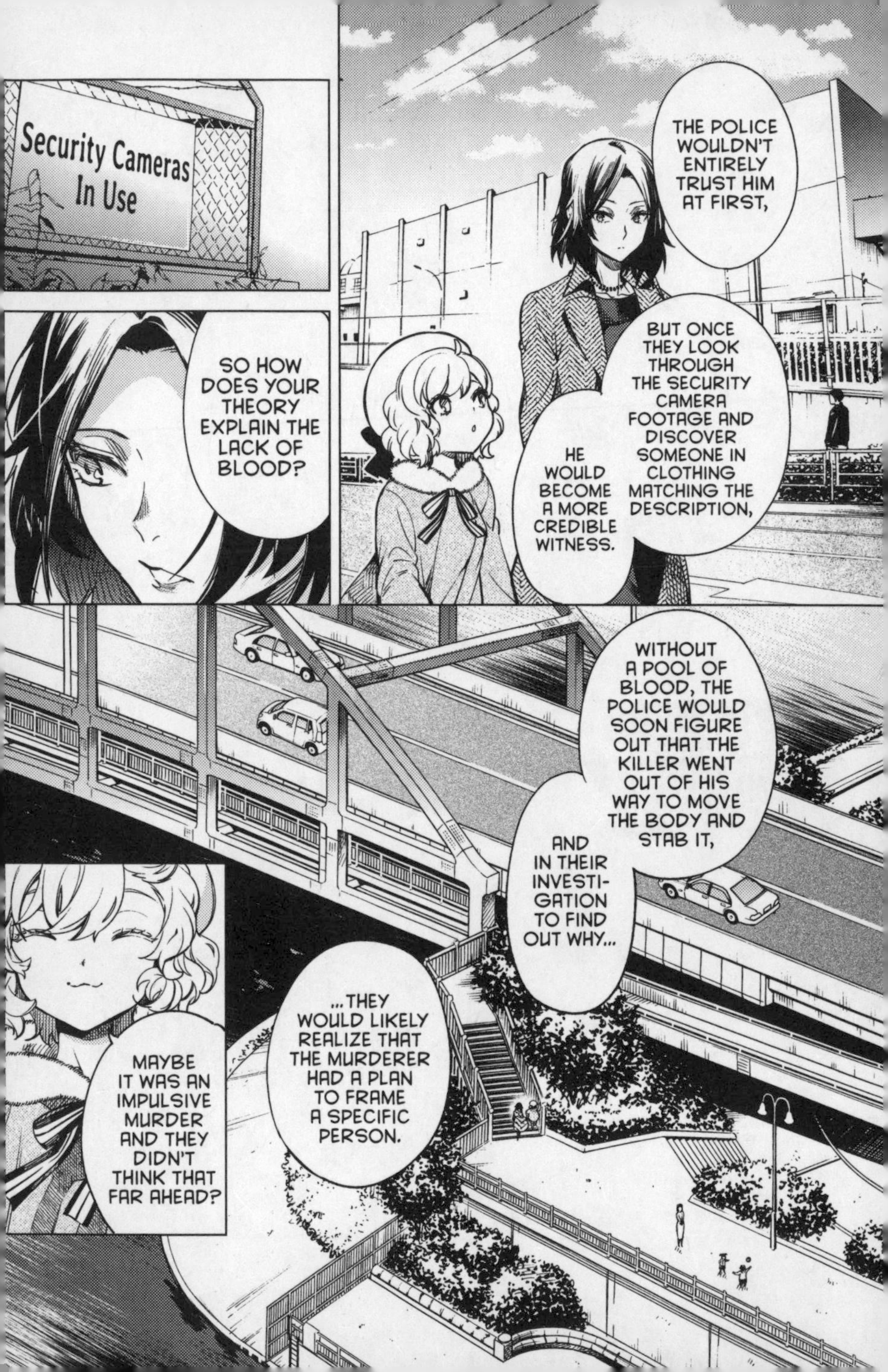
THE POLICE WOULDN'T ENTIRELY TRUST HIM AT FIRST,
BUT ONCE THEY LOOK THROUGH THE SECURITY CAMERA FOOTAGE AND DISCOVER SOMEONE IN CLOTHING MATCHING THE DESCRIPTION,
HE WOULD BECOME A MORE CREDIBLE WITNESS.
Security Cameras In Use
SO HOW DOES YOUR THEORY EXPLAIN THE LACK OF BLOOD?
WITHOUT A POOL OF BLOOD, THE POLICE WOULD SOON FIGURE OUT THAT THE KILLER WENT OUT OF HIS WAY TO MOVE THE BODY AND STAB IT,
AND IN THEIR INVESTIGATION TO FIND OUT WHY...
...THEY WOULD LIKELY REALIZE THAT THE MURDERER HAD A PLAN TO FRAME A SPECIFIC PERSON.
MAYBE IT WAS AN IMPULSIVE MURDER AND THEY DIDN'T THINK THAT FAR AHEAD?

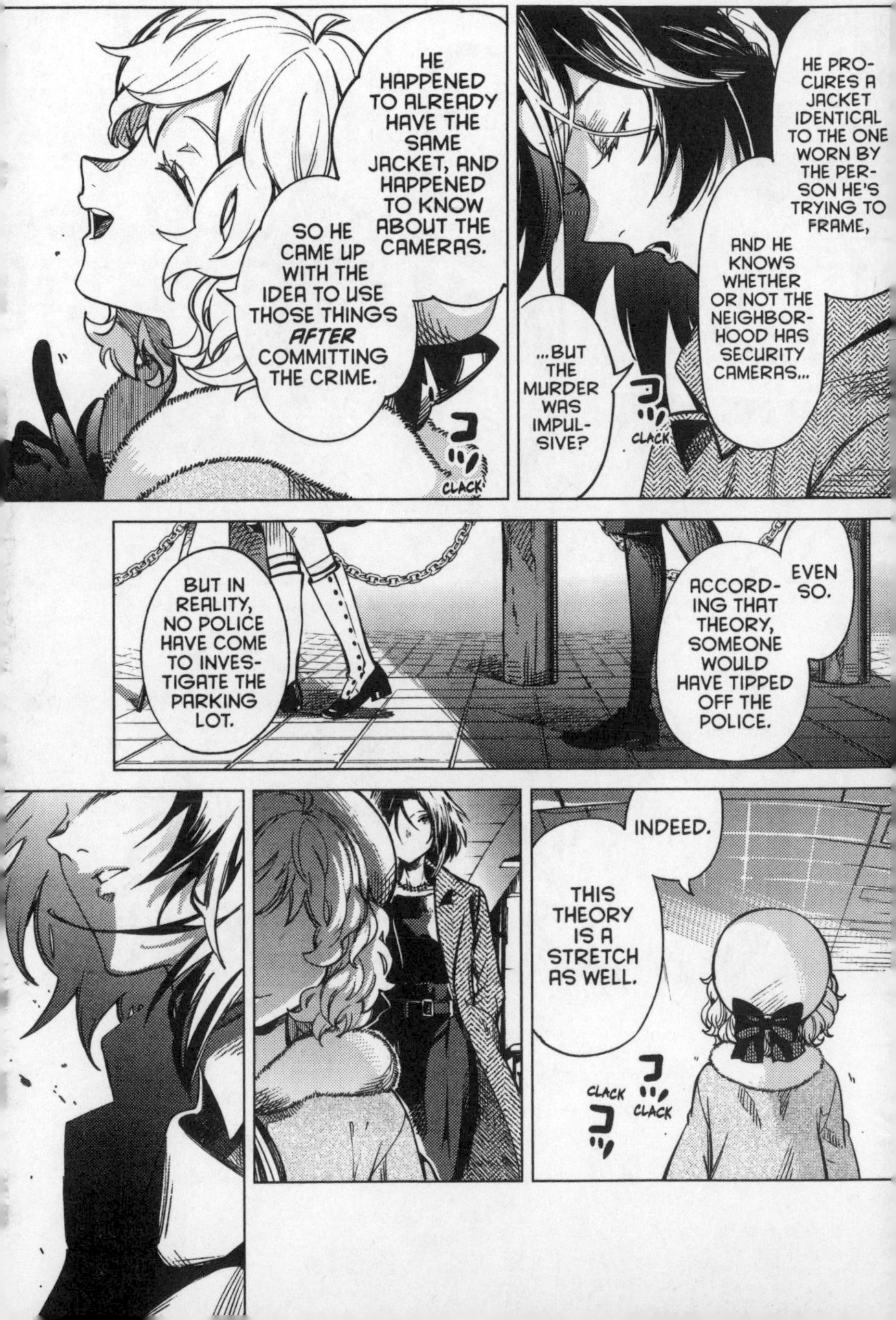
HE PROCURES A JACKET IDENTICAL TO THE ONE WORN BY THE PERSON HE'S TRYING TO FRAME,
AND HE KNOWS WHETHER OR NOT THE NEIGHBORHOOD HAS SECURITY CAMERAS...
CLACK
...BUT THE MURDER WAS IMPULSIVE?
HE HAPPENED TO ALREADY HAVE THE SAME JACKET, AND HAPPENED TO KNOW ABOUT THE CAMERAS.
SO HE CAME UP WITH THE IDEA TO USE THOSE THINGS *AFTER* COMMITTING THE CRIME.
CLACK
EVEN SO.
ACCORDING THAT THEORY, SOMEONE WOULD HAVE TIPPED OFF THE POLICE.
BUT IN REALITY, NO POLICE HAVE COME TO INVESTIGATE THE PARKING LOT.
INDEED.
THIS THEORY IS A STRETCH AS WELL.
CLACK
CLACK

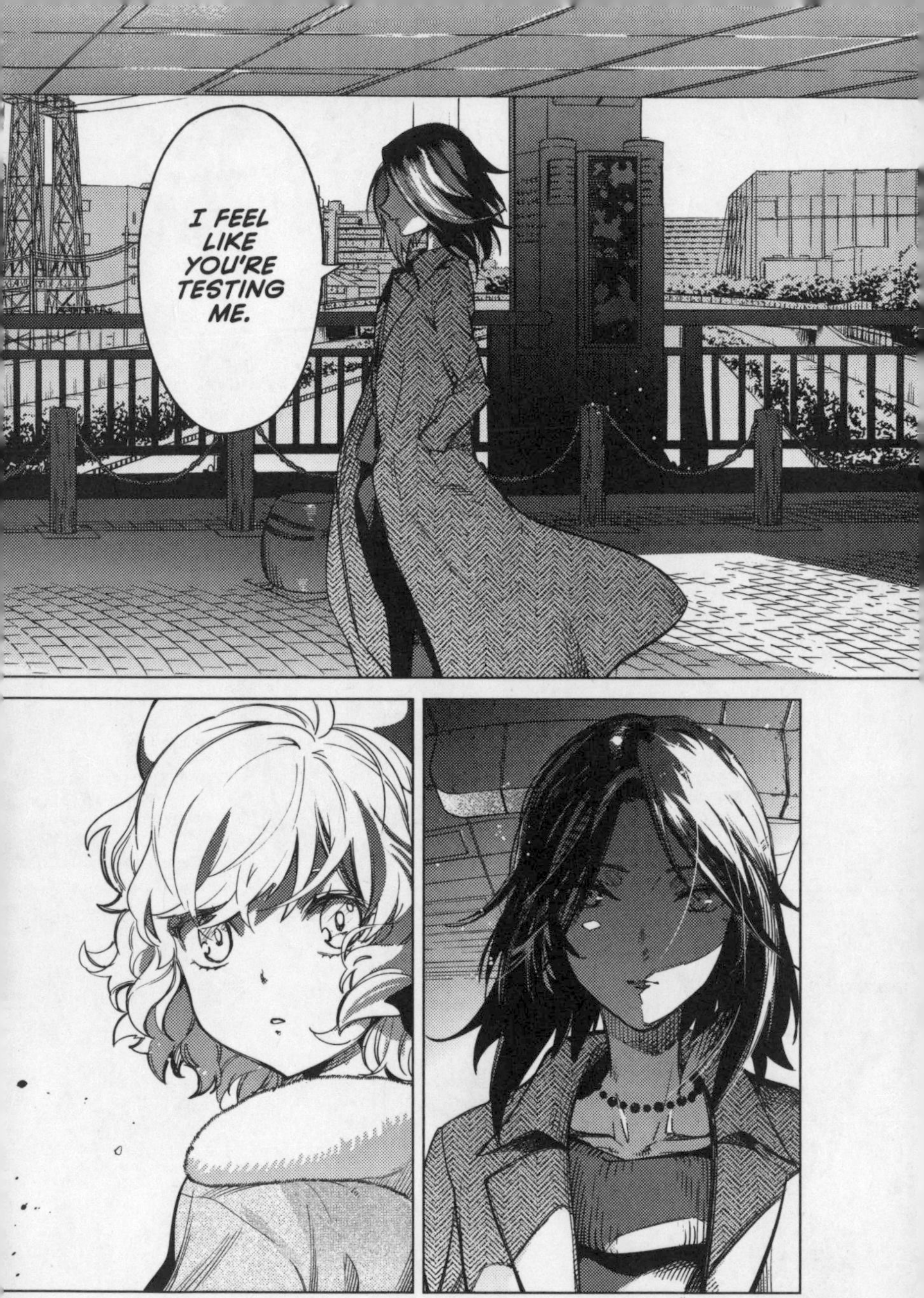
I FEEL LIKE YOU'RE TESTING ME.

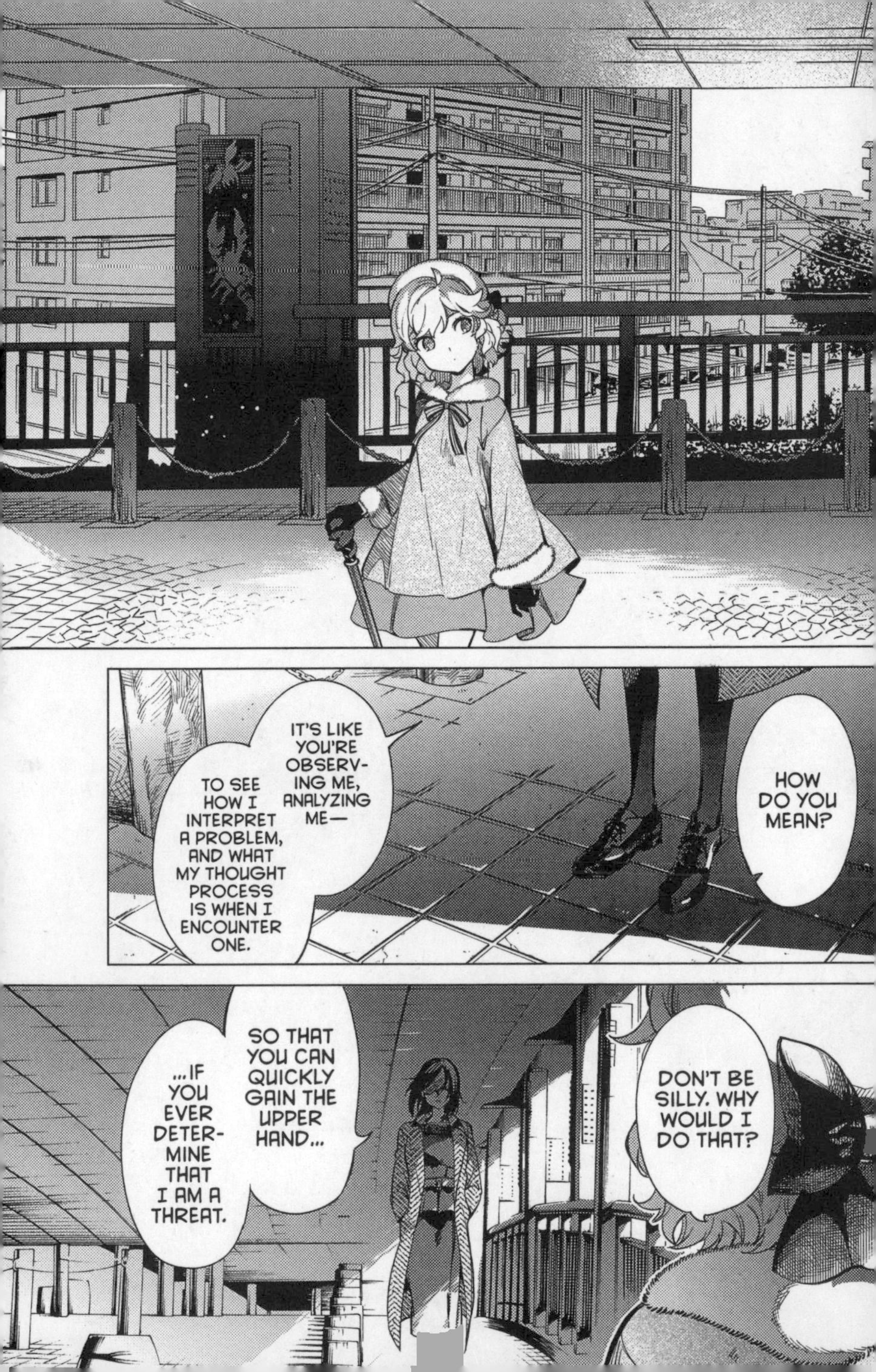
HOW DO YOU MEAN?
IT'S LIKE YOU'RE OBSERV-ING ME, ANALYZING ME—
TO SEE HOW I INTERPRET A PROBLEM, AND WHAT MY THOUGHT PROCESS IS WHEN I ENCOUNTER ONE.
DON'T BE SILLY. WHY WOULD I DO THAT?
SO THAT YOU CAN QUICKLY GAIN THE UPPER HAND...
...IF YOU EVER DETER-MINE THAT I AM A THREAT.

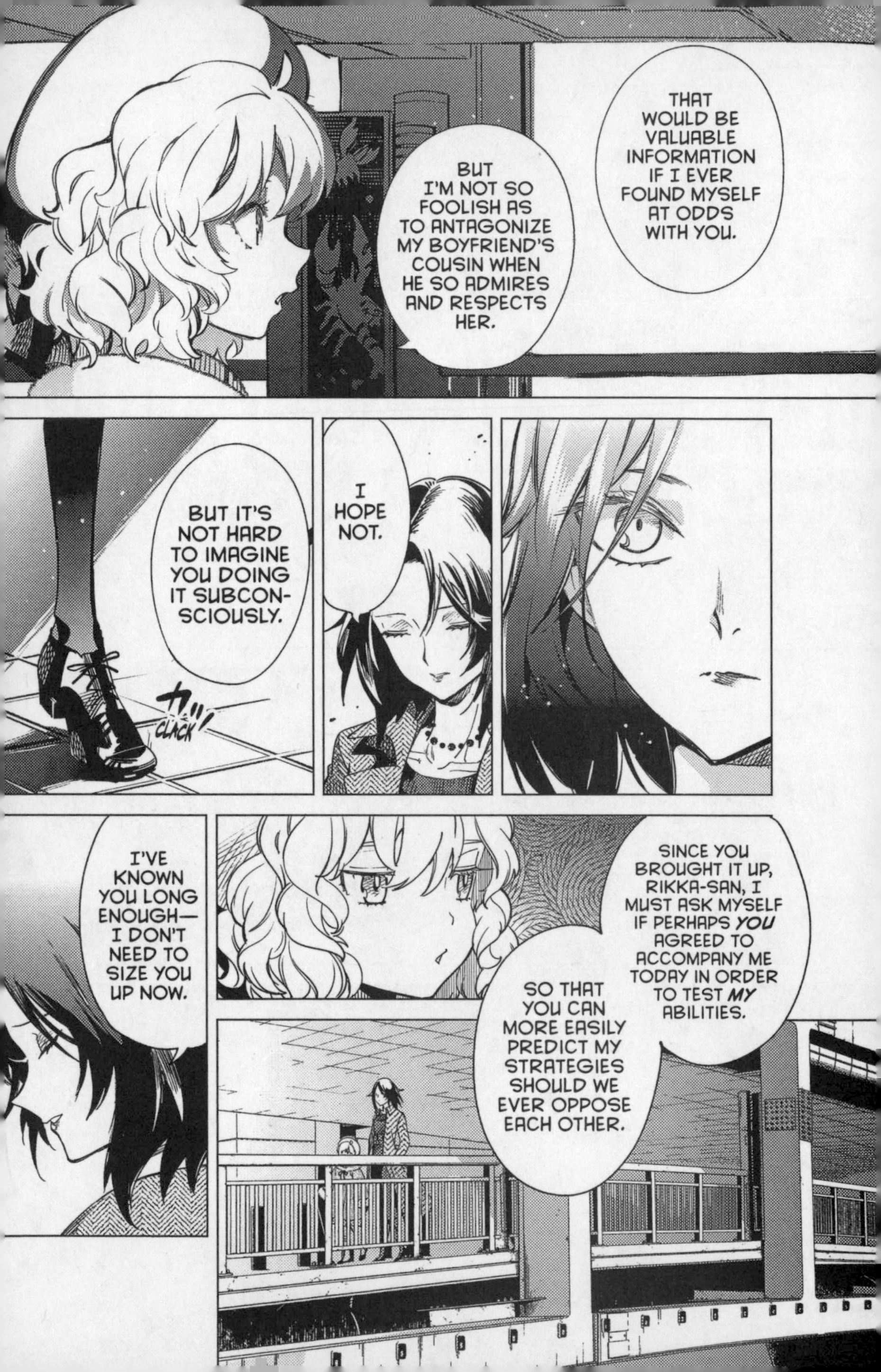
THAT WOULD BE VALUABLE INFORMATION IF I EVER FOUND MYSELF AT ODDS WITH YOU.
BUT I'M NOT SO FOOLISH AS TO ANTAGONIZE MY BOYFRIEND'S COUSIN WHEN HE SO ADMIRES AND RESPECTS HER.
I HOPE NOT.
BUT IT'S NOT HARD TO IMAGINE YOU DOING IT SUBCON-SCIOUSLY.
CLACK
SINCE YOU BROUGHT IT UP, RIKKA-SAN, I MUST ASK MYSELF IF PERHAPS *YOU* AGREED TO ACCOMPANY ME TODAY IN ORDER TO TEST *MY* ABILITIES.
SO THAT YOU CAN MORE EASILY PREDICT MY STRATEGIES SHOULD WE EVER OPPOSE EACH OTHER.
I'VE KNOWN YOU LONG ENOUGH— I DON'T NEED TO SIZE YOU UP NOW.

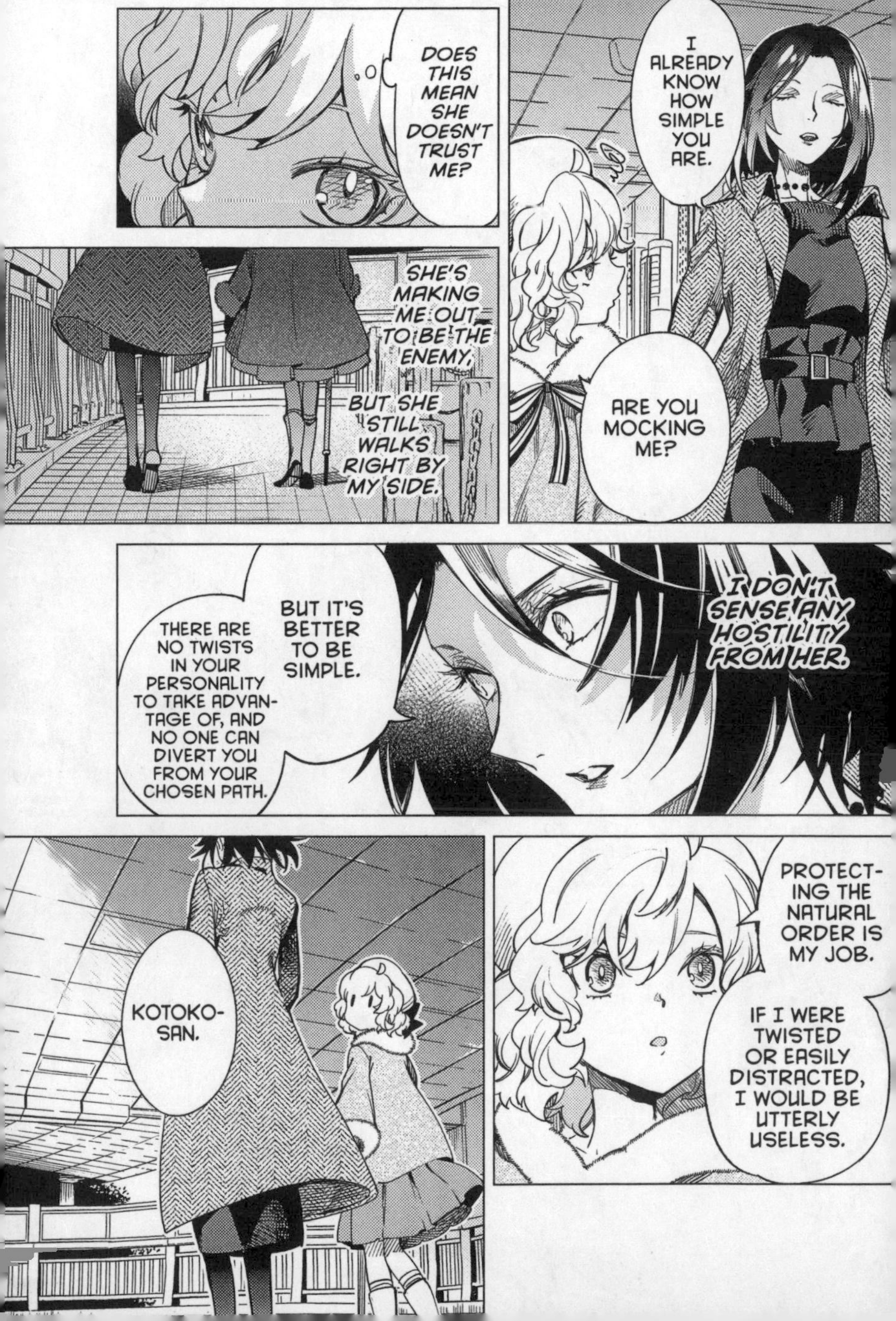
I ALREADY KNOW HOW SIMPLE YOU ARE.
ARE YOU MOCKING ME?
DOES THIS MEAN SHE DOESN'T TRUST ME?
SHE'S MAKING ME OUT TO BE THE ENEMY,
BUT SHE STILL WALKS RIGHT BY MY SIDE.
I DON'T SENSE ANY HOSTILITY FROM HER.
BUT IT'S BETTER TO BE SIMPLE.
THERE ARE NO TWISTS IN YOUR PERSONALITY TO TAKE ADVANTAGE OF, AND NO ONE CAN DIVERT YOU FROM YOUR CHOSEN PATH.
PROTECTING THE NATURAL ORDER IS MY JOB.
IF I WERE TWISTED OR EASILY DISTRACTED, I WOULD BE UTTERLY USELESS.
KOTOKO-SAN.

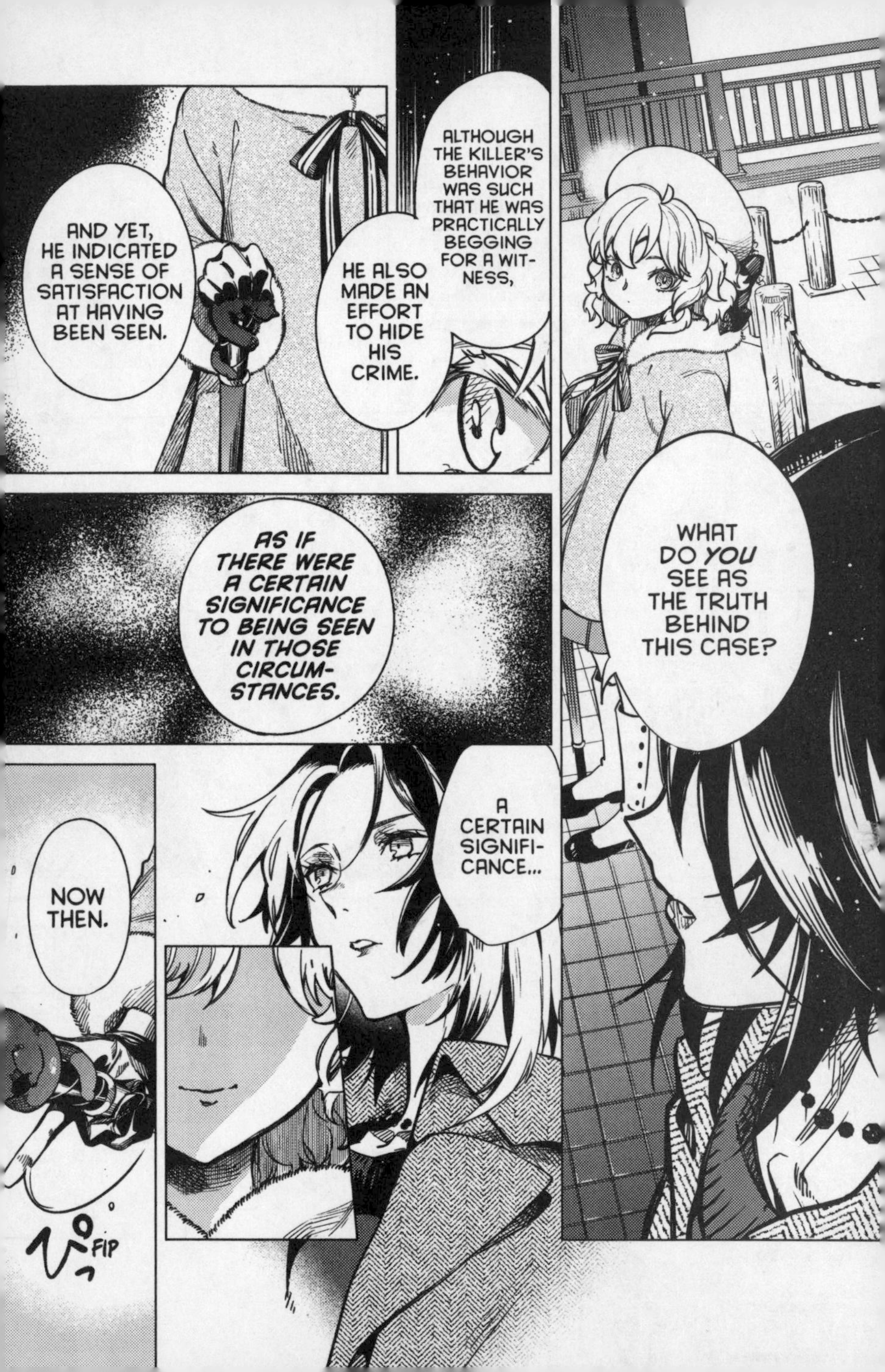
WHAT DO *YOU* SEE AS THE TRUTH BEHIND THIS CASE?
ALTHOUGH THE KILLER'S BEHAVIOR WAS SUCH THAT HE WAS PRACTICALLY BEGGING FOR A WIT-NESS,
HE ALSO MADE AN EFFORT TO HIDE HIS CRIME.
AND YET, HE INDICATED A SENSE OF SATISFACTION AT HAVING BEEN SEEN.
AS IF THERE WERE A CERTAIN SIGNIFICANCE TO BEING SEEN IN THOSE CIRCUM-STANCES.
A CERTAIN SIGNIFI-CANCE...
NOW THEN.
FIP

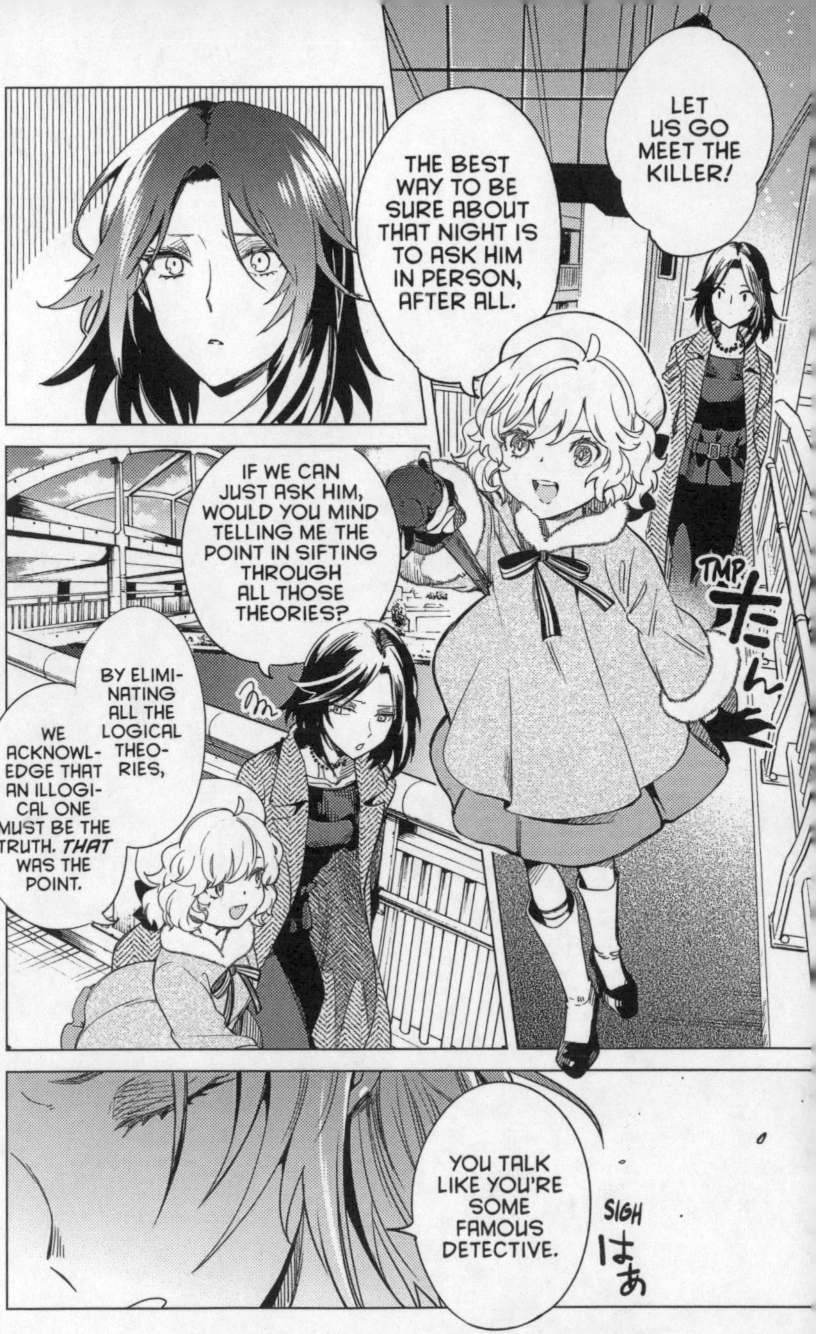
LET US GO MEET THE KILLER!
TMP たん
THE BEST WAY TO BE SURE ABOUT THAT NIGHT IS TO ASK HIM IN PERSON, AFTER ALL.
IF WE CAN JUST ASK HIM, WOULD YOU MIND TELLING ME THE POINT IN SIFTING THROUGH ALL THOSE THEORIES?
BY ELIMINATING ALL THE LOGICAL THEORIES,
WE ACKNOWLEDGE THAT AN ILLOGICAL ONE MUST BE THE TRUTH. *THAT* WAS THE POINT.
SIGH はあ
YOU TALK LIKE YOU'RE SOME FAMOUS DETECTIVE.

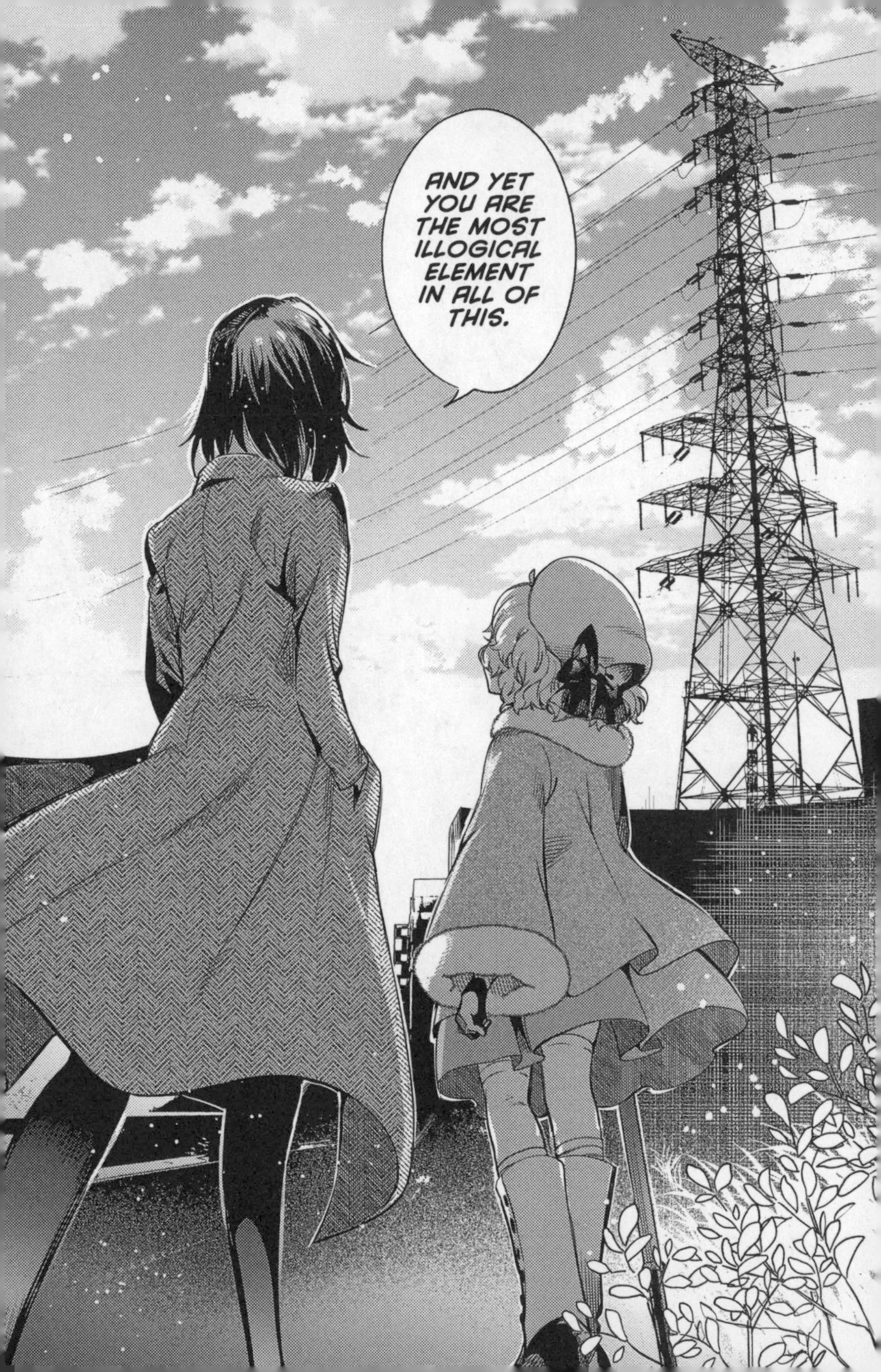
AND YET YOU ARE THE MOST ILLOGICAL ELEMENT IN ALL OF THIS.

IN/SPECTRE

CHAPTER 37:
"WHAT WAS SEEN PART 3"

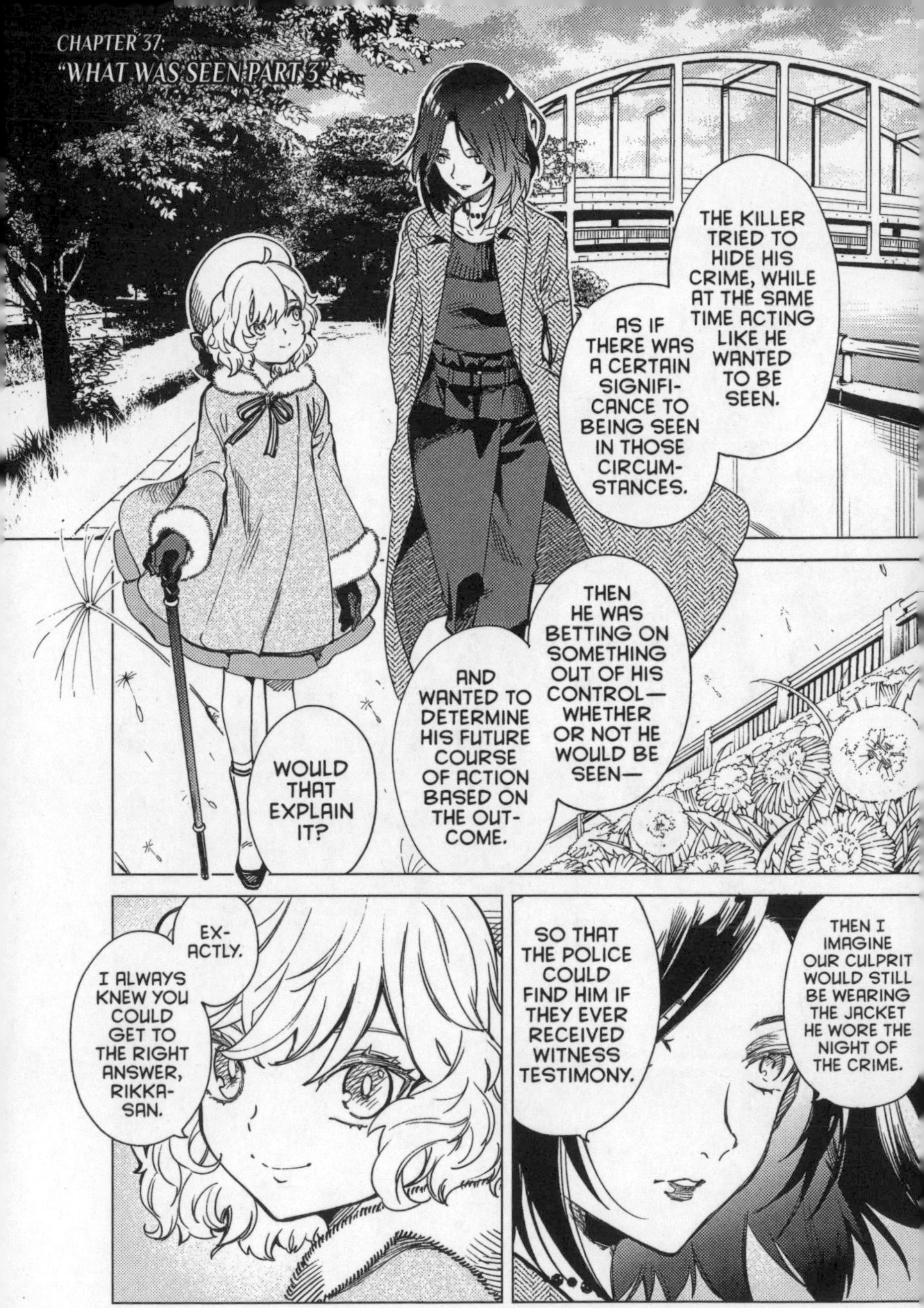
THE KILLER TRIED TO HIDE HIS CRIME, WHILE AT THE SAME TIME ACTING LIKE HE WANTED TO BE SEEN.
AS IF THERE WAS A CERTAIN SIGNIFI-CANCE TO BEING SEEN IN THOSE CIRCUM-STANCES.
THEN HE WAS BETTING ON SOMETHING OUT OF HIS CONTROL—WHETHER OR NOT HE WOULD BE SEEN—
AND WANTED TO DETERMINE HIS FUTURE COURSE OF ACTION BASED ON THE OUT-COME.
WOULD THAT EXPLAIN IT?
THEN I IMAGINE OUR CULPRIT WOULD STILL BE WEARING THE JACKET HE WORE THE NIGHT OF THE CRIME.
SO THAT THE POLICE COULD FIND HIM IF THEY EVER RECEIVED WITNESS TESTIMONY.
EX-ACTLY.
I ALWAYS KNEW YOU COULD GET TO THE RIGHT ANSWER, RIKKA-SAN.

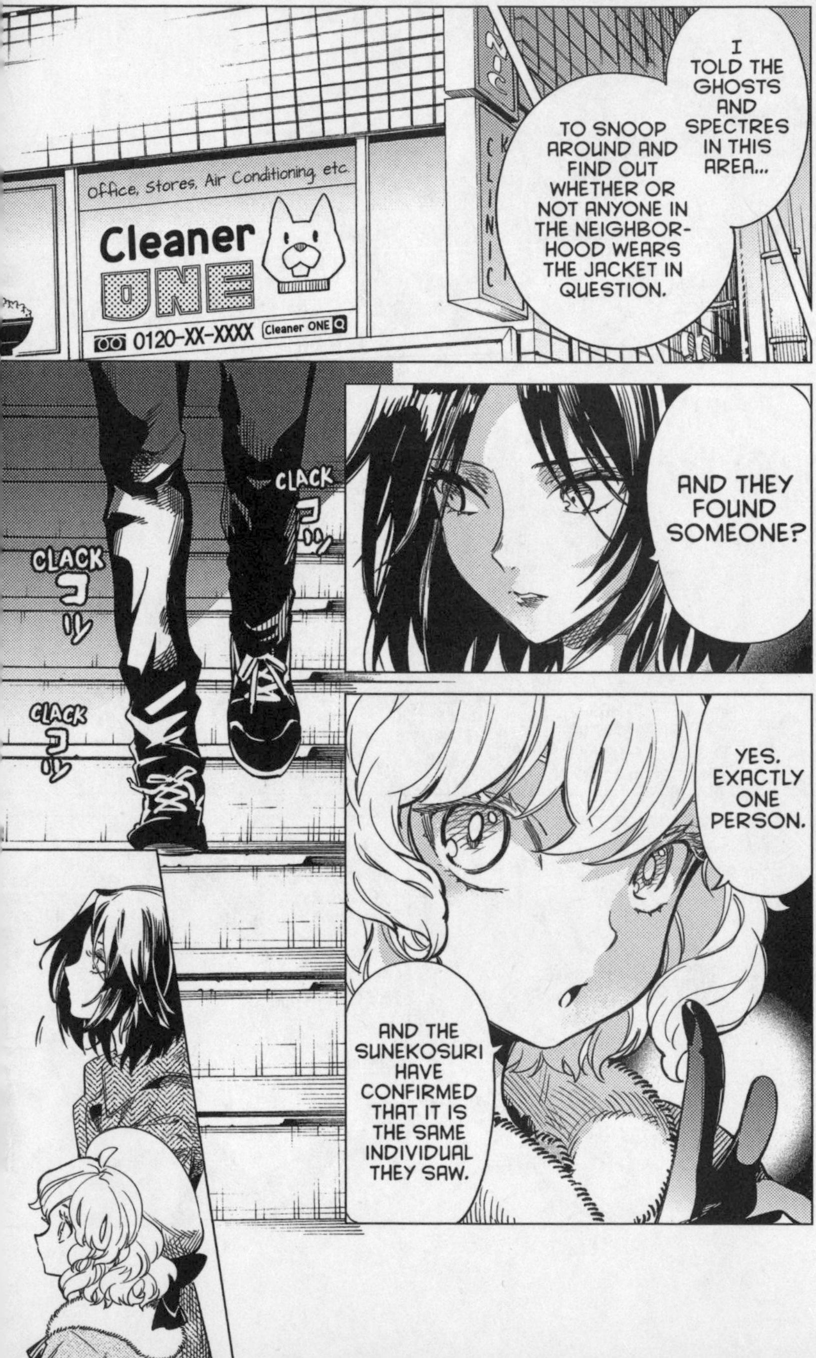
I TOLD THE GHOSTS AND SPECTRES IN THIS AREA...
TO SNOOP AROUND AND FIND OUT WHETHER OR NOT ANYONE IN THE NEIGHBOR-HOOD WEARS THE JACKET IN QUESTION.
Office, Stores, Air Conditioning etc.
Cleaner ONE
0120-XX-XXXX
Cleaner ONE
CLINIC
AND THEY FOUND SOMEONE?
CLACK
CLACK
CLACK
YES. EXACTLY ONE PERSON.
AND THE SUNEKOSURI HAVE CONFIRMED THAT IT IS THE SAME INDIVIDUAL THEY SAW.

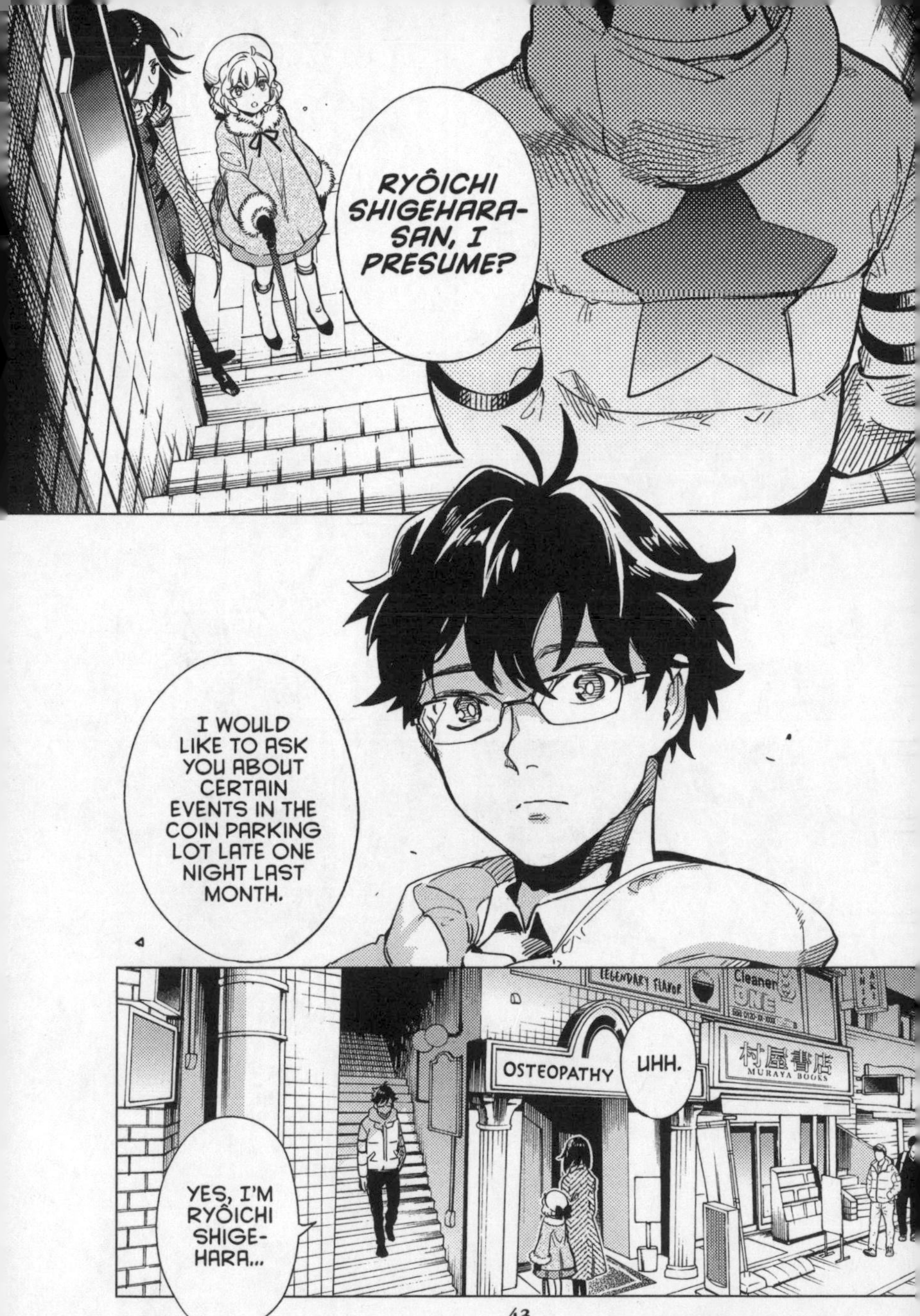

RYÔICHI SHIGEHARA-SAN, I PRESUME?
I WOULD LIKE TO ASK YOU ABOUT CERTAIN EVENTS IN THE COIN PARKING LOT LATE ONE NIGHT LAST MONTH.
LEGENDARY FLAVOR
Cleaner ONE
村屋書店
MURAYA BOOKS
UHH.
OSTEOPATHY
YES, I'M RYÔICHI SHIGE-HARA...

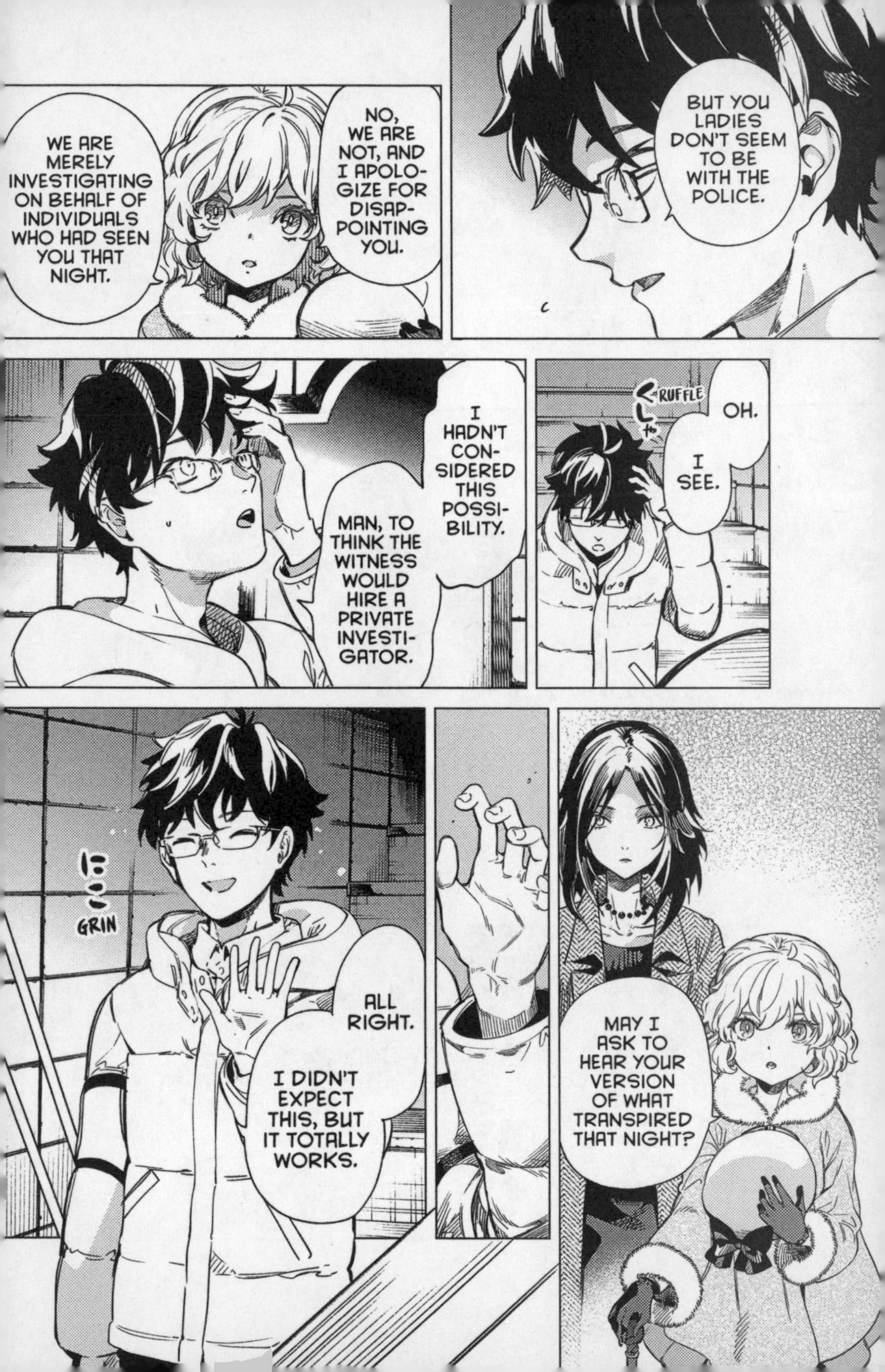
BUT YOU LADIES DON'T SEEM TO BE WITH THE POLICE.
NO, WE ARE NOT, AND I APOLOGIZE FOR DISAPPOINTING YOU.
WE ARE MERELY INVESTIGATING ON BEHALF OF INDIVIDUALS WHO HAD SEEN YOU THAT NIGHT.
OH.
I SEE.
RUFFLE
I HADN'T CONSIDERED THIS POSSIBILITY.
MAN, TO THINK THE WITNESS WOULD HIRE A PRIVATE INVESTIGATOR.
MAY I ASK TO HEAR YOUR VERSION OF WHAT TRANSPIRED THAT NIGHT?
ALL RIGHT.
I DIDN'T EXPECT THIS, BUT IT TOTALLY WORKS.
GRIN

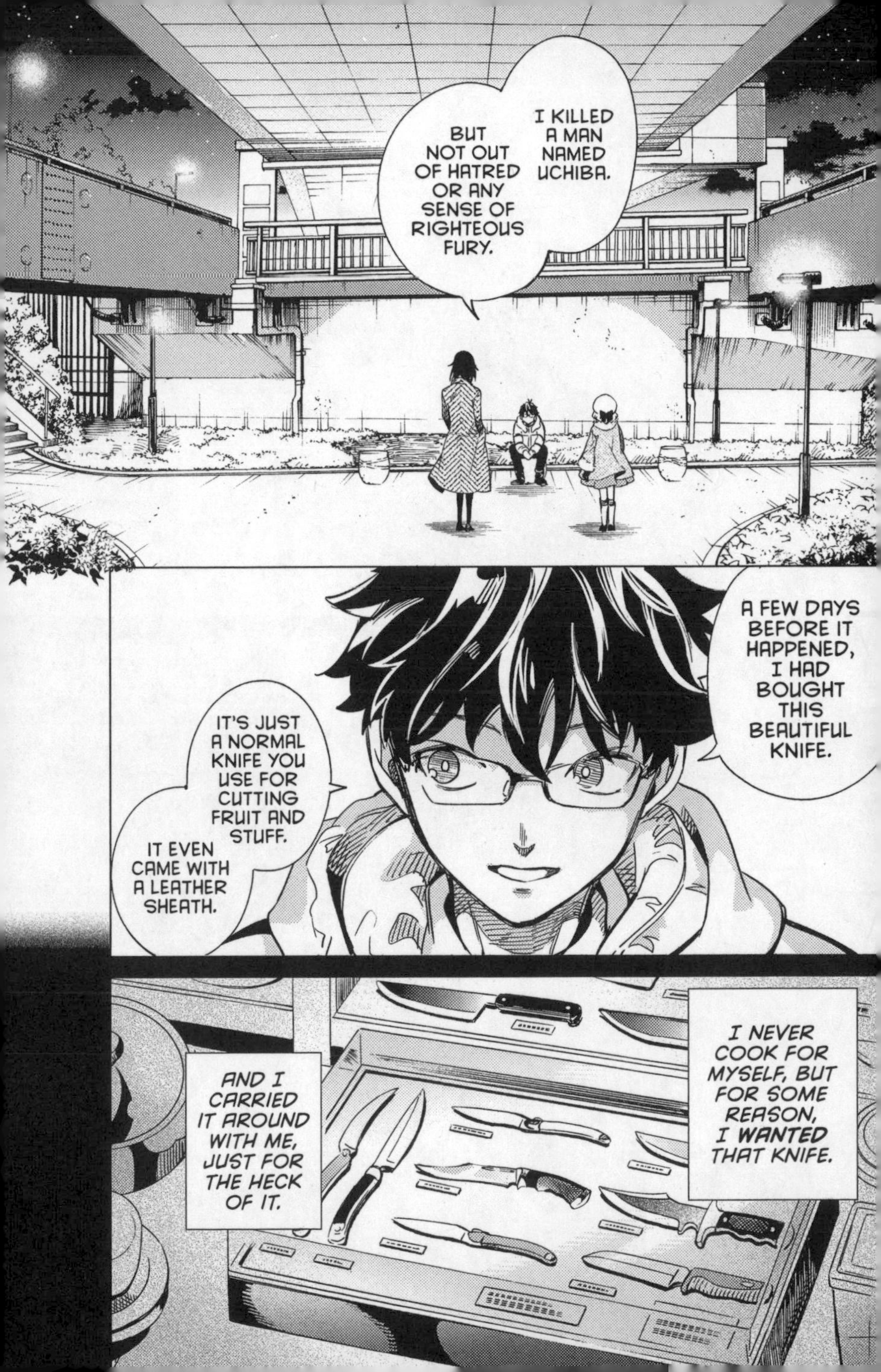
I KILLED A MAN NAMED UCHIBA.
BUT NOT OUT OF HATRED OR ANY SENSE OF RIGHTEOUS FURY.
A FEW DAYS BEFORE IT HAPPENED, I HAD BOUGHT THIS BEAUTIFUL KNIFE.
IT'S JUST A NORMAL KNIFE YOU USE FOR CUTTING FRUIT AND STUFF.
IT EVEN CAME WITH A LEATHER SHEATH.
I NEVER COOK FOR MYSELF, BUT FOR SOME REASON, I WANTED THAT KNIFE.
AND I CARRIED IT AROUND WITH ME, JUST FOR THE HECK OF IT.

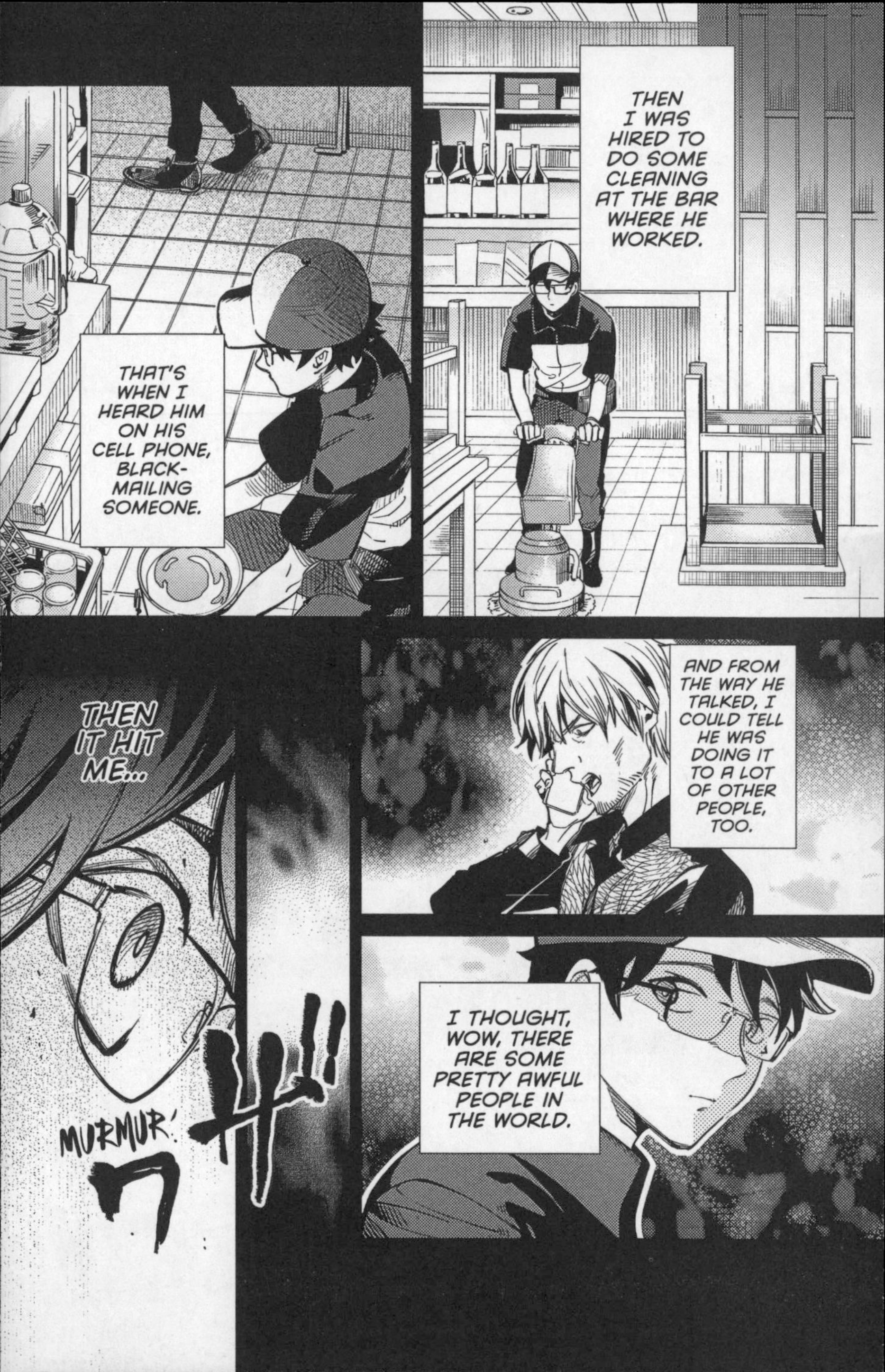
THEN I WAS HIRED TO DO SOME CLEANING AT THE BAR WHERE HE WORKED.
THAT'S WHEN I HEARD HIM ON HIS CELL PHONE, BLACK-MAILING SOMEONE.
AND FROM THE WAY HE TALKED, I COULD TELL HE WAS DOING IT TO A LOT OF OTHER PEOPLE, TOO.
I THOUGHT, WOW, THERE ARE SOME PRETTY AWFUL PEOPLE IN THE WORLD.
THEN IT HIT ME...
MURMUR

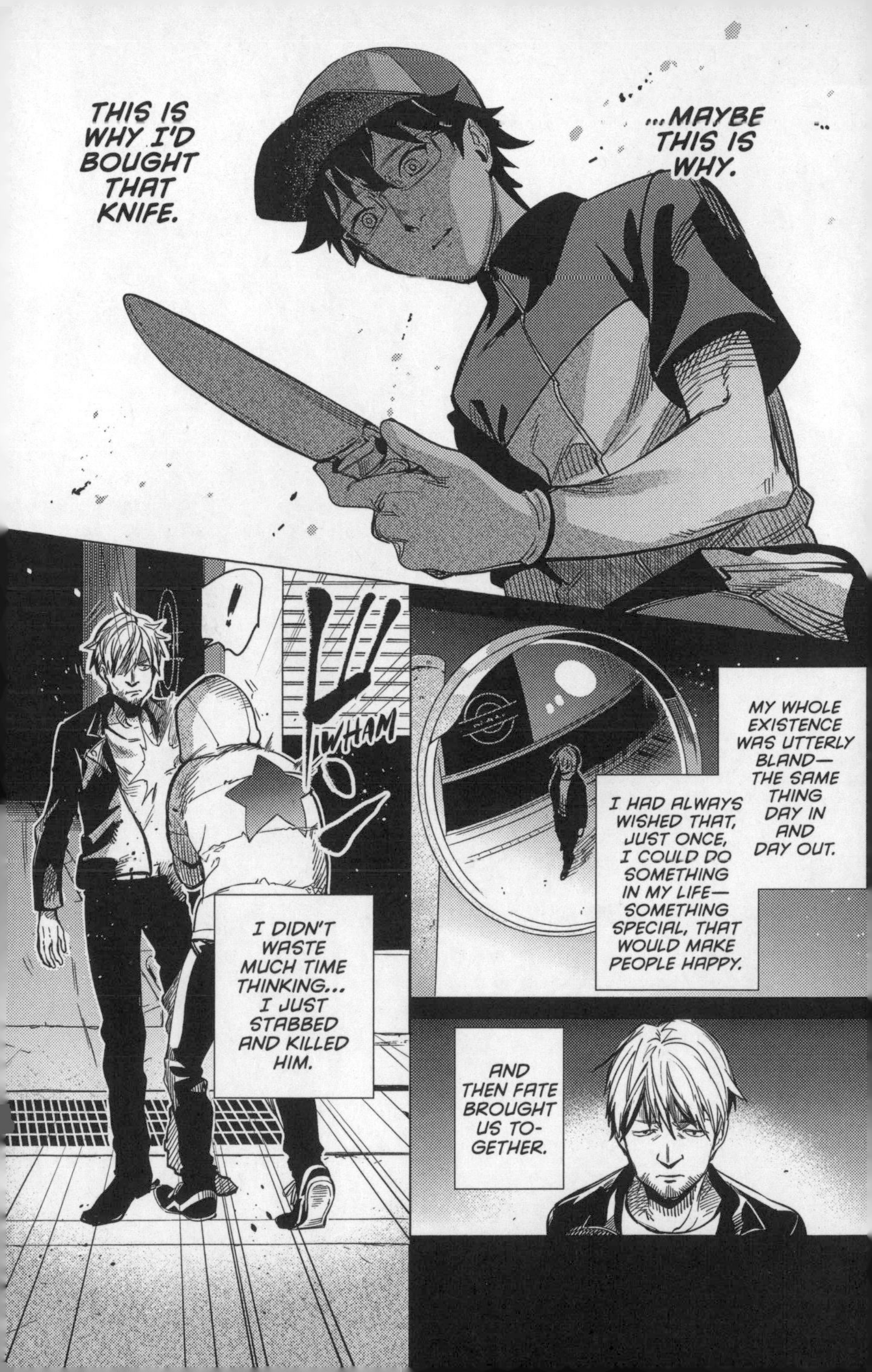
...MAYBE THIS IS WHY.
THIS IS WHY I'D BOUGHT THAT KNIFE.
MY WHOLE EXISTENCE WAS UTTERLY BLAND—THE SAME THING DAY IN AND DAY OUT.
I HAD ALWAYS WISHED THAT, JUST ONCE, I COULD DO SOMETHING IN MY LIFE—SOMETHING SPECIAL, THAT WOULD MAKE PEOPLE HAPPY.
AND THEN FATE BROUGHT US TO-GETHER.
!
WHAM
I DIDN'T WASTE MUCH TIME THINKING... I JUST STABBED AND KILLED HIM.

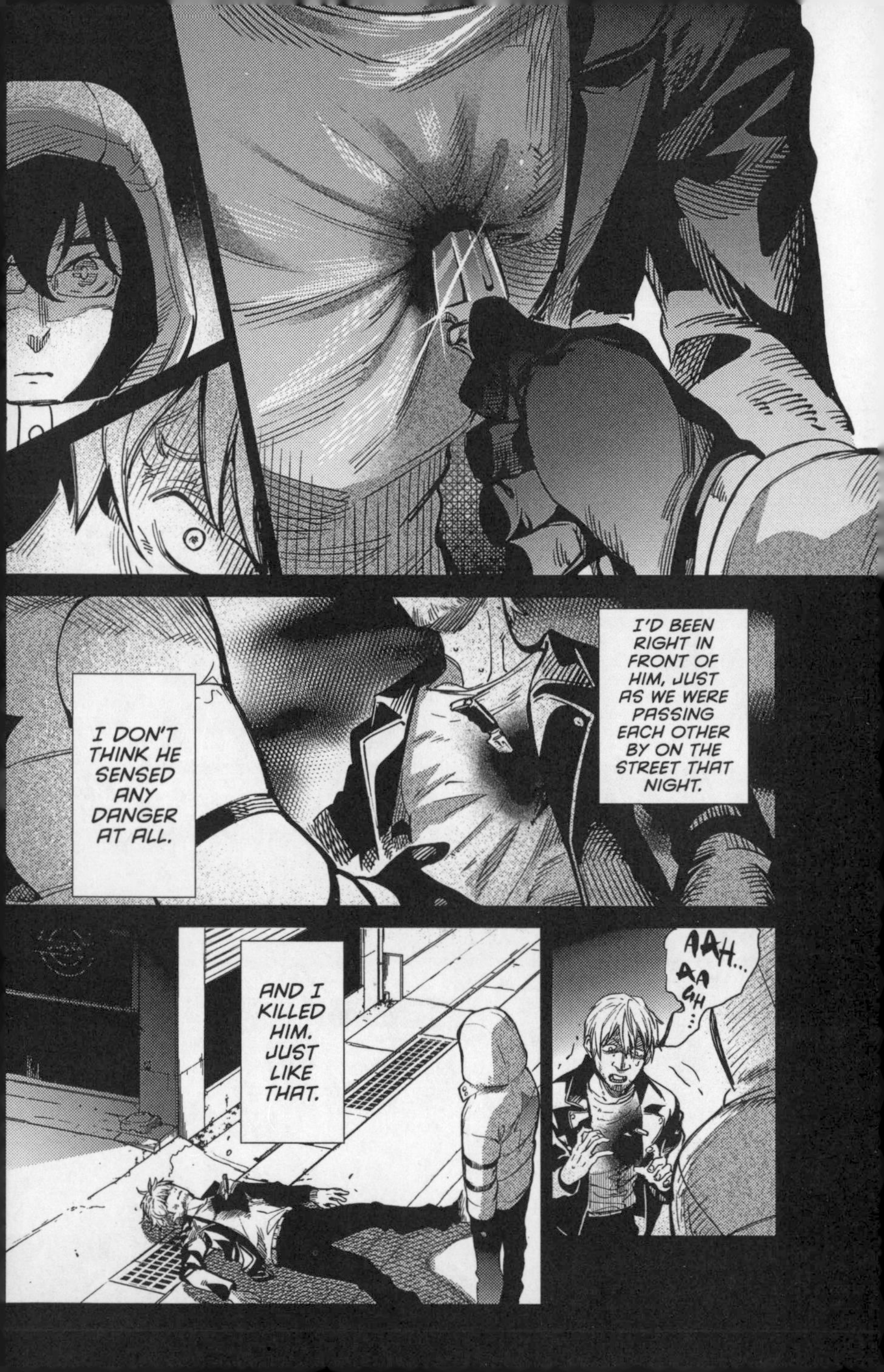
I'D BEEN RIGHT IN FRONT OF HIM, JUST AS WE WERE PASSING EACH OTHER BY ON THE STREET THAT NIGHT.
I DON'T THINK HE SENSED ANY DANGER AT ALL.
AAH... AAGH...
AND I KILLED HIM. JUST LIKE THAT.

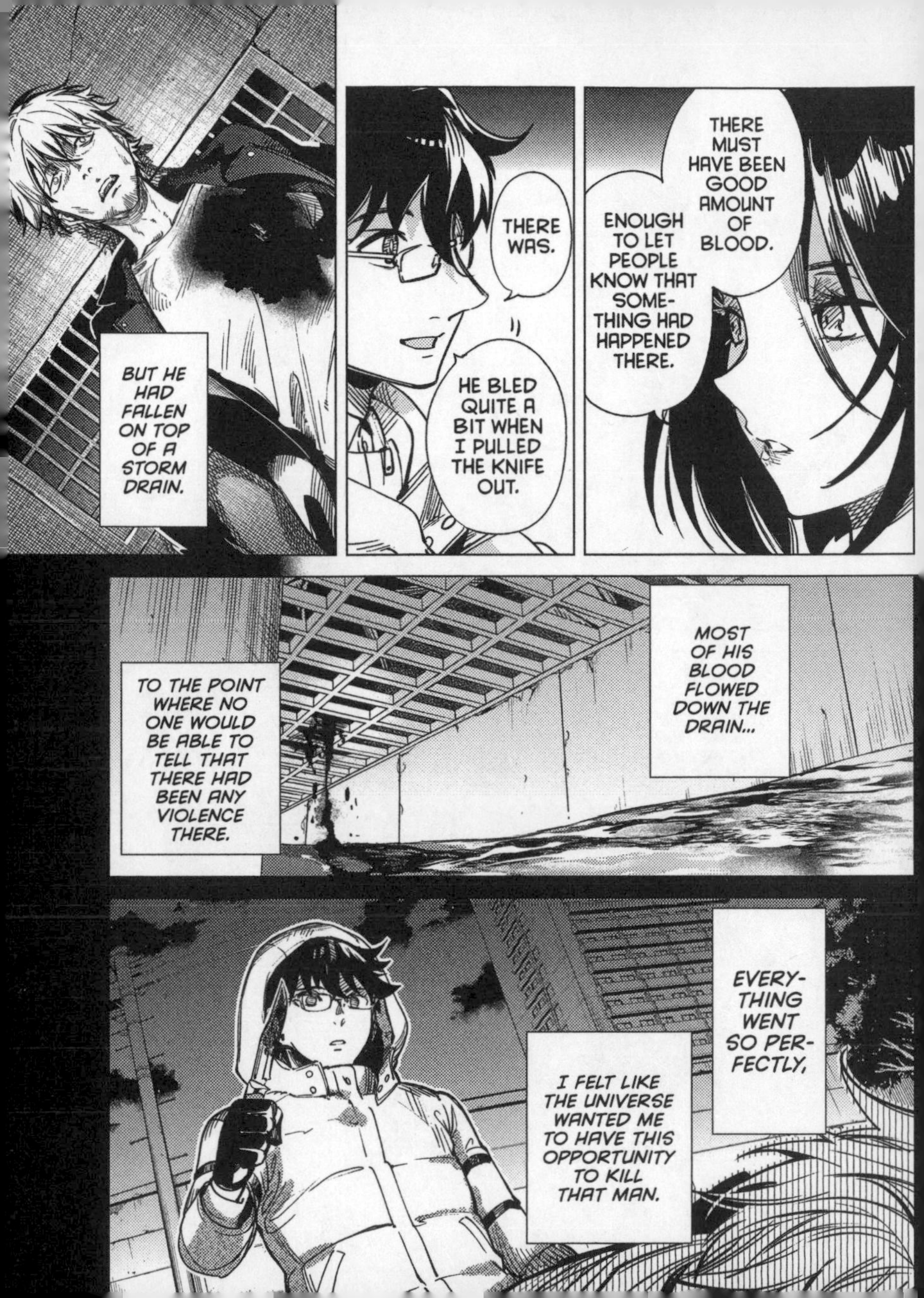
THERE MUST HAVE BEEN GOOD AMOUNT OF BLOOD.
ENOUGH TO LET PEOPLE KNOW THAT SOME-THING HAD HAPPENED THERE.
THERE WAS.
HE BLED QUITE A BIT WHEN I PULLED THE KNIFE OUT.
BUT HE HAD FALLEN ON TOP OF A STORM DRAIN.
MOST OF HIS BLOOD FLOWED DOWN THE DRAIN...
TO THE POINT WHERE NO ONE WOULD BE ABLE TO TELL THAT THERE HAD BEEN ANY VIOLENCE THERE.
EVERY-THING WENT SO PER-FECTLY,
I FELT LIKE THE UNIVERSE WANTED ME TO HAVE THIS OPPORTUNITY TO KILL THAT MAN.

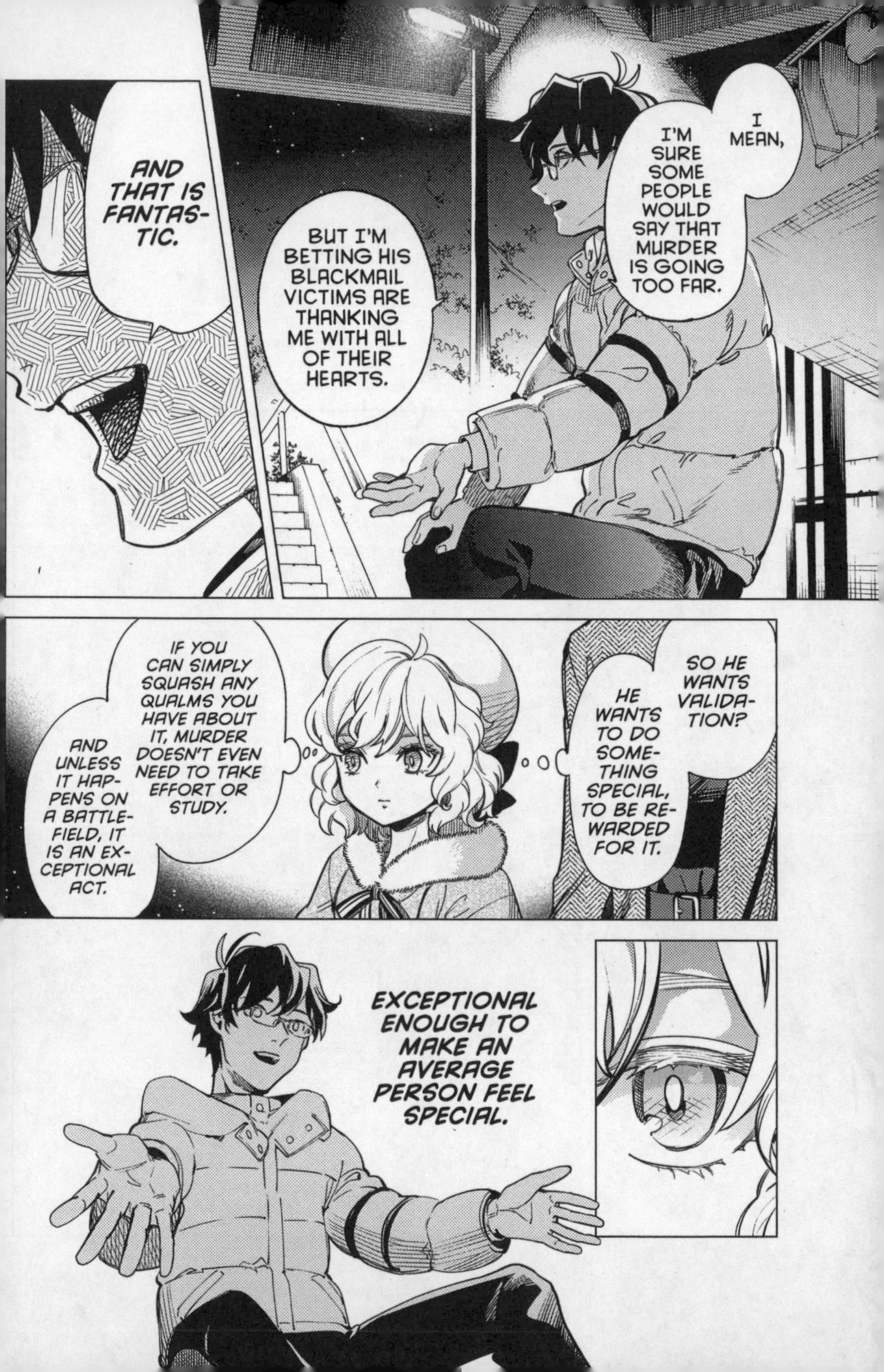
I MEAN, I'M SURE SOME PEOPLE WOULD SAY THAT MURDER IS GOING TOO FAR.
BUT I'M BETTING HIS BLACKMAIL VICTIMS ARE THANKING ME WITH ALL OF THEIR HEARTS.
AND THAT IS FANTASTIC.
SO HE WANTS VALIDATION?
HE WANTS TO DO SOMETHING SPECIAL, TO BE REWARDED FOR IT.
IF YOU CAN SIMPLY SQUASH ANY QUALMS YOU HAVE ABOUT IT, MURDER DOESN'T EVEN NEED TO TAKE EFFORT OR STUDY.
AND UNLESS IT HAPPENS ON A BATTLEFIELD, IT IS AN EXCEPTIONAL ACT.
EXCEPTIONAL ENOUGH TO MAKE AN AVERAGE PERSON FEEL SPECIAL.

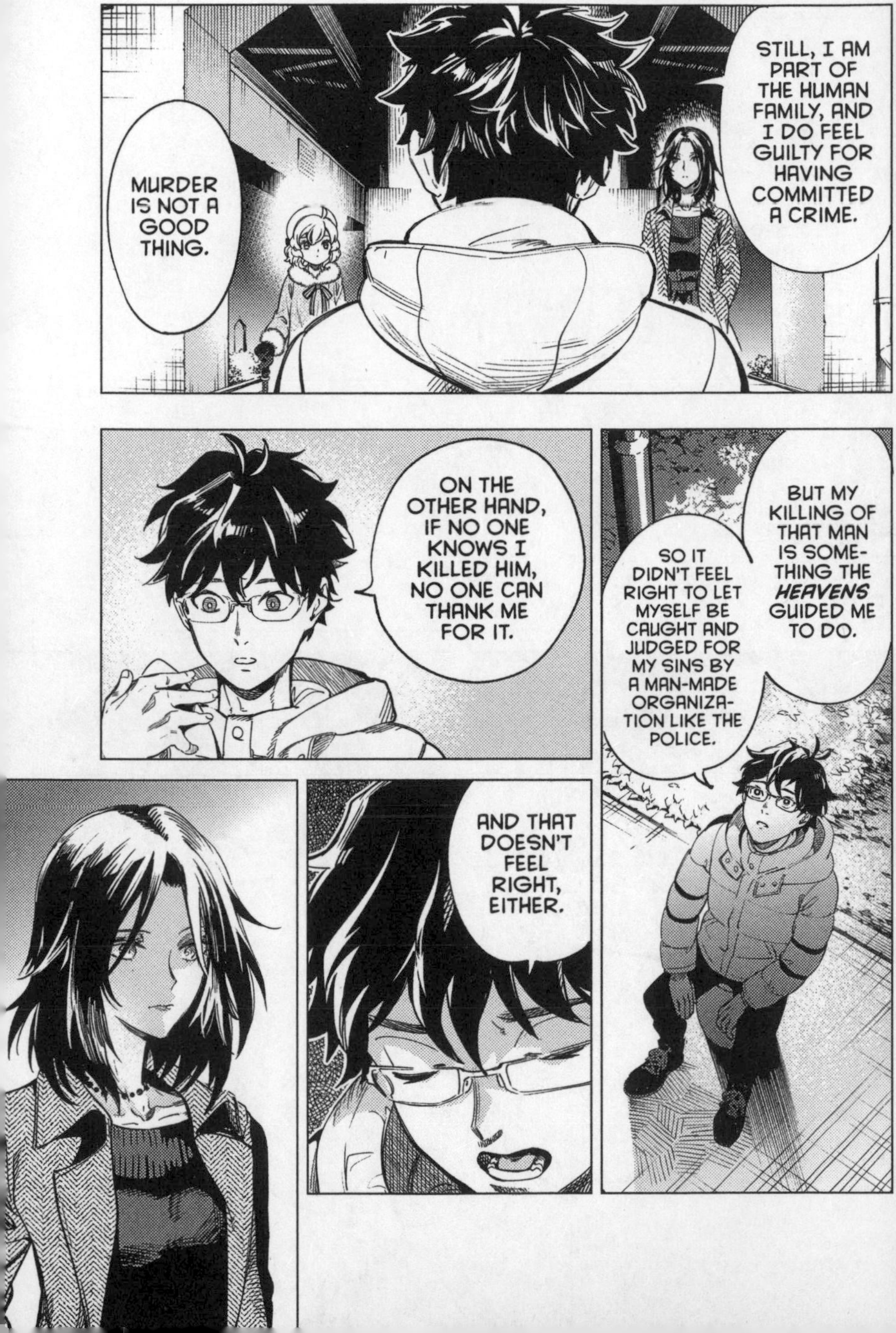
STILL, I AM PART OF THE HUMAN FAMILY, AND I DO FEEL GUILTY FOR HAVING COMMITTED A CRIME.
MURDER IS NOT A GOOD THING.
BUT MY KILLING OF THAT MAN IS SOME-THING THE *HEAVENS* GUIDED ME TO DO.
SO IT DIDN'T FEEL RIGHT TO LET MYSELF BE CAUGHT AND JUDGED FOR MY SINS BY A MAN-MADE ORGANIZA-TION LIKE THE POLICE.
ON THE OTHER HAND, IF NO ONE KNOWS I KILLED HIM, NO ONE CAN THANK ME FOR IT.
AND THAT DOESN'T FEEL RIGHT, EITHER.

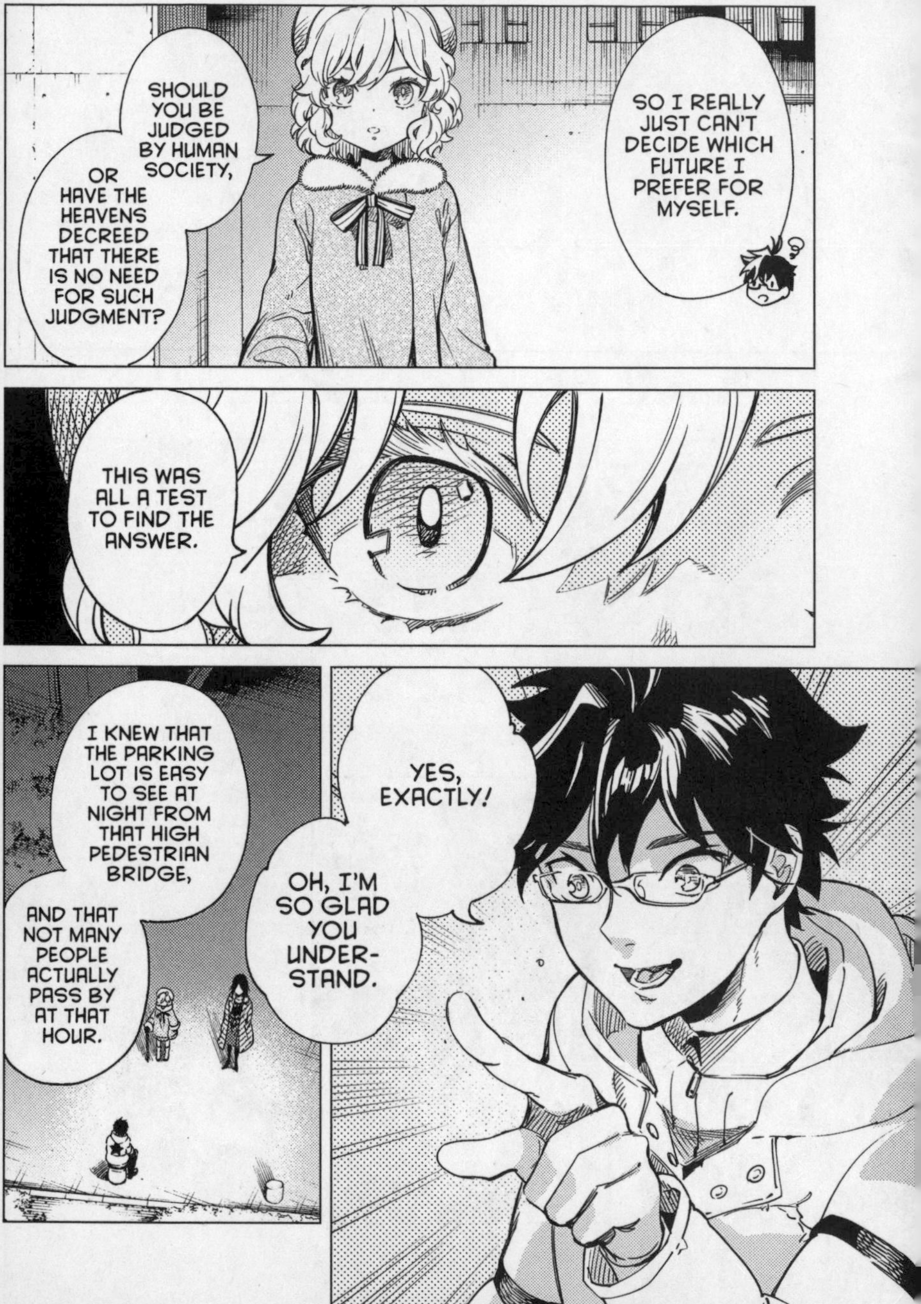
SO I REALLY JUST CAN'T DECIDE WHICH FUTURE I PREFER FOR MYSELF.
SHOULD YOU BE JUDGED BY HUMAN SOCIETY,
OR HAVE THE HEAVENS DECREED THAT THERE IS NO NEED FOR SUCH JUDGMENT?
THIS WAS ALL A TEST TO FIND THE ANSWER.
YES, EXACTLY!
OH, I'M SO GLAD YOU UNDER-STAND.
I KNEW THAT THE PARKING LOT IS EASY TO SEE AT NIGHT FROM THAT HIGH PEDESTRIAN BRIDGE,
AND THAT NOT MANY PEOPLE ACTUALLY PASS BY AT THAT HOUR.

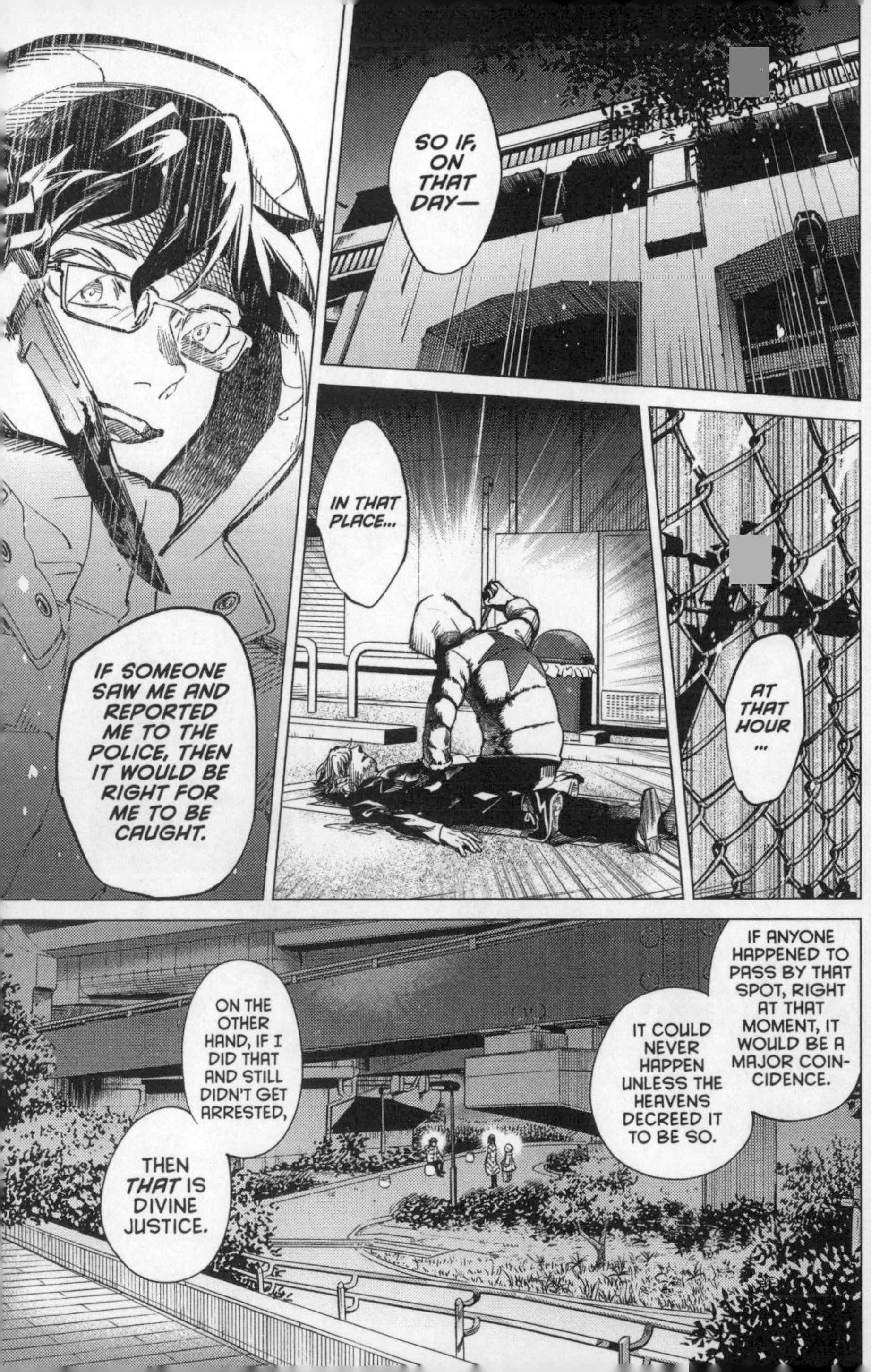
SO IF, ON THAT DAY—
AT THAT HOUR...
IN THAT PLACE...
IF SOMEONE SAW ME AND REPORTED ME TO THE POLICE, THEN IT WOULD BE RIGHT FOR ME TO BE CAUGHT.
IF ANYONE HAPPENED TO PASS BY THAT SPOT, RIGHT AT THAT MOMENT, IT WOULD BE A MAJOR COINCIDENCE.
IT COULD NEVER HAPPEN UNLESS THE HEAVENS DECREED IT TO BE SO.
ON THE OTHER HAND, IF I DID THAT AND STILL DIDN'T GET ARRESTED,
THEN THAT IS DIVINE JUSTICE.

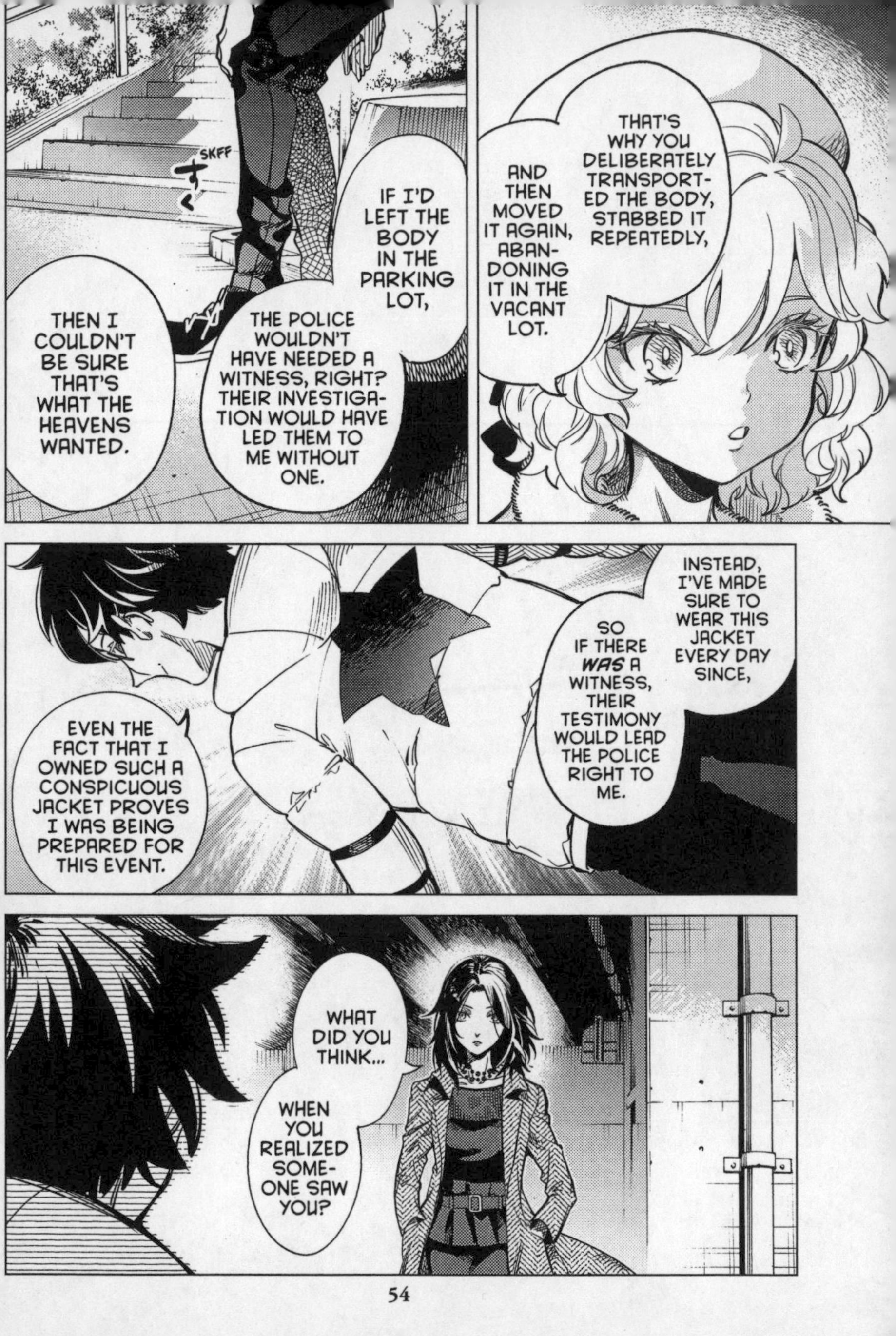
THAT'S WHY YOU DELIBERATELY TRANSPORTED THE BODY, STABBED IT REPEATEDLY,
AND THEN MOVED IT AGAIN, ABANDONING IT IN THE VACANT LOT.
IF I'D LEFT THE BODY IN THE PARKING LOT,
THE POLICE WOULDN'T HAVE NEEDED A WITNESS, RIGHT? THEIR INVESTIGATION WOULD HAVE LED THEM TO ME WITHOUT ONE.
SKFF
THEN I COULDN'T BE SURE THAT'S WHAT THE HEAVENS WANTED.
INSTEAD, I'VE MADE SURE TO WEAR THIS JACKET EVERY DAY SINCE,
SO IF THERE ***WAS*** A WITNESS, THEIR TESTIMONY WOULD LEAD THE POLICE RIGHT TO ME.
EVEN THE FACT THAT I OWNED SUCH A CONSPICUOUS JACKET PROVES I WAS BEING PREPARED FOR THIS EVENT.
WHAT DID YOU THINK...
WHEN YOU REALIZED SOMEONE SAW YOU?

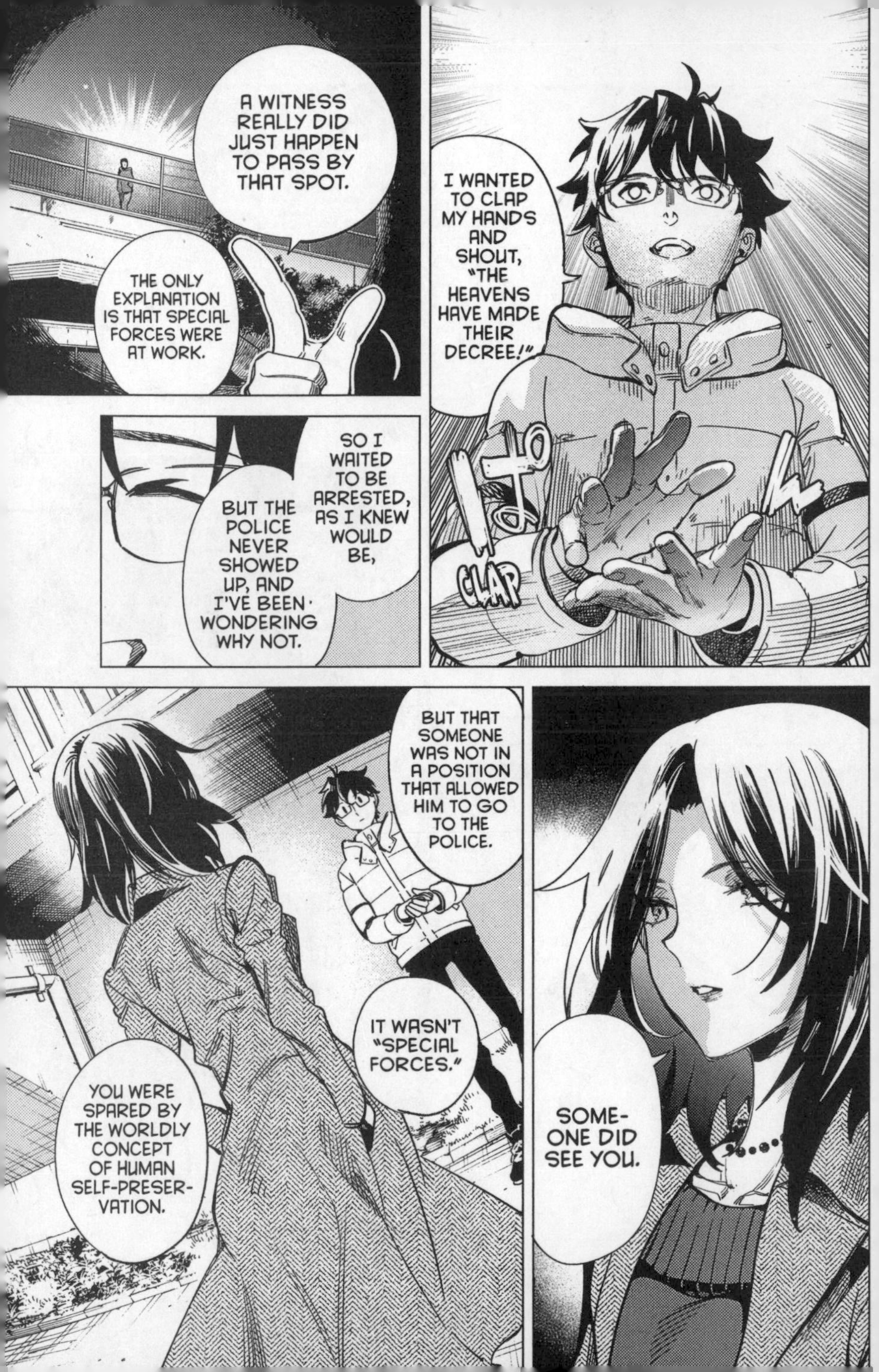
I WANTED TO CLAP MY HANDS AND SHOUT, "THE HEAVENS HAVE MADE THEIR DECREE!"
CLAP
A WITNESS REALLY DID JUST HAPPEN TO PASS BY THAT SPOT.
THE ONLY EXPLANATION IS THAT SPECIAL FORCES WERE AT WORK.
SO I WAITED TO BE ARRESTED, AS I KNEW WOULD BE,
BUT THE POLICE NEVER SHOWED UP, AND I'VE BEEN WONDERING WHY NOT.
SOME-ONE DID SEE YOU.
BUT THAT SOMEONE WAS NOT IN A POSITION THAT ALLOWED HIM TO GO TO THE POLICE.
IT WASN'T "SPECIAL FORCES."
YOU WERE SPARED BY THE WORLDLY CONCEPT OF HUMAN SELF-PRESER-VATION.

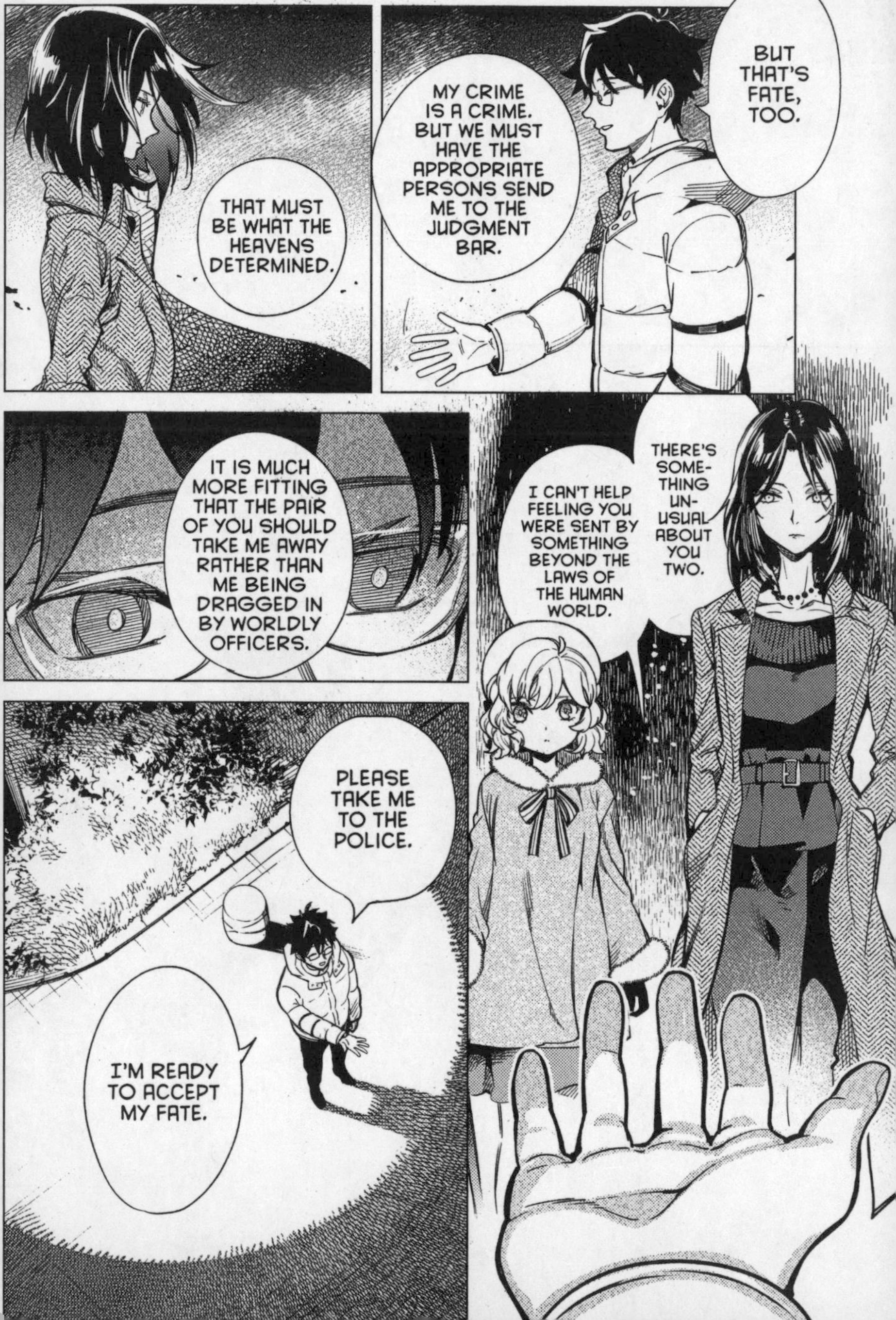
BUT THAT'S FATE, TOO.
MY CRIME IS A CRIME. BUT WE MUST HAVE THE APPROPRIATE PERSONS SEND ME TO THE JUDGMENT BAR.
THAT MUST BE WHAT THE HEAVENS DETERMINED.
THERE'S SOME-THING UN-USUAL ABOUT YOU TWO.
I CAN'T HELP FEELING YOU WERE SENT BY SOMETHING BEYOND THE LAWS OF THE HUMAN WORLD.
IT IS MUCH MORE FITTING THAT THE PAIR OF YOU SHOULD TAKE ME AWAY RATHER THAN ME BEING DRAGGED IN BY WORLDLY OFFICERS.
PLEASE TAKE ME TO THE POLICE.
I'M READY TO ACCEPT MY FATE.

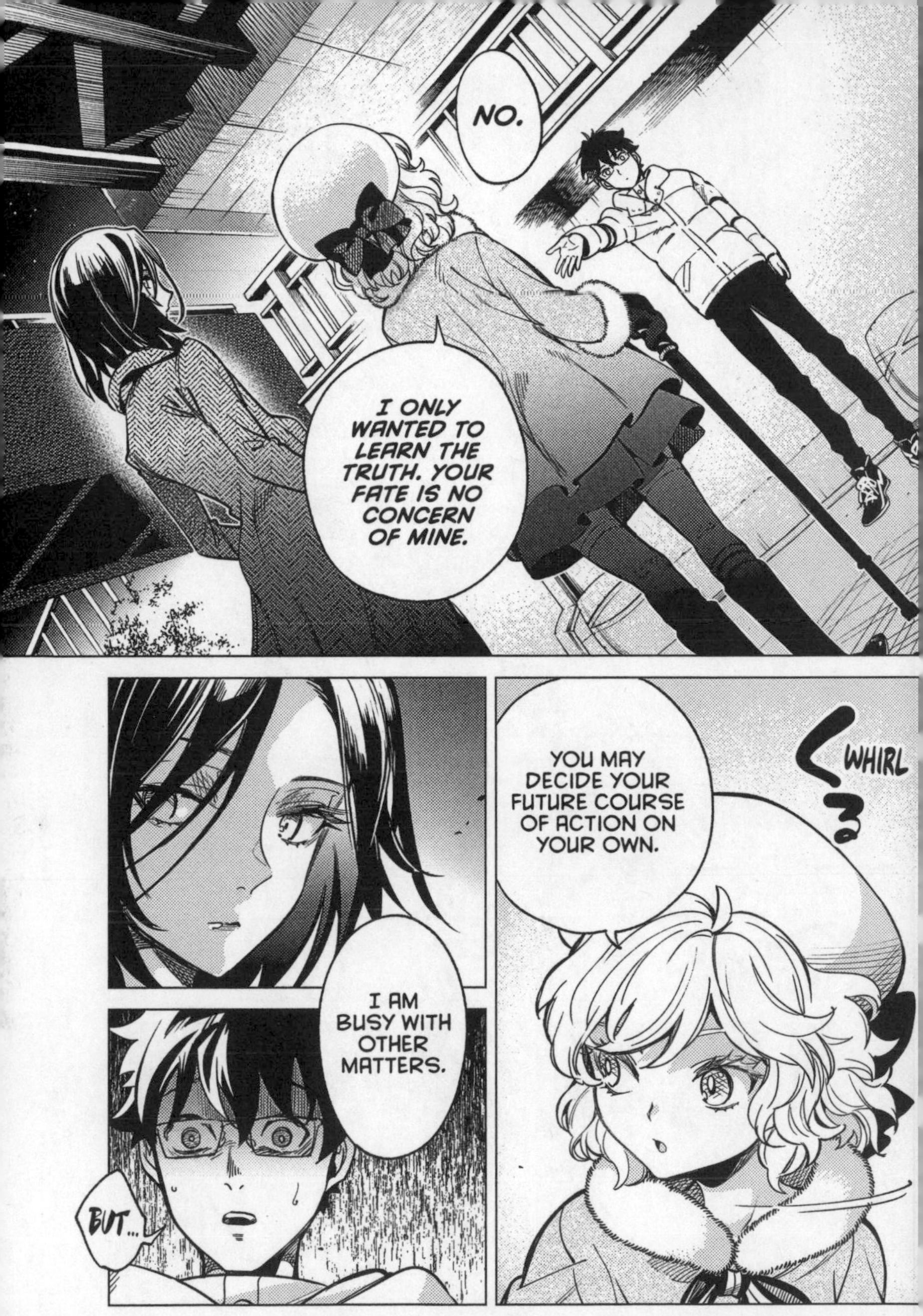
NO.
I ONLY WANTED TO LEARN THE TRUTH. YOUR FATE IS NO CONCERN OF MINE.
WHIRL
YOU MAY DECIDE YOUR FUTURE COURSE OF ACTION ON YOUR OWN.
I AM BUSY WITH OTHER MATTERS.
BUT...

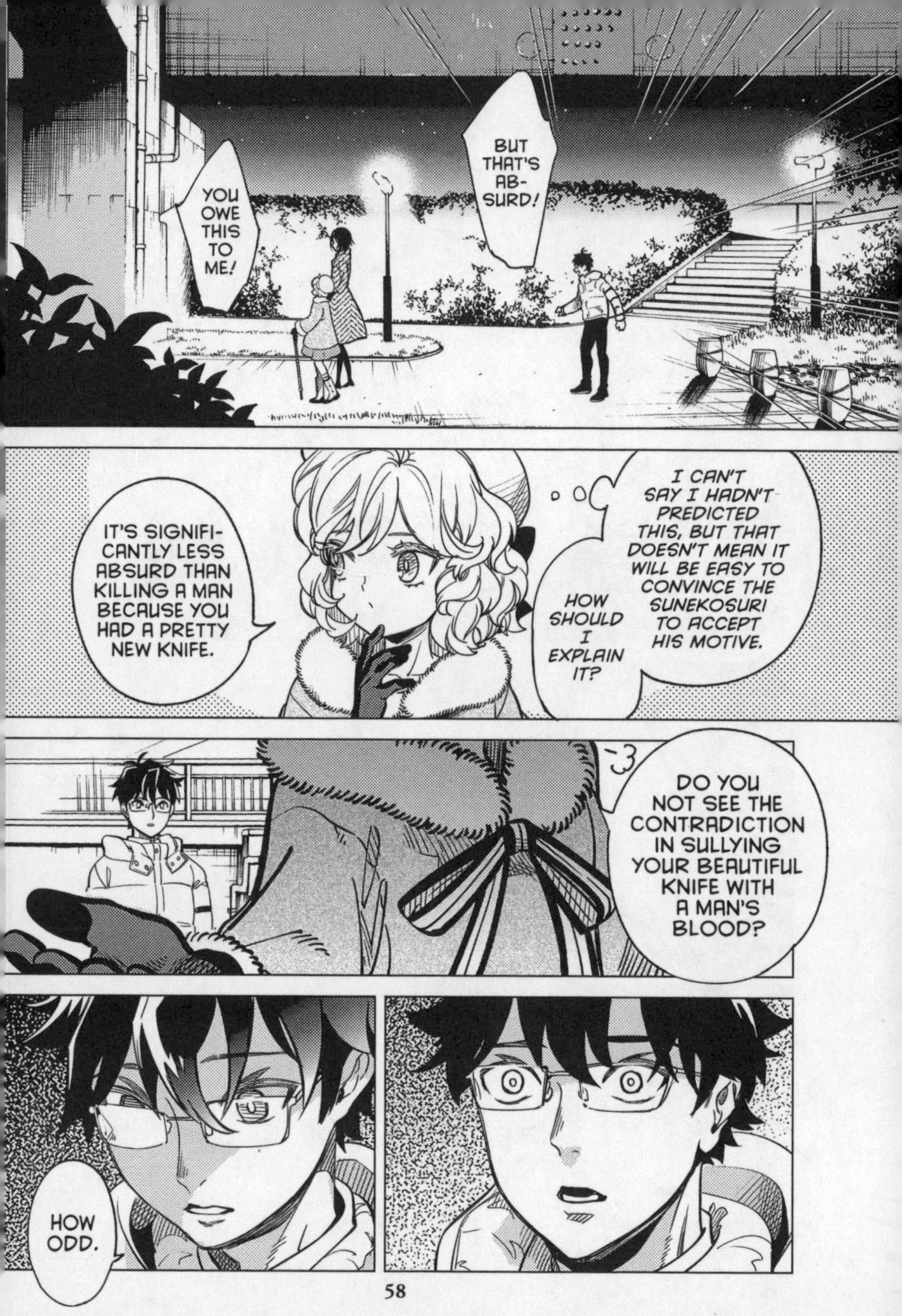
BUT THAT'S AB-SURD!
YOU OWE THIS TO ME!
I CAN'T SAY I HADN'T PREDICTED THIS, BUT THAT DOESN'T MEAN IT WILL BE EASY TO CONVINCE THE SUNEKOSURI TO ACCEPT HIS MOTIVE.
HOW SHOULD I EXPLAIN IT?
IT'S SIGNIFI-CANTLY LESS ABSURD THAN KILLING A MAN BECAUSE YOU HAD A PRETTY NEW KNIFE.
DO YOU NOT SEE THE CONTRADICTION IN SULLYING YOUR BEAUTIFUL KNIFE WITH A MAN'S BLOOD?
HOW ODD.

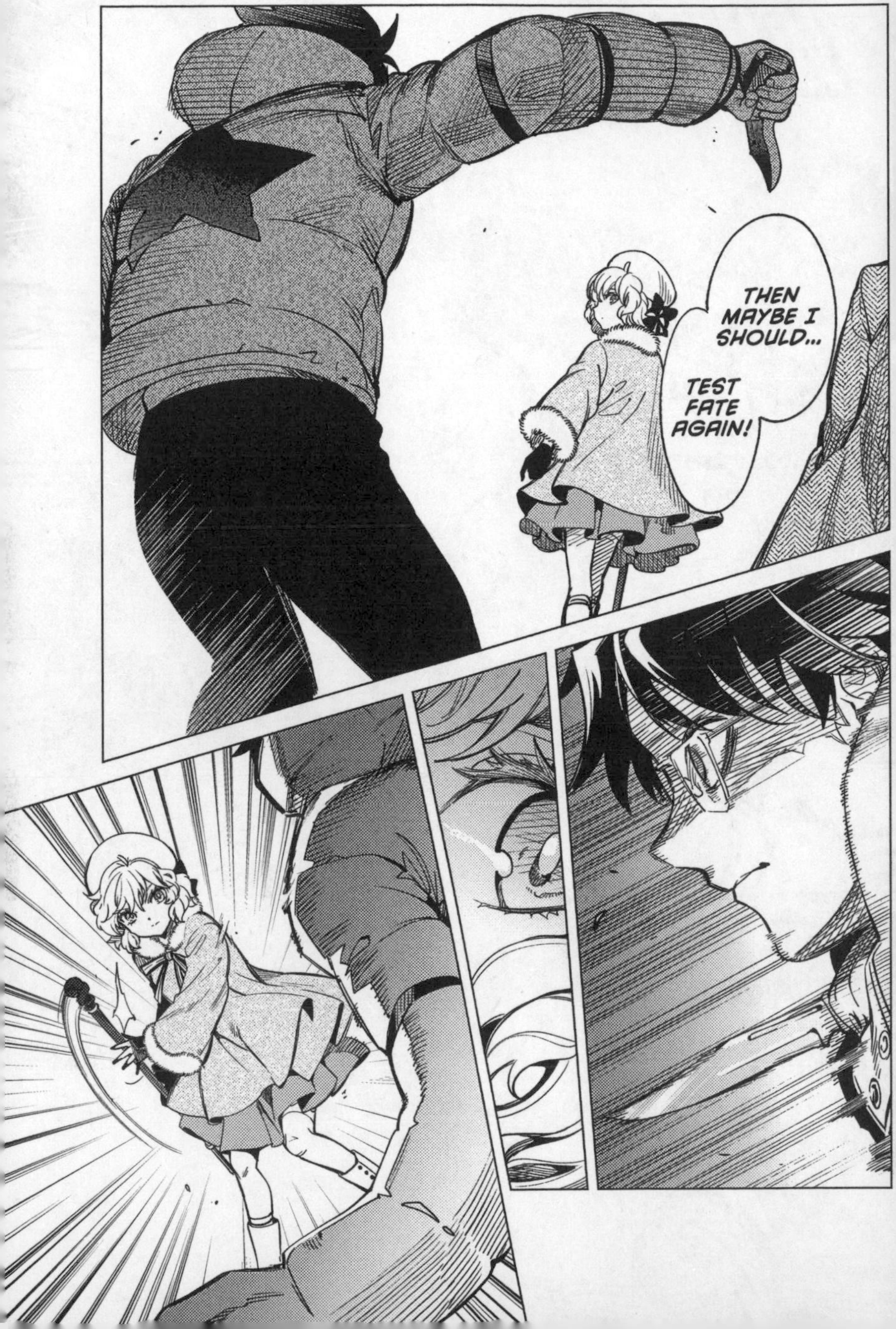
THEN MAYBE I SHOULD...
TEST FATE AGAIN!

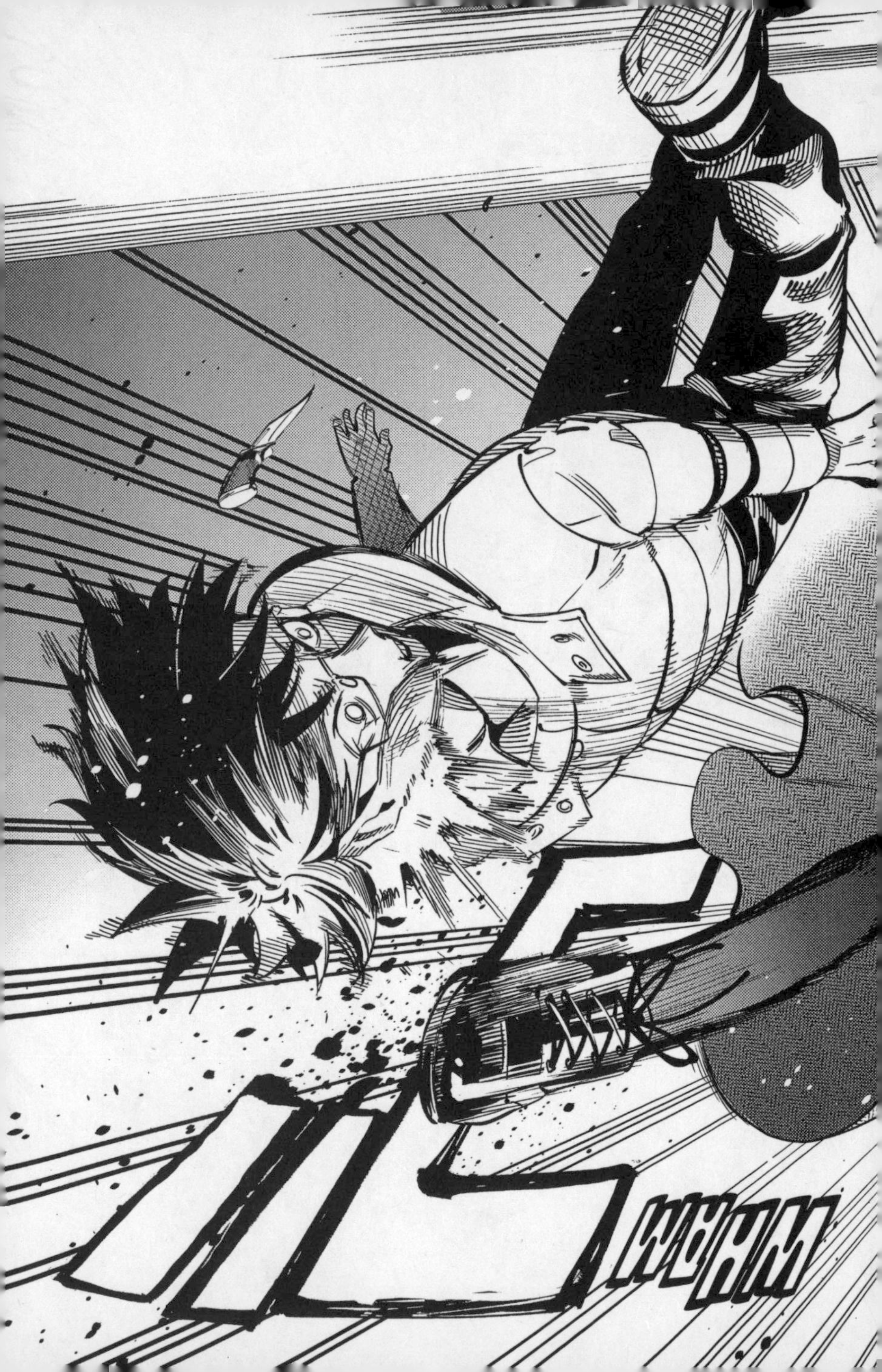

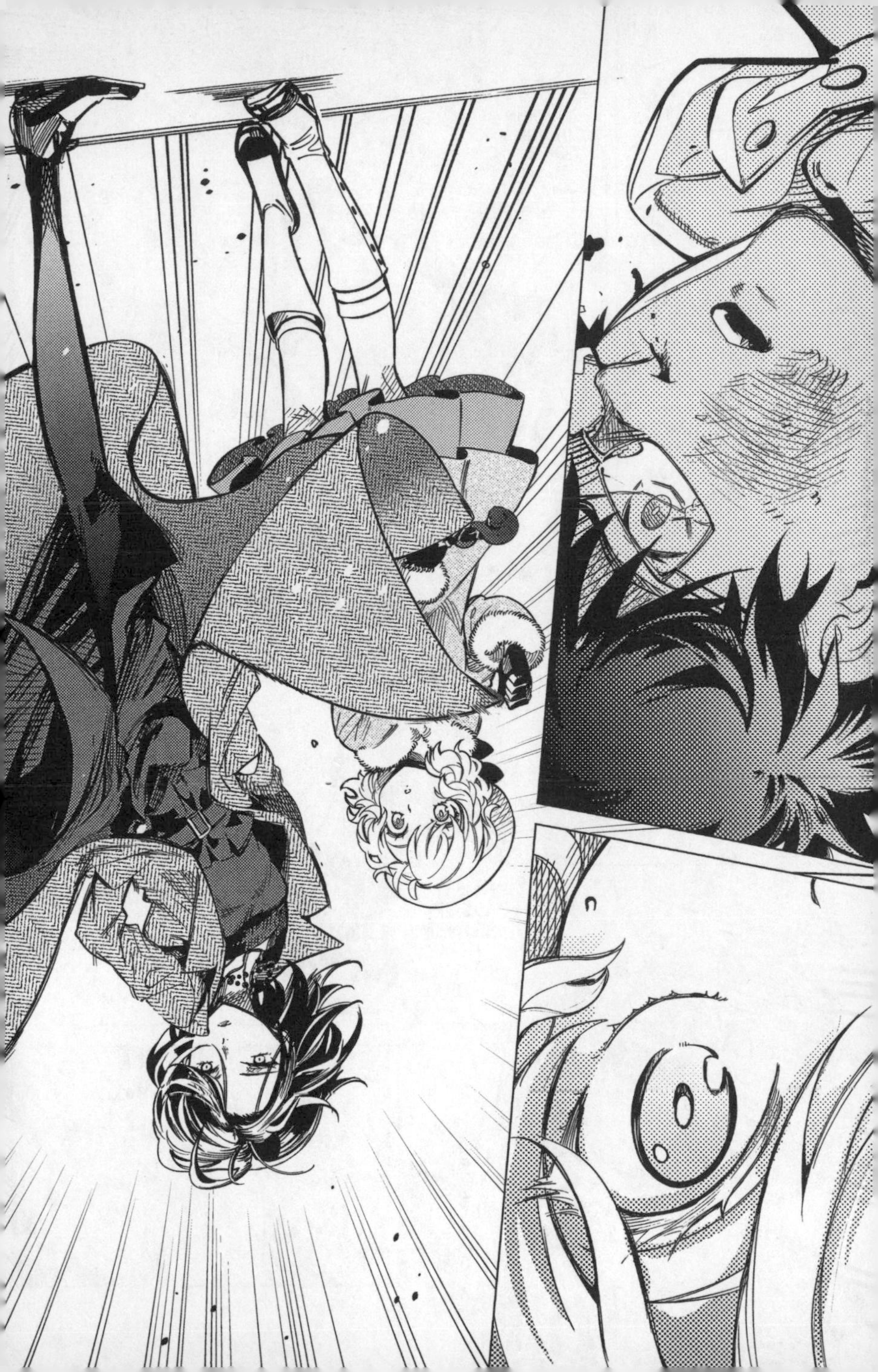

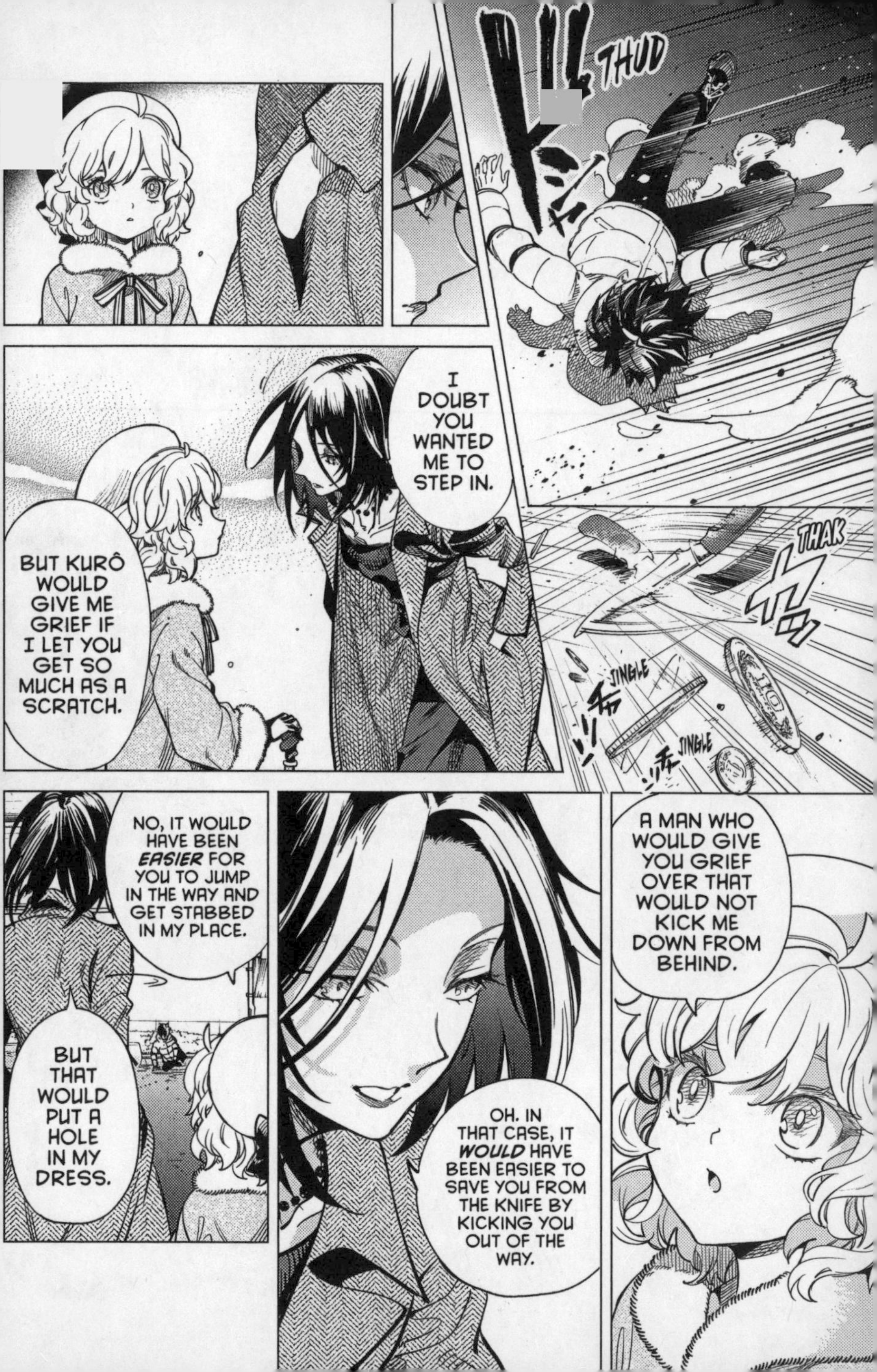
THUD
THAK
JINGLE
JINGLE
I DOUBT YOU WANTED ME TO STEP IN.
BUT KURÔ WOULD GIVE ME GRIEF IF I LET YOU GET SO MUCH AS A SCRATCH.
A MAN WHO WOULD GIVE YOU GRIEF OVER THAT WOULD NOT KICK ME DOWN FROM BEHIND.
OH. IN THAT CASE, IT *WOULD* HAVE BEEN EASIER TO SAVE YOU FROM THE KNIFE BY KICKING YOU OUT OF THE WAY.
NO, IT WOULD HAVE BEEN *EASIER* FOR YOU TO JUMP IN THE WAY AND GET STABBED IN MY PLACE.
BUT THAT WOULD PUT A HOLE IN MY DRESS.

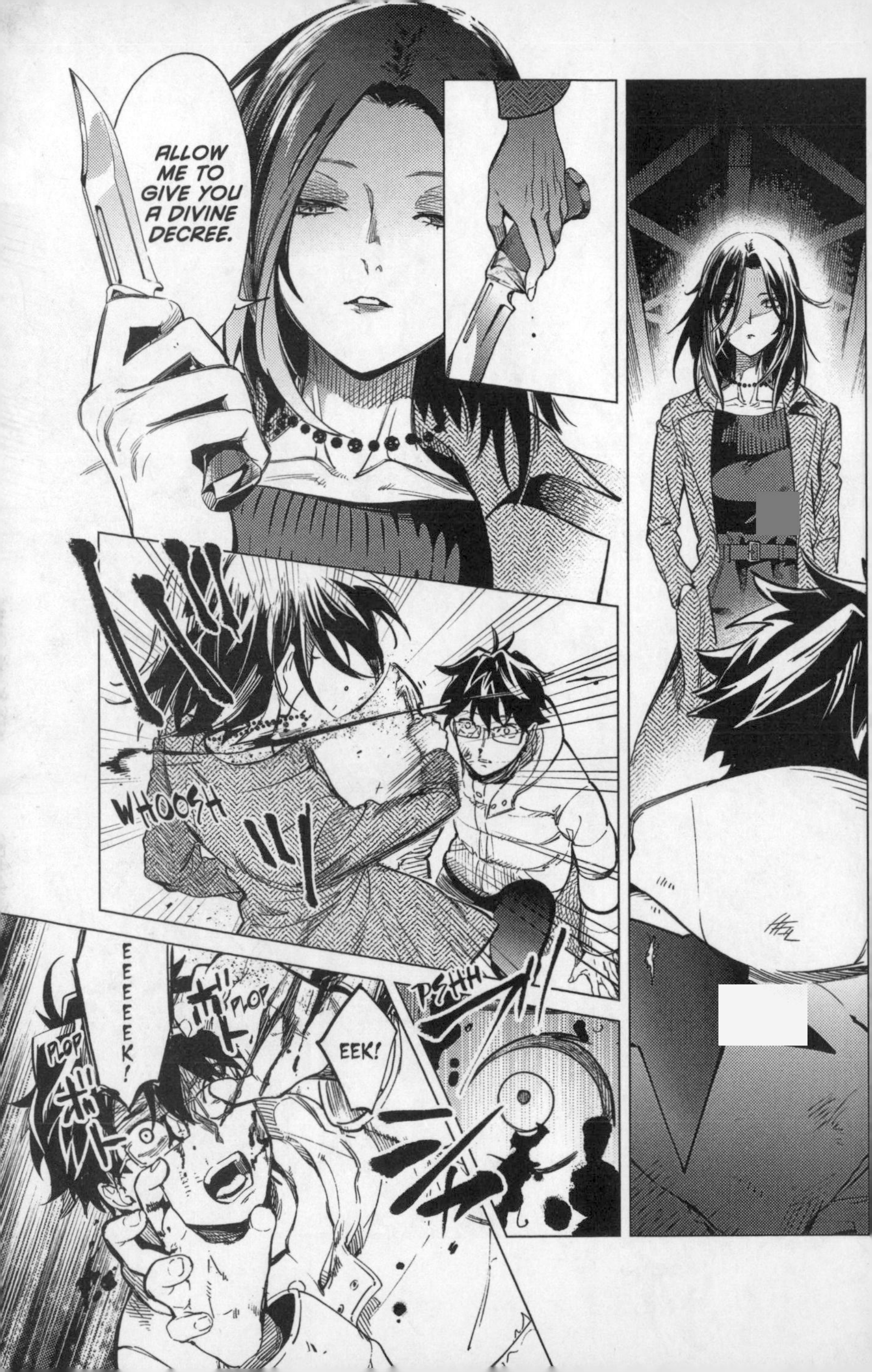
ALLOW ME TO GIVE YOU A DIVINE DECREE.
WHOOSH
PSHH
EEK!
PLOP
EEEEEEK!
PLOP

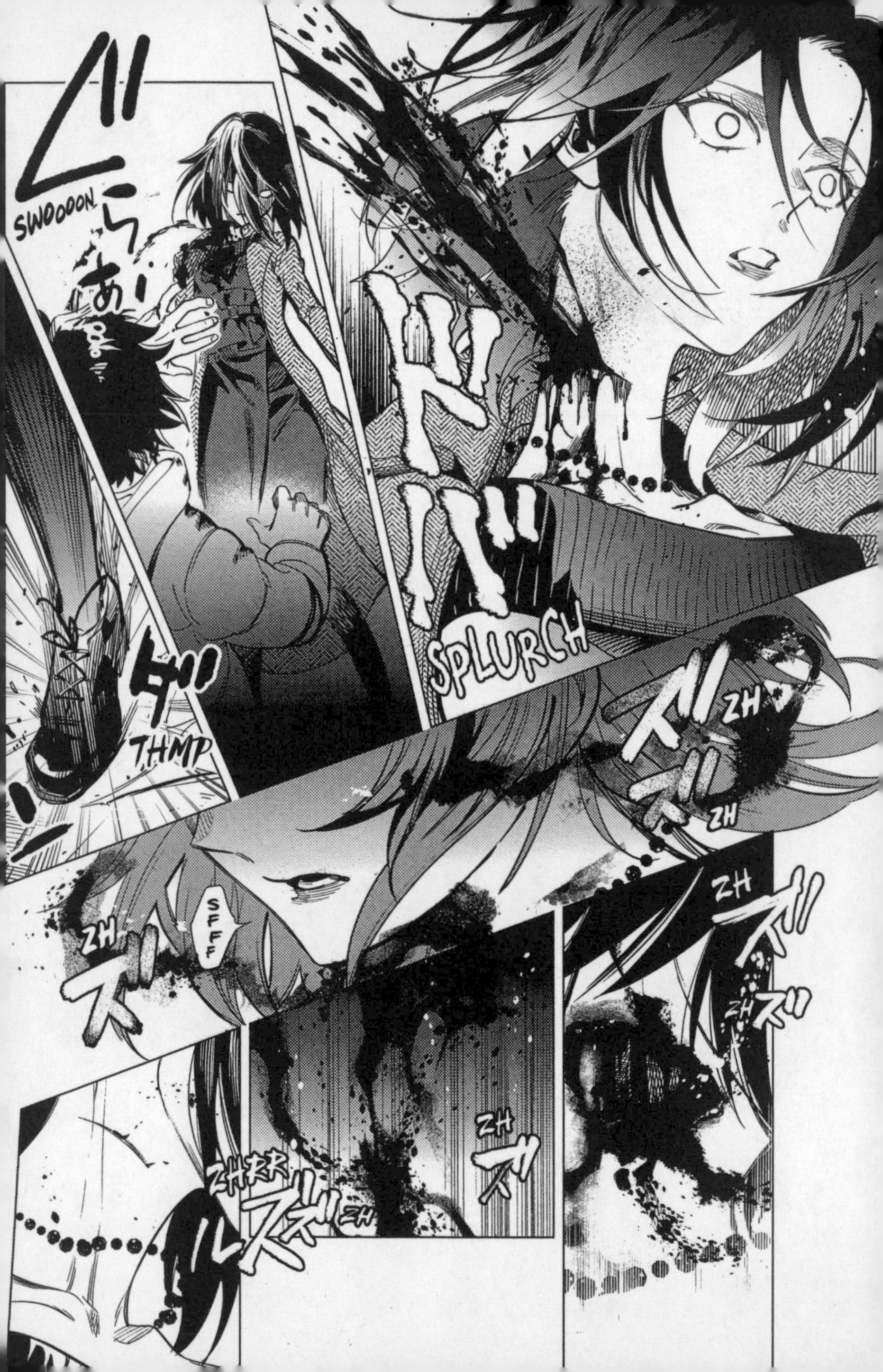
SPLURCH
SWOOOON
THMP
ZH
ZH
SFFF
ZH
ZH
ZH
ZH
ZHRR
ZH

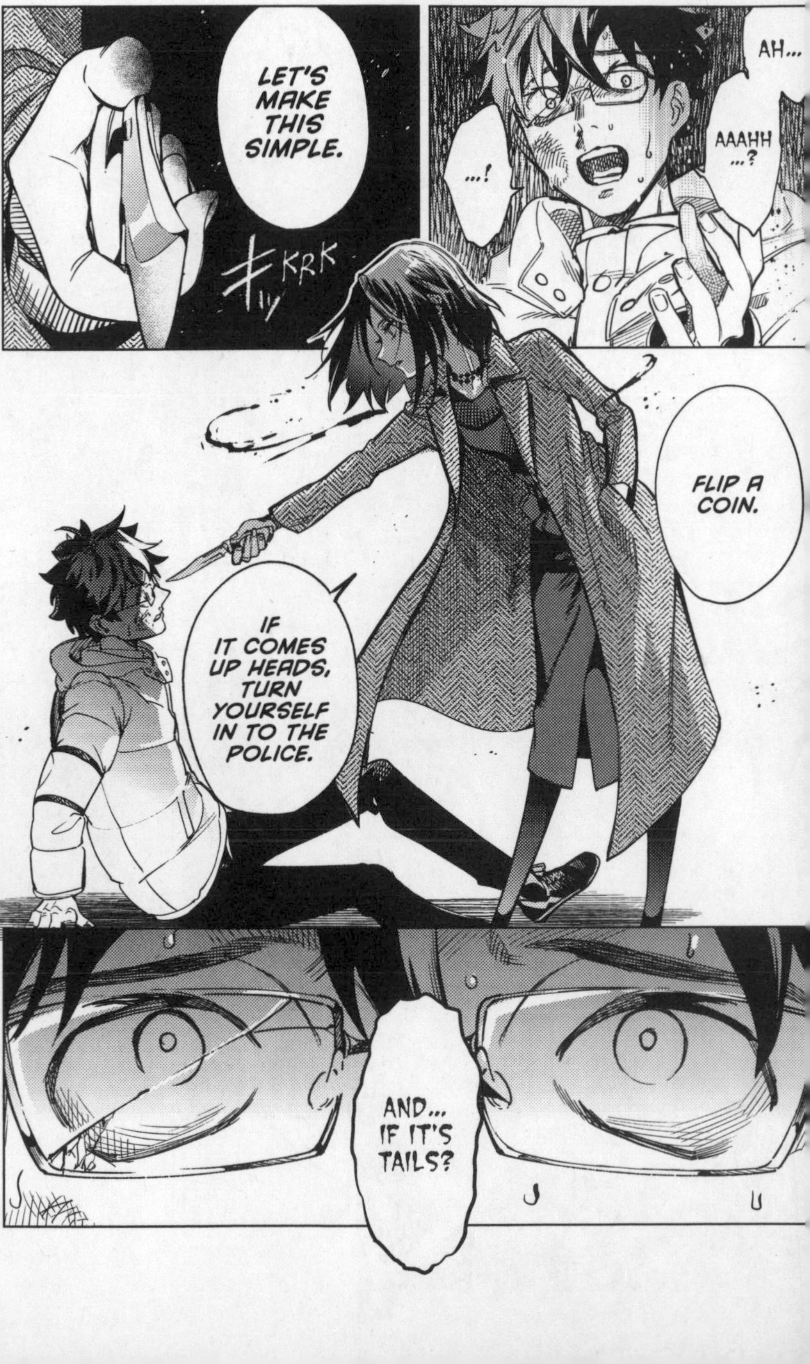
AH...
AAAHH ...?
...!
LET'S MAKE THIS SIMPLE.
KRK
FLIP A COIN.
IF IT COMES UP HEADS, TURN YOURSELF IN TO THE POLICE.
AND... IF IT'S TAILS?

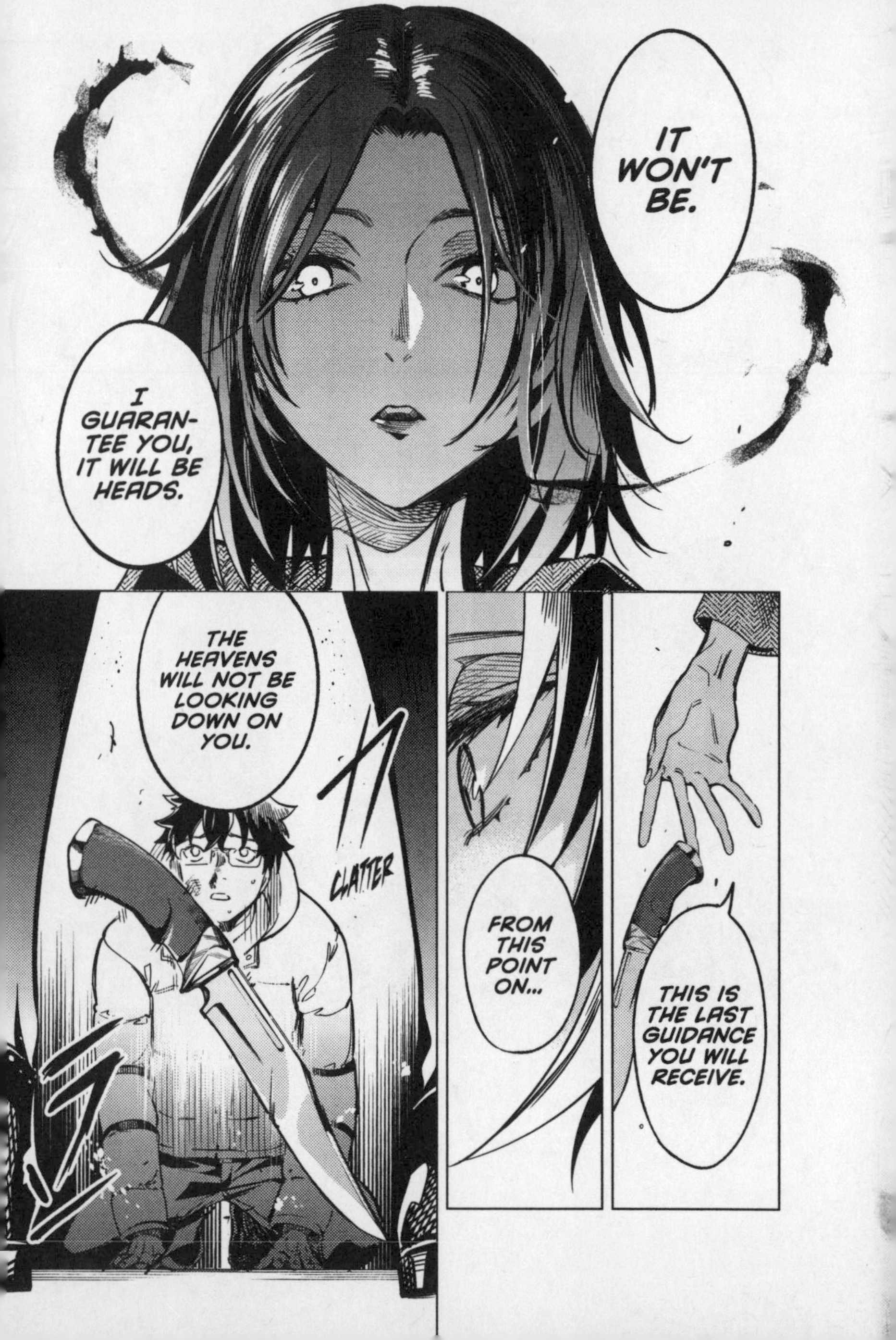
IT WON'T BE.
I GUARANTEE YOU, IT WILL BE HEADS.
THIS IS THE LAST GUIDANCE YOU WILL RECEIVE.
FROM THIS POINT ON...
THE HEAVENS WILL NOT BE LOOKING DOWN ON YOU.
CLATTER

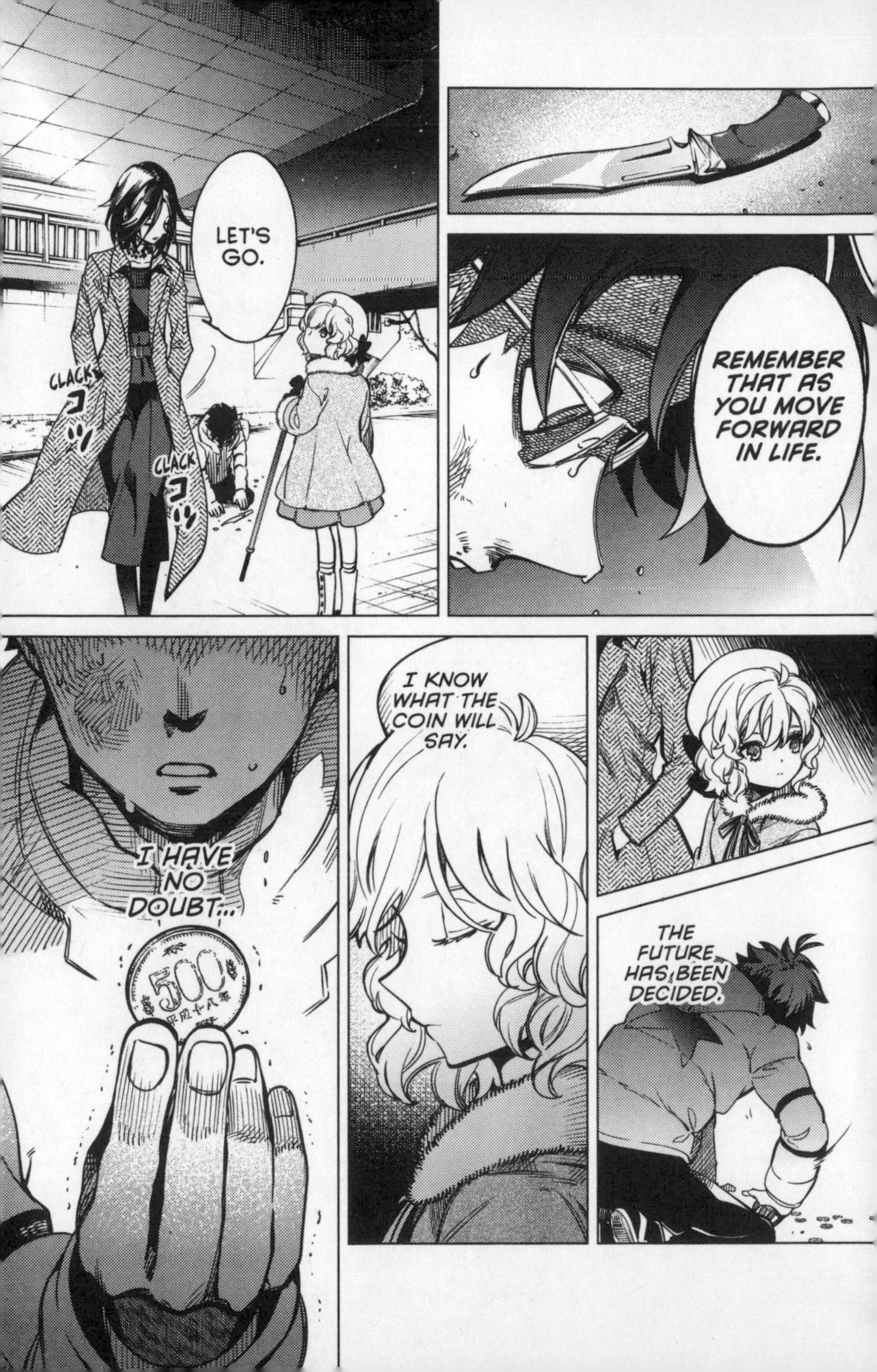
REMEMBER THAT AS YOU MOVE FORWARD IN LIFE.
LET'S GO.
CLACK
CLACK
THE FUTURE HAS BEEN DECIDED.
I KNOW WHAT THE COIN WILL SAY.
I HAVE NO DOUBT...
500

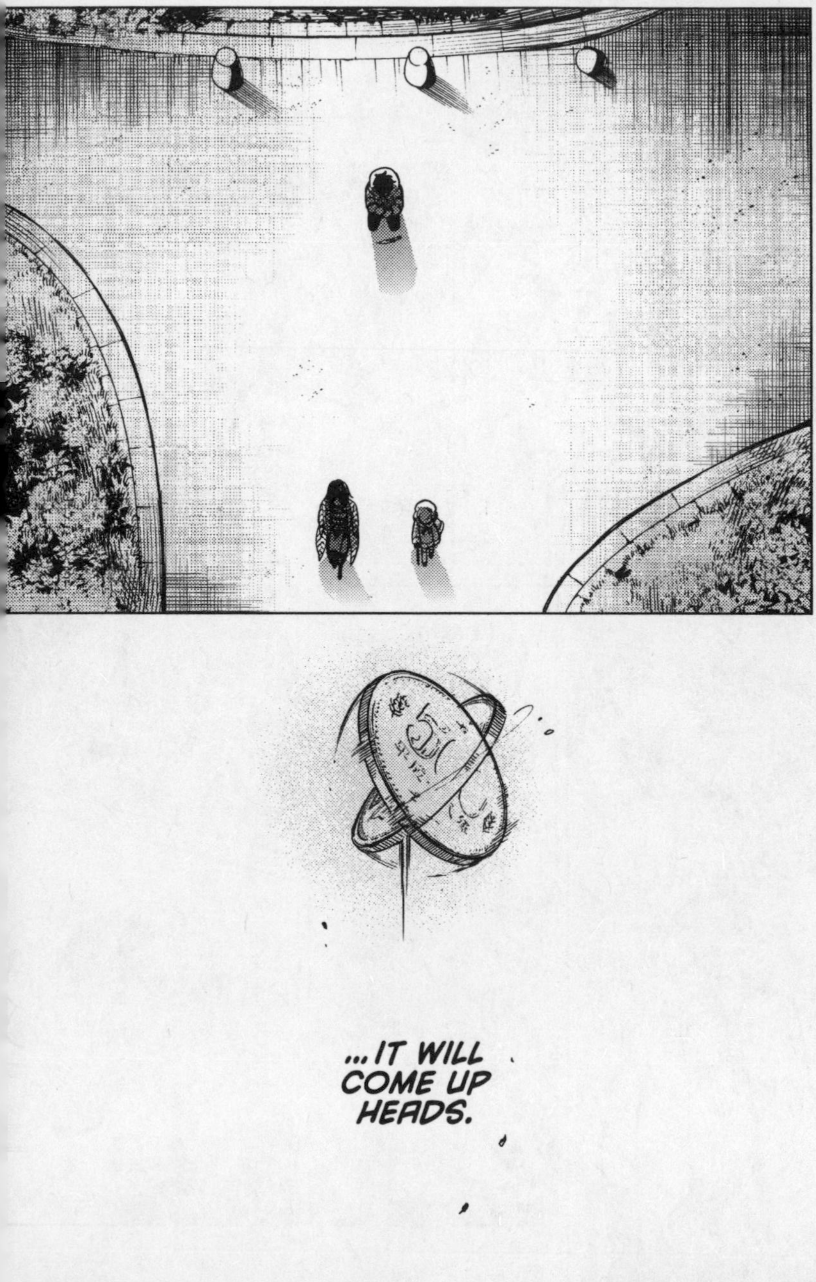
...IT WILL COME UP HEADS.

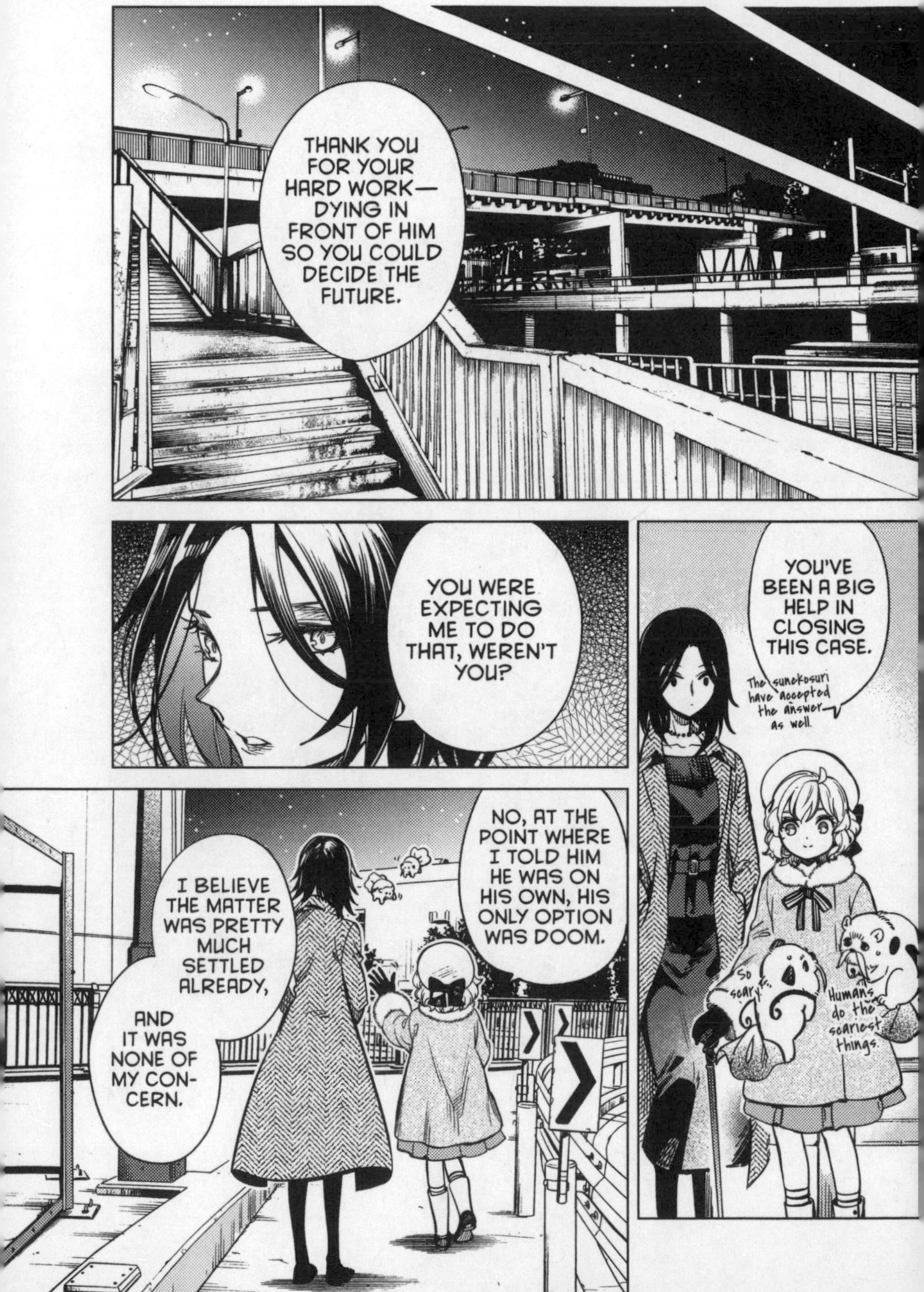
THANK YOU FOR YOUR HARD WORK—DYING IN FRONT OF HIM SO YOU COULD DECIDE THE FUTURE.
YOU'VE BEEN A BIG HELP IN CLOSING THIS CASE.
The sunekosuri have accepted the answer as well.
So scary.
Humans do the scariest things.
YOU WERE EXPECTING ME TO DO THAT, WEREN'T YOU?
NO, AT THE POINT WHERE I TOLD HIM HE WAS ON HIS OWN, HIS ONLY OPTION WAS DOOM.
I BELIEVE THE MATTER WAS PRETTY MUCH SETTLED ALREADY,
AND IT WAS NONE OF MY CON-CERN.

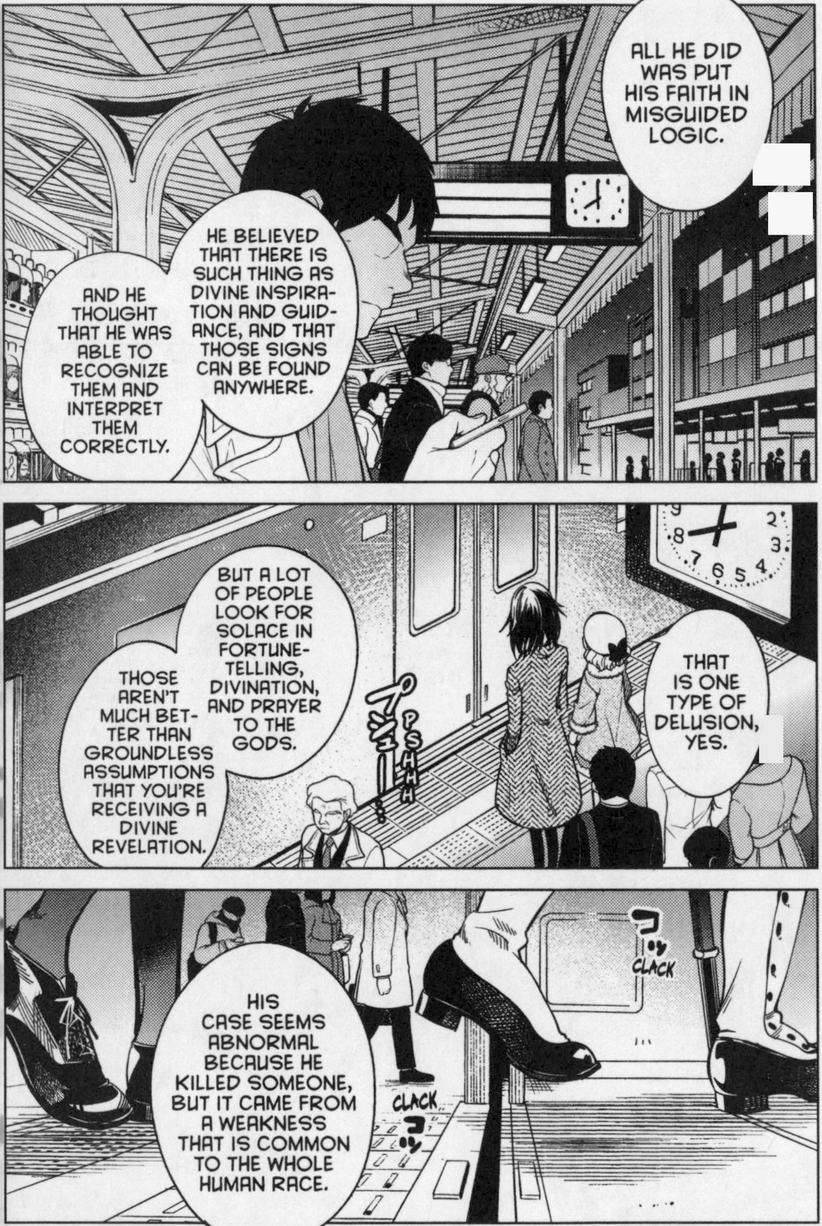
ALL HE DID WAS PUT HIS FAITH IN MISGUIDED LOGIC.
HE BELIEVED THAT THERE IS SUCH THING AS DIVINE INSPIRATION AND GUIDANCE, AND THAT THOSE SIGNS CAN BE FOUND ANYWHERE.
AND HE THOUGHT THAT HE WAS ABLE TO RECOGNIZE THEM AND INTERPRET THEM CORRECTLY.
THAT IS ONE TYPE OF DELUSION, YES.
PSHHH
BUT A LOT OF PEOPLE LOOK FOR SOLACE IN FORTUNE-TELLING, DIVINATION, AND PRAYER TO THE GODS.
THOSE AREN'T MUCH BETTER THAN GROUNDLESS ASSUMPTIONS THAT YOU'RE RECEIVING A DIVINE REVELATION.
CLACK
CLACK
HIS CASE SEEMS ABNORMAL BECAUSE HE KILLED SOMEONE, BUT IT CAME FROM A WEAKNESS THAT IS COMMON TO THE WHOLE HUMAN RACE.

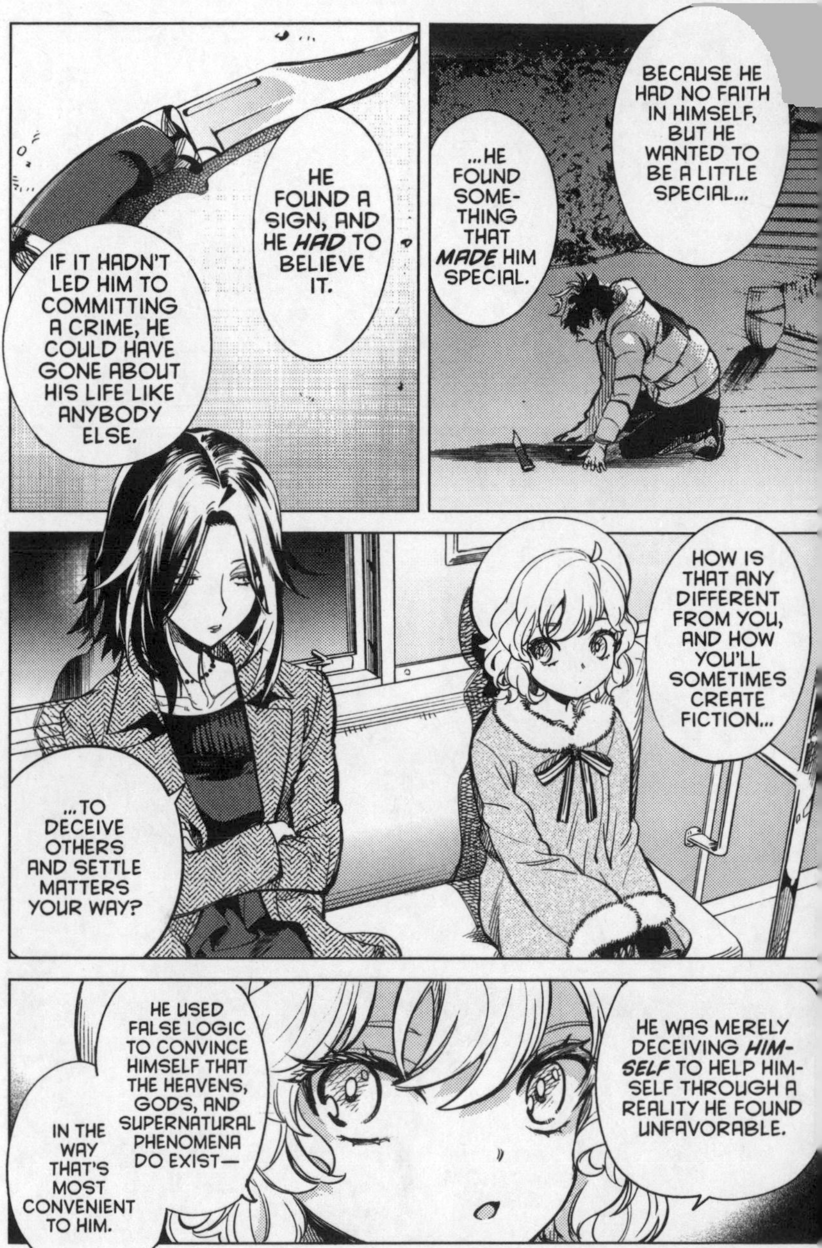
BECAUSE HE HAD NO FAITH IN HIMSELF, BUT HE WANTED TO BE A LITTLE SPECIAL...
...HE FOUND SOME-THING THAT *MADE* HIM SPECIAL.
HE FOUND A SIGN, AND HE *HAD* TO BELIEVE IT.
IF IT HADN'T LED HIM TO COMMITTING A CRIME, HE COULD HAVE GONE ABOUT HIS LIFE LIKE ANYBODY ELSE.
HOW IS THAT ANY DIFFERENT FROM YOU, AND HOW YOU'LL SOMETIMES CREATE FICTION...
...TO DECEIVE OTHERS AND SETTLE MATTERS YOUR WAY?
HE WAS MERELY DECEIVING *HIM-SELF* TO HELP HIM-SELF THROUGH A REALITY HE FOUND UNFAVORABLE.
HE USED FALSE LOGIC TO CONVINCE HIMSELF THAT THE HEAVENS, GODS, AND SUPERNATURAL PHENOMENA DO EXIST—
IN THE WAY THAT'S MOST CONVENIENT TO HIM.

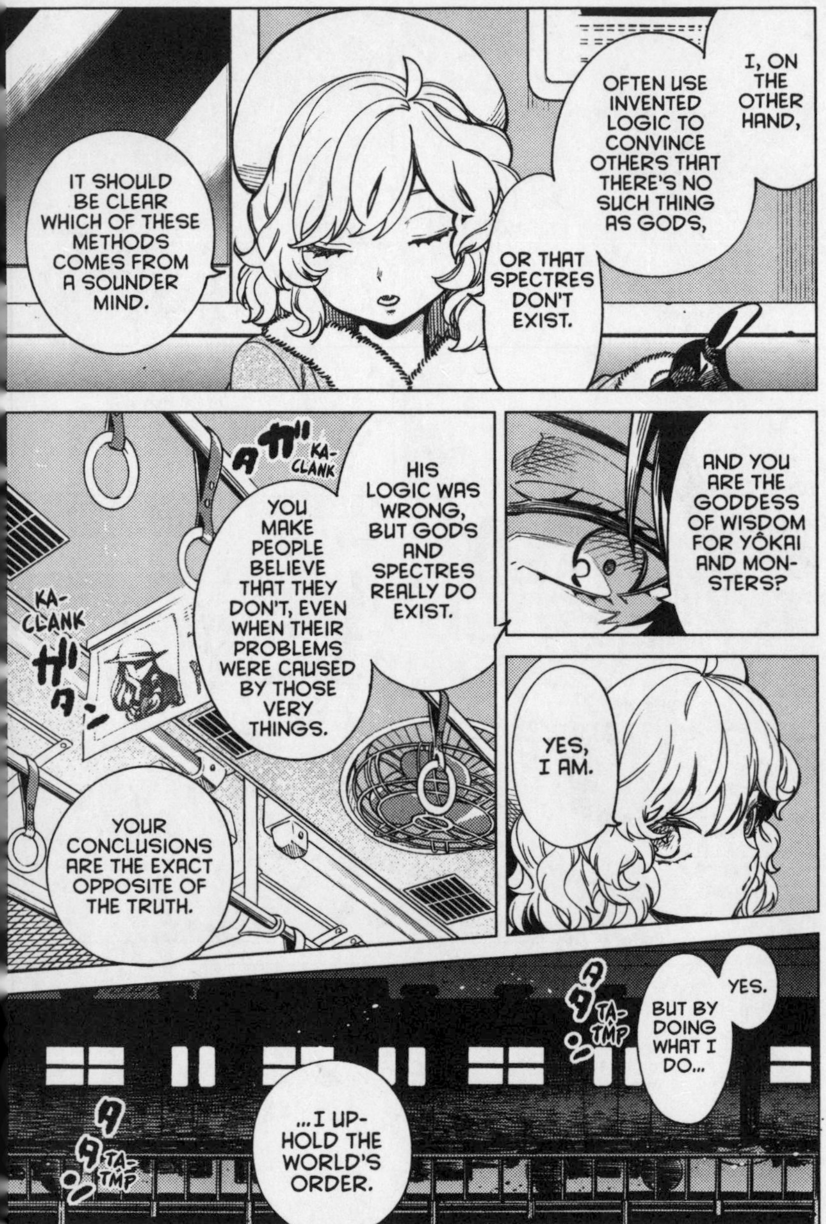
I, ON THE OTHER HAND,
OFTEN USE INVENTED LOGIC TO CONVINCE OTHERS THAT THERE'S NO SUCH THING AS GODS,
OR THAT SPECTRES DON'T EXIST.
IT SHOULD BE CLEAR WHICH OF THESE METHODS COMES FROM A SOUNDER MIND.
AND YOU ARE THE GODDESS OF WISDOM FOR YÔKAI AND MONSTERS?
YES, I AM.
HIS LOGIC WAS WRONG, BUT GODS AND SPECTRES REALLY DO EXIST.
KA-CLANK
YOU MAKE PEOPLE BELIEVE THAT THEY DON'T, EVEN WHEN THEIR PROBLEMS WERE CAUSED BY THOSE VERY THINGS.
KA-CLANK
YOUR CONCLUSIONS ARE THE EXACT OPPOSITE OF THE TRUTH.
YES.
BUT BY DOING WHAT I DO...
TA-TMP
...I UPHOLD THE WORLD'S ORDER.
TA-TMP

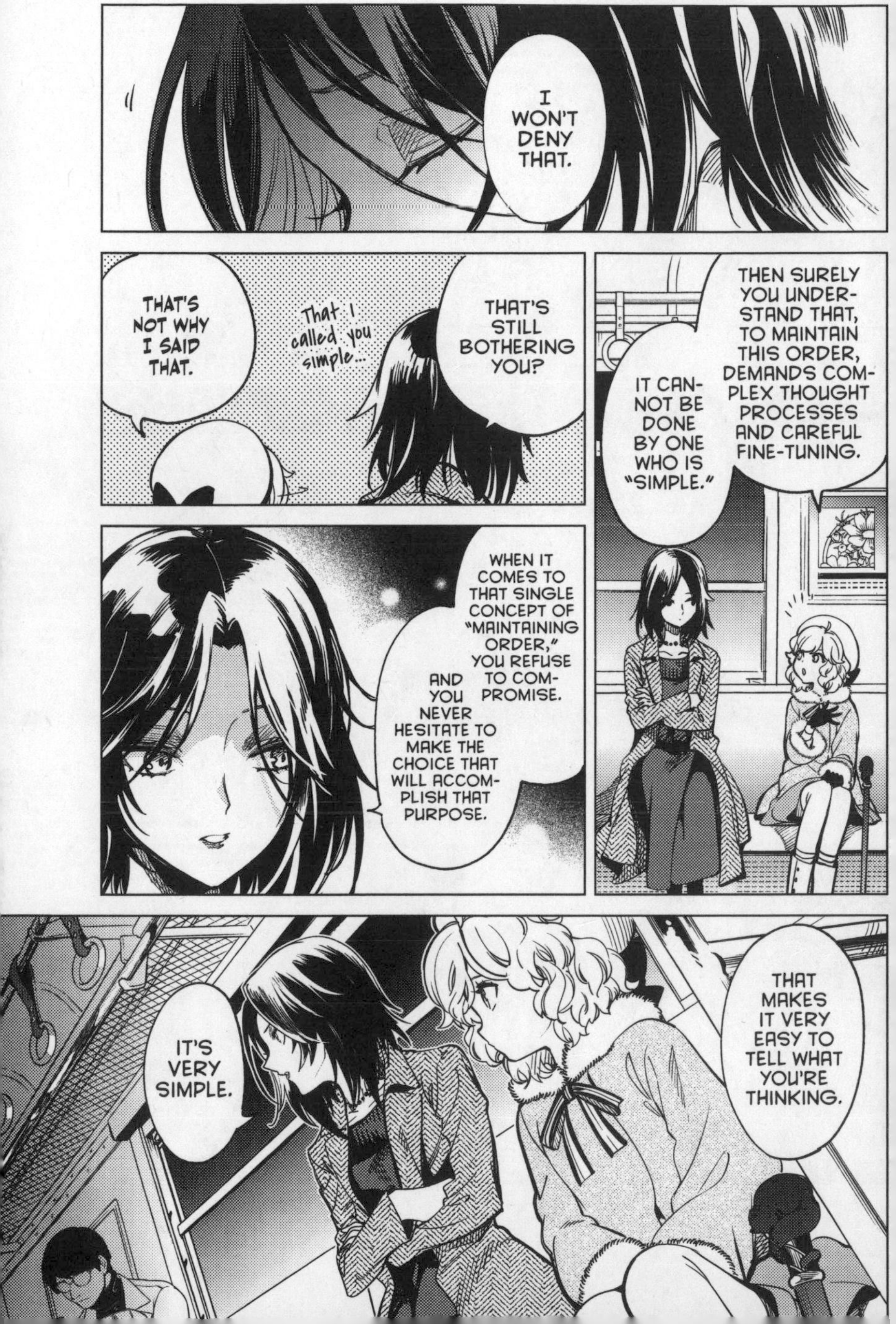
I WON'T DENY THAT.
THEN SURELY YOU UNDERSTAND THAT, TO MAINTAIN THIS ORDER, DEMANDS COMPLEX THOUGHT PROCESSES AND CAREFUL FINE-TUNING.
IT CANNOT BE DONE BY ONE WHO IS "SIMPLE."
THAT'S STILL BOTHERING YOU?
That I called you simple...
THAT'S NOT WHY I SAID THAT.
WHEN IT COMES TO THAT SINGLE CONCEPT OF "MAINTAINING ORDER," YOU REFUSE TO COMPROMISE.
AND YOU NEVER HESITATE TO MAKE THE CHOICE THAT WILL ACCOMPLISH THAT PURPOSE.
THAT MAKES IT VERY EASY TO TELL WHAT YOU'RE THINKING.
IT'S VERY SIMPLE.

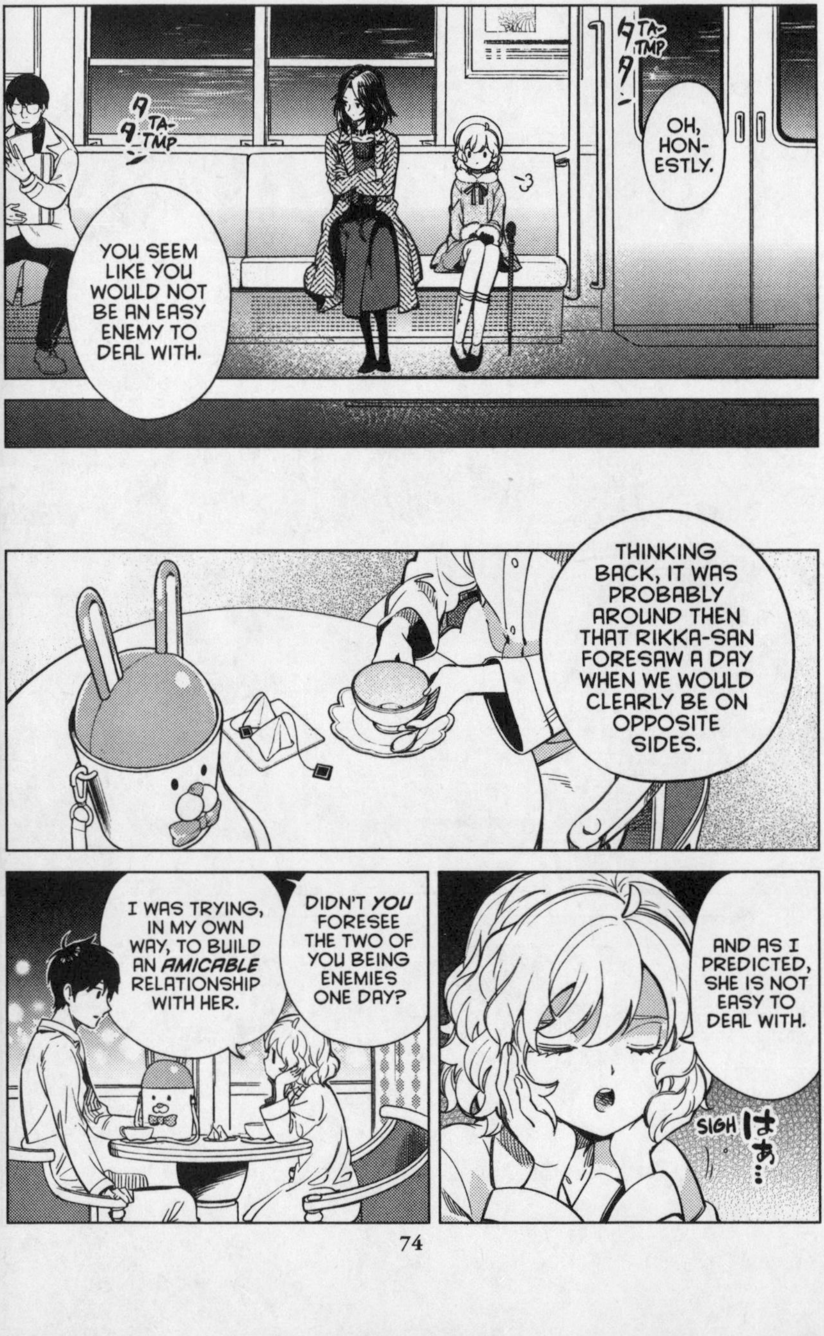

TA-TMP
OH, HON-ESTLY.
TA-TMP
YOU SEEM LIKE YOU WOULD NOT BE AN EASY ENEMY TO DEAL WITH.
THINKING BACK, IT WAS PROBABLY AROUND THEN THAT RIKKA-SAN FORESAW A DAY WHEN WE WOULD CLEARLY BE ON OPPOSITE SIDES.
AND AS I PREDICTED, SHE IS NOT EASY TO DEAL WITH.
SIGH はあ…
DIDN'T *YOU* FORESEE THE TWO OF YOU BEING ENEMIES ONE DAY?
I WAS TRYING, IN MY OWN WAY, TO BUILD AN *AMICABLE* RELATIONSHIP WITH HER.

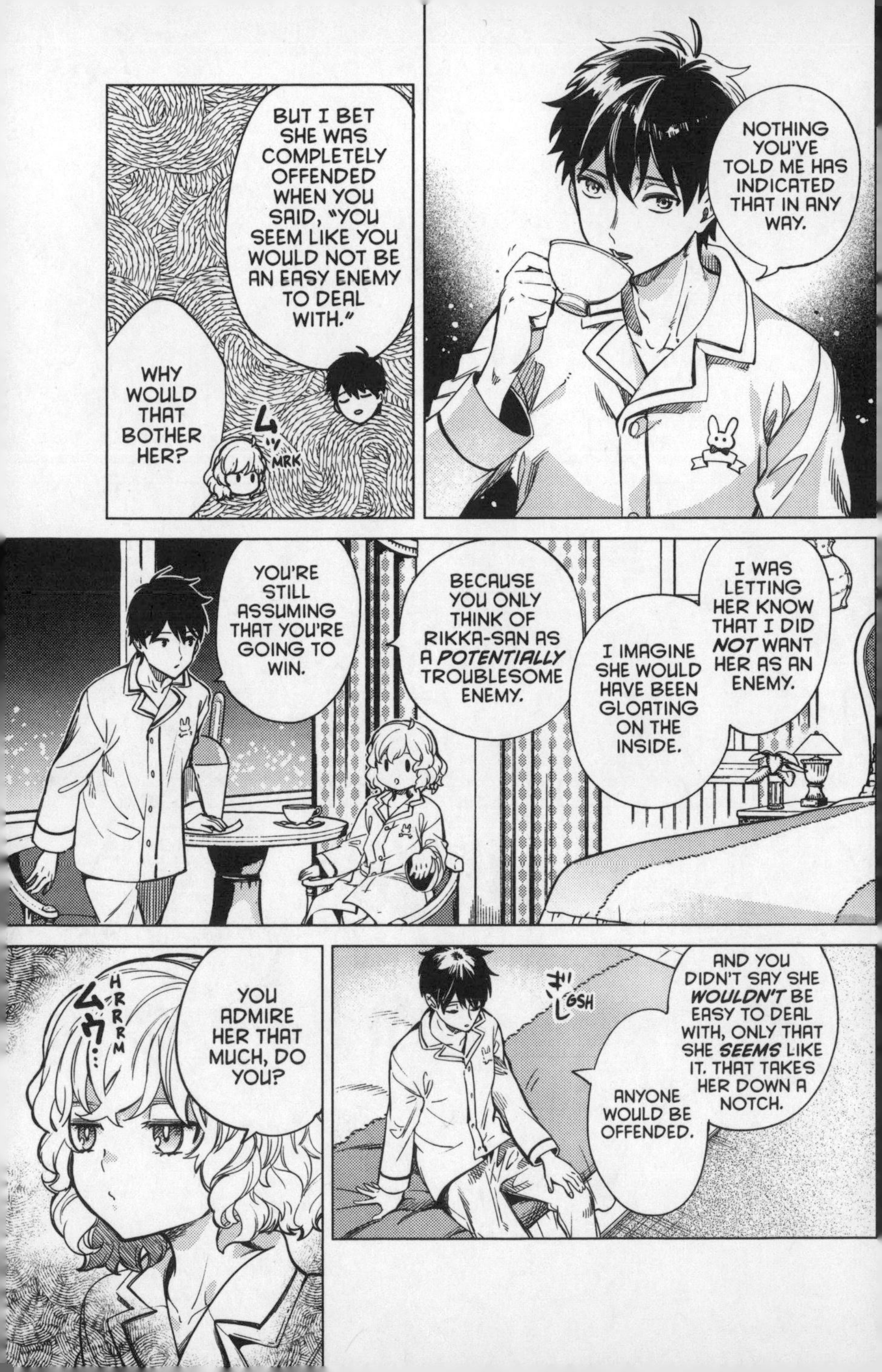
NOTHING YOU'VE TOLD ME HAS INDICATED THAT IN ANY WAY.
BUT I BET SHE WAS COMPLETELY OFFENDED WHEN YOU SAID, "YOU SEEM LIKE YOU WOULD NOT BE AN EASY ENEMY TO DEAL WITH."
WHY WOULD THAT BOTHER HER?
MRK
I WAS LETTING HER KNOW THAT I DID ***NOT*** WANT HER AS AN ENEMY.
I IMAGINE SHE WOULD HAVE BEEN GLOATING ON THE INSIDE.
BECAUSE YOU ONLY THINK OF RIKKA-SAN AS A ***POTENTIALLY*** TROUBLESOME ENEMY.
YOU'RE STILL ASSUMING THAT YOU'RE GOING TO WIN.
AND YOU DIDN'T SAY SHE ***WOULDN'T*** BE EASY TO DEAL WITH, ONLY THAT SHE ***SEEMS*** LIKE IT. THAT TAKES HER DOWN A NOTCH.
ANYONE WOULD BE OFFENDED.
GSH
YOU ADMIRE HER THAT MUCH, DO YOU?
HRRRM...

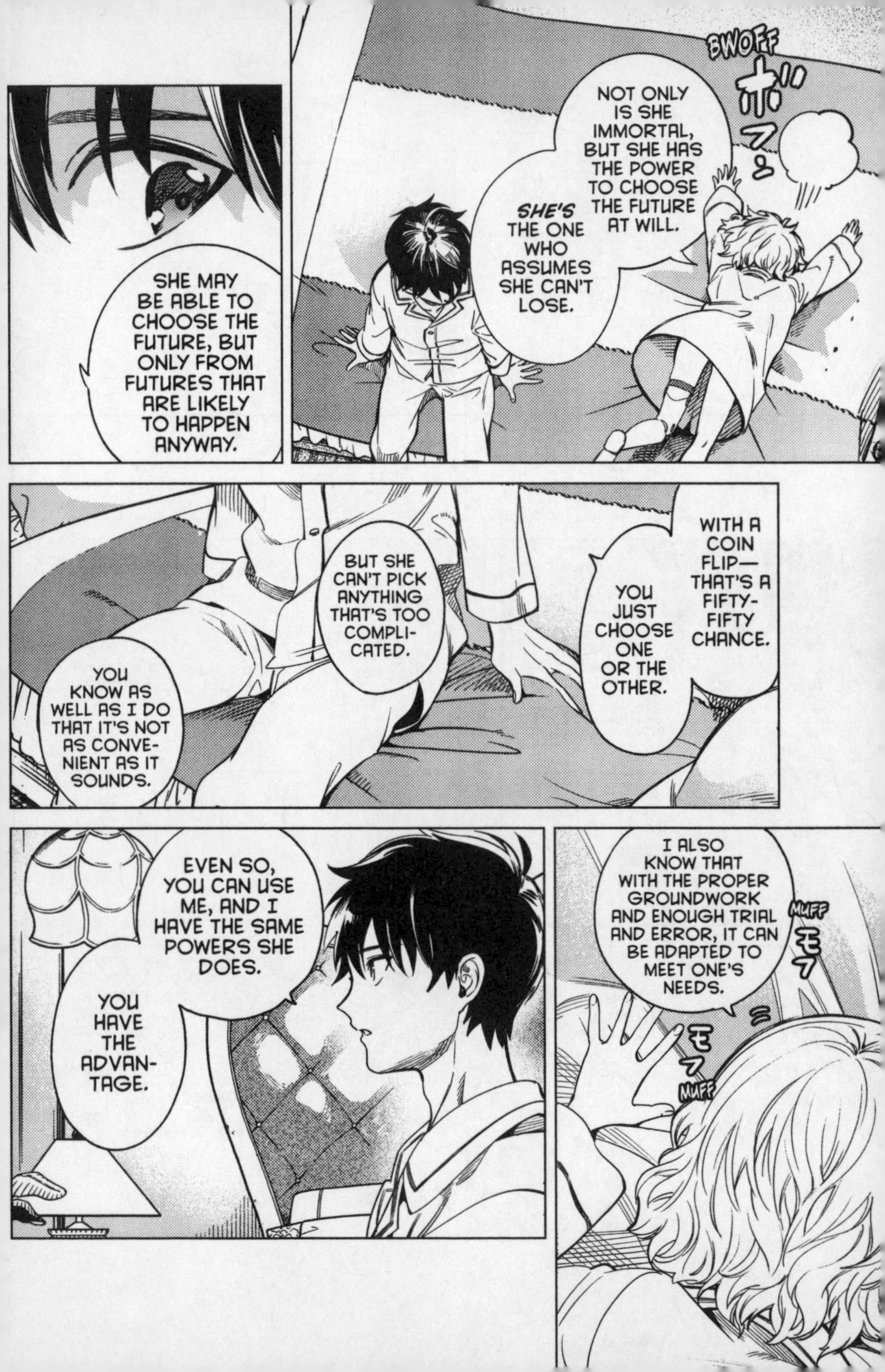
BWOFF
NOT ONLY IS SHE IMMORTAL, BUT SHE HAS THE POWER TO CHOOSE THE FUTURE AT WILL.
SHE'S THE ONE WHO ASSUMES SHE CAN'T LOSE.
SHE MAY BE ABLE TO CHOOSE THE FUTURE, BUT ONLY FROM FUTURES THAT ARE LIKELY TO HAPPEN ANYWAY.
WITH A COIN FLIP—THAT'S A FIFTY-FIFTY CHANCE.
YOU JUST CHOOSE ONE OR THE OTHER.
BUT SHE CAN'T PICK ANYTHING THAT'S TOO COMPLI-CATED.
YOU KNOW AS WELL AS I DO THAT IT'S NOT AS CONVE-NIENT AS IT SOUNDS.
I ALSO KNOW THAT WITH THE PROPER GROUNDWORK AND ENOUGH TRIAL AND ERROR, IT CAN BE ADAPTED TO MEET ONE'S NEEDS.
MUFF
MUFF
EVEN SO, YOU CAN USE ME, AND I HAVE THE SAME POWERS SHE DOES.
YOU HAVE THE ADVAN-TAGE.

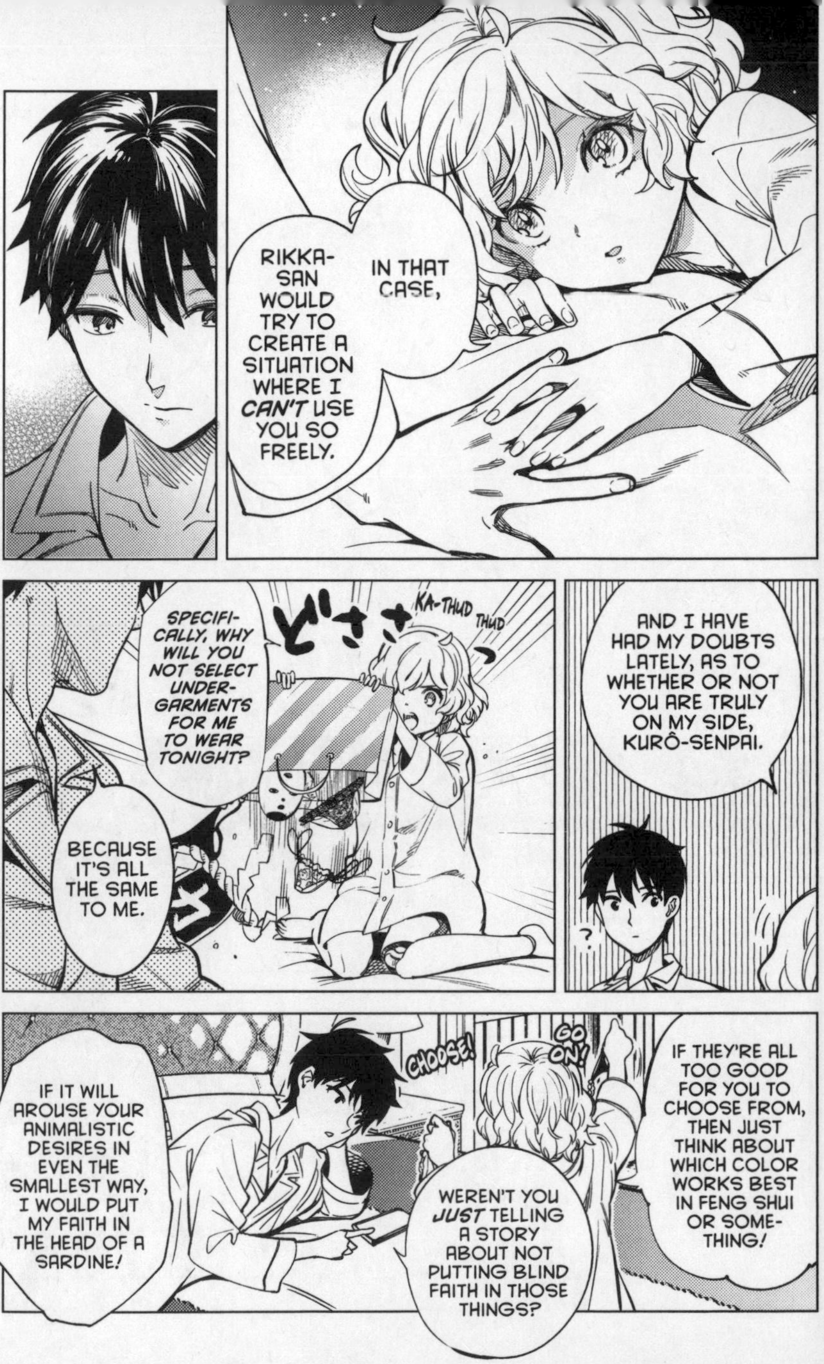
IN THAT CASE,
RIKKA-SAN WOULD TRY TO CREATE A SITUATION WHERE I *CAN'T* USE YOU SO FREELY.
AND I HAVE HAD MY DOUBTS LATELY, AS TO WHETHER OR NOT YOU ARE TRULY ON MY SIDE, KURÔ-SENPAI.
?
KA-THUD THUD
SPECIFICALLY, WHY WILL YOU NOT SELECT UNDERGARMENTS FOR ME TO WEAR TONIGHT?
BECAUSE IT'S ALL THE SAME TO ME.
IF THEY'RE ALL TOO GOOD FOR YOU TO CHOOSE FROM, THEN JUST THINK ABOUT WHICH COLOR WORKS BEST IN FENG SHUI OR SOMETHING!
GO ON!
CHOOSE!
WEREN'T YOU *JUST* TELLING A STORY ABOUT NOT PUTTING BLIND FAITH IN THOSE THINGS?
IF IT WILL AROUSE YOUR ANIMALISTIC DESIRES IN EVEN THE SMALLEST WAY, I WOULD PUT MY FAITH IN THE HEAD OF A SARDINE!

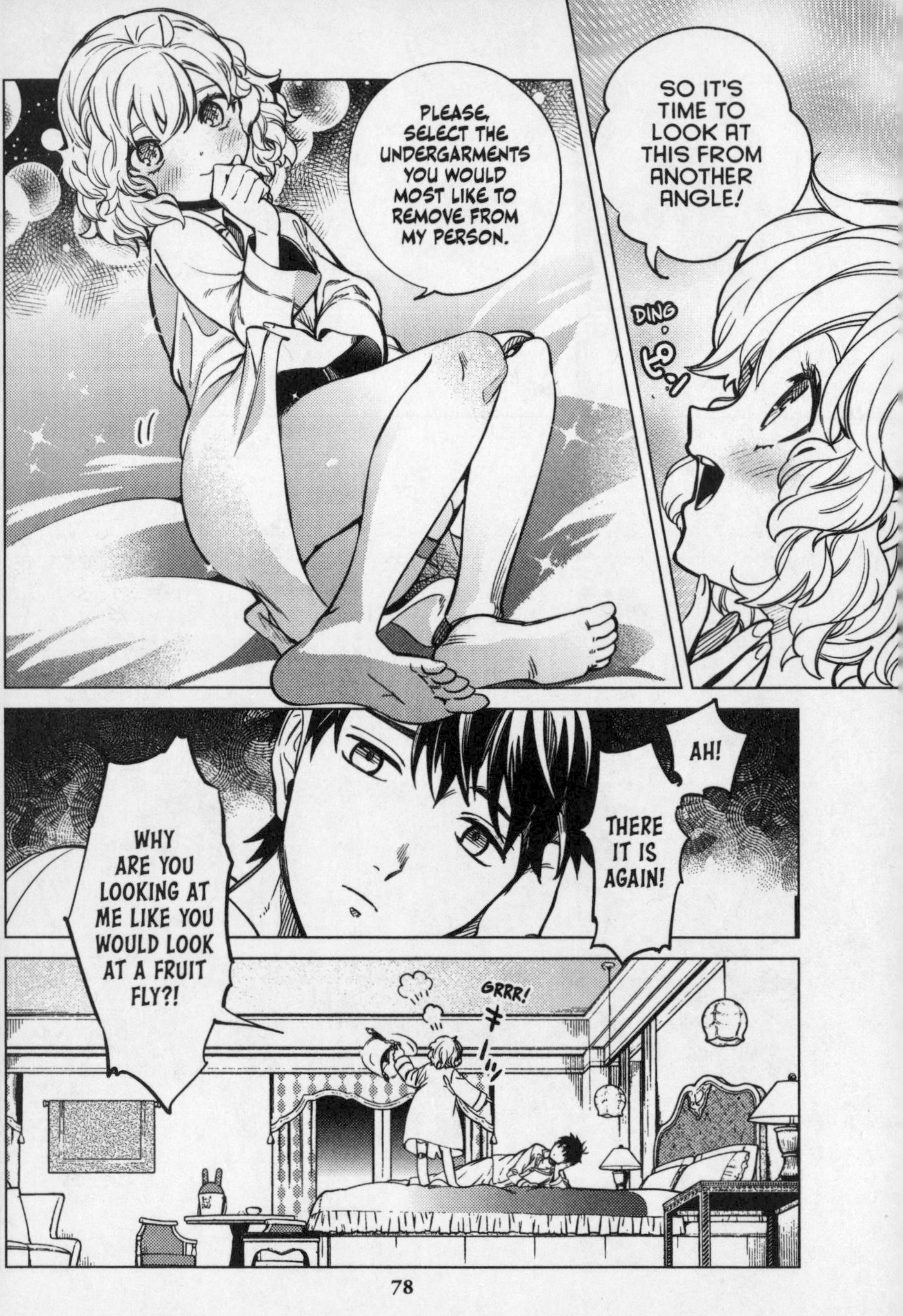
SO IT'S TIME TO LOOK AT THIS FROM ANOTHER ANGLE!
DING
PLEASE, SELECT THE UNDERGARMENTS YOU WOULD MOST LIKE TO REMOVE FROM MY PERSON.
AH!
THERE IT IS AGAIN!
WHY ARE YOU LOOKING AT ME LIKE YOU WOULD LOOK AT A FRUIT FLY?!
GRRR!

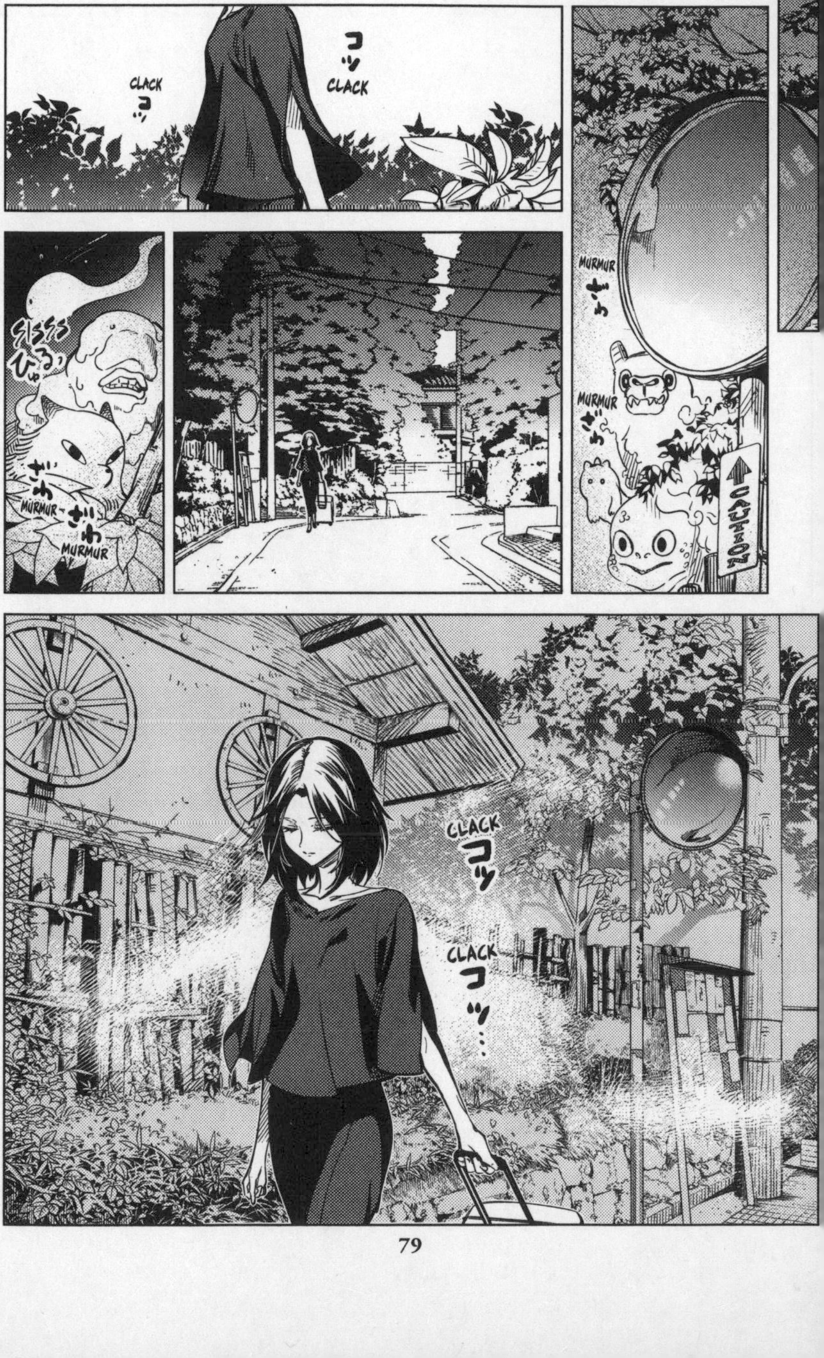
ざわ
MURMUR
ざわ
MURMUR
CAUTION
コッ
CLACK
コッ
CLACK
ひゅるっ
SISSSS
ざわ
MURMUR
ざわ
MURMUR
CLACK
コッ
CLACK
コッ…

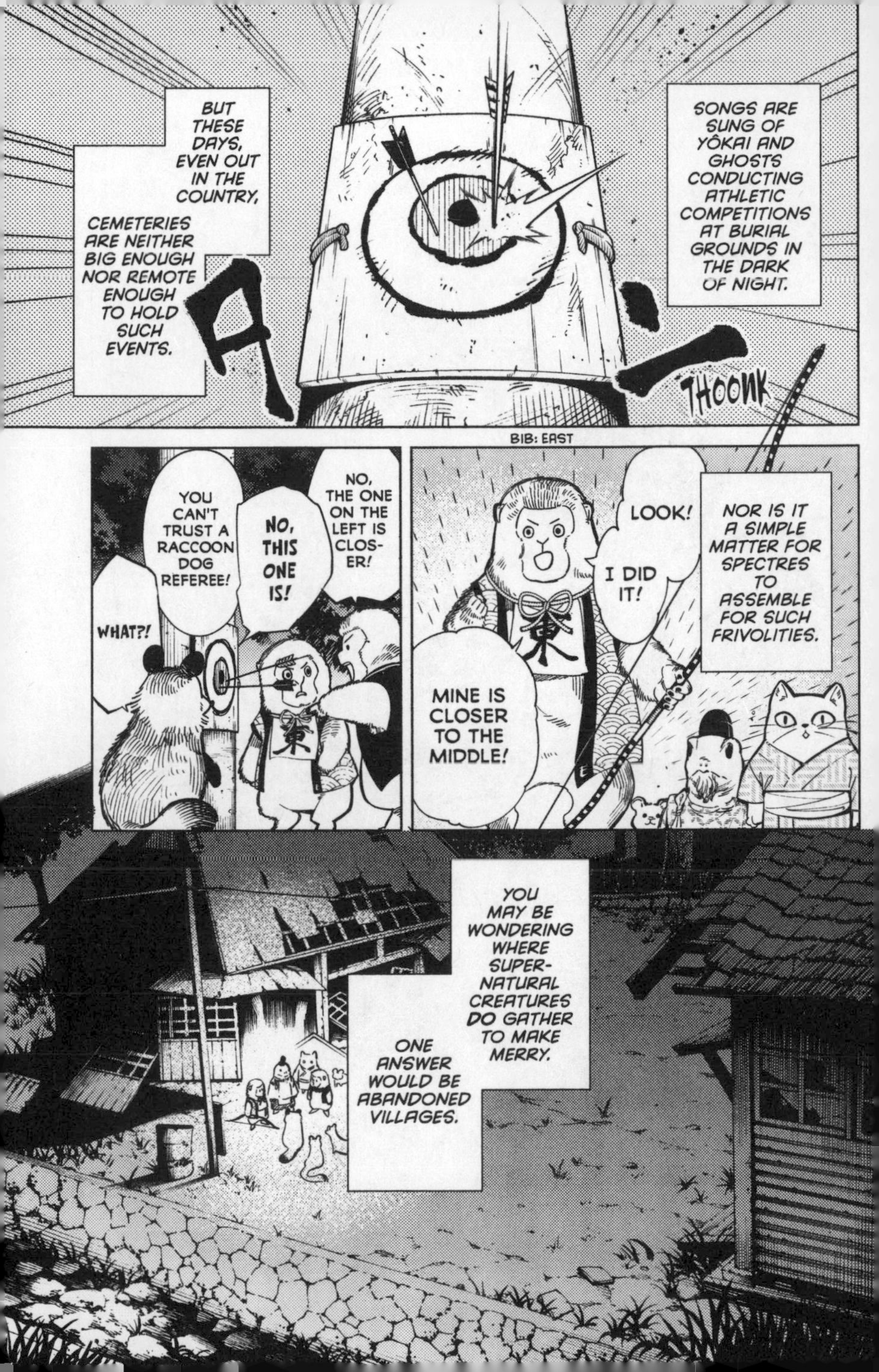
SONGS ARE SUNG OF YÔKAI AND GHOSTS CONDUCTING ATHLETIC COMPETITIONS AT BURIAL GROUNDS IN THE DARK OF NIGHT.
BUT THESE DAYS, EVEN OUT IN THE COUNTRY,
CEMETERIES ARE NEITHER BIG ENOUGH NOR REMOTE ENOUGH TO HOLD SUCH EVENTS.
THOONK
BIB: EAST
NOR IS IT A SIMPLE MATTER FOR SPECTRES TO ASSEMBLE FOR SUCH FRIVOLITIES.
LOOK!
I DID IT!
MINE IS CLOSER TO THE MIDDLE!
NO, THE ONE ON THE LEFT IS CLOS-ER!
NO, THIS ONE IS!
YOU CAN'T TRUST A RACCOON DOG REFEREE!
WHAT?!
YOU MAY BE WONDERING WHERE SUPER-NATURAL CREATURES DO GATHER TO MAKE MERRY.
ONE ANSWER WOULD BE ABANDONED VILLAGES.

CHAPTER 38: "HIT THE BULL'S EYE WIDE OF THE MARK"

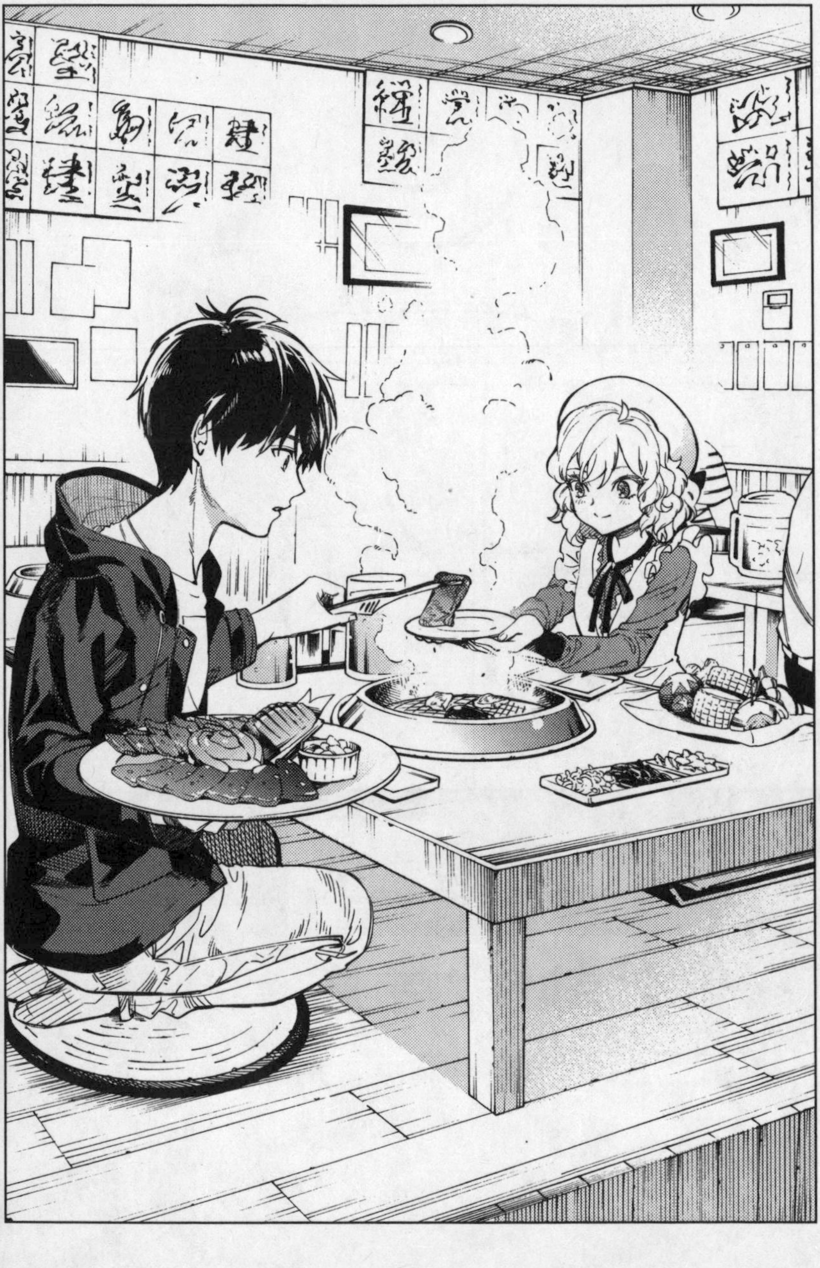

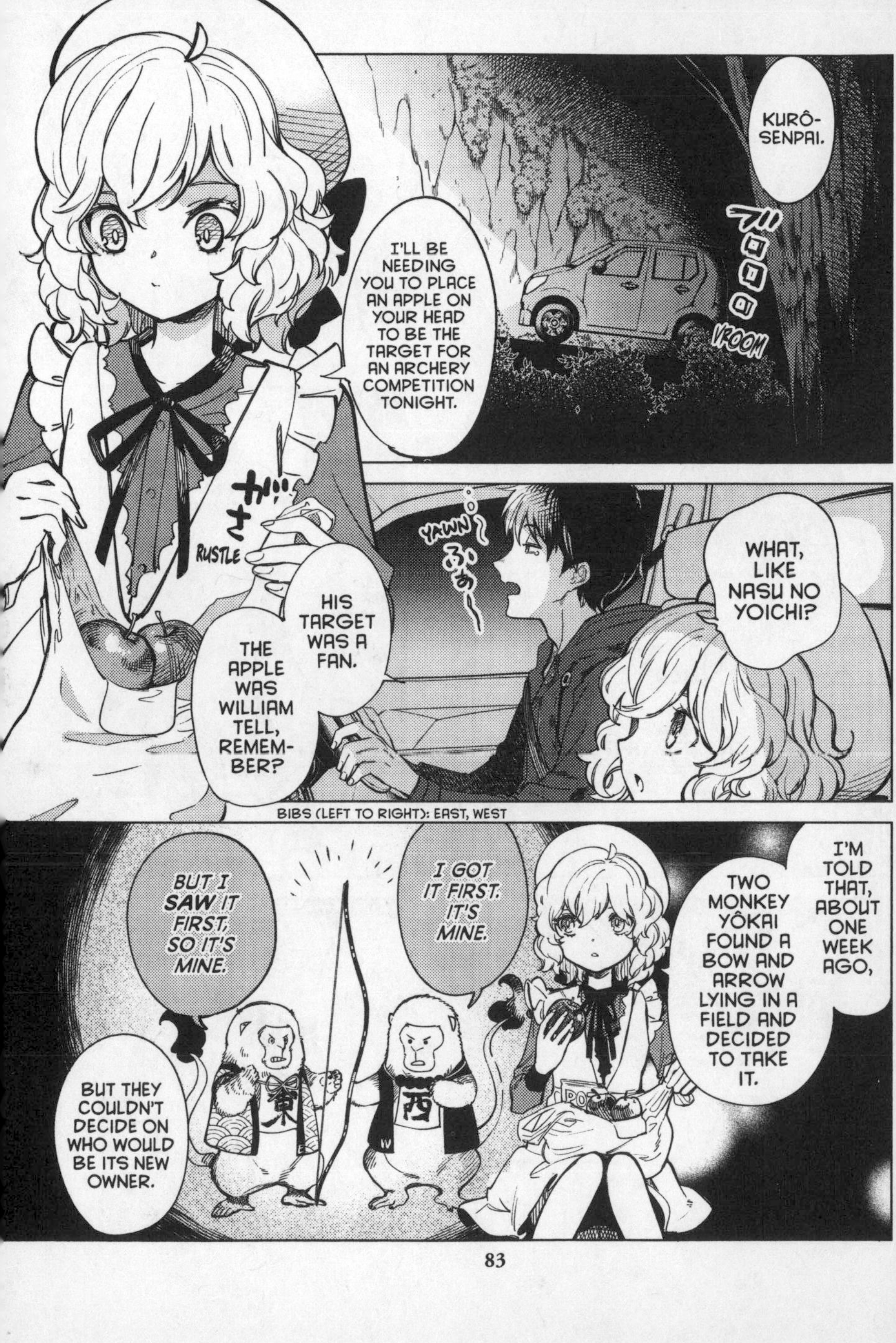
KURÔ-SENPAI.
ブロロロ
VROOM
I'LL BE NEEDING YOU TO PLACE AN APPLE ON YOUR HEAD TO BE THE TARGET FOR AN ARCHERY COMPETITION TONIGHT.
WHAT, LIKE NASU NO YOICHI?
ふぁ~
YAWN
HIS TARGET WAS A FAN.
THE APPLE WAS WILLIAM TELL, REMEMBER?
がさ
RUSTLE
BIBS (LEFT TO RIGHT): EAST, WEST
I'M TOLD THAT, ABOUT ONE WEEK AGO,
TWO MONKEY YÔKAI FOUND A BOW AND ARROW LYING IN A FIELD AND DECIDED TO TAKE IT.
I GOT IT FIRST. IT'S MINE.
BUT I SAW IT FIRST, SO IT'S MINE.
BUT THEY COULDN'T DECIDE ON WHO WOULD BE ITS NEW OWNER.

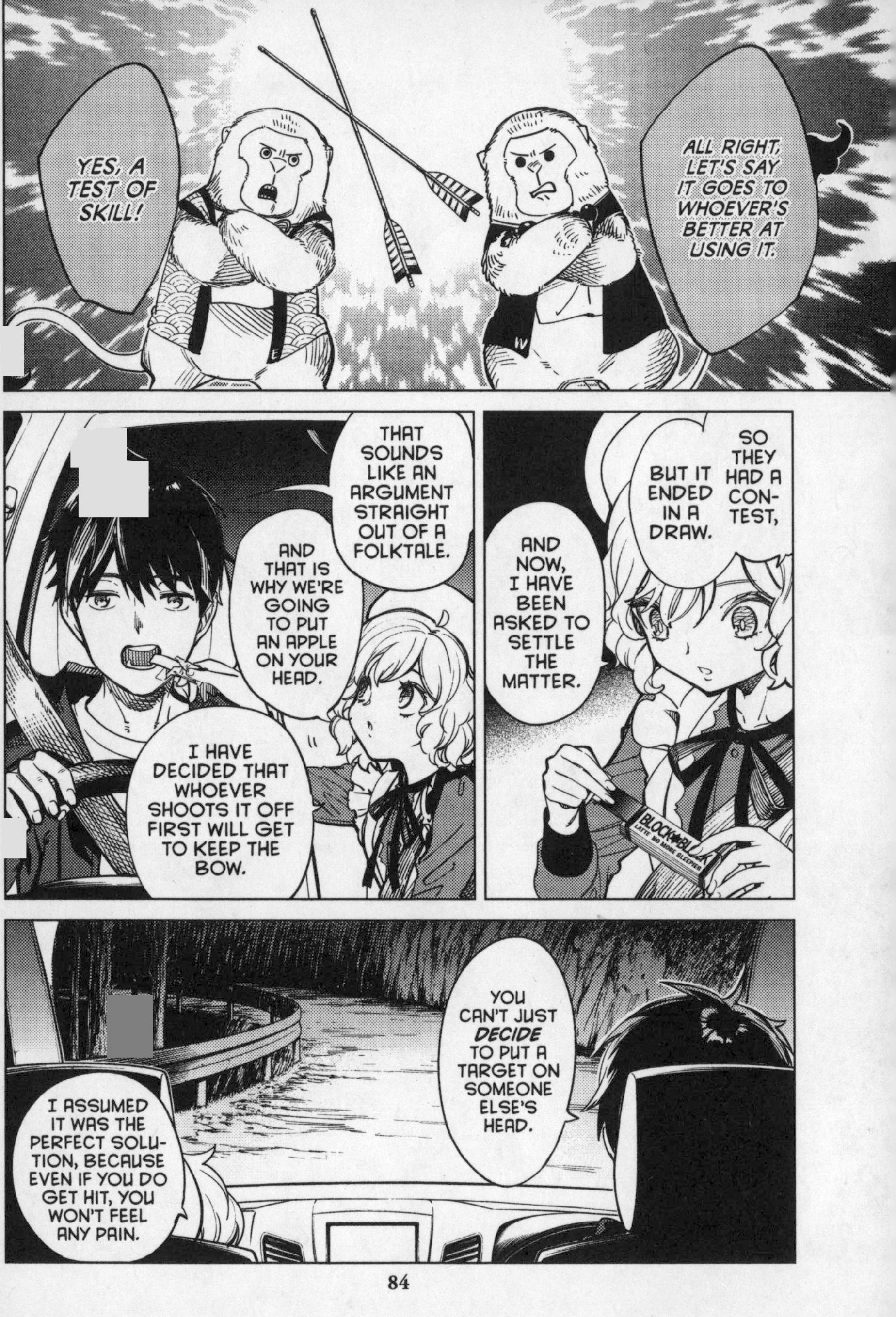
ALL RIGHT, LET'S SAY IT GOES TO WHOEVER'S BETTER AT USING IT.
YES, A TEST OF SKILL!
SO THEY HAD A CON-TEST,
BUT IT ENDED IN A DRAW.
AND NOW, I HAVE BEEN ASKED TO SETTLE THE MATTER.
BLOCK★BLOCK
LATTE NO MORE SLEEPER
THAT SOUNDS LIKE AN ARGUMENT STRAIGHT OUT OF A FOLKTALE.
AND THAT IS WHY WE'RE GOING TO PUT AN APPLE ON YOUR HEAD.
I HAVE DECIDED THAT WHOEVER SHOOTS IT OFF FIRST WILL GET TO KEEP THE BOW.
YOU CAN'T JUST *DECIDE* TO PUT A TARGET ON SOMEONE ELSE'S HEAD.
I ASSUMED IT WAS THE PERFECT SOLU-TION, BECAUSE EVEN IF YOU DO GET HIT, YOU WON'T FEEL ANY PAIN.

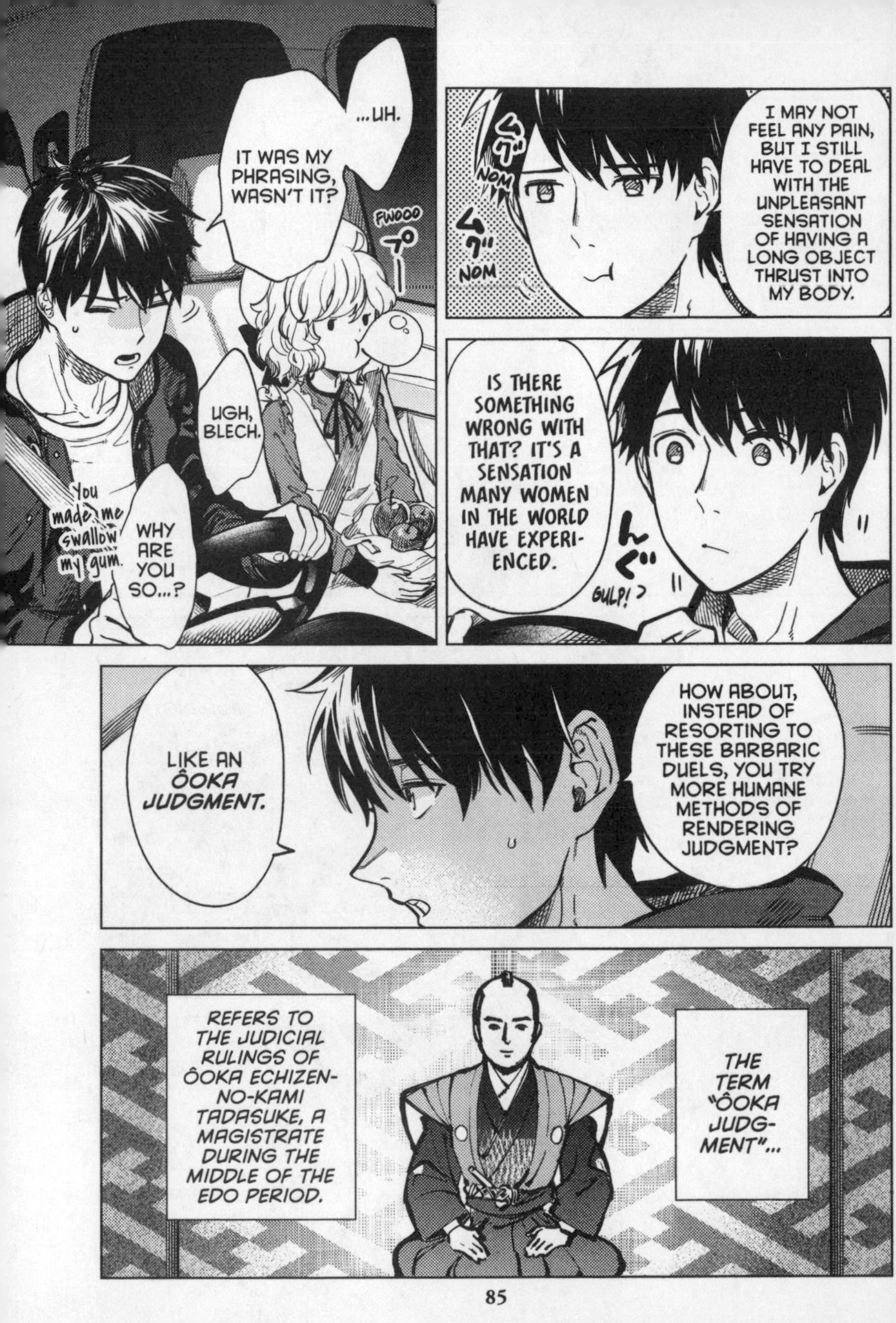
I MAY NOT FEEL ANY PAIN, BUT I STILL HAVE TO DEAL WITH THE UNPLEASANT SENSATION OF HAVING A LONG OBJECT THRUST INTO MY BODY.
NOM
NOM
IS THERE SOMETHING WRONG WITH THAT? IT'S A SENSATION MANY WOMEN IN THE WORLD HAVE EXPERIENCED.
GULP!
...UH.
IT WAS MY PHRASING, WASN'T IT?
FWOOO
UGH, BLECH.
WHY ARE YOU SO...?
You made me swallow my gum.
HOW ABOUT, INSTEAD OF RESORTING TO THESE BARBARIC DUELS, YOU TRY MORE HUMANE METHODS OF RENDERING JUDGMENT?
LIKE AN ÔOKA JUDGMENT.
THE TERM "ÔOKA JUDGMENT"...
REFERS TO THE JUDICIAL RULINGS OF ÔOKA ECHIZEN-NO-KAMI TADASUKE, A MAGISTRATE DURING THE MIDDLE OF THE EDO PERIOD.

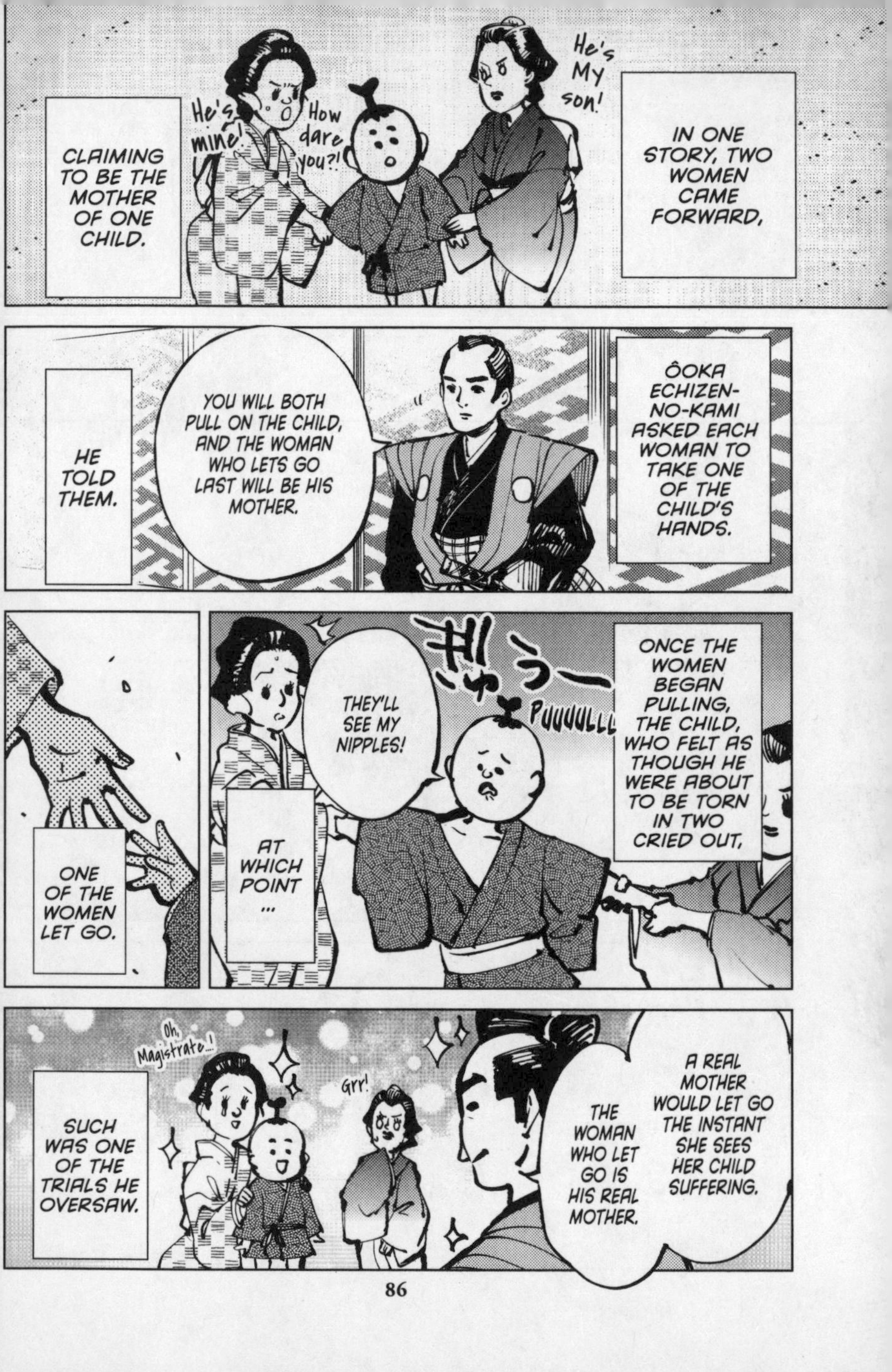
IN ONE STORY, TWO WOMEN CAME FORWARD,
He's My son!
How dare you?!
He's mine!
CLAIMING TO BE THE MOTHER OF ONE CHILD.
ÔOKA ECHIZEN-NO-KAMI ASKED EACH WOMAN TO TAKE ONE OF THE CHILD'S HANDS.
YOU WILL BOTH PULL ON THE CHILD, AND THE WOMAN WHO LETS GO LAST WILL BE HIS MOTHER.
HE TOLD THEM.
ONCE THE WOMEN BEGAN PULLING, THE CHILD, WHO FELT AS THOUGH HE WERE ABOUT TO BE TORN IN TWO CRIED OUT,
ぎゅうー
PUUUULLL
THEY'LL SEE MY NIPPLES!
AT WHICH POINT ...
ONE OF THE WOMEN LET GO.
A REAL MOTHER WOULD LET GO THE INSTANT SHE SEES HER CHILD SUFFERING.
THE WOMAN WHO LET GO IS HIS REAL MOTHER.
Grr!
Oh, Magistrate...!
SUCH WAS ONE OF THE TRIALS HE OVERSAW.

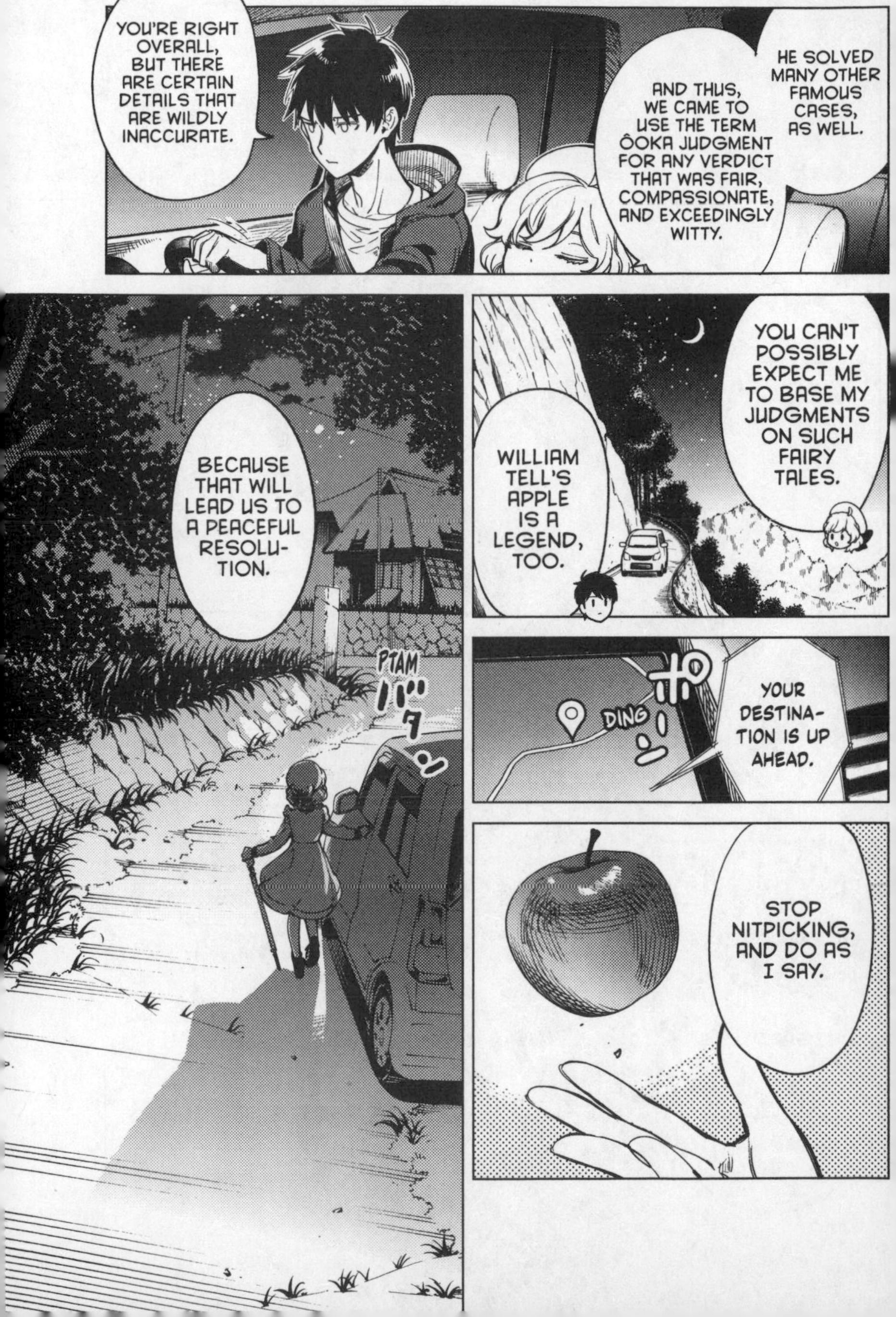
HE SOLVED MANY OTHER FAMOUS CASES, AS WELL.
AND THUS, WE CAME TO USE THE TERM ÔOKA JUDGMENT FOR ANY VERDICT THAT WAS FAIR, COMPASSIONATE, AND EXCEEDINGLY WITTY.
YOU'RE RIGHT OVERALL, BUT THERE ARE CERTAIN DETAILS THAT ARE WILDLY INACCURATE.
YOU CAN'T POSSIBLY EXPECT ME TO BASE MY JUDGMENTS ON SUCH FAIRY TALES.
WILLIAM TELL'S APPLE IS A LEGEND, TOO.
YOUR DESTINATION IS UP AHEAD.
DING
STOP NITPICKING, AND DO AS I SAY.
BECAUSE THAT WILL LEAD US TO A PEACEFUL RESOLUTION.
PTAM

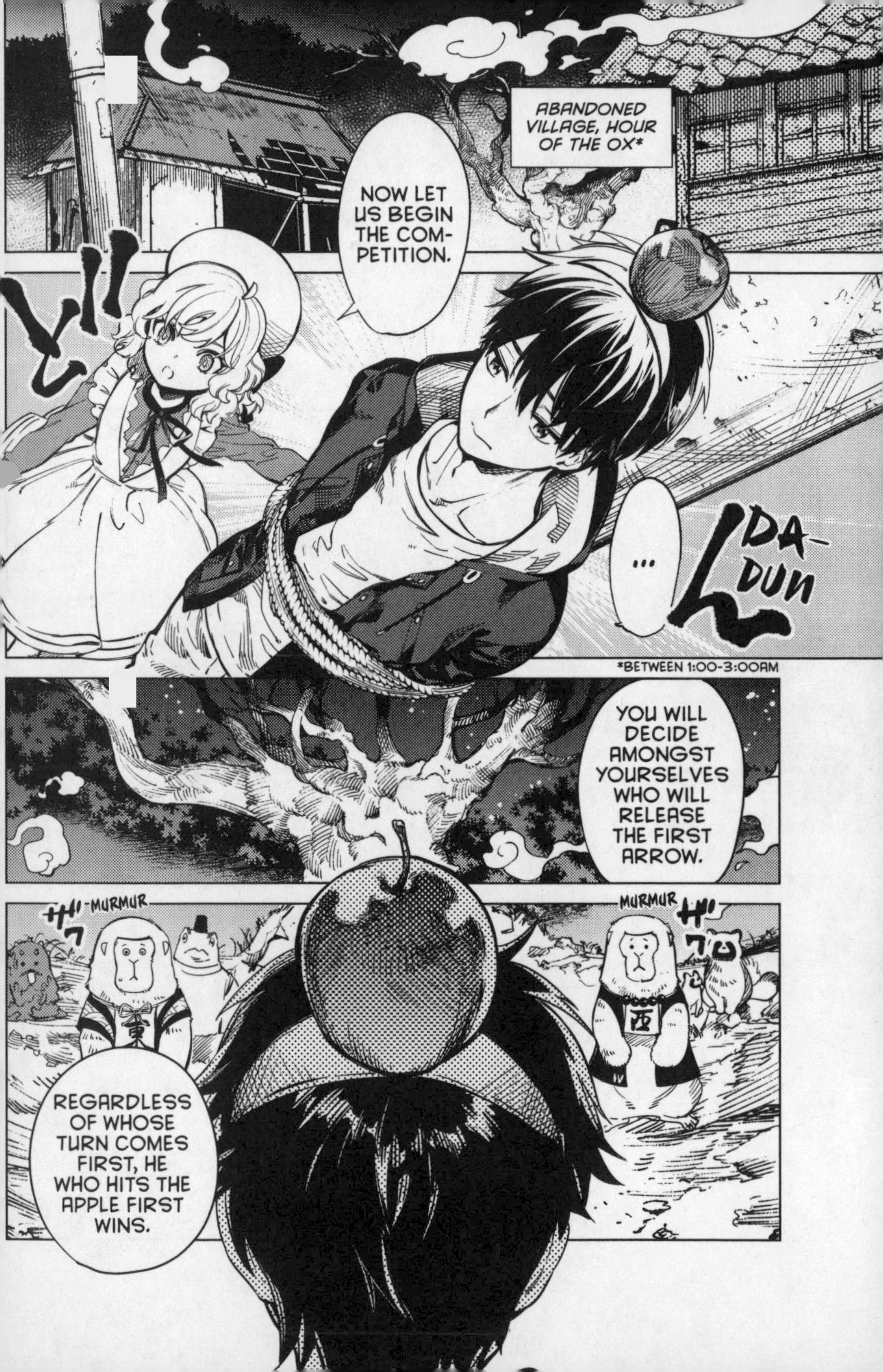
ABANDONED VILLAGE, HOUR OF THE OX*
NOW LET US BEGIN THE COMPETITION.
DA-DUN
...
*BETWEEN 1:00-3:00AM
YOU WILL DECIDE AMONGST YOURSELVES WHO WILL RELEASE THE FIRST ARROW.
MURMUR
MURMUR
REGARDLESS OF WHOSE TURN COMES FIRST, HE WHO HITS THE APPLE FIRST WINS.

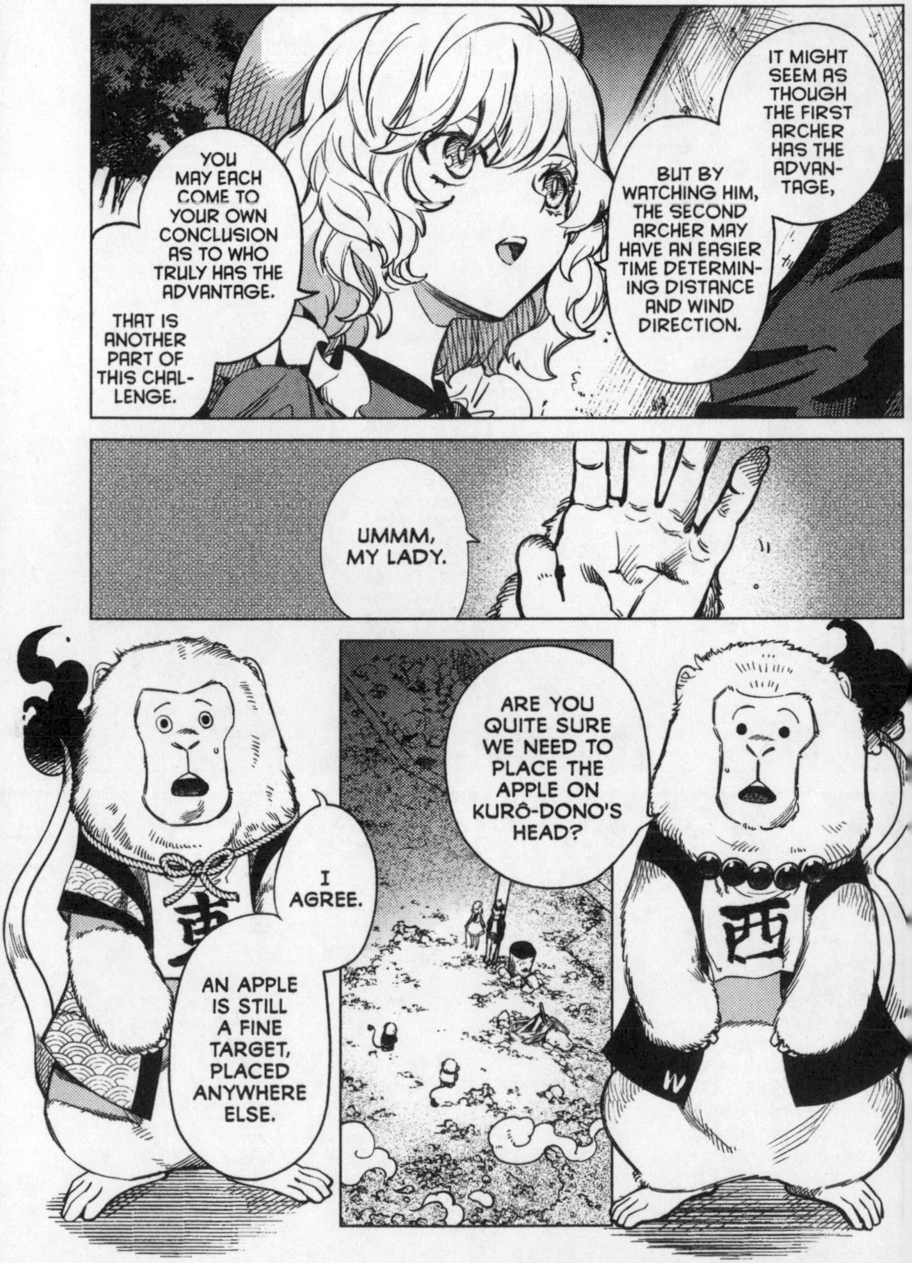
IT MIGHT SEEM AS THOUGH THE FIRST ARCHER HAS THE ADVAN-TAGE,
BUT BY WATCHING HIM, THE SECOND ARCHER MAY HAVE AN EASIER TIME DETERMIN-ING DISTANCE AND WIND DIRECTION.
YOU MAY EACH COME TO YOUR OWN CONCLUSION AS TO WHO TRULY HAS THE ADVANTAGE.
THAT IS ANOTHER PART OF THIS CHAL-LENGE.
UMMM, MY LADY.
ARE YOU QUITE SURE WE NEED TO PLACE THE APPLE ON KURÔ-DONO'S HEAD?
西
I AGREE.
AN APPLE IS STILL A FINE TARGET, PLACED ANYWHERE ELSE.

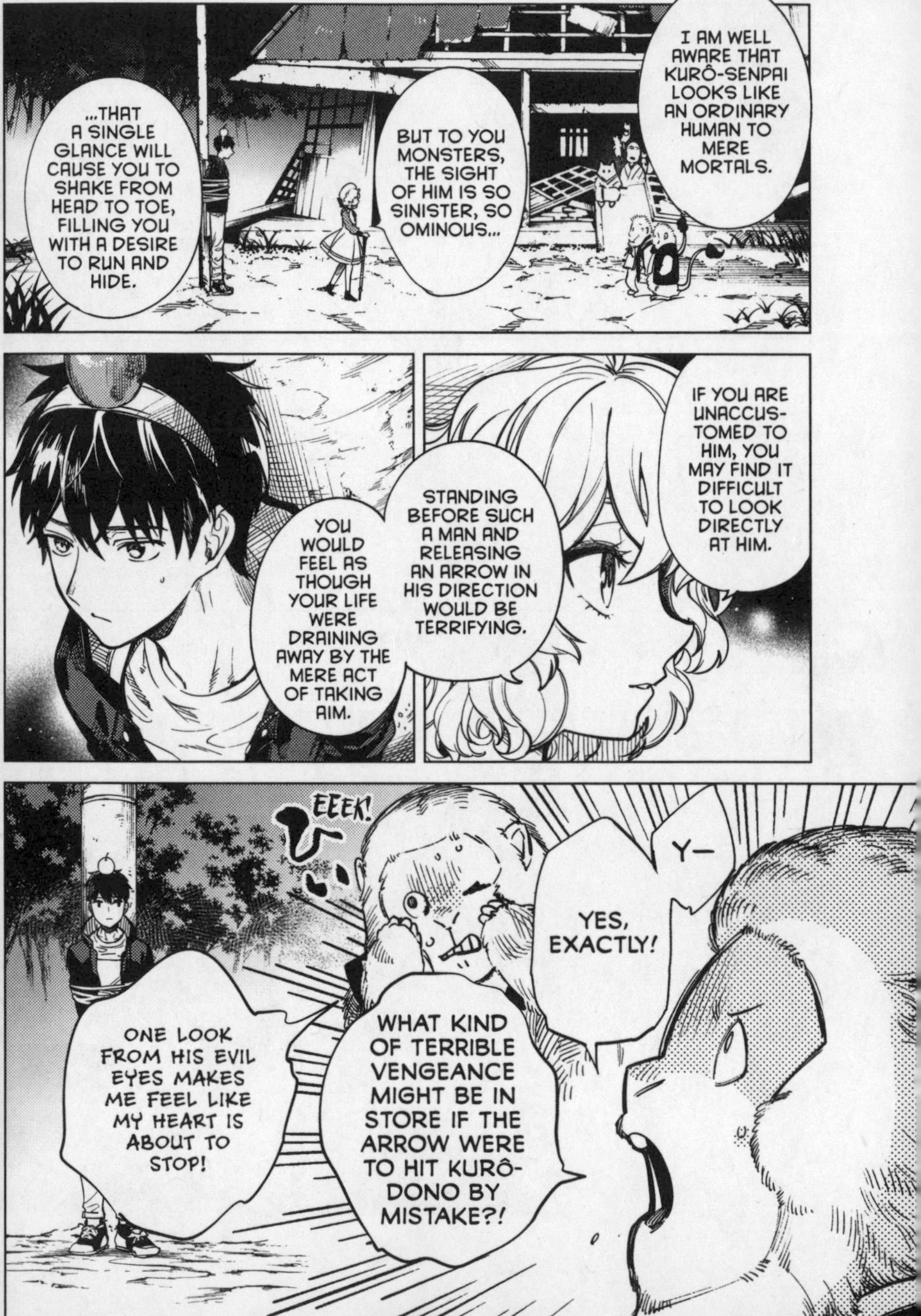
I AM WELL AWARE THAT KURÔ-SENPAI LOOKS LIKE AN ORDINARY HUMAN TO MERE MORTALS.
BUT TO YOU MONSTERS, THE SIGHT OF HIM IS SO SINISTER, SO OMINOUS...
...THAT A SINGLE GLANCE WILL CAUSE YOU TO SHAKE FROM HEAD TO TOE, FILLING YOU WITH A DESIRE TO RUN AND HIDE.
IF YOU ARE UNACCUS-TOMED TO HIM, YOU MAY FIND IT DIFFICULT TO LOOK DIRECTLY AT HIM.
STANDING BEFORE SUCH A MAN AND RELEASING AN ARROW IN HIS DIRECTION WOULD BE TERRIFYING.
YOU WOULD FEEL AS THOUGH YOUR LIFE WERE DRAINING AWAY BY THE MERE ACT OF TAKING AIM.
Y—
YES, EXACTLY!
EEEK!
WHAT KIND OF TERRIBLE VENGEANCE MIGHT BE IN STORE IF THE ARROW WERE TO HIT KURÔ-DONO BY MISTAKE?!
ONE LOOK FROM HIS EVIL EYES MAKES ME FEEL LIKE MY HEART IS ABOUT TO STOP!

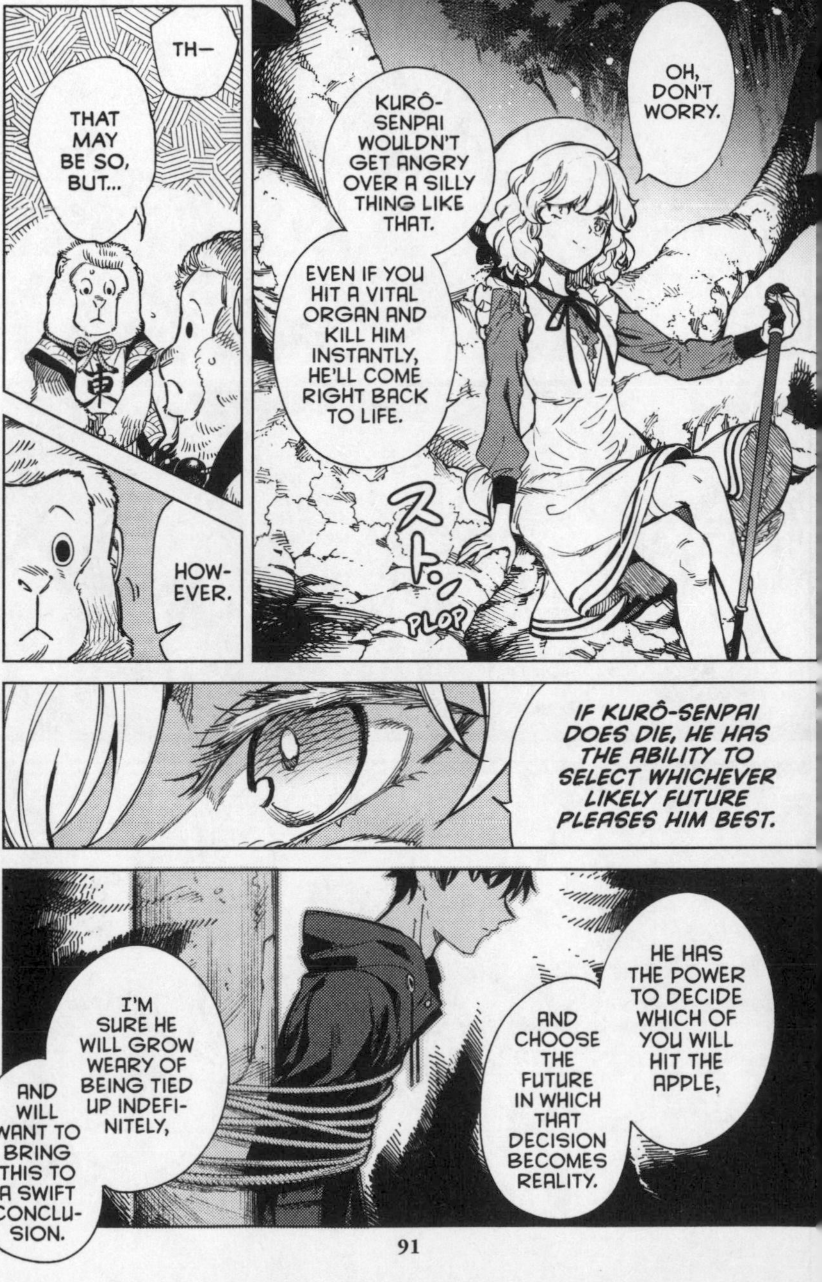
OH, DON'T WORRY.
KURÔ-SENPAI WOULDN'T GET ANGRY OVER A SILLY THING LIKE THAT.
EVEN IF YOU HIT A VITAL ORGAN AND KILL HIM INSTANTLY, HE'LL COME RIGHT BACK TO LIFE.
PLOP
TH—
THAT MAY BE SO, BUT...
HOW-EVER.
IF KURÔ-SENPAI DOES DIE, HE HAS THE ABILITY TO SELECT WHICHEVER LIKELY FUTURE PLEASES HIM BEST.
HE HAS THE POWER TO DECIDE WHICH OF YOU WILL HIT THE APPLE,
AND CHOOSE THE FUTURE IN WHICH THAT DECISION BECOMES REALITY.
I'M SURE HE WILL GROW WEARY OF BEING TIED UP INDEFINITELY,
AND WILL WANT TO BRING THIS TO A SWIFT CONCLUSION.

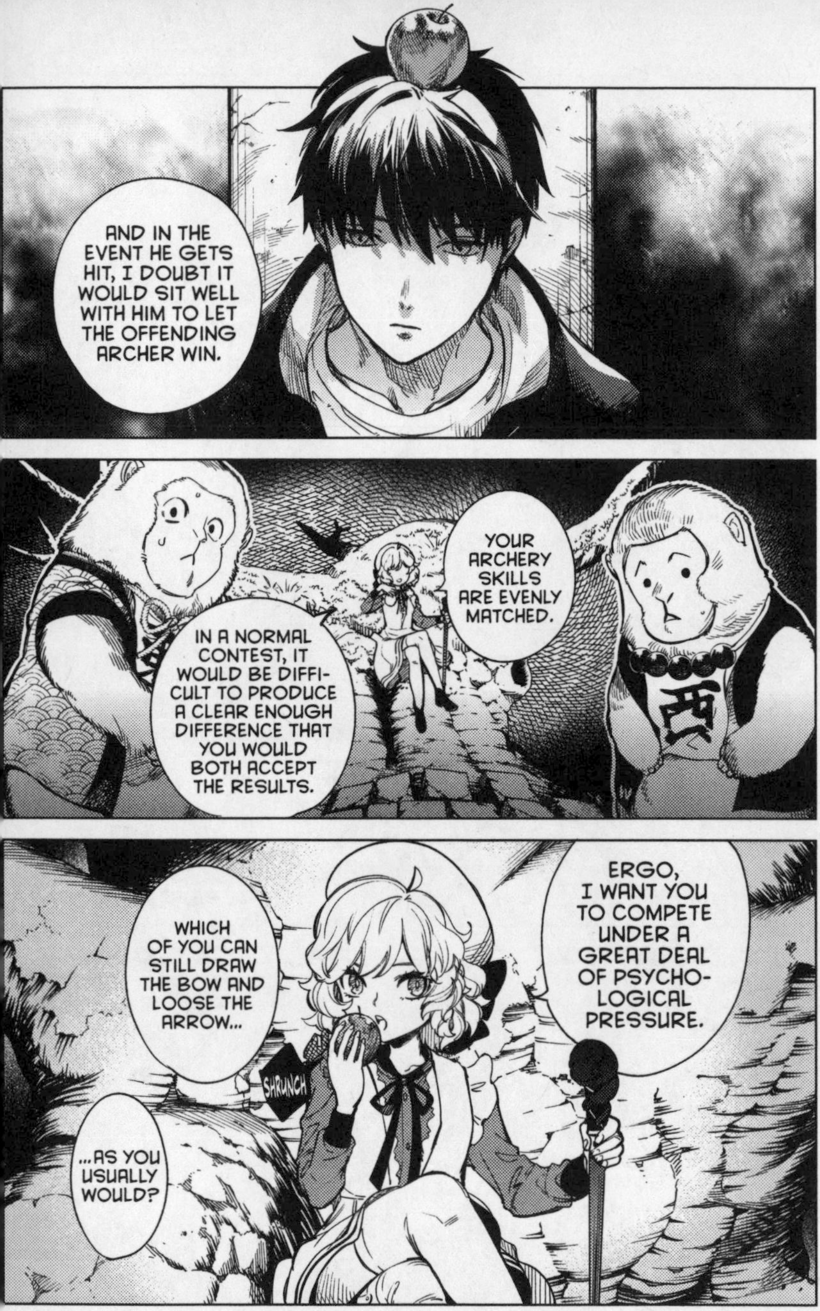
AND IN THE EVENT HE GETS HIT, I DOUBT IT WOULD SIT WELL WITH HIM TO LET THE OFFENDING ARCHER WIN.
YOUR ARCHERY SKILLS ARE EVENLY MATCHED.
IN A NORMAL CONTEST, IT WOULD BE DIFFICULT TO PRODUCE A CLEAR ENOUGH DIFFERENCE THAT YOU WOULD BOTH ACCEPT THE RESULTS.
ERGO, I WANT YOU TO COMPETE UNDER A GREAT DEAL OF PSYCHOLOGICAL PRESSURE.
WHICH OF YOU CAN STILL DRAW THE BOW AND LOOSE THE ARROW...
SHRUNCH
...AS YOU USUALLY WOULD?

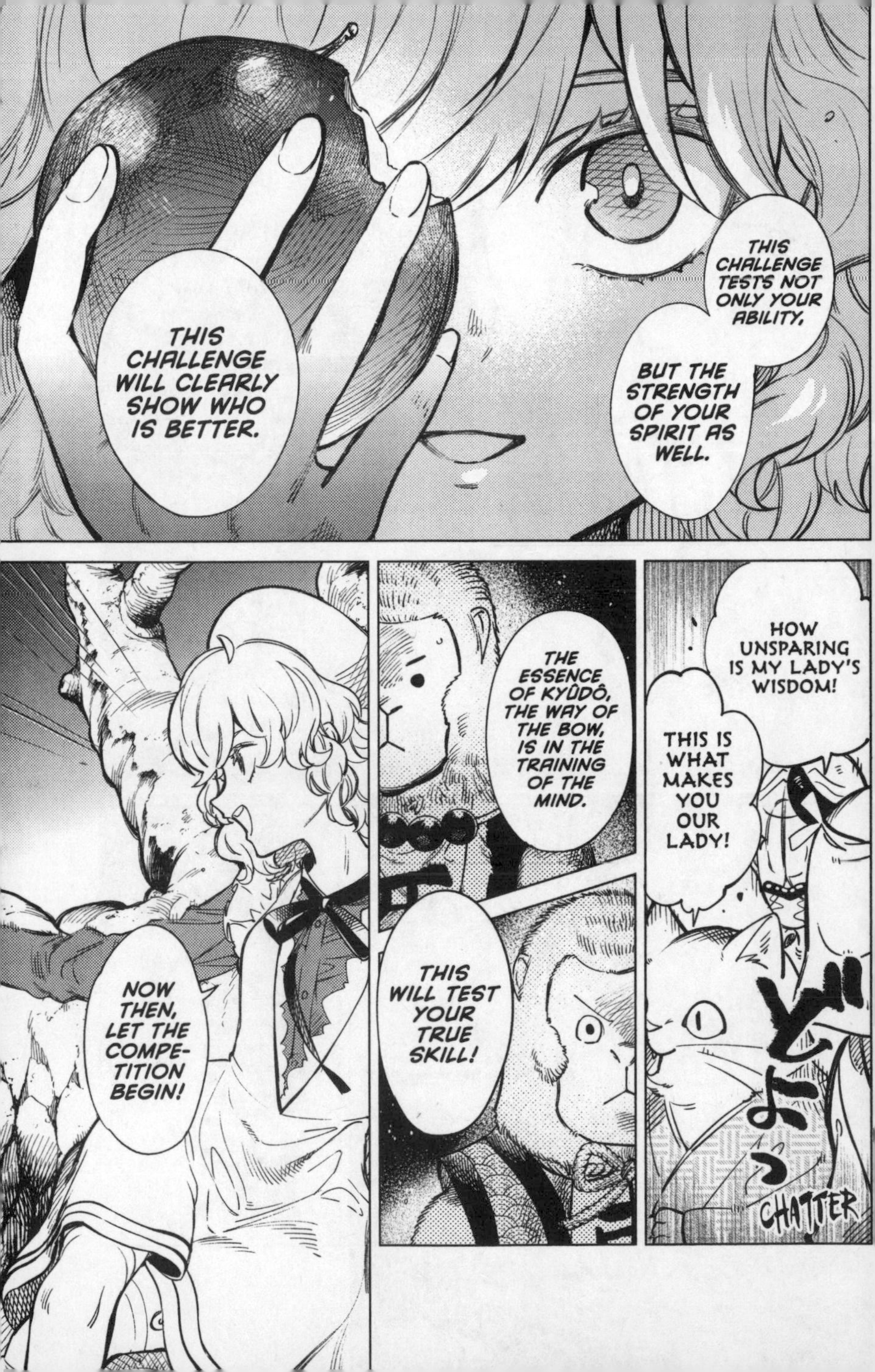
THIS CHALLENGE TESTS NOT ONLY YOUR ABILITY,
BUT THE STRENGTH OF YOUR SPIRIT AS WELL.
THIS CHALLENGE WILL CLEARLY SHOW WHO IS BETTER.
HOW UNSPARING IS MY LADY'S WISDOM!
THIS IS WHAT MAKES YOU OUR LADY!
CHATTER
THE ESSENCE OF KYÛDÔ, THE WAY OF THE BOW, IS IN THE TRAINING OF THE MIND.
THIS WILL TEST YOUR TRUE SKILL!
NOW THEN, LET THE COMPE-TITION BEGIN!

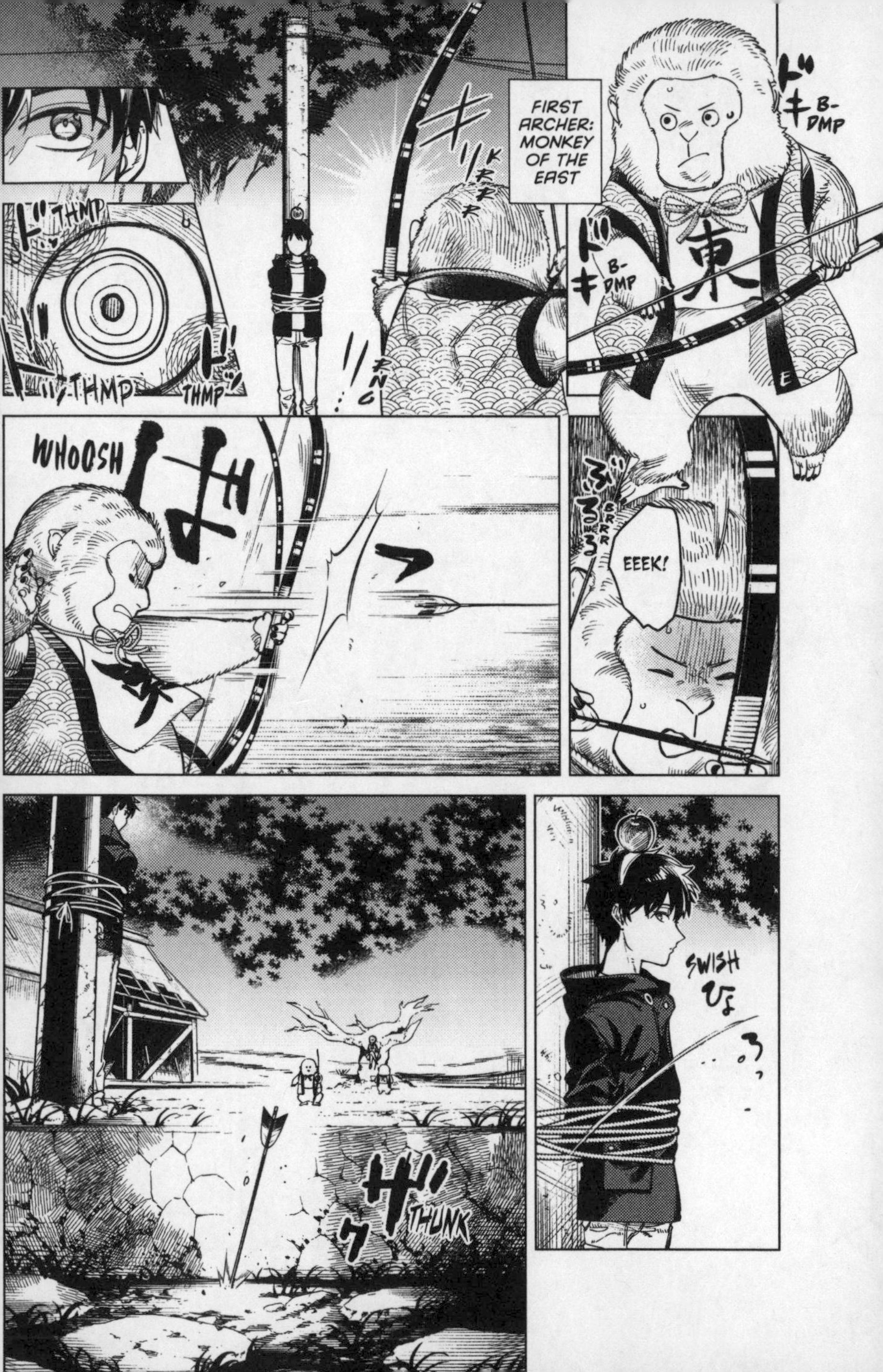
FIRST ARCHER: MONKEY OF THE EAST
B-DMP
B-DMP
東
KRRR
THMP
THMP
THMP
WHOOSH
ERRR
EEEK!
SWISH
THUNK

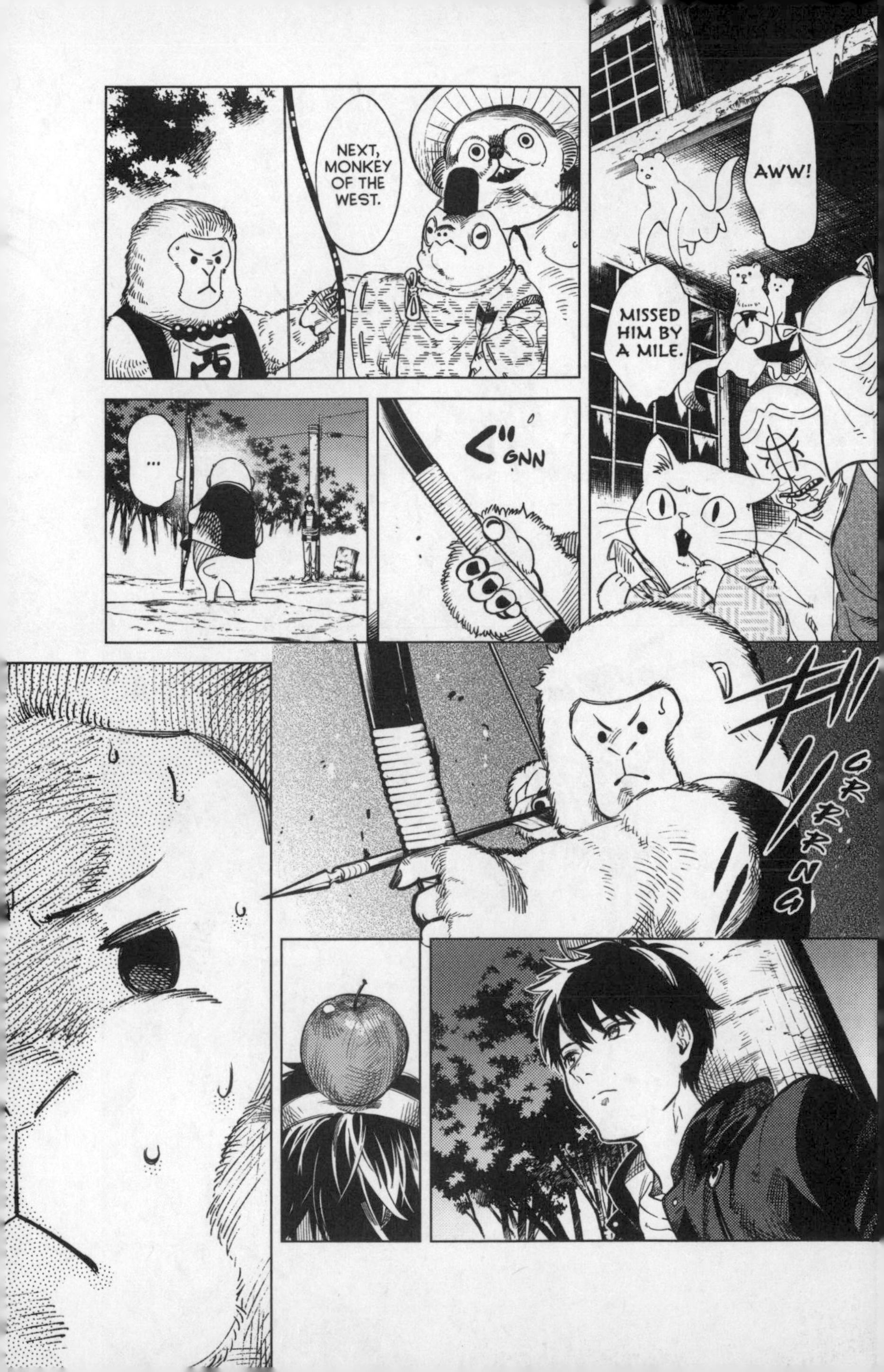
AWW!
MISSED HIM BY A MILE.
NEXT, MONKEY OF THE WEST.
GNN
...
GRRRNG

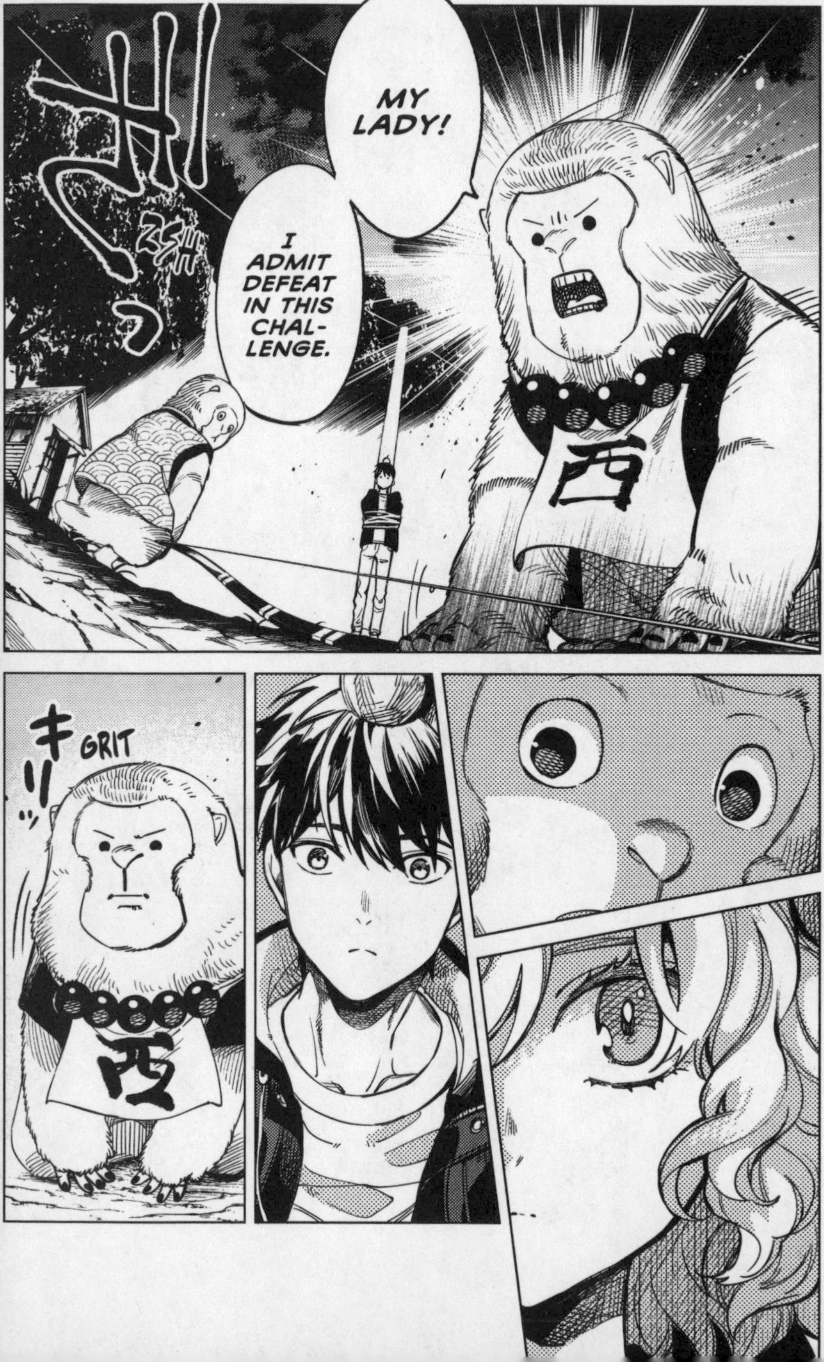
MY LADY!
I ADMIT DEFEAT IN THIS CHAL-LENGE.
ZSH
GRIT

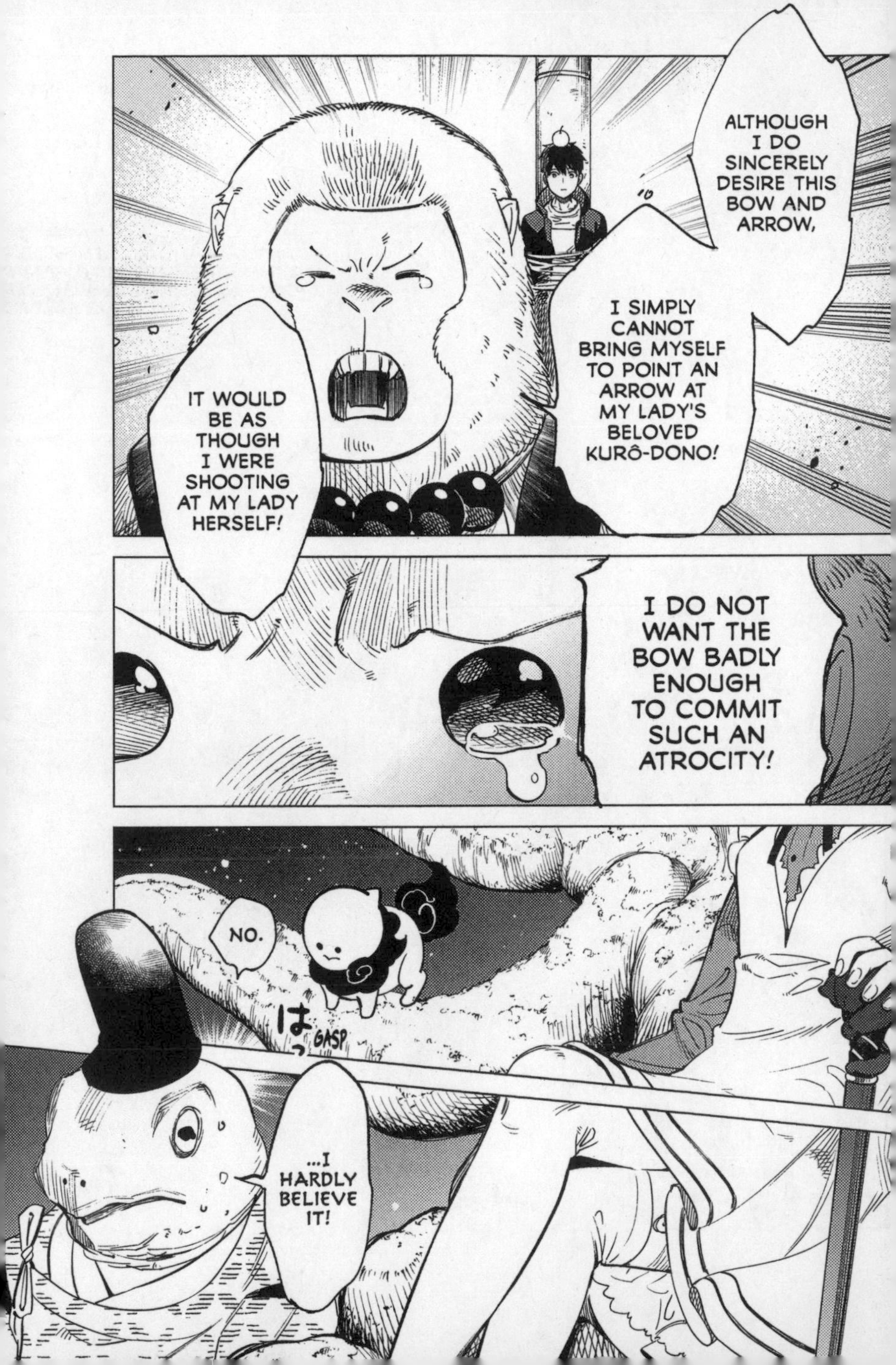
ALTHOUGH I DO SINCERELY DESIRE THIS BOW AND ARROW,
I SIMPLY CANNOT BRING MYSELF TO POINT AN ARROW AT MY LADY'S BELOVED KURÔ-DONO!
IT WOULD BE AS THOUGH I WERE SHOOTING AT MY LADY HERSELF!
I DO NOT WANT THE BOW BADLY ENOUGH TO COMMIT SUCH AN ATROCITY!
NO.
はっ GASP
...I HARDLY BELIEVE IT!

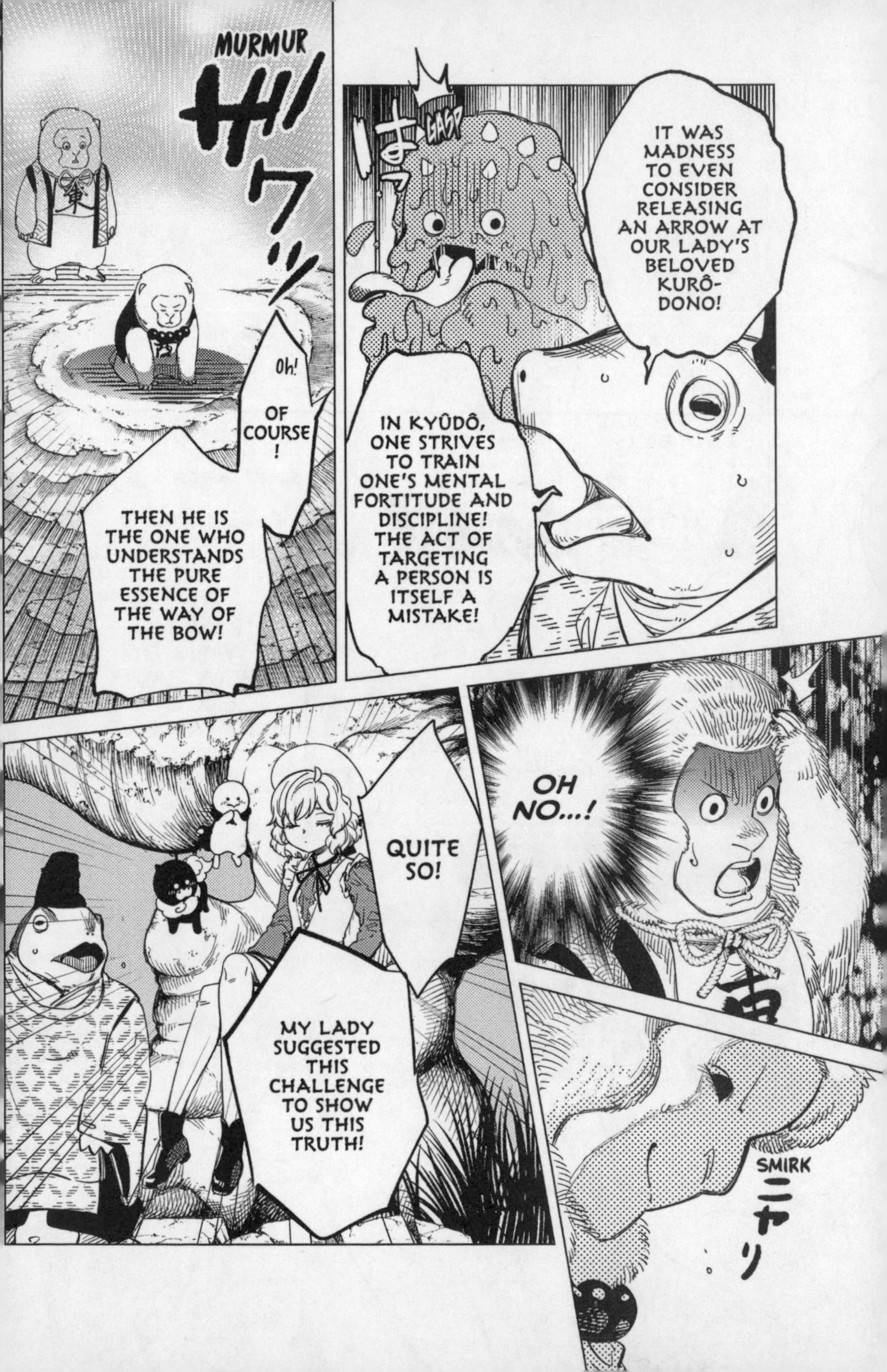
GASP
はっ
IT WAS MADNESS TO EVEN CONSIDER RELEASING AN ARROW AT OUR LADY'S BELOVED KURÔ-DONO!
IN KYÛDÔ, ONE STRIVES TO TRAIN ONE'S MENTAL FORTITUDE AND DISCIPLINE! THE ACT OF TARGETING A PERSON IS ITSELF A MISTAKE!
MURMUR
ザワッ
Oh!
OF COURSE!
THEN HE IS THE ONE WHO UNDERSTANDS THE PURE ESSENCE OF THE WAY OF THE BOW!
OH NO...!
SMIRK
ニヤリ
QUITE SO!
MY LADY SUGGESTED THIS CHALLENGE TO SHOW US THIS TRUTH!

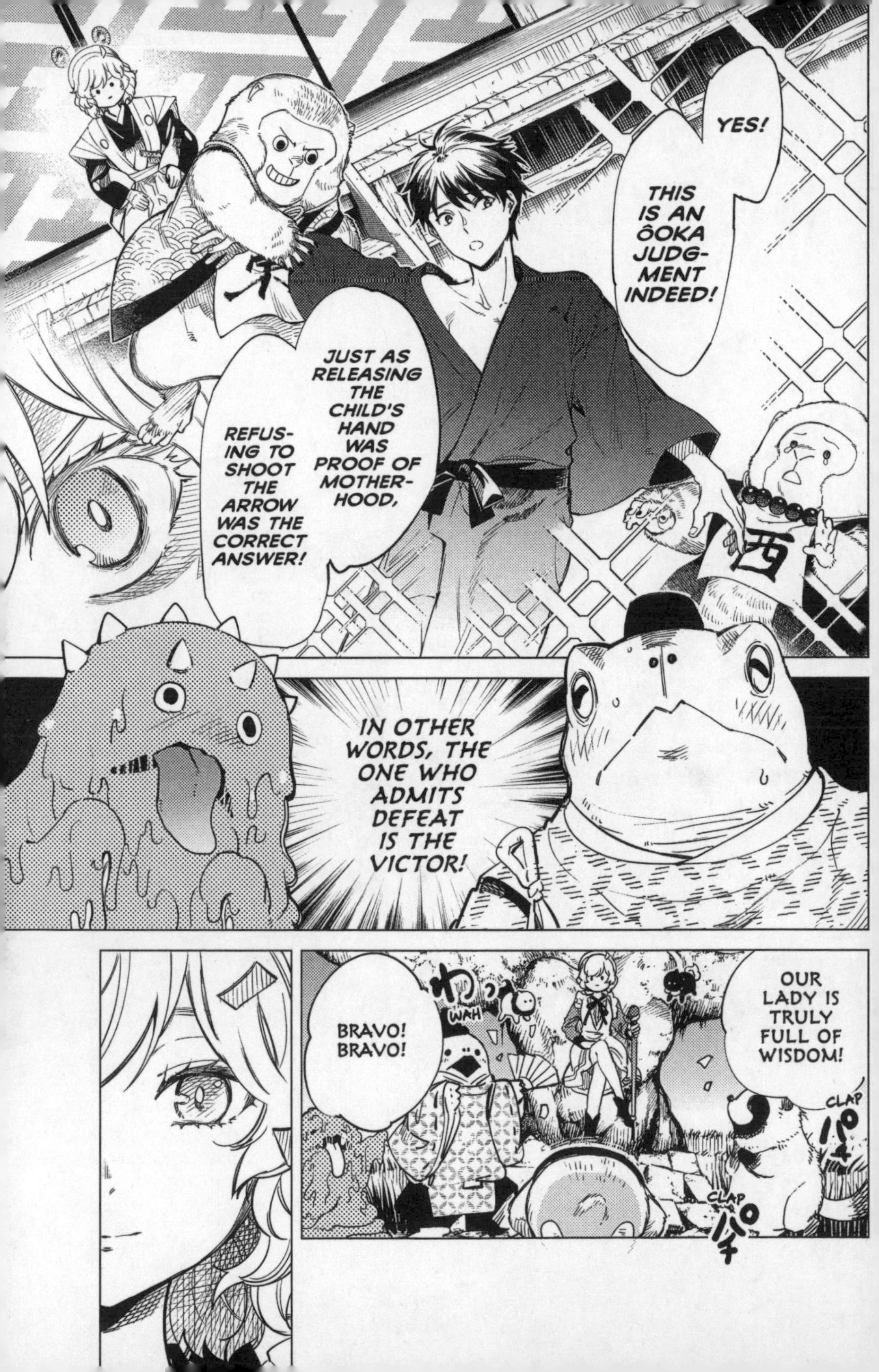
YES!
THIS IS AN ÔOKA JUDGMENT INDEED!
JUST AS RELEASING THE CHILD'S HAND WAS PROOF OF MOTHERHOOD,
REFUSING TO SHOOT THE ARROW WAS THE CORRECT ANSWER!
IN OTHER WORDS, THE ONE WHO ADMITS DEFEAT IS THE VICTOR!
OUR LADY IS TRULY FULL OF WISDOM!
CLAP
CLAP
わっ
WAH
BRAVO! BRAVO!

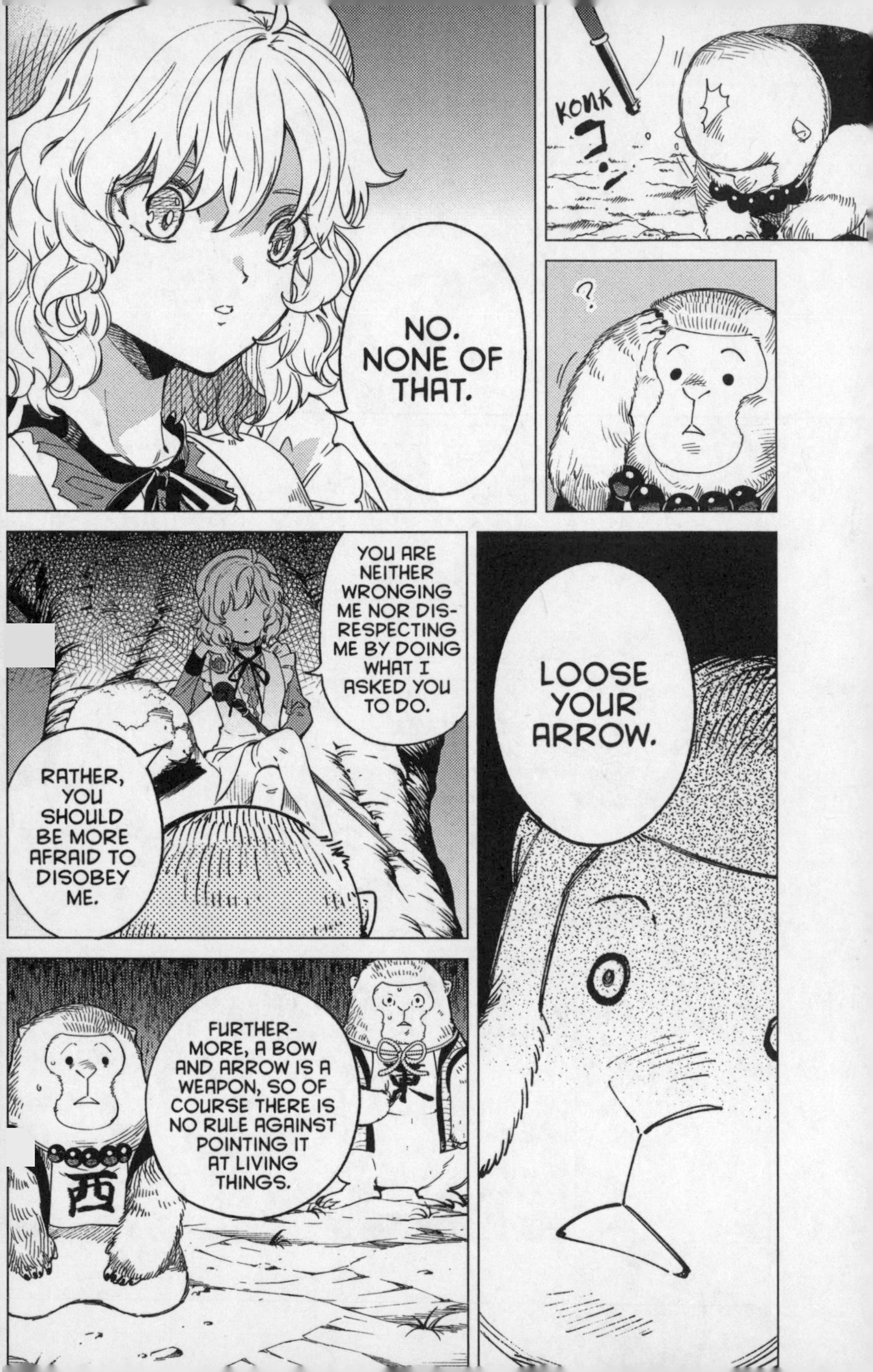
KONK
?
NO. NONE OF THAT.
LOOSE YOUR ARROW.
YOU ARE NEITHER WRONGING ME NOR DIS-RESPECTING ME BY DOING WHAT I ASKED YOU TO DO.
RATHER, YOU SHOULD BE MORE AFRAID TO DISOBEY ME.
FURTHER-MORE, A BOW AND ARROW IS A WEAPON, SO OF COURSE THERE IS NO RULE AGAINST POINTING IT AT LIVING THINGS.
西

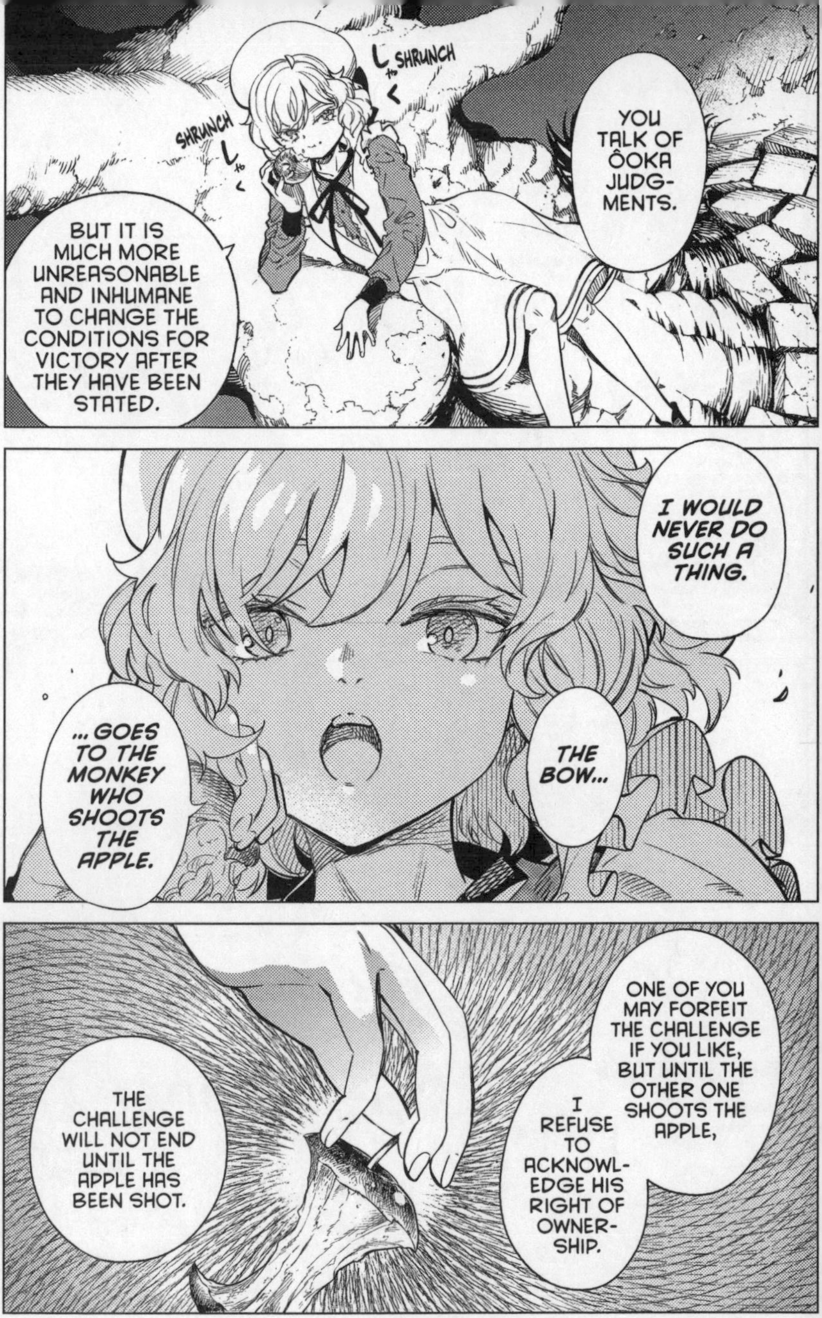
YOU TALK OF ÔOKA JUDGMENTS.
SHRUNCH
SHRUNCH
BUT IT IS MUCH MORE UNREASONABLE AND INHUMANE TO CHANGE THE CONDITIONS FOR VICTORY AFTER THEY HAVE BEEN STATED.
I WOULD NEVER DO SUCH A THING.
THE BOW...
...GOES TO THE MONKEY WHO SHOOTS THE APPLE.
ONE OF YOU MAY FORFEIT THE CHALLENGE IF YOU LIKE, BUT UNTIL THE OTHER ONE SHOOTS THE APPLE,
I REFUSE TO ACKNOWLEDGE HIS RIGHT OF OWNERSHIP.
THE CHALLENGE WILL NOT END UNTIL THE APPLE HAS BEEN SHOT.

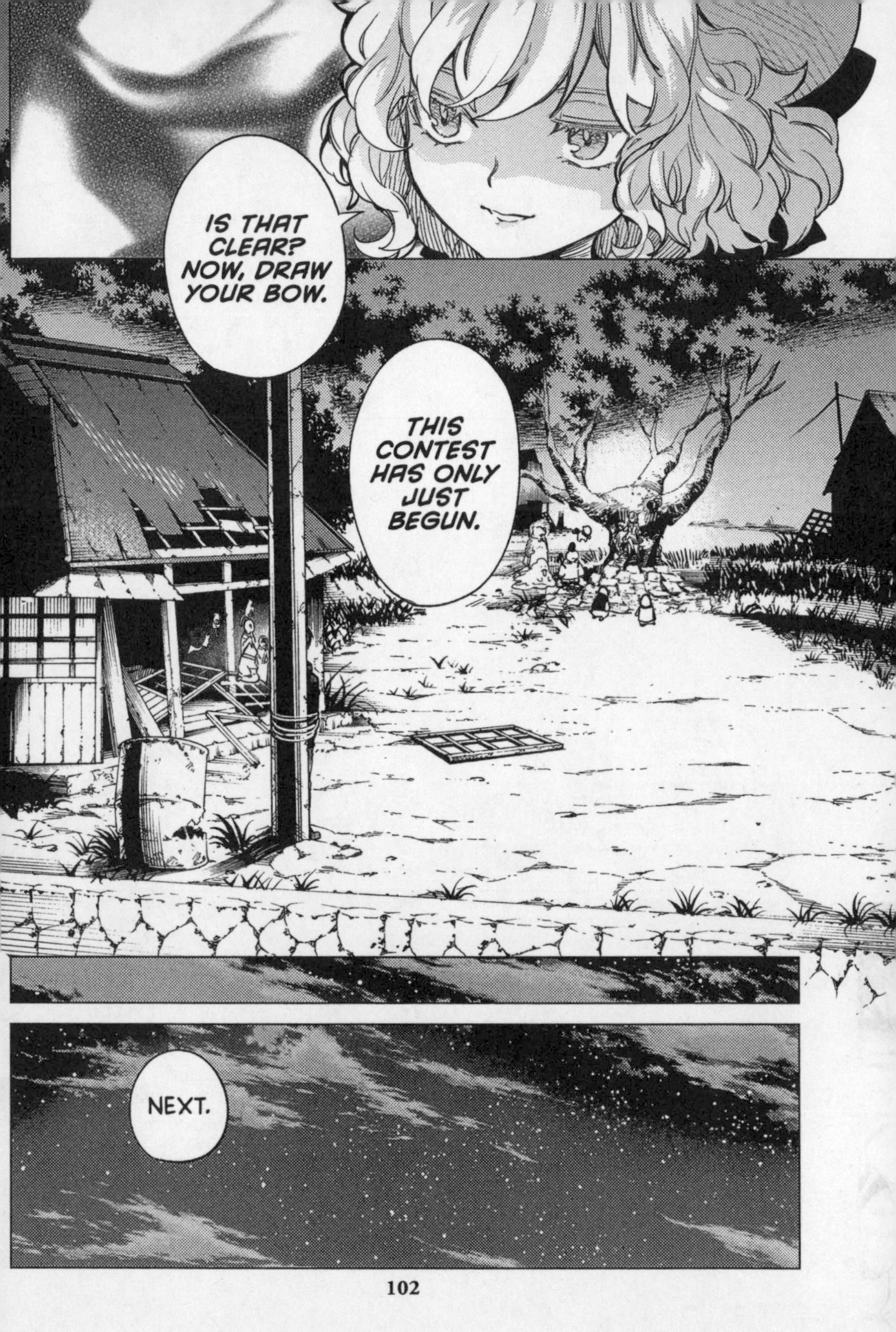
IS THAT CLEAR? NOW, DRAW YOUR BOW.
THIS CONTEST HAS ONLY JUST BEGUN.
NEXT.

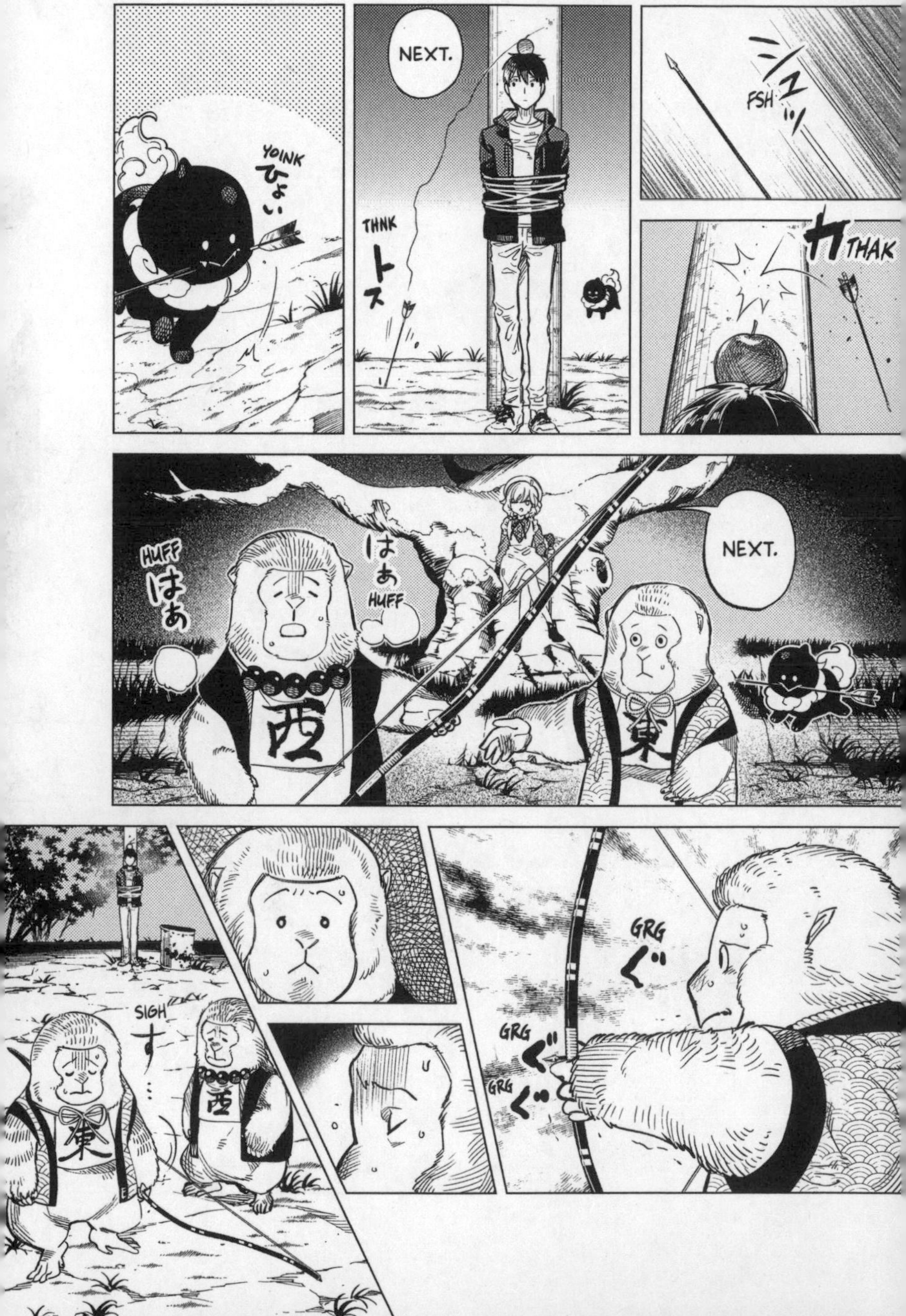
FSH
シュッ
カ THAK
NEXT.
THNK
トス
YOINK
ひょい
NEXT.
はぁ
HUFF
HUFF
はぁ
GRG
ぐ
GRG
ぐ
GRG
ぐ
SIGH
す…

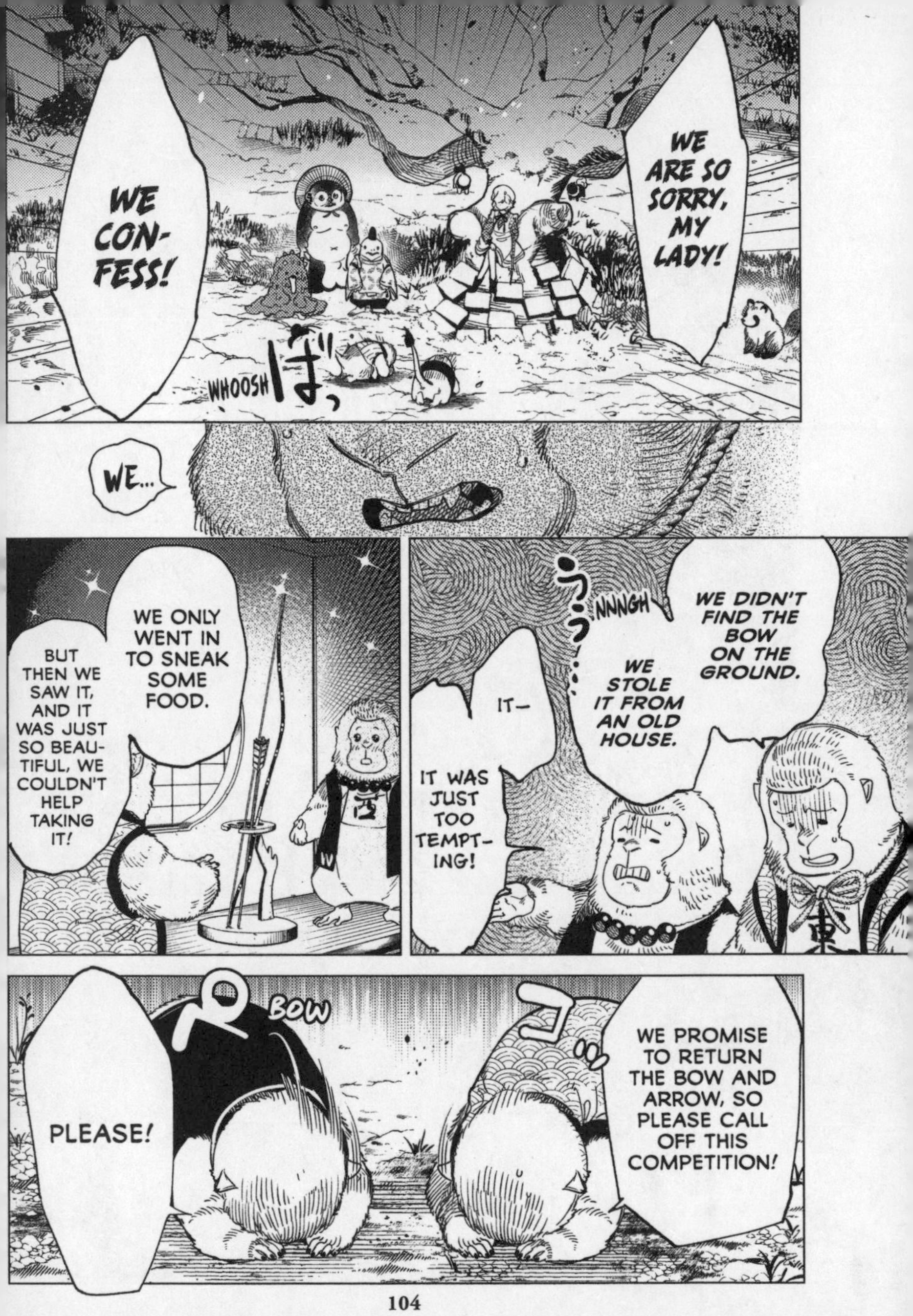
WE ARE SO SORRY, MY LADY!
WE CONFESS!
WHOOSH
ばっ
WE...
WE DIDN'T FIND THE BOW ON THE GROUND.
WE STOLE IT FROM AN OLD HOUSE.
NNNGH
うう...
IT—
IT WAS JUST TOO TEMPTING!
WE ONLY WENT IN TO SNEAK SOME FOOD.
BUT THEN WE SAW IT, AND IT WAS JUST SO BEAUTIFUL, WE COULDN'T HELP TAKING IT!
WE PROMISE TO RETURN THE BOW AND ARROW, SO PLEASE CALL OFF THIS COMPETITION!
BOW
PLEASE!

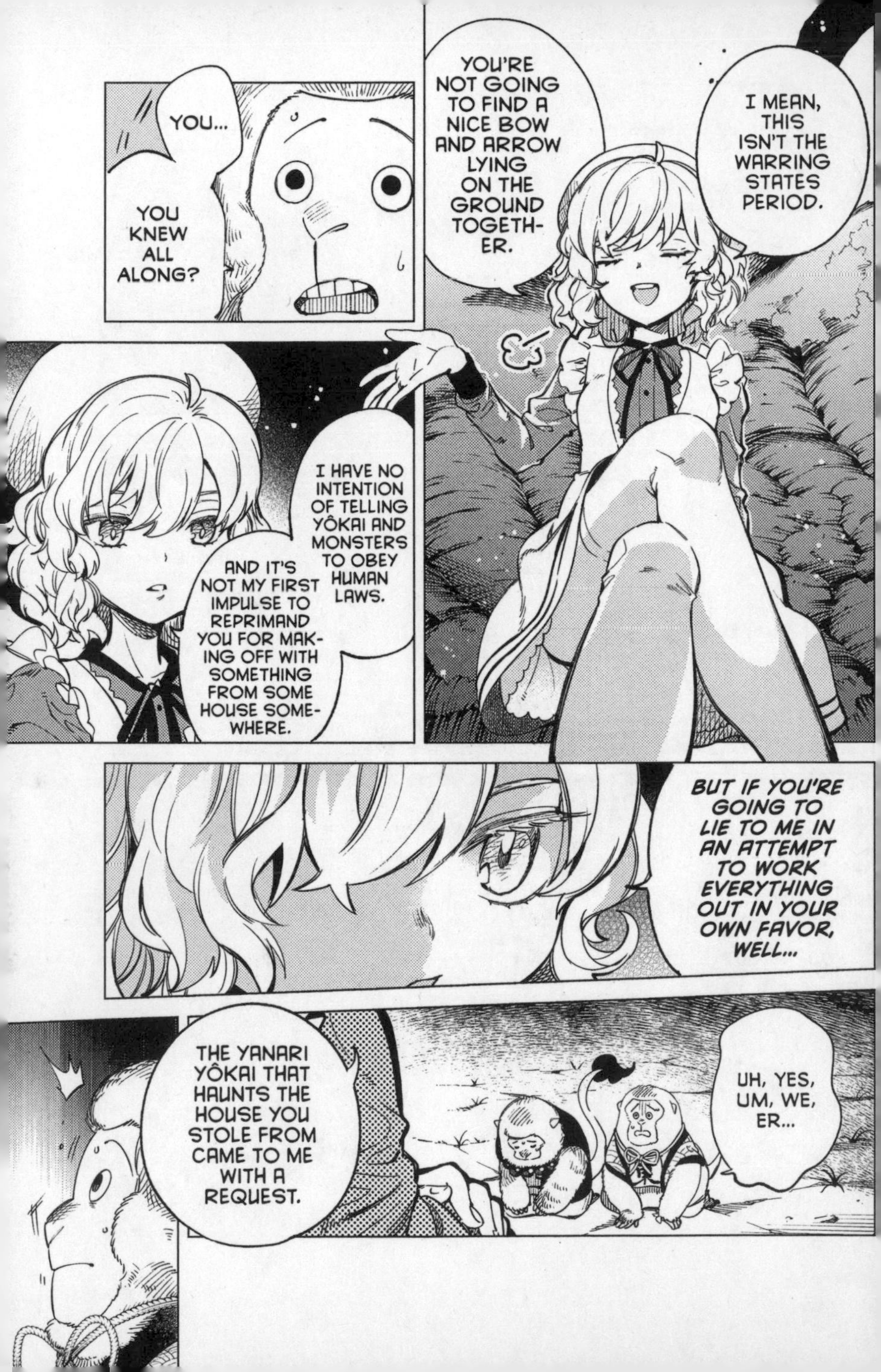
I MEAN, THIS ISN'T THE WARRING STATES PERIOD.
YOU'RE NOT GOING TO FIND A NICE BOW AND ARROW LYING ON THE GROUND TOGETH-ER.
YOU...
YOU KNEW ALL ALONG?
I HAVE NO INTENTION OF TELLING YÔKAI AND MONSTERS TO OBEY HUMAN LAWS.
AND IT'S NOT MY FIRST IMPULSE TO REPRIMAND YOU FOR MAK-ING OFF WITH SOMETHING FROM SOME HOUSE SOME-WHERE.
BUT IF YOU'RE GOING TO LIE TO ME IN AN ATTEMPT TO WORK EVERYTHING OUT IN YOUR OWN FAVOR, WELL...
UH, YES, UM, WE, ER...
THE YANARI YÔKAI THAT HAUNTS THE HOUSE YOU STOLE FROM CAME TO ME WITH A REQUEST.

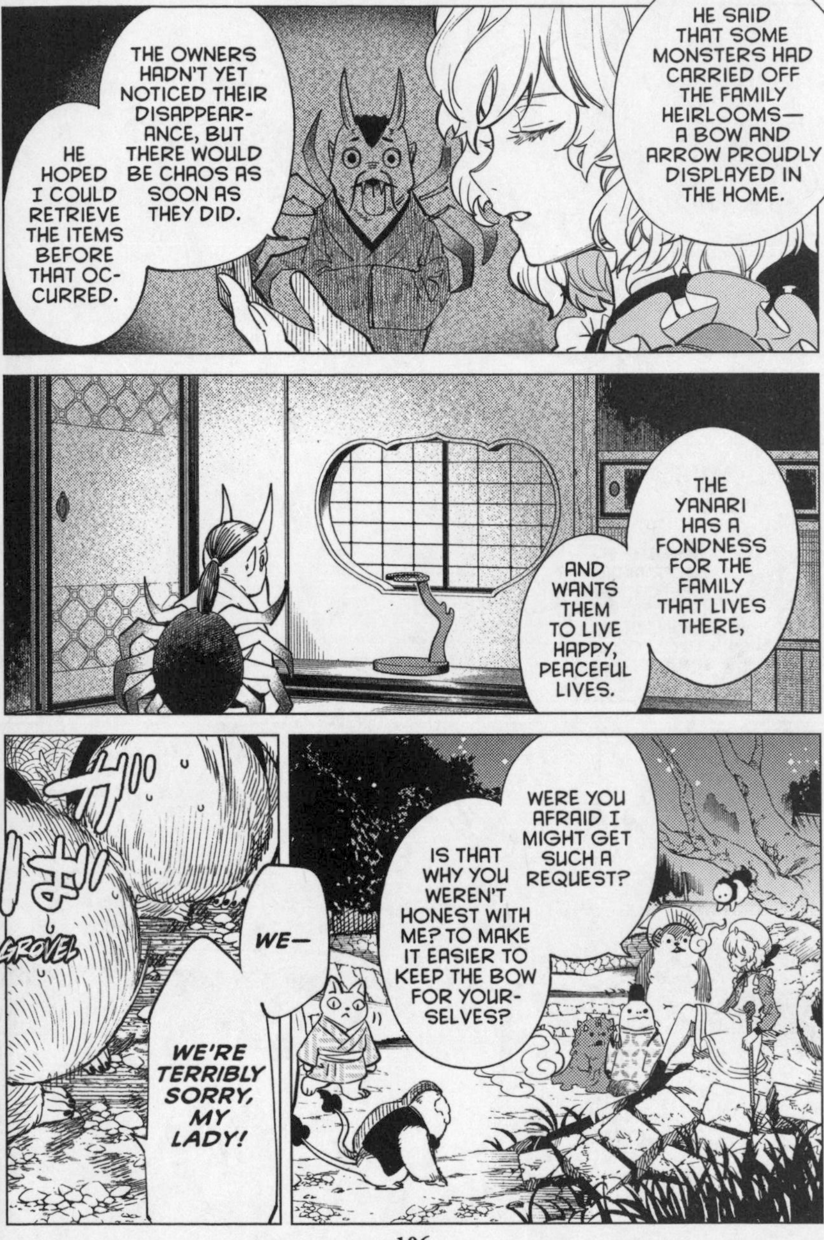
HE SAID THAT SOME MONSTERS HAD CARRIED OFF THE FAMILY HEIRLOOMS—A BOW AND ARROW PROUDLY DISPLAYED IN THE HOME.
THE OWNERS HADN'T YET NOTICED THEIR DISAPPEARANCE, BUT THERE WOULD BE CHAOS AS SOON AS THEY DID.
HE HOPED I COULD RETRIEVE THE ITEMS BEFORE THAT OCCURRED.
THE YANARI HAS A FONDNESS FOR THE FAMILY THAT LIVES THERE,
AND WANTS THEM TO LIVE HAPPY, PEACEFUL LIVES.
WERE YOU AFRAID I MIGHT GET SUCH A REQUEST?
IS THAT WHY YOU WEREN'T HONEST WITH ME? TO MAKE IT EASIER TO KEEP THE BOW FOR YOURSELVES?
WE—
GROVEL
WE'RE TERRIBLY SORRY, MY LADY!

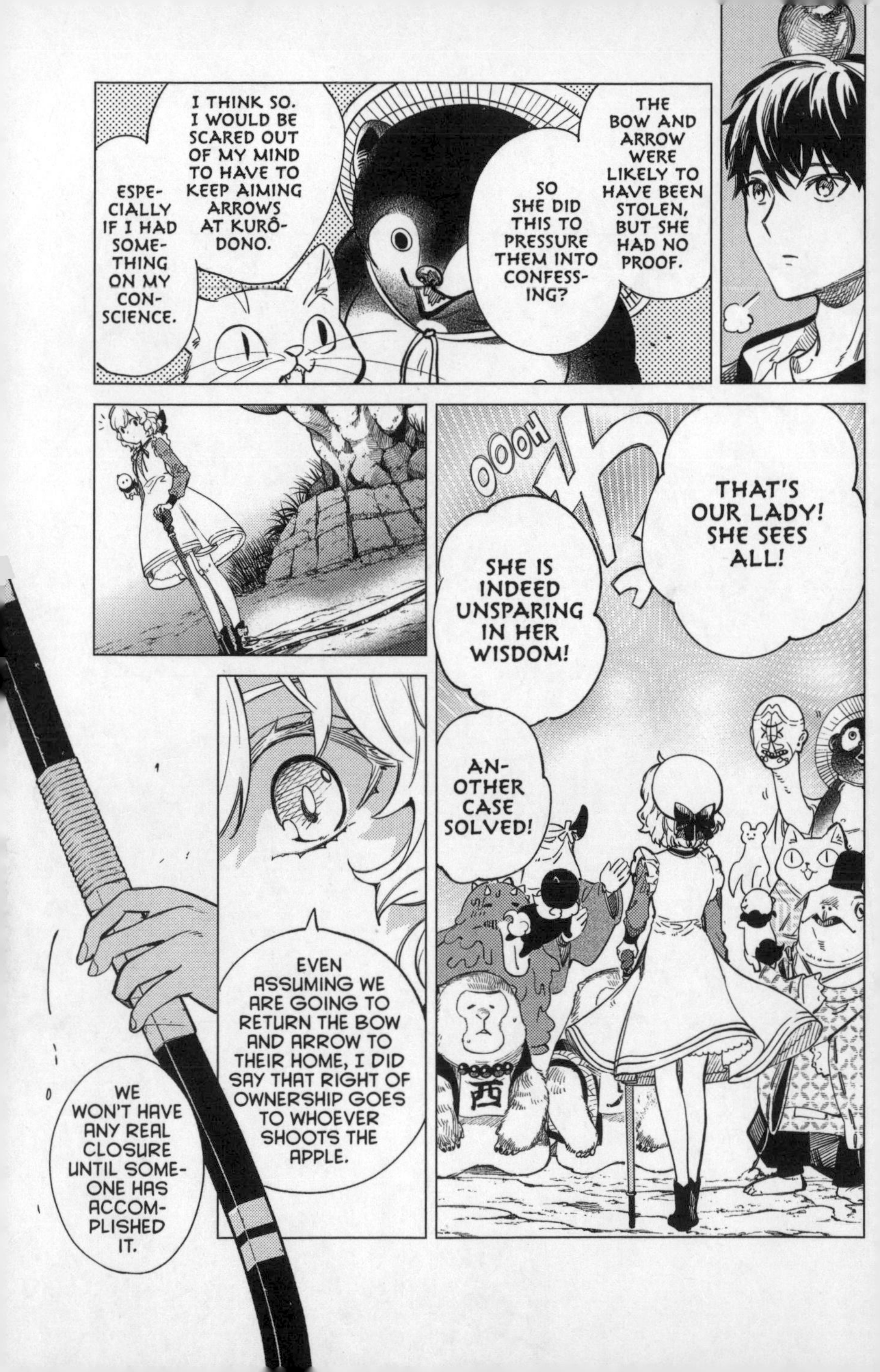
THE BOW AND ARROW WERE LIKELY TO HAVE BEEN STOLEN, BUT SHE HAD NO PROOF.
SO SHE DID THIS TO PRESSURE THEM INTO CONFESSING?
I THINK SO. I WOULD BE SCARED OUT OF MY MIND TO HAVE TO KEEP AIMING ARROWS AT KURÔ-DONO.
ESPECIALLY IF I HAD SOMETHING ON MY CONSCIENCE.
OOOH
THAT'S OUR LADY! SHE SEES ALL!
SHE IS INDEED UNSPARING IN HER WISDOM!
ANOTHER CASE SOLVED!
EVEN ASSUMING WE ARE GOING TO RETURN THE BOW AND ARROW TO THEIR HOME, I DID SAY THAT RIGHT OF OWNERSHIP GOES TO WHOEVER SHOOTS THE APPLE.
WE WON'T HAVE ANY REAL CLOSURE UNTIL SOMEONE HAS ACCOMPLISHED IT.

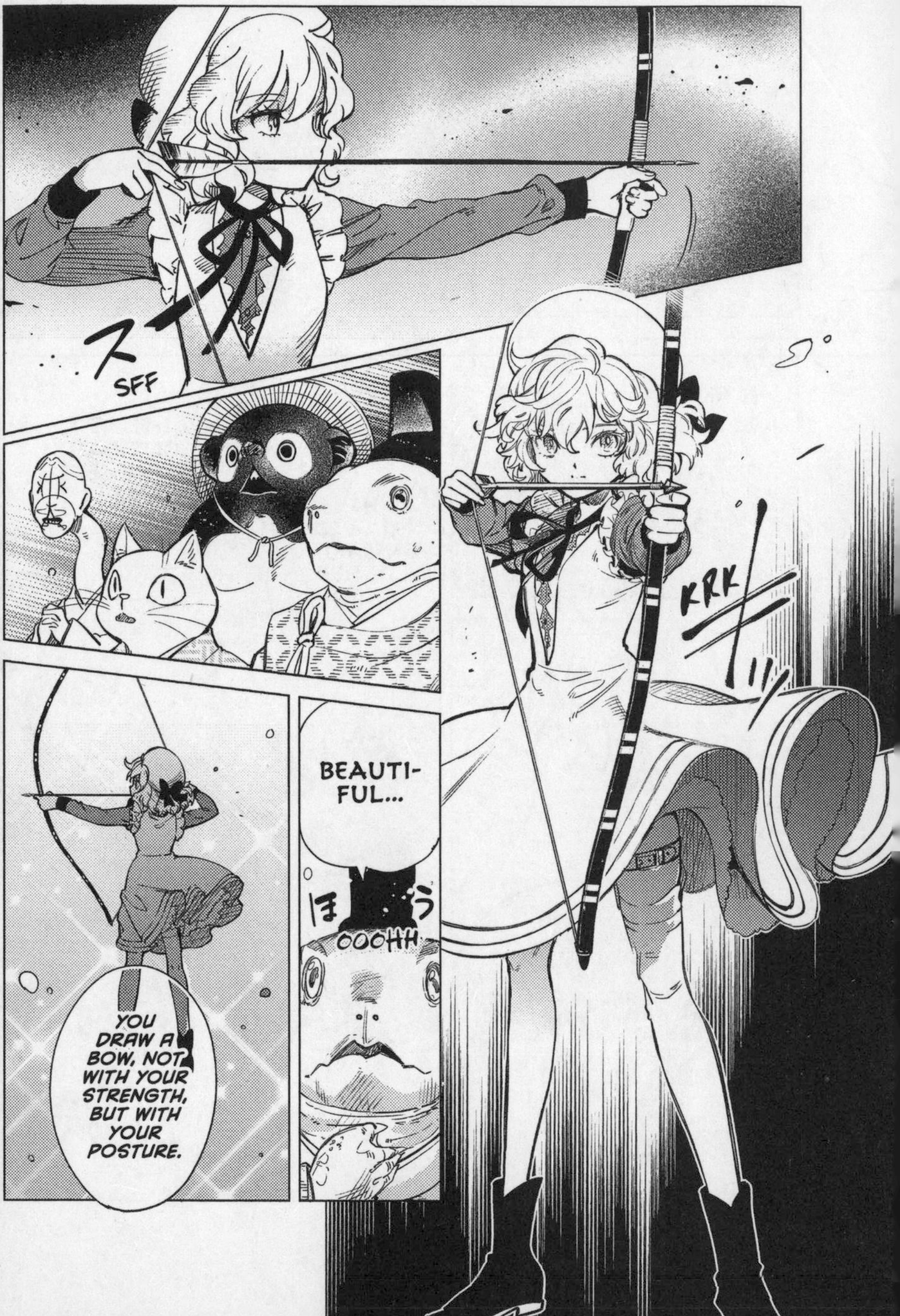
SFF
KRK
BEAUTI-
FUL...
OOOHH
YOU DRAW A BOW, NOT WITH YOUR STRENGTH, BUT WITH YOUR POSTURE.

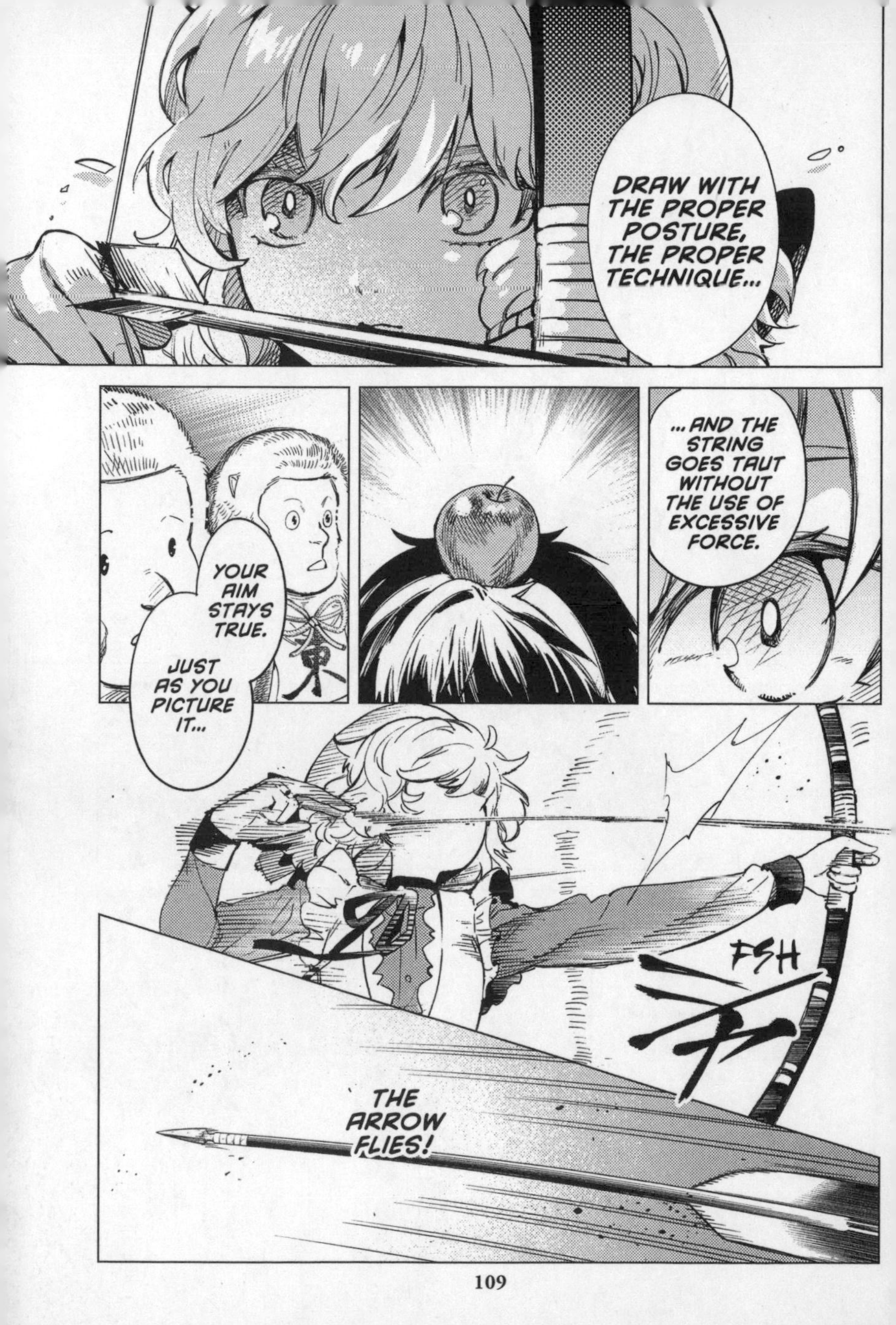
DRAW WITH THE PROPER POSTURE, THE PROPER TECHNIQUE...
...AND THE STRING GOES TAUT WITHOUT THE USE OF EXCESSIVE FORCE.
YOUR AIM STAYS TRUE.
JUST AS YOU PICTURE IT...
FSH
THE ARROW FLIES!

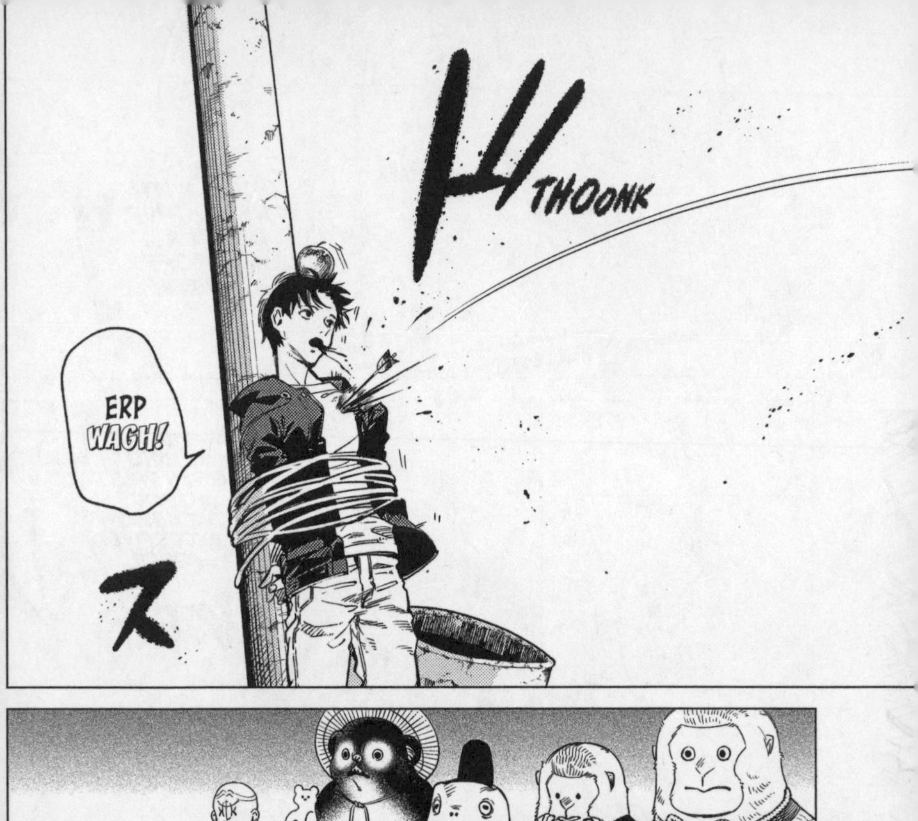
THOONK
ERP WAGH!
PERHAPS I MIS-JUDGED THE HEIGHT A BIT.
BUT I'VE GOT THE FEEL FOR IT NOW.

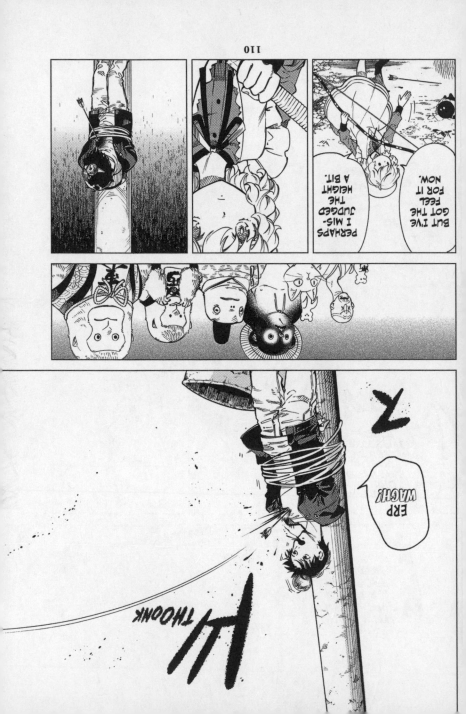

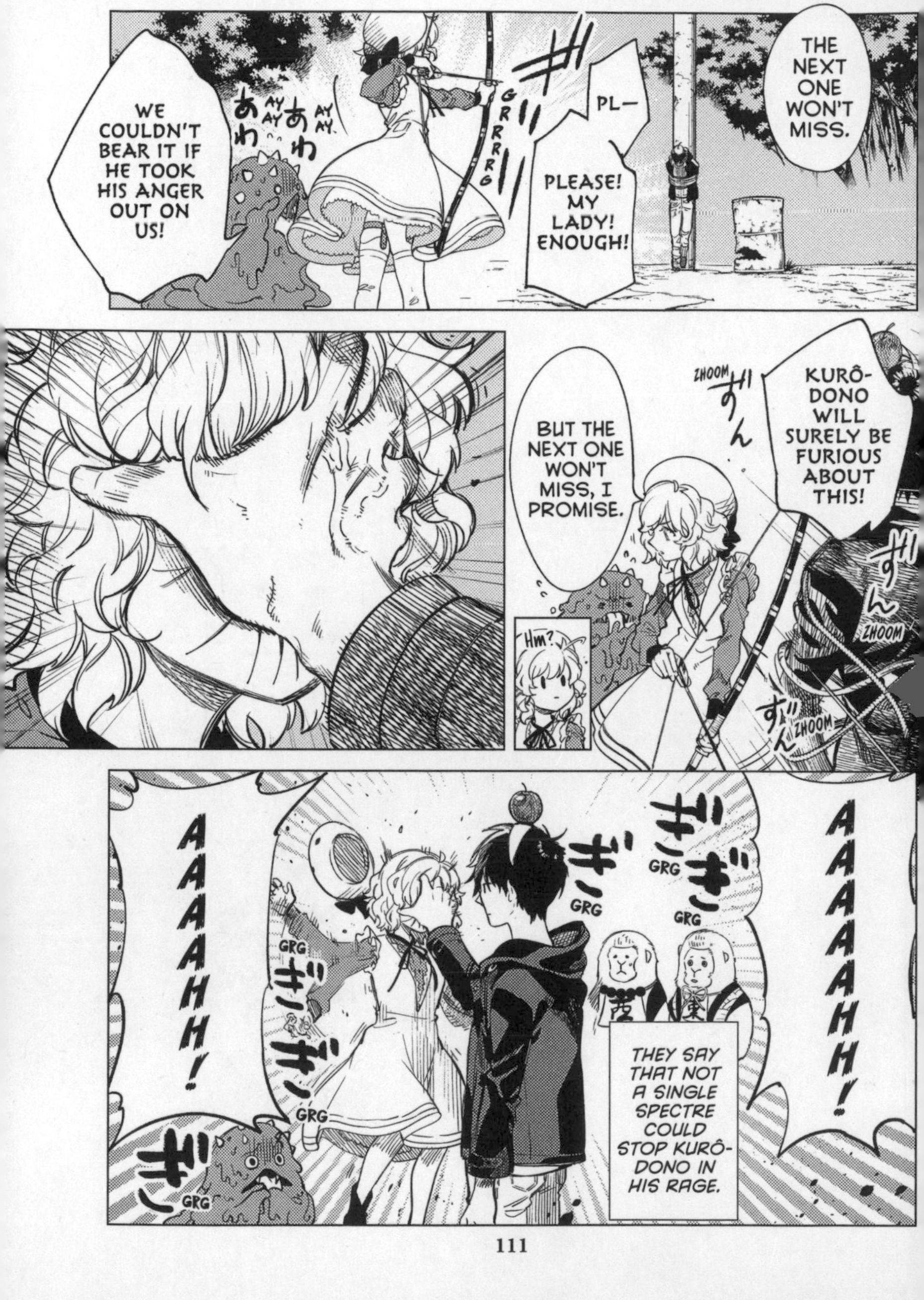
THE NEXT ONE WON'T MISS.
PL—
PLEASE! MY LADY! ENOUGH!
GRRRRG
AY AY
AY AY
WE COULDN'T BEAR IT IF HE TOOK HIS ANGER OUT ON US!
ZHOOM
ZHOOM
KURÔ-DONO WILL SURELY BE FURIOUS ABOUT THIS!
ZHOOM
BUT THE NEXT ONE WON'T MISS, I PROMISE.
Hm?
AAAAAAHH!
GRG
GRG
GRG
THEY SAY THAT NOT A SINGLE SPECTRE COULD STOP KURÔ-DONO IN HIS RAGE.
GRG
GRG
GRG
AAAAAHH!

Device to keep the apple
from falling

CHAPTER 39: "THE RETALIATION AND DEFEAT OF KOTOKO IWANAGA PART 1"

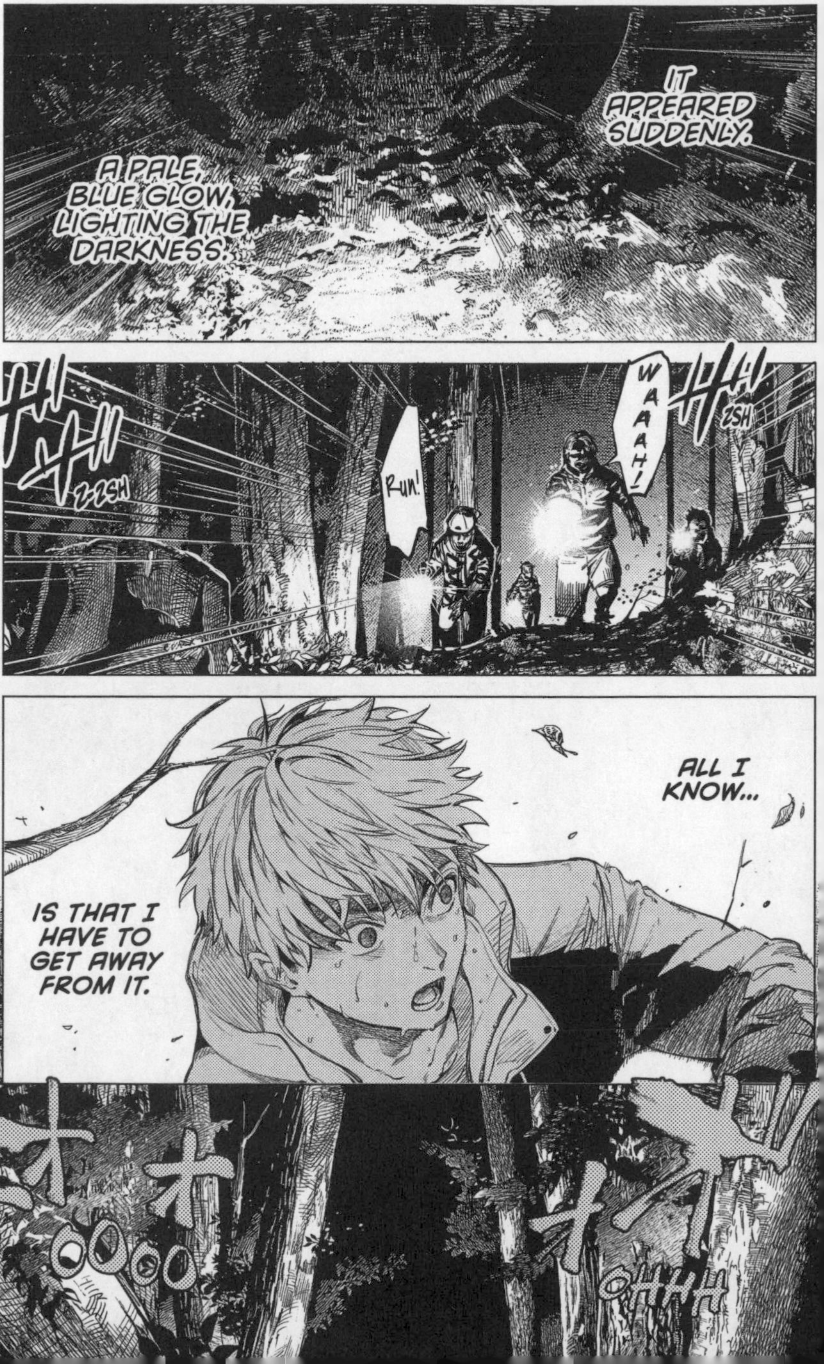
IT APPEARED SUDDENLY.
A PALE, BLUE GLOW, LIGHTING THE DARKNESS.
ZSH
WAAAH!
Run!
Z-ZSH
ALL I KNOW...
IS THAT I HAVE TO GET AWAY FROM IT.
OHHH
OOOO

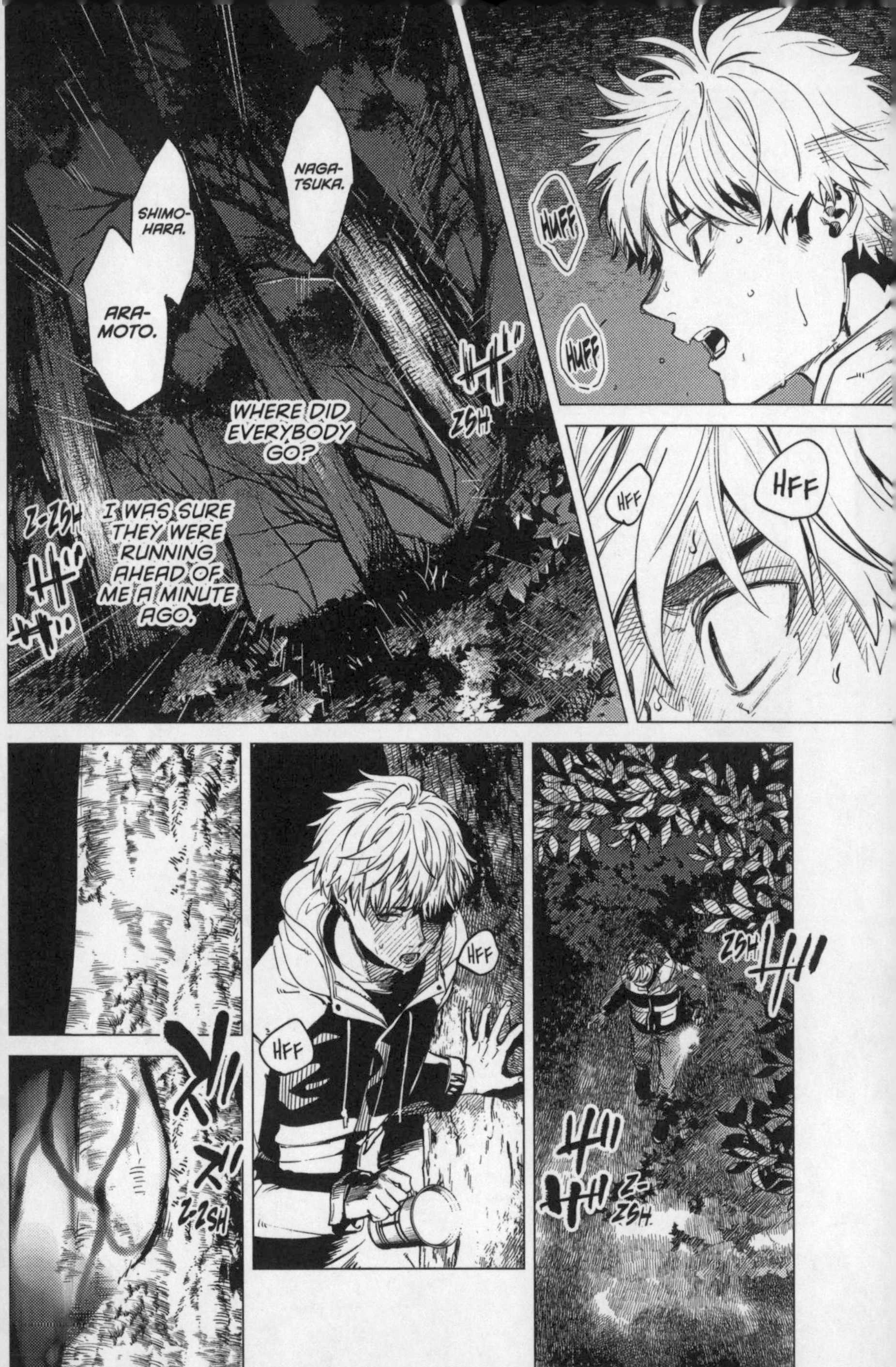
HUFF
HUFF
HFF
HFF
NAGA-TSUKA.
SHIMO-HARA.
ARA-MOTO.
ZSH
WHERE DID EVERYBODY GO?
Z-ZSH
I WAS SURE THEY WERE RUNNING AHEAD OF ME A MINUTE AGO.
ZSH
Z-ZSH
HFF
HFF
Z-ZSH

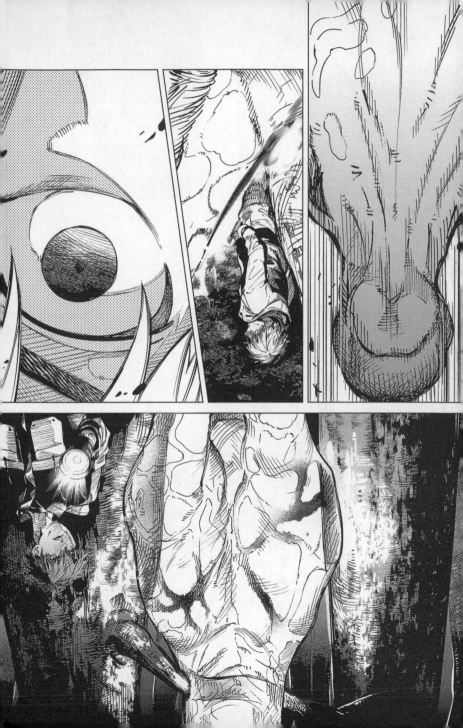

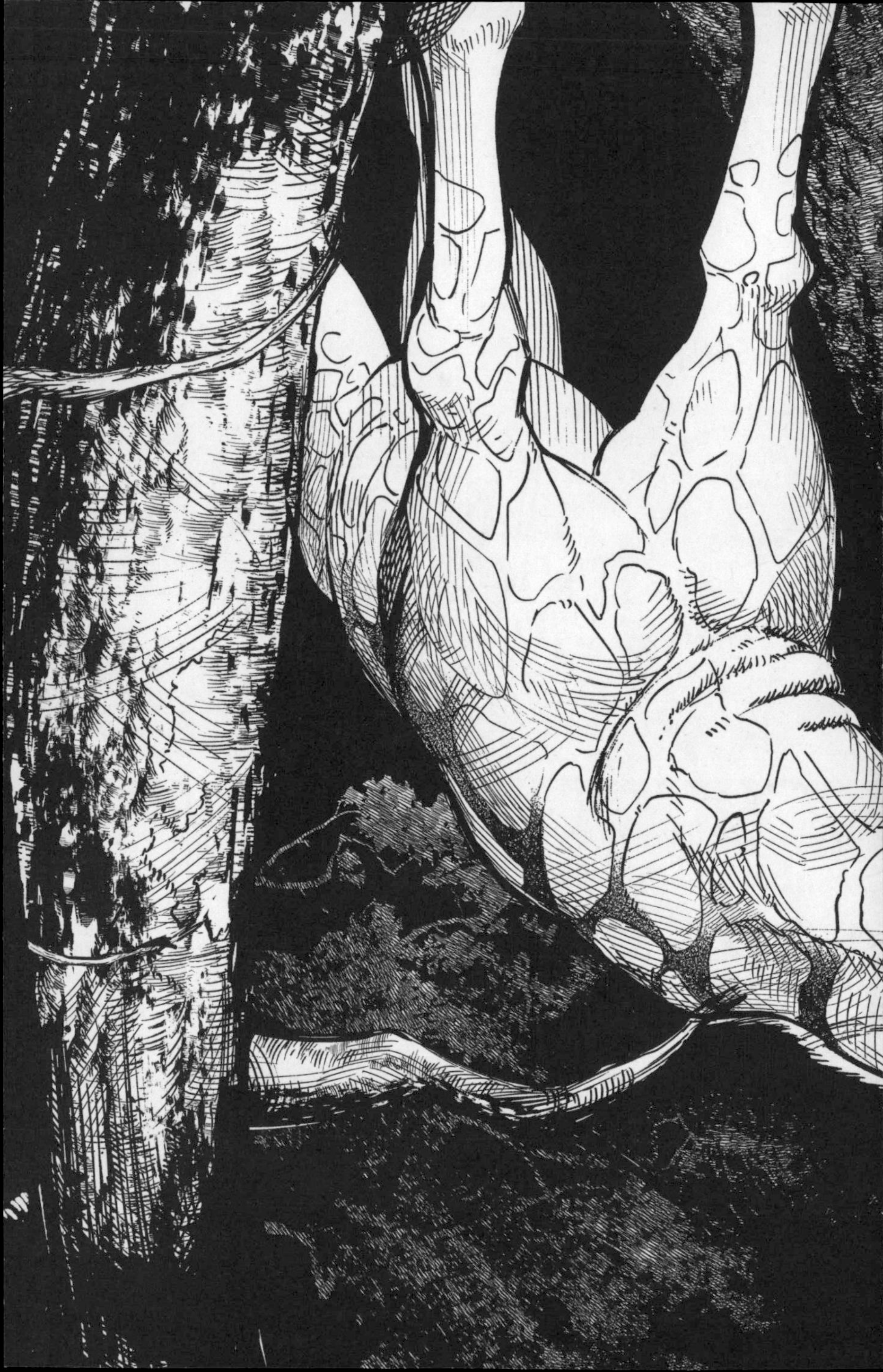

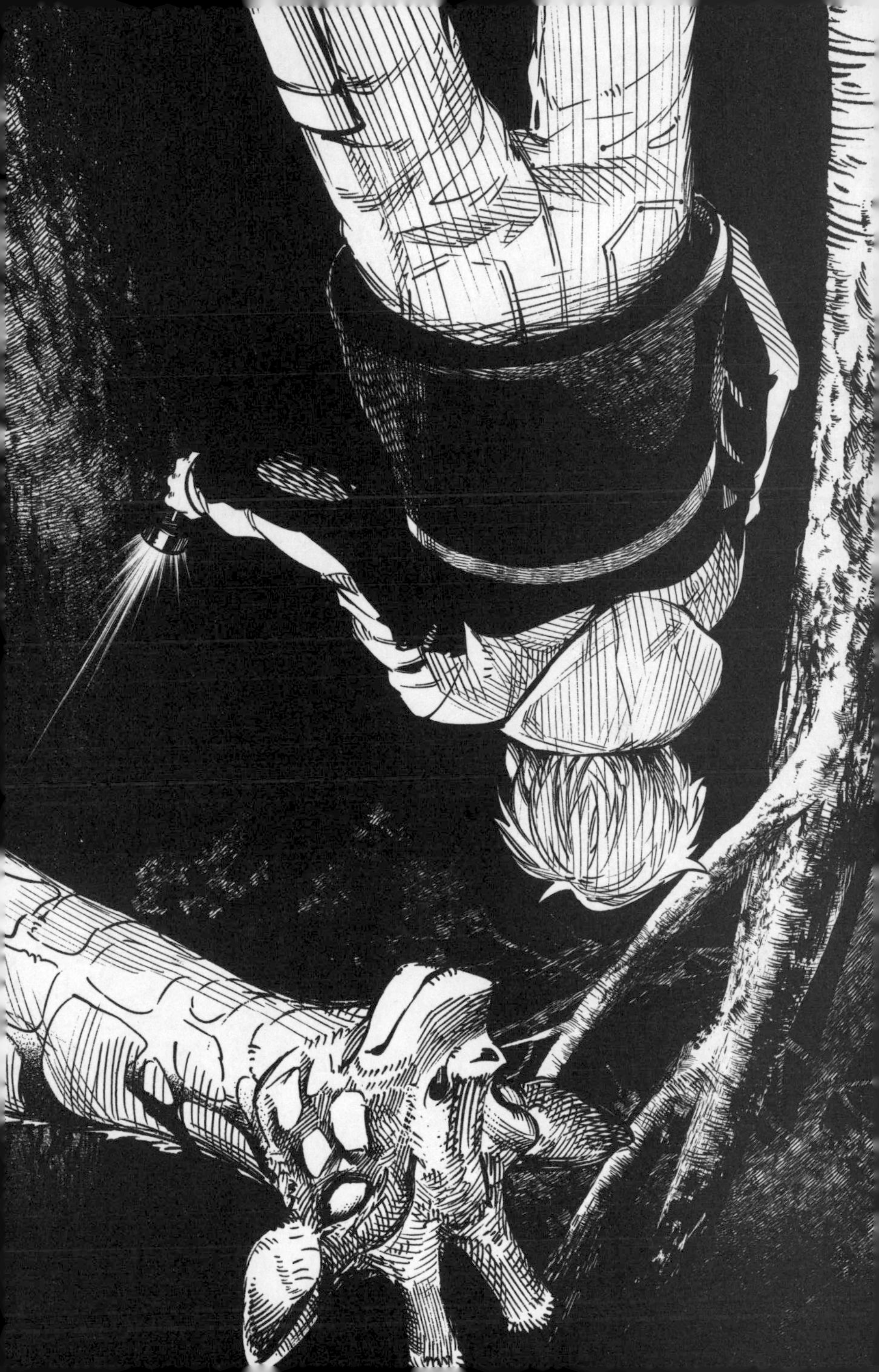

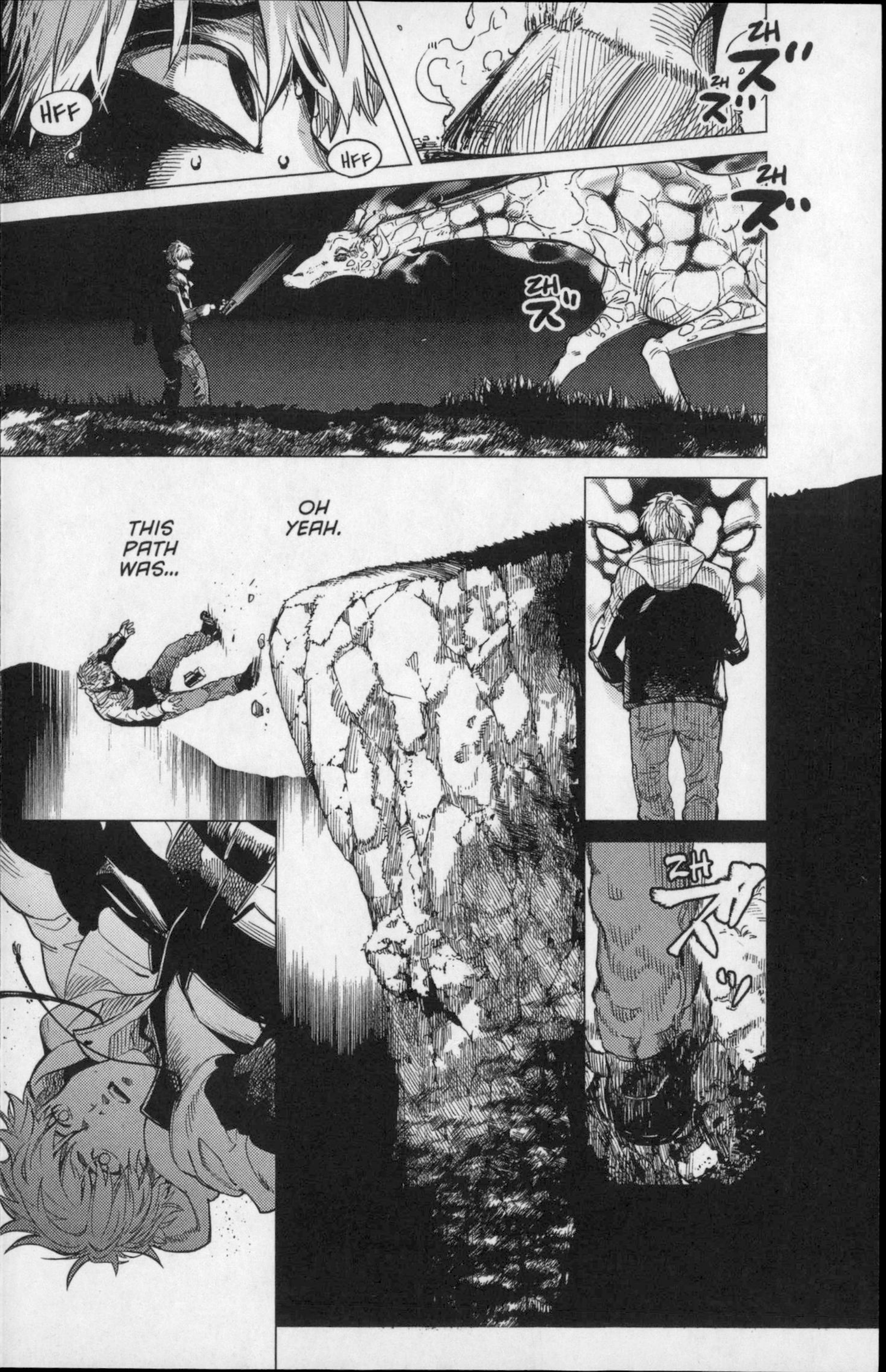
ZH ZH
HFF
HFF
ZH
ZH
OH YEAH.
THIS PATH WAS...
ZH

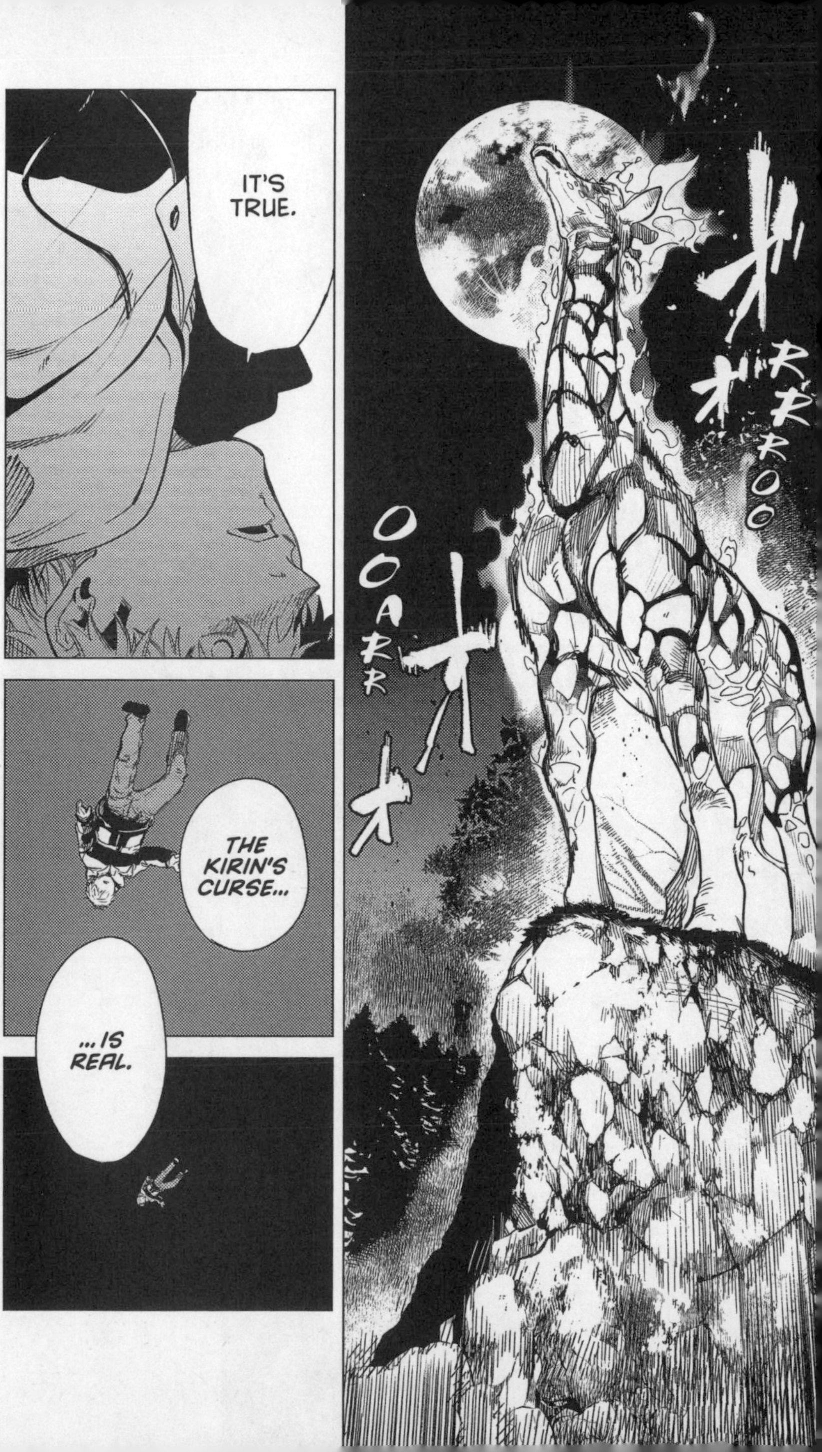
RRRROO
OOARR
IT'S TRUE.
THE KIRIN'S CURSE...
...IS REAL.

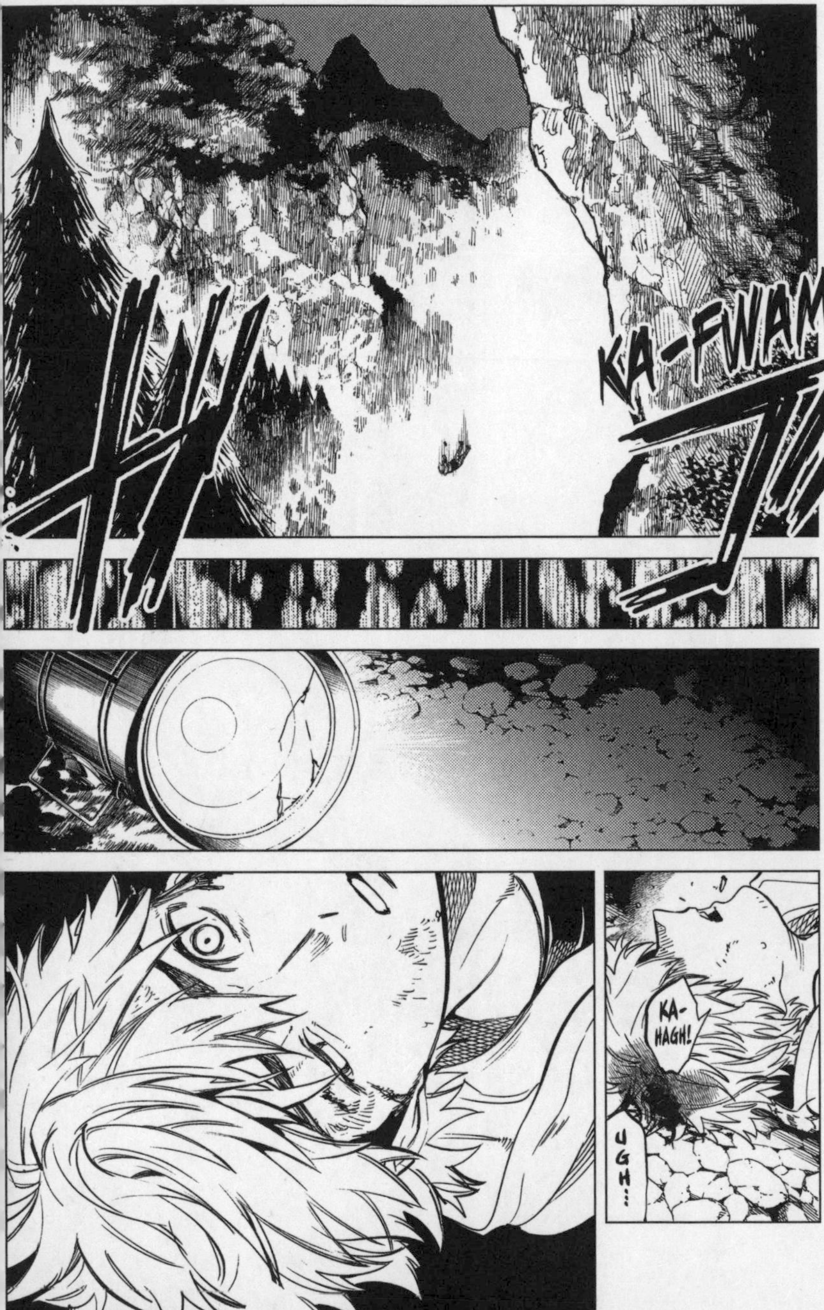
KA-FWAM
KA-HAGH!
UGH...

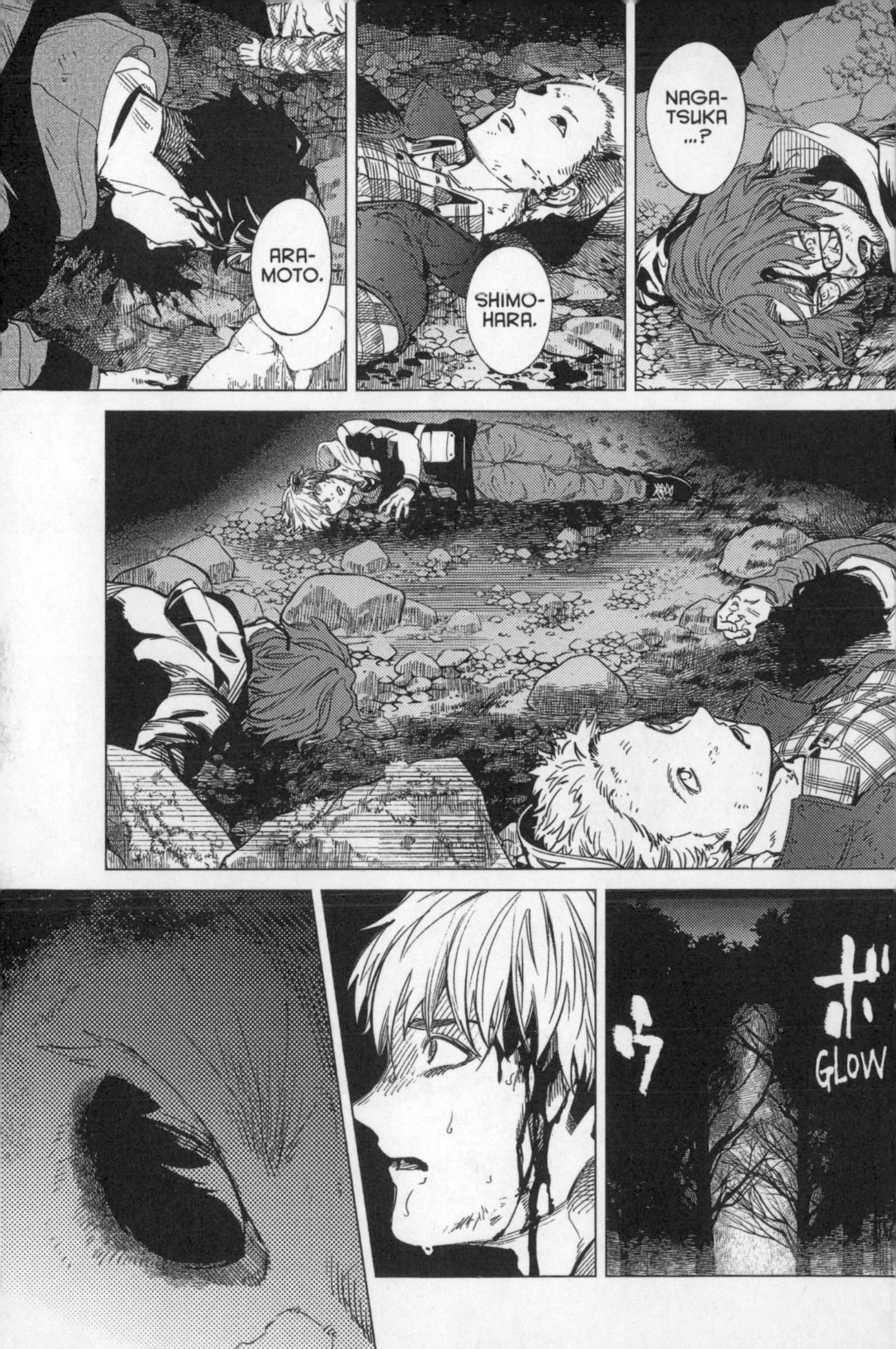
NAGA-TSUKA ...?
SHIMO-HARA.
ARA-MOTO.
ボ
う
GLOW

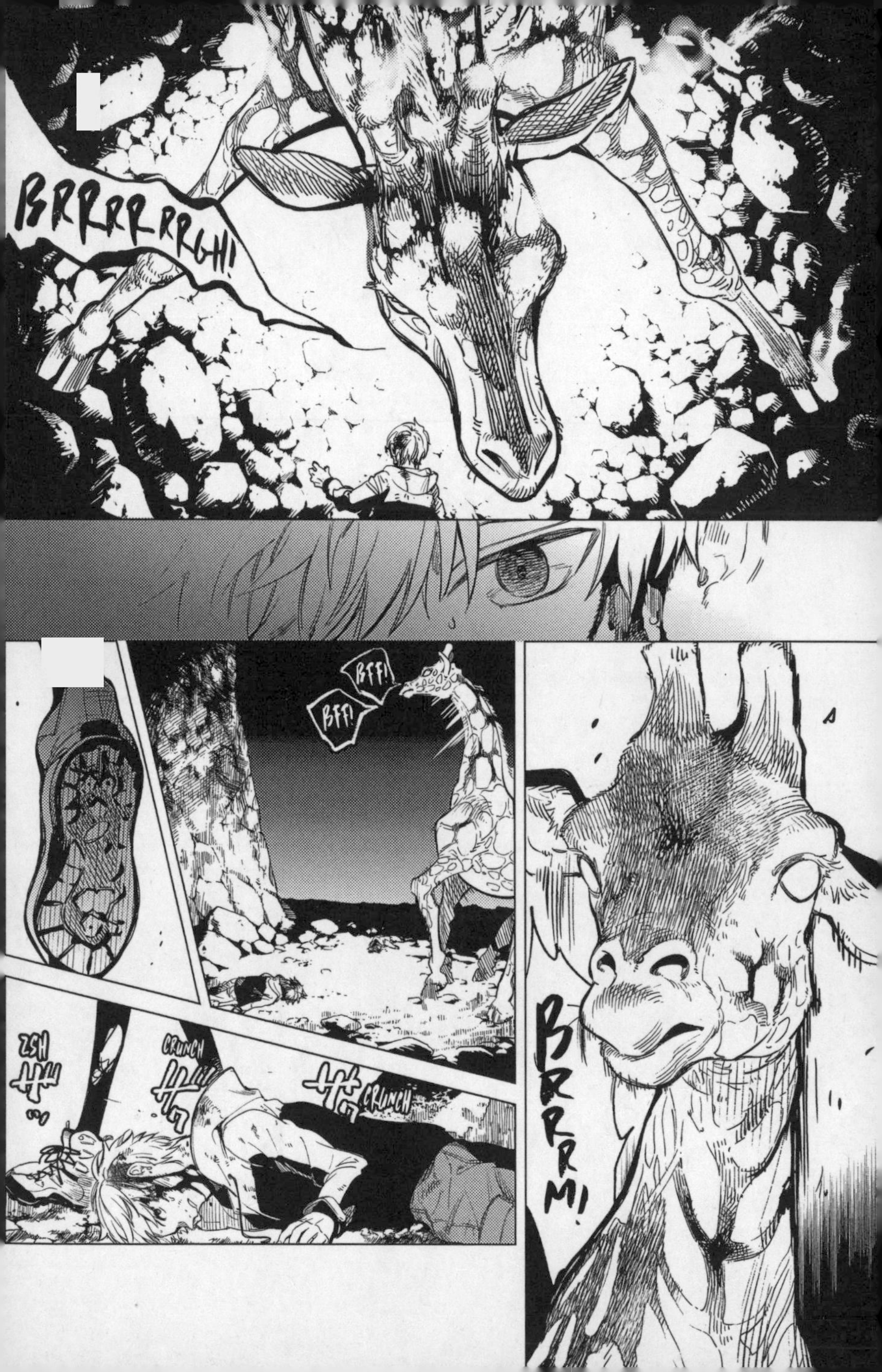
BRRRRRRGH!
BRRRRM!
BFF!
BFF!
CRUNCH
CRUNCH
ZSH

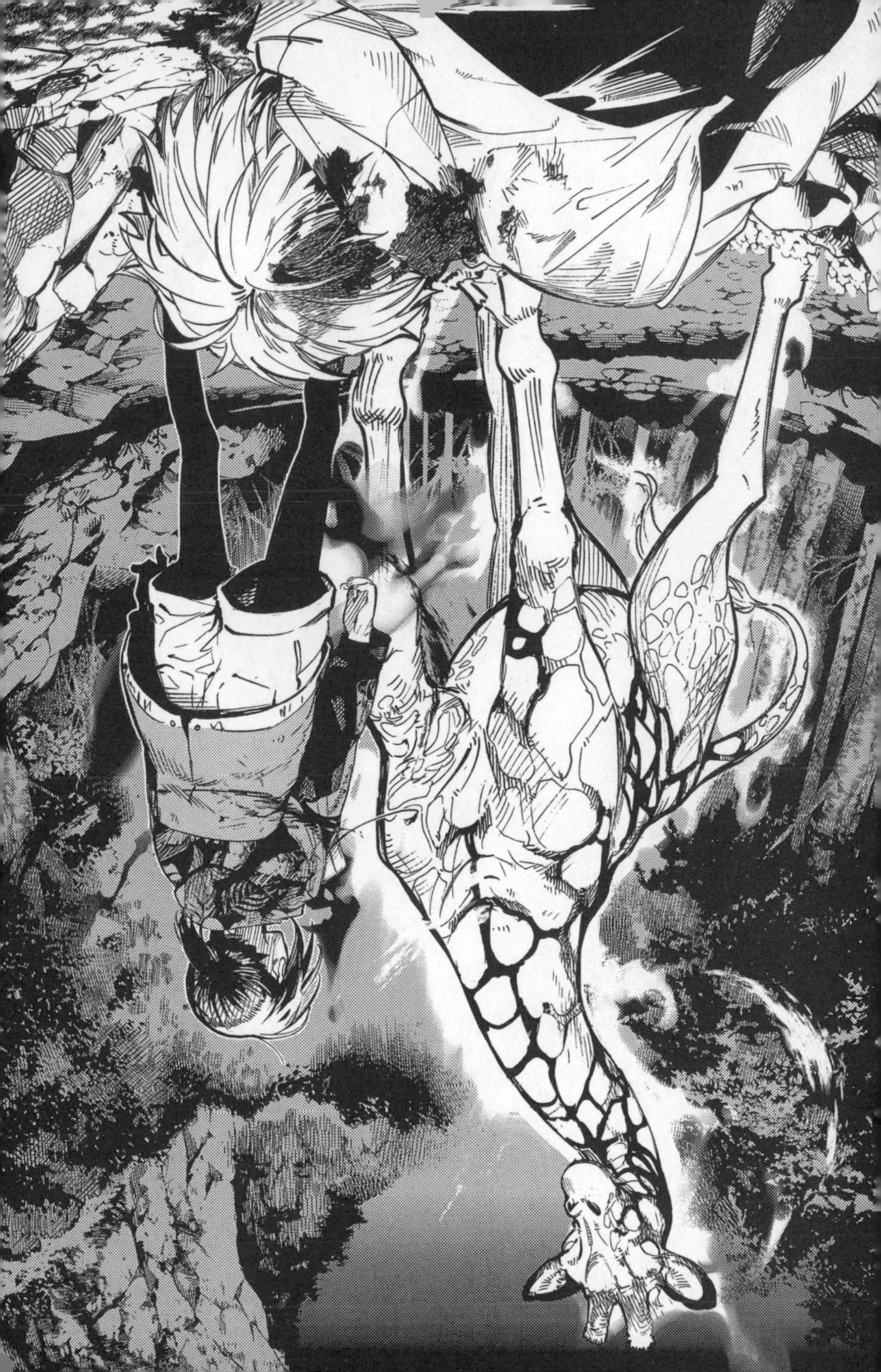

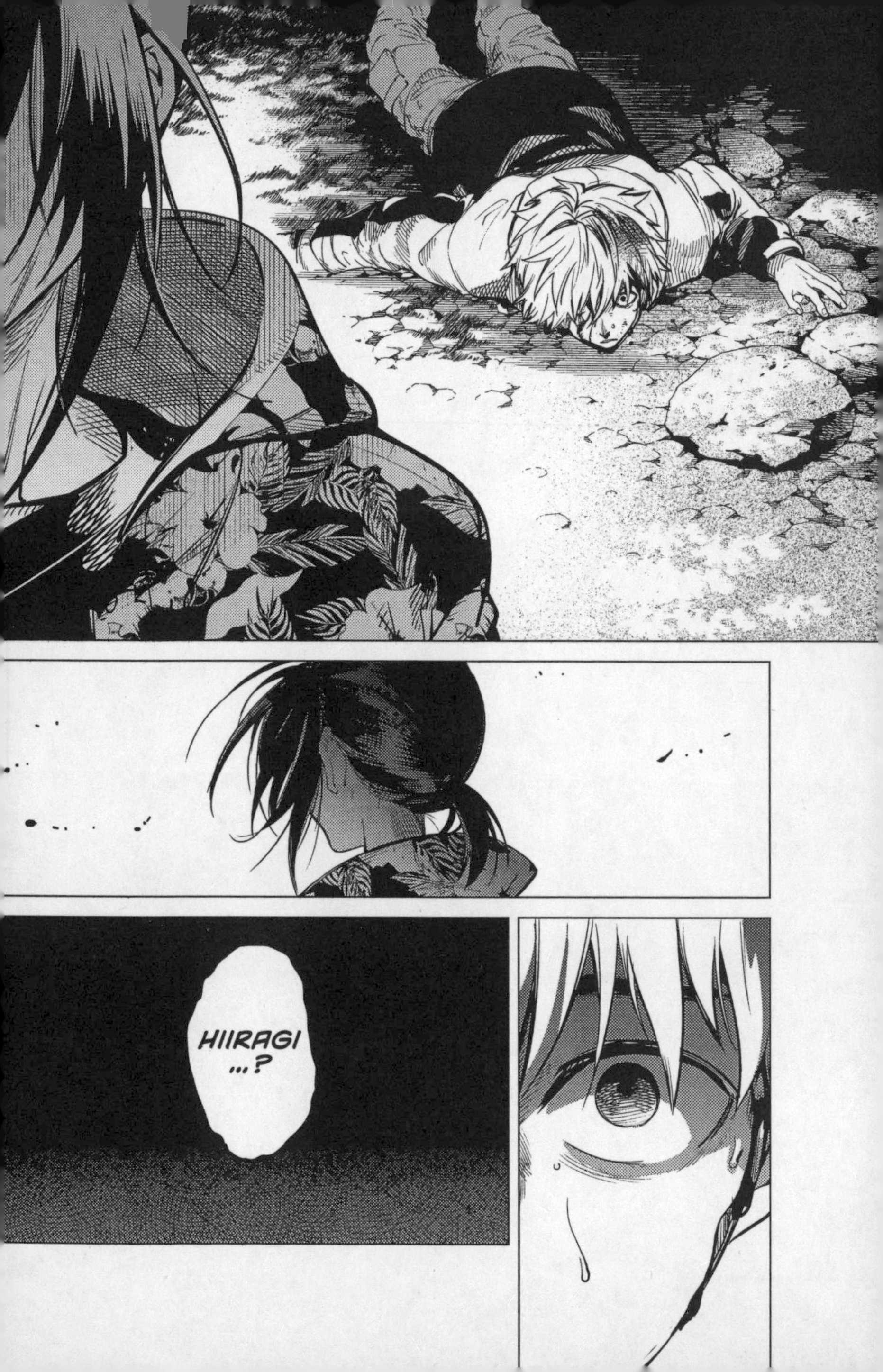
HIIRAGI ...?

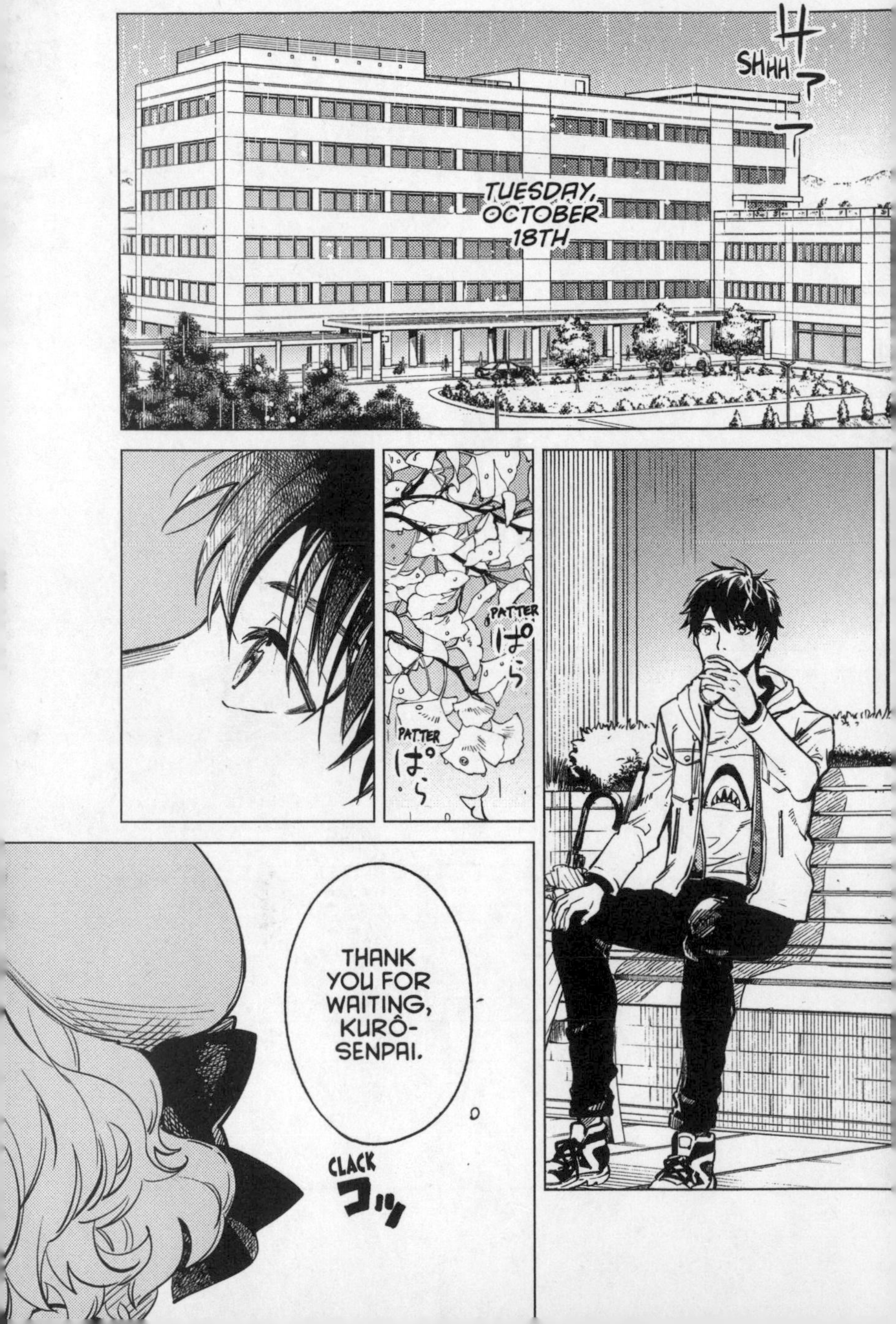
SHHH
TUESDAY, OCTOBER 18TH
PATTER
ぱら
PATTER
ぱら
THANK YOU FOR WAITING, KURÔ-SENPAI.
CLACK
コッ

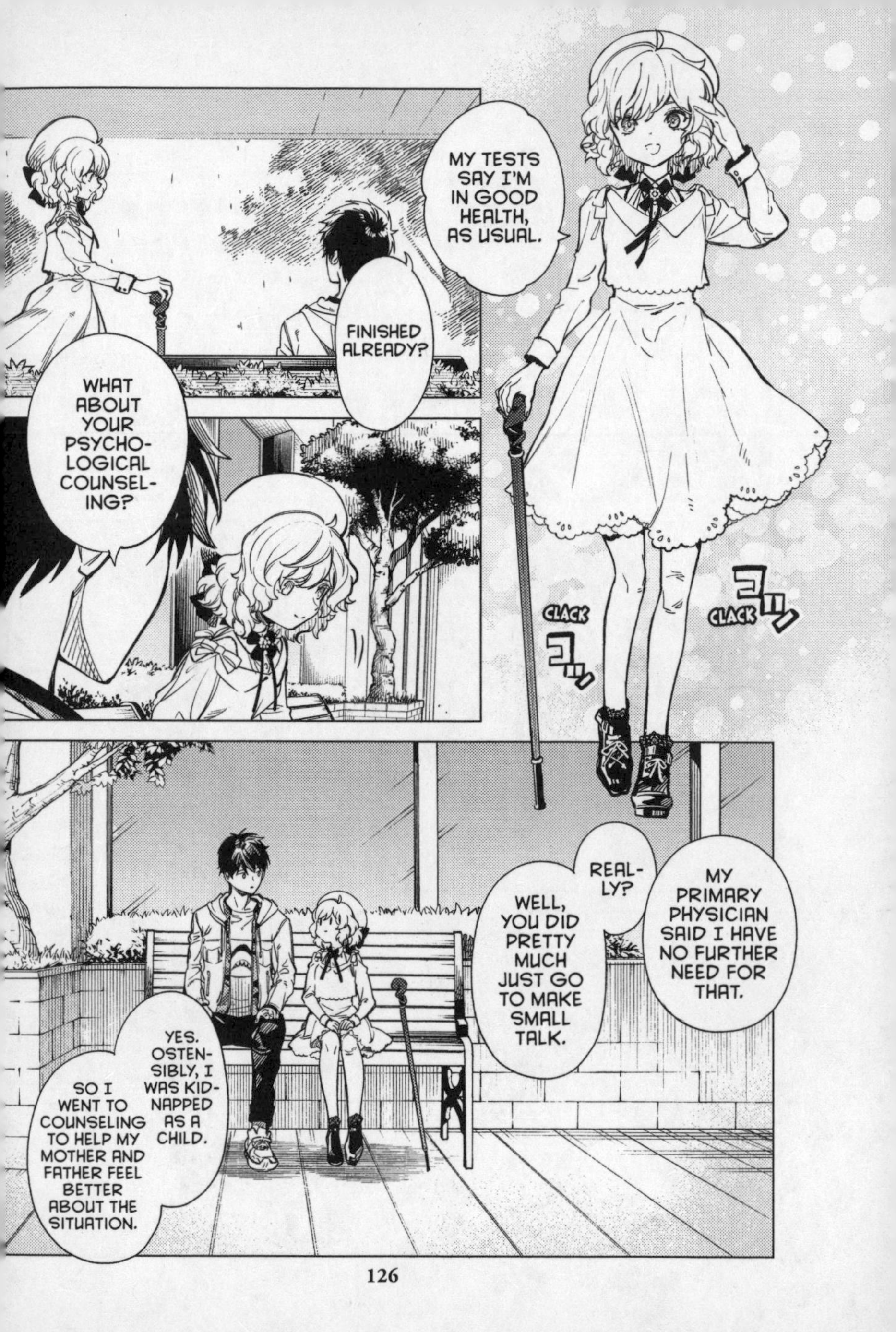
MY TESTS SAY I'M IN GOOD HEALTH, AS USUAL.
CLACK
CLACK
FINISHED ALREADY?
WHAT ABOUT YOUR PSYCHO-LOGICAL COUNSEL-ING?
MY PRIMARY PHYSICIAN SAID I HAVE NO FURTHER NEED FOR THAT.
REAL-LY?
WELL, YOU DID PRETTY MUCH JUST GO TO MAKE SMALL TALK.
YES. OSTEN-SIBLY, I WAS KID-NAPPED AS A CHILD.
SO I WENT TO COUNSELING TO HELP MY MOTHER AND FATHER FEEL BETTER ABOUT THE SITUATION.

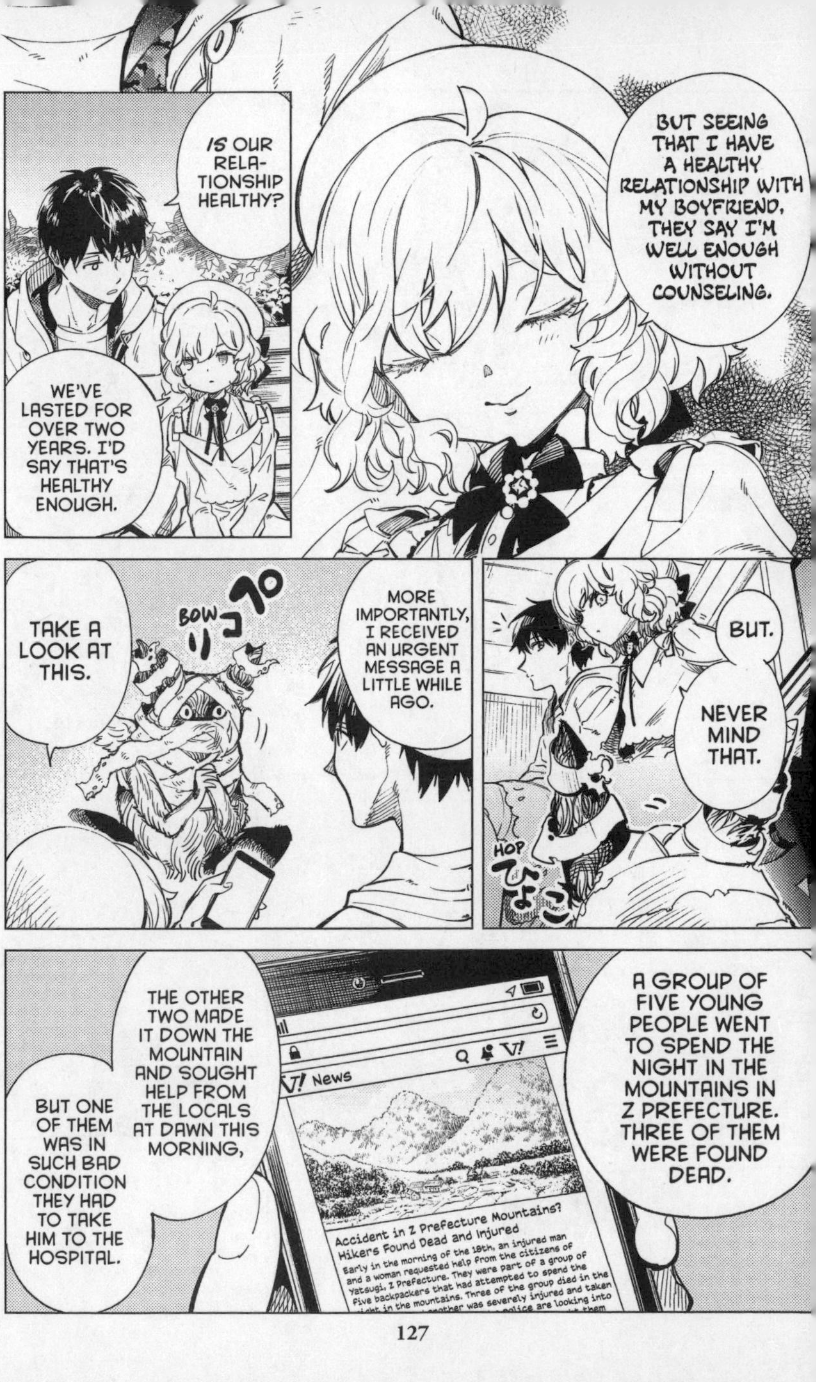
BUT SEEING THAT I HAVE A HEALTHY RELATIONSHIP WITH MY BOYFRIEND, THEY SAY I'M WELL ENOUGH WITHOUT COUNSELING.
IS OUR RELA-TIONSHIP HEALTHY?
WE'VE LASTED FOR OVER TWO YEARS. I'D SAY THAT'S HEALTHY ENOUGH.
BUT.
NEVER MIND THAT.
HOP
MORE IMPORTANTLY, I RECEIVED AN URGENT MESSAGE A LITTLE WHILE AGO.
BOW
TAKE A LOOK AT THIS.
A GROUP OF FIVE YOUNG PEOPLE WENT TO SPEND THE NIGHT IN THE MOUNTAINS IN Z PREFECTURE. THREE OF THEM WERE FOUND DEAD.
V! News
Accident in Z Prefecture Mountains?
Hikers Found Dead and Injured
Early in the morning of the 19th, an injured man and a woman requested help from the citizens of Yatsugi, Z Prefecture. They were part of a group of five backpackers that had attempted to spend the
THE OTHER TWO MADE IT DOWN THE MOUNTAIN AND SOUGHT HELP FROM THE LOCALS AT DAWN THIS MORNING,
BUT ONE OF THEM WAS IN SUCH BAD CONDITION THEY HAD TO TAKE HIM TO THE HOSPITAL.

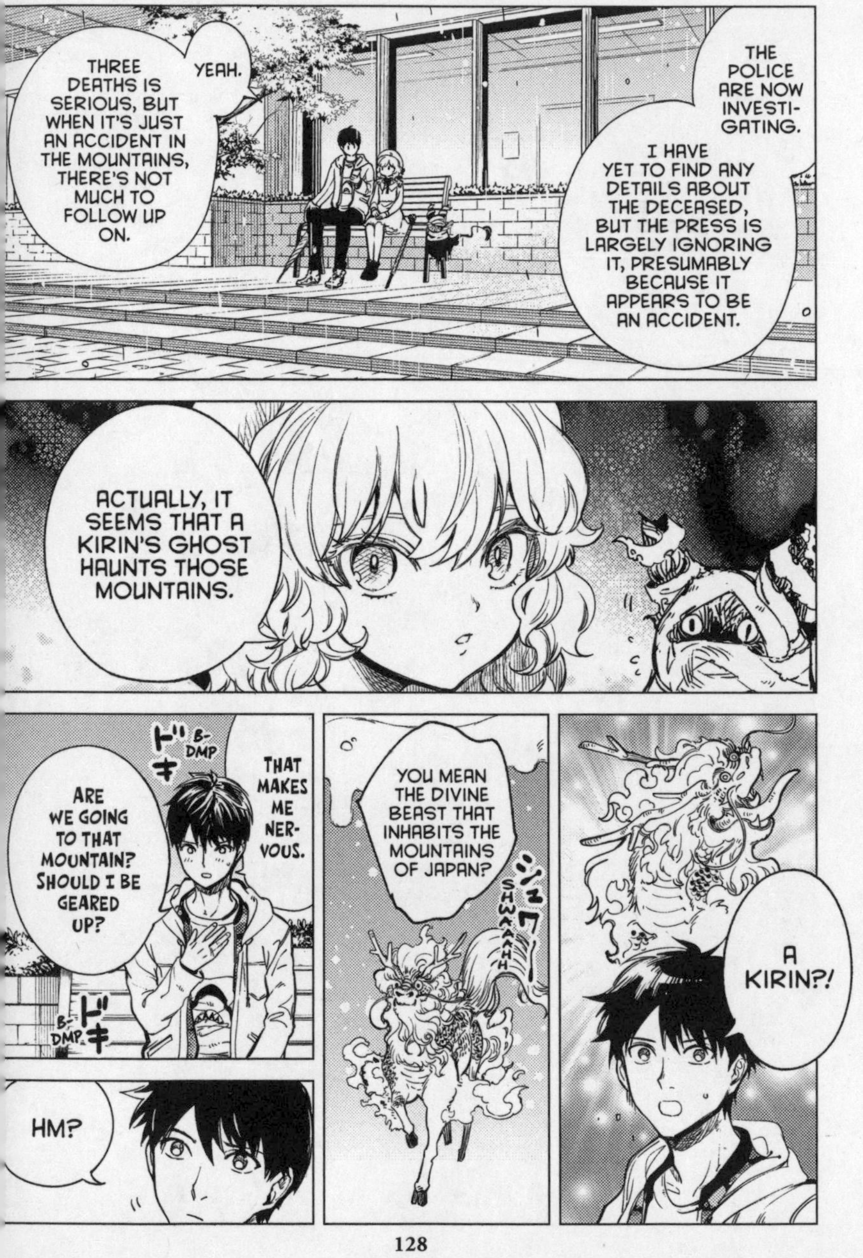
THE POLICE ARE NOW INVESTI-GATING.
I HAVE YET TO FIND ANY DETAILS ABOUT THE DECEASED, BUT THE PRESS IS LARGELY IGNORING IT, PRESUMABLY BECAUSE IT APPEARS TO BE AN ACCIDENT.
YEAH.
THREE DEATHS IS SERIOUS, BUT WHEN IT'S JUST AN ACCIDENT IN THE MOUNTAINS, THERE'S NOT MUCH TO FOLLOW UP ON.
ACTUALLY, IT SEEMS THAT A KIRIN'S GHOST HAUNTS THOSE MOUNTAINS.
A KIRIN?!
YOU MEAN THE DIVINE BEAST THAT INHABITS THE MOUNTAINS OF JAPAN?
SHWAAAHH
B-DMP
THAT MAKES ME NER-VOUS.
ARE WE GOING TO THAT MOUNTAIN? SHOULD I BE GEARED UP?
B-DMP
HM?

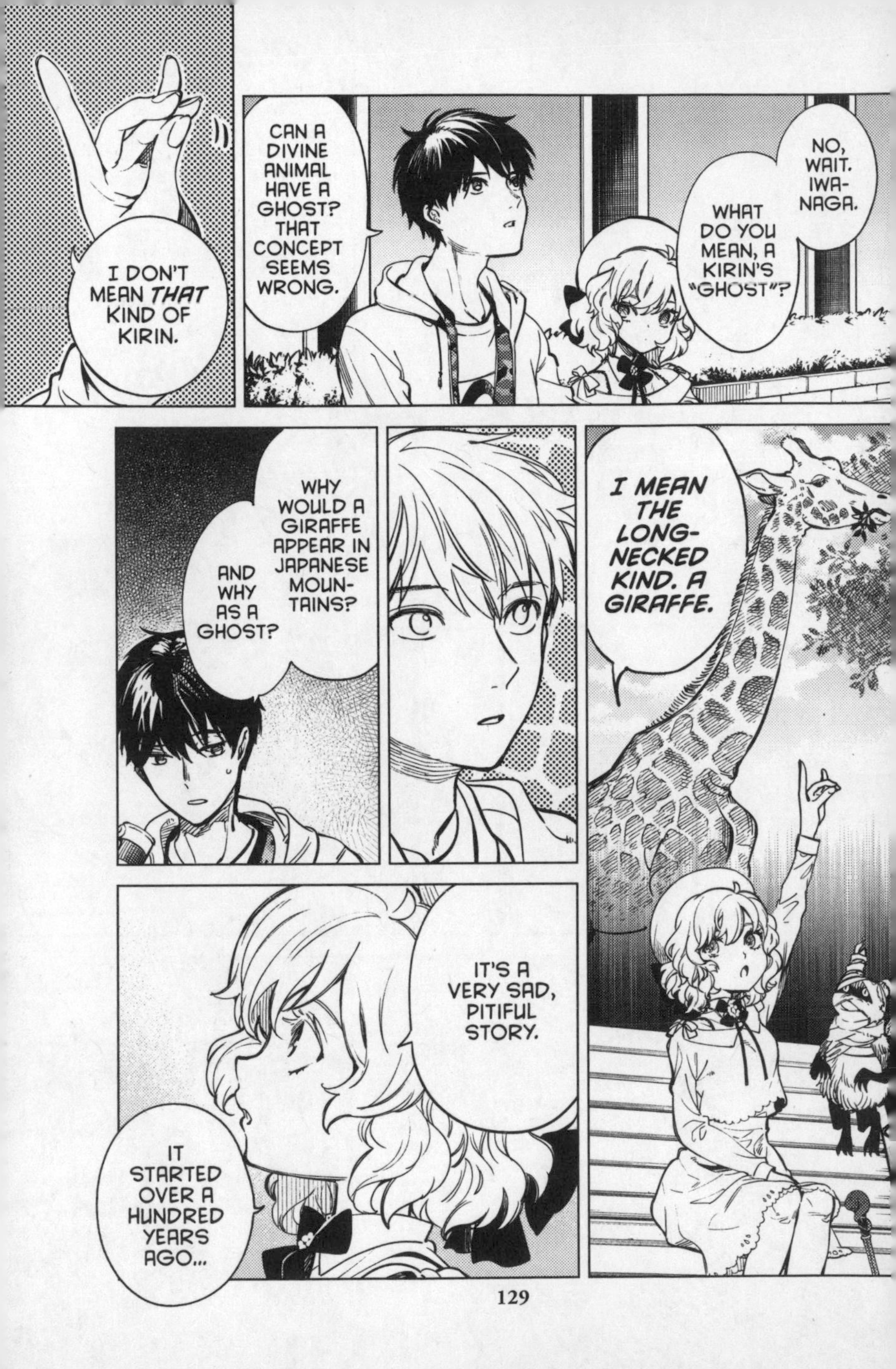
NO, WAIT. IWA-NAGA.
WHAT DO YOU MEAN, A KIRIN'S "GHOST"?
CAN A DIVINE ANIMAL HAVE A GHOST? THAT CONCEPT SEEMS WRONG.
I DON'T MEAN *THAT* KIND OF KIRIN.
I MEAN THE LONG-NECKED KIND. A GIRAFFE.
WHY WOULD A GIRAFFE APPEAR IN JAPANESE MOUN-TAINS?
AND WHY AS A GHOST?
IT'S A VERY SAD, PITIFUL STORY.
IT STARTED OVER A HUNDRED YEARS AGO...

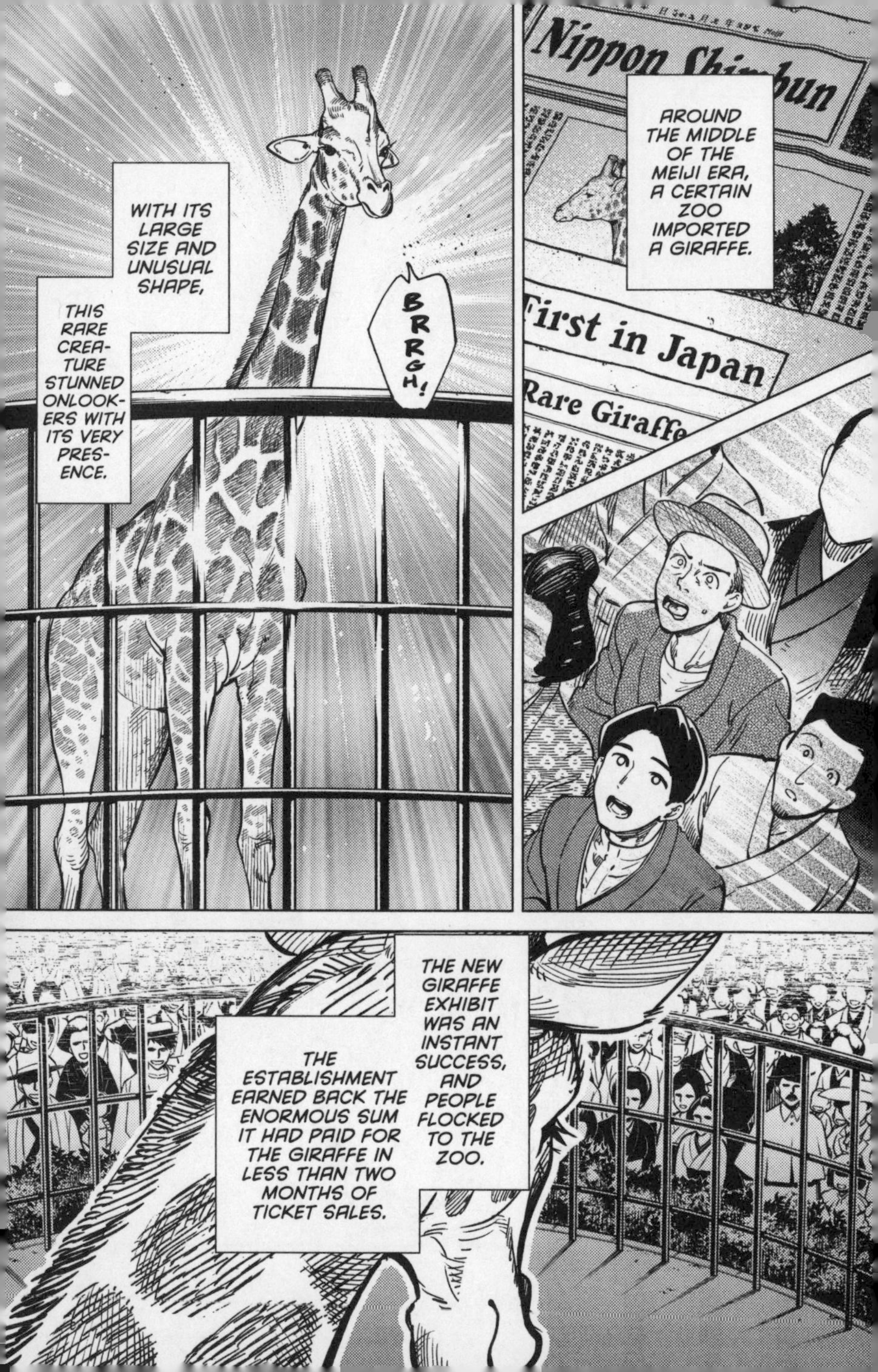
Nippon Shimbun
AROUND THE MIDDLE OF THE MEIJI ERA, A CERTAIN ZOO IMPORTED A GIRAFFE.
First in Japan
Rare Giraffe
WITH ITS LARGE SIZE AND UNUSUAL SHAPE,
THIS RARE CREA-TURE STUNNED ONLOOK-ERS WITH ITS VERY PRES-ENCE.
BRRGH!
THE NEW GIRAFFE EXHIBIT WAS AN INSTANT SUCCESS, AND PEOPLE FLOCKED TO THE ZOO.
THE ESTABLISHMENT EARNED BACK THE ENORMOUS SUM IT HAD PAID FOR THE GIRAFFE IN LESS THAN TWO MONTHS OF TICKET SALES.

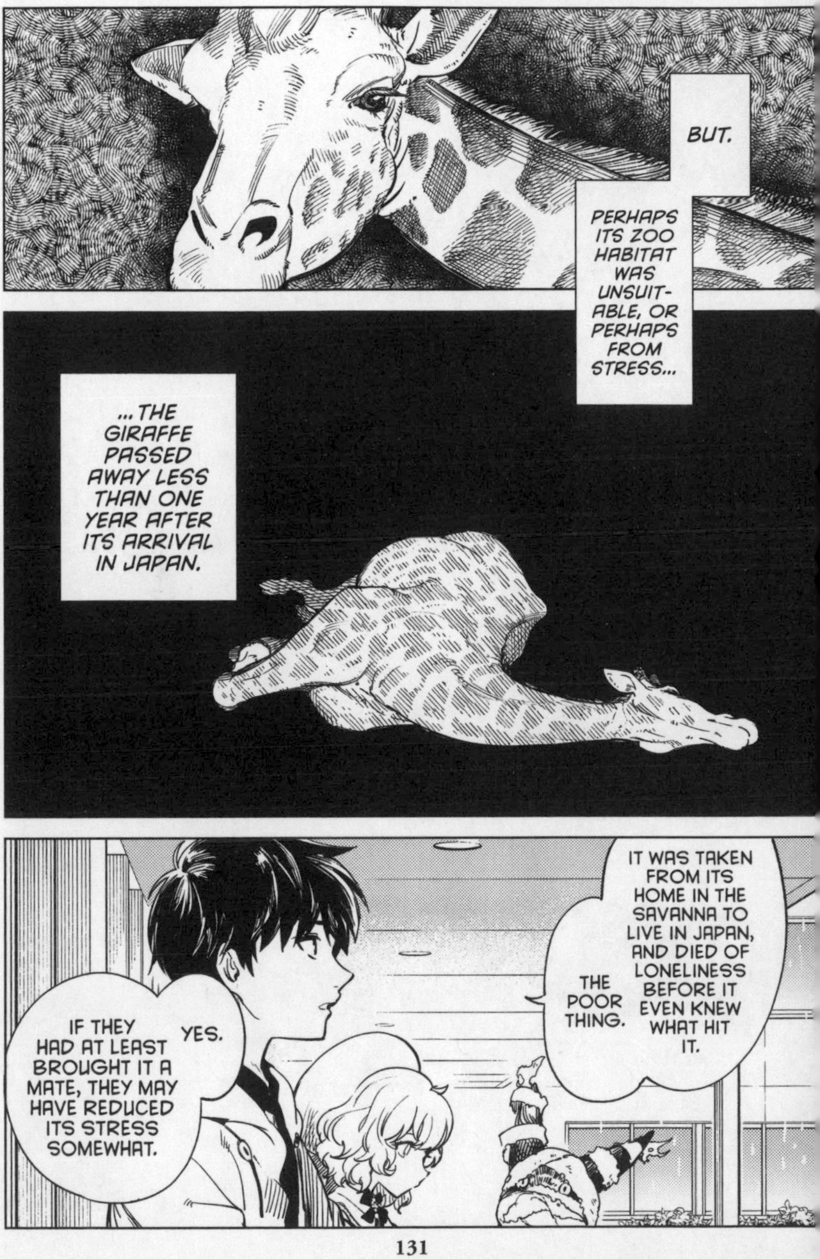
BUT.
PERHAPS ITS ZOO HABITAT WAS UNSUIT-ABLE, OR PERHAPS FROM STRESS...
...THE GIRAFFE PASSED AWAY LESS THAN ONE YEAR AFTER ITS ARRIVAL IN JAPAN.
IT WAS TAKEN FROM ITS HOME IN THE SAVANNA TO LIVE IN JAPAN, AND DIED OF LONELINESS BEFORE IT EVEN KNEW WHAT HIT IT.
THE POOR THING.
YES.
IF THEY HAD AT LEAST BROUGHT IT A MATE, THEY MAY HAVE REDUCED ITS STRESS SOMEWHAT.

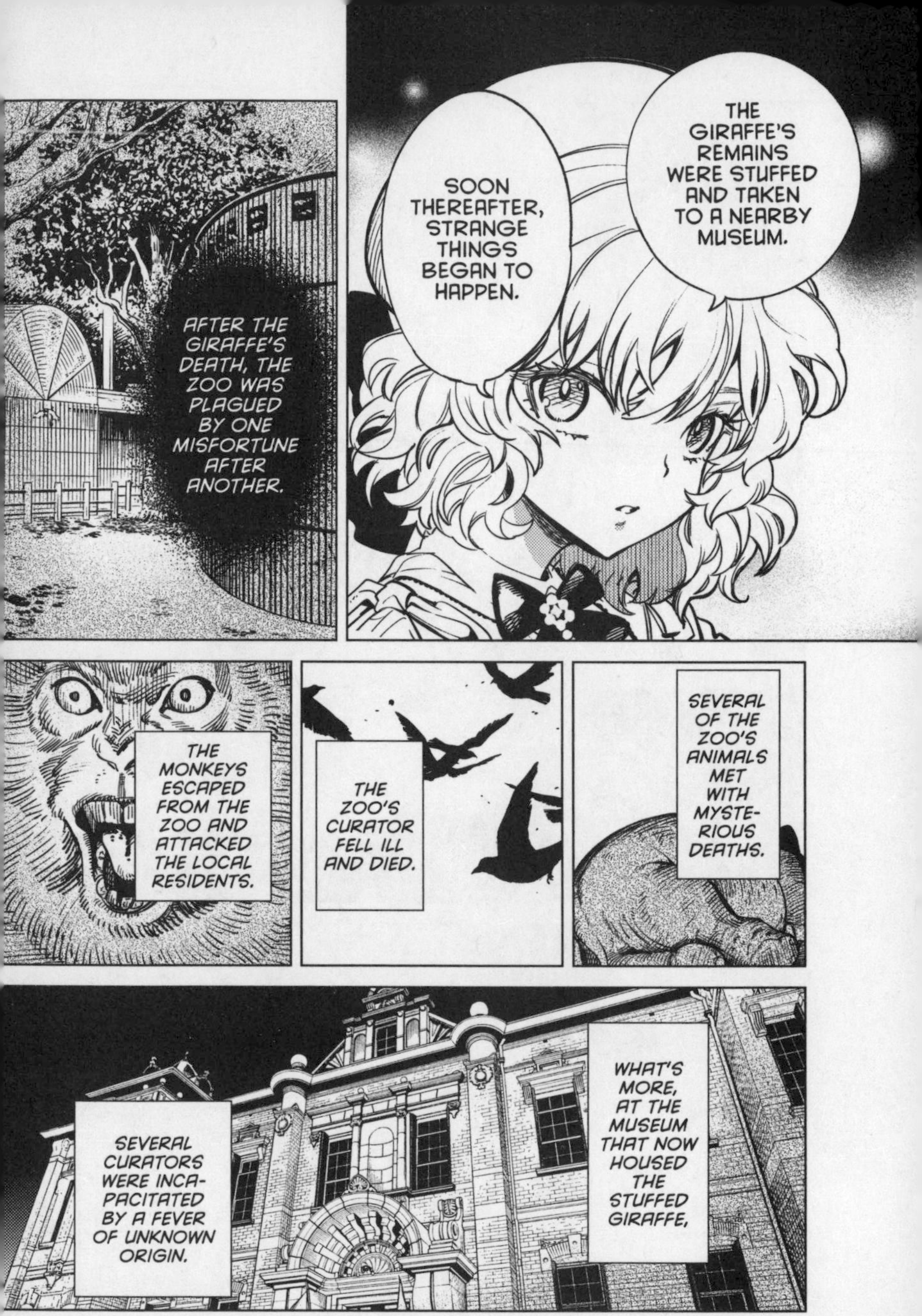
THE GIRAFFE'S REMAINS WERE STUFFED AND TAKEN TO A NEARBY MUSEUM.
SOON THEREAFTER, STRANGE THINGS BEGAN TO HAPPEN.
AFTER THE GIRAFFE'S DEATH, THE ZOO WAS PLAGUED BY ONE MISFORTUNE AFTER ANOTHER.
SEVERAL OF THE ZOO'S ANIMALS MET WITH MYSTE-RIOUS DEATHS.
THE ZOO'S CURATOR FELL ILL AND DIED.
THE MONKEYS ESCAPED FROM THE ZOO AND ATTACKED THE LOCAL RESIDENTS.
WHAT'S MORE, AT THE MUSEUM THAT NOW HOUSED THE STUFFED GIRAFFE,
SEVERAL CURATORS WERE INCA-PACITATED BY A FEVER OF UNKNOWN ORIGIN.

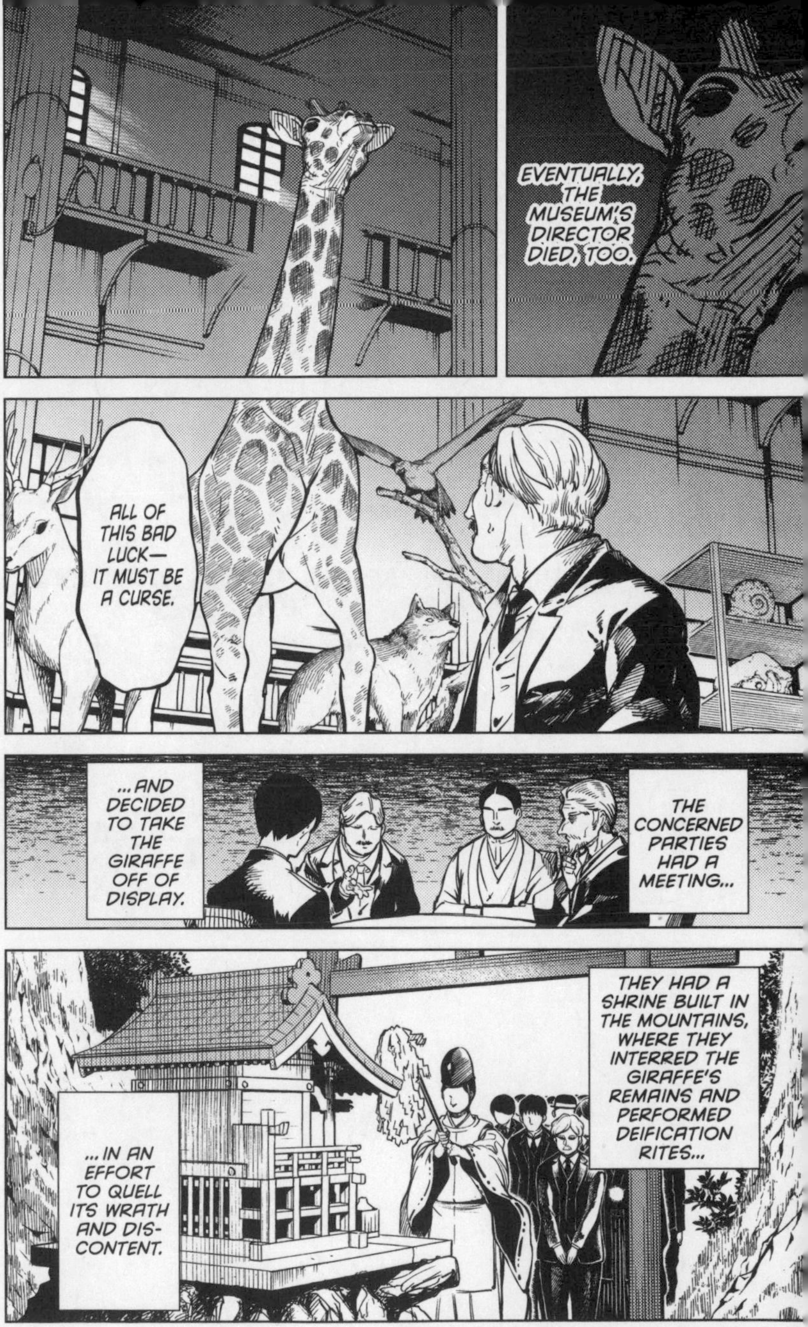
EVENTUALLY, THE MUSEUM'S DIRECTOR DIED, TOO.
ALL OF THIS BAD LUCK— IT MUST BE A CURSE.
THE CONCERNED PARTIES HAD A MEETING...
...AND DECIDED TO TAKE THE GIRAFFE OFF OF DISPLAY.
THEY HAD A SHRINE BUILT IN THE MOUNTAINS, WHERE THEY INTERRED THE GIRAFFE'S REMAINS AND PERFORMED DEIFICATION RITES...
...IN AN EFFORT TO QUELL ITS WRATH AND DIS-CONTENT.

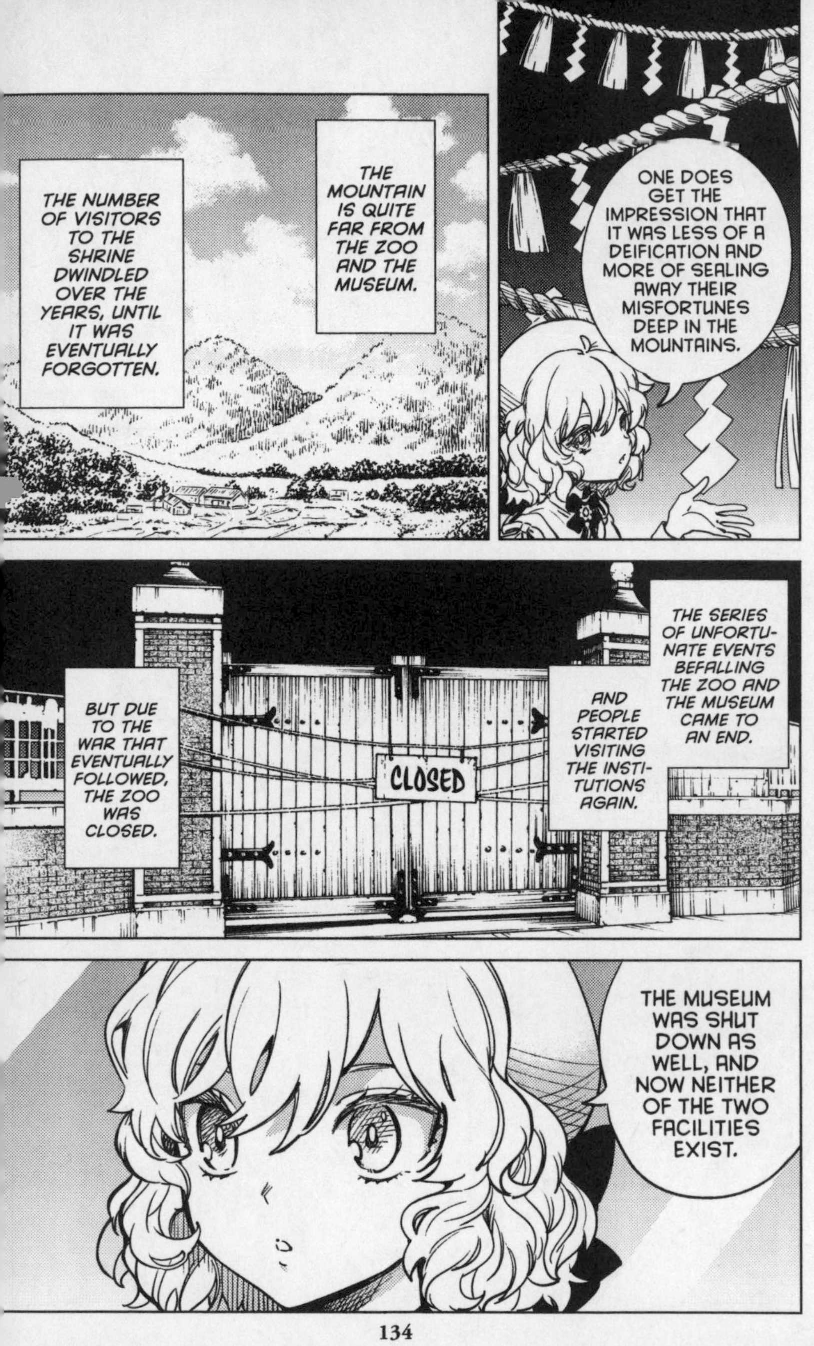
ONE DOES GET THE IMPRESSION THAT IT WAS LESS OF A DEIFICATION AND MORE OF SEALING AWAY THEIR MISFORTUNES DEEP IN THE MOUNTAINS.
THE MOUNTAIN IS QUITE FAR FROM THE ZOO AND THE MUSEUM.
THE NUMBER OF VISITORS TO THE SHRINE DWINDLED OVER THE YEARS, UNTIL IT WAS EVENTUALLY FORGOTTEN.
THE SERIES OF UNFORTUNATE EVENTS BEFALLING THE ZOO AND THE MUSEUM CAME TO AN END.
AND PEOPLE STARTED VISITING THE INSTITUTIONS AGAIN.
CLOSED
BUT DUE TO THE WAR THAT EVENTUALLY FOLLOWED, THE ZOO WAS CLOSED.
THE MUSEUM WAS SHUT DOWN AS WELL, AND NOW NEITHER OF THE TWO FACILITIES EXIST.

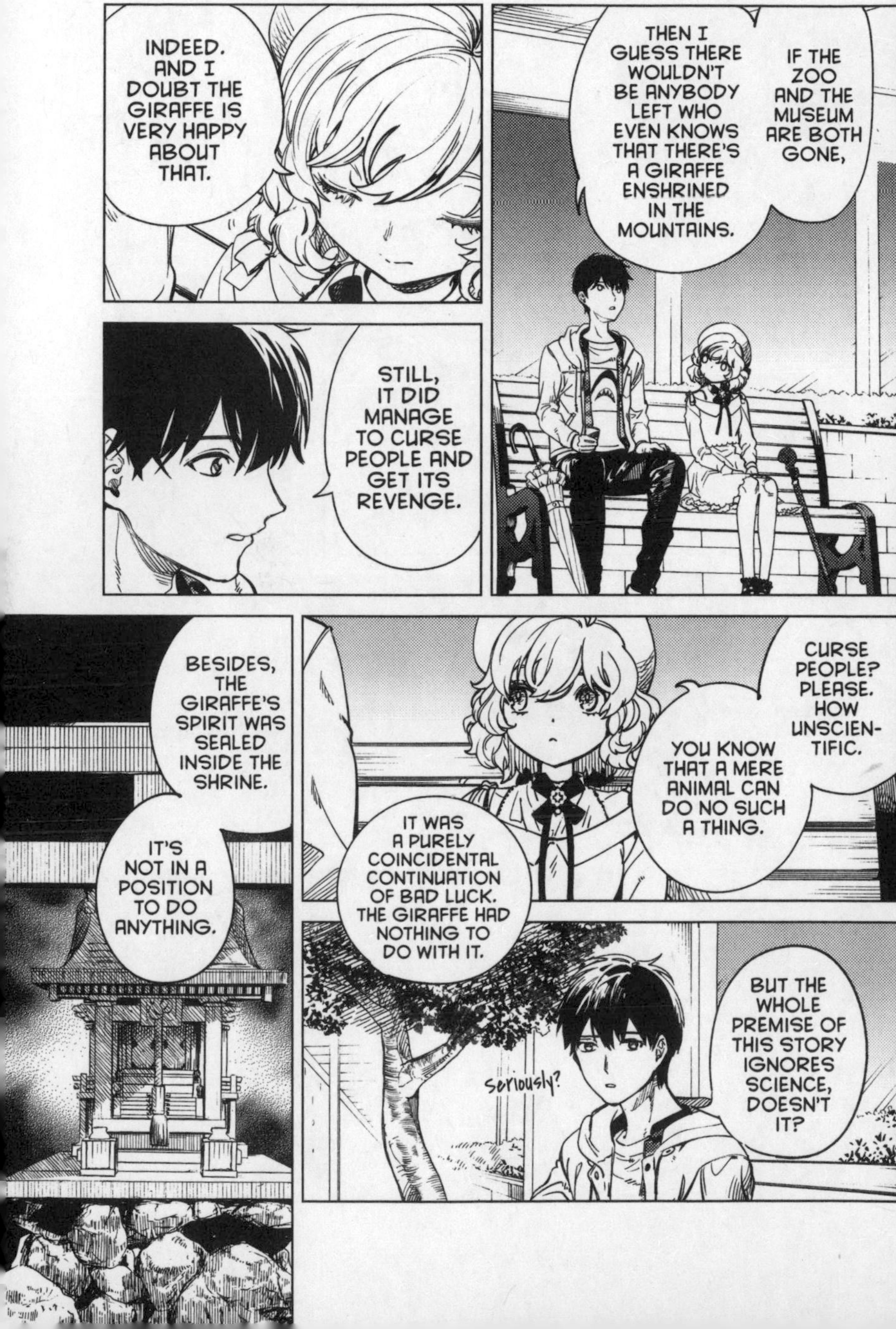
IF THE ZOO AND THE MUSEUM ARE BOTH GONE,
THEN I GUESS THERE WOULDN'T BE ANYBODY LEFT WHO EVEN KNOWS THAT THERE'S A GIRAFFE ENSHRINED IN THE MOUNTAINS.
INDEED. AND I DOUBT THE GIRAFFE IS VERY HAPPY ABOUT THAT.
STILL, IT DID MANAGE TO CURSE PEOPLE AND GET ITS REVENGE.
CURSE PEOPLE? PLEASE. HOW UNSCIEN-TIFIC.
YOU KNOW THAT A MERE ANIMAL CAN DO NO SUCH A THING.
IT WAS A PURELY COINCIDENTAL CONTINUATION OF BAD LUCK. THE GIRAFFE HAD NOTHING TO DO WITH IT.
BUT THE WHOLE PREMISE OF THIS STORY IGNORES SCIENCE, DOESN'T IT?
seriously?
BESIDES, THE GIRAFFE'S SPIRIT WAS SEALED INSIDE THE SHRINE.
IT'S NOT IN A POSITION TO DO ANYTHING.

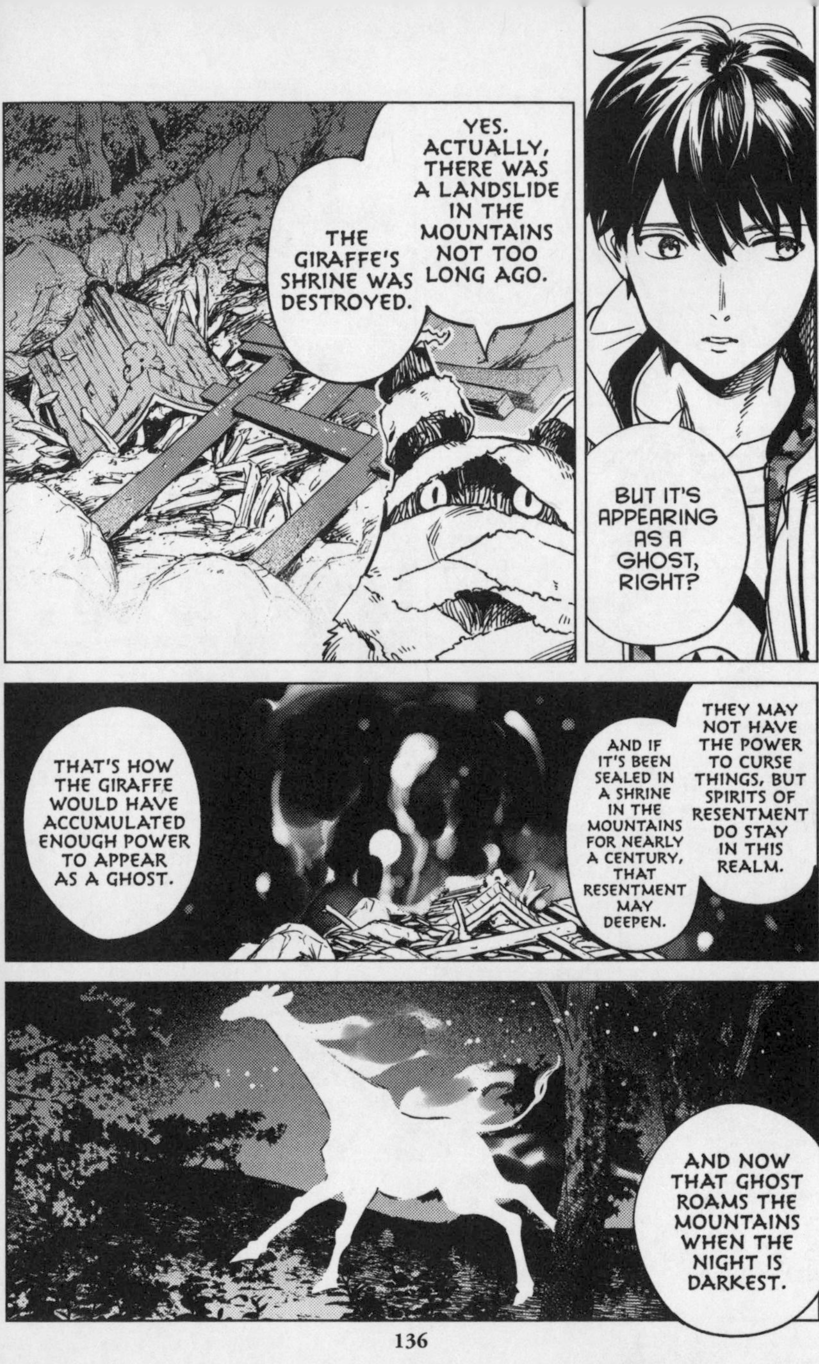
BUT IT'S APPEARING AS A GHOST, RIGHT?
YES. ACTUALLY, THERE WAS A LANDSLIDE IN THE MOUNTAINS NOT TOO LONG AGO.
THE GIRAFFE'S SHRINE WAS DESTROYED.
THEY MAY NOT HAVE THE POWER TO CURSE THINGS, BUT SPIRITS OF RESENTMENT DO STAY IN THIS REALM.
AND IF IT'S BEEN SEALED IN A SHRINE IN THE MOUNTAINS FOR NEARLY A CENTURY, THAT RESENTMENT MAY DEEPEN.
THAT'S HOW THE GIRAFFE WOULD HAVE ACCUMULATED ENOUGH POWER TO APPEAR AS A GHOST.
AND NOW THAT GHOST ROAMS THE MOUNTAINS WHEN THE NIGHT IS DARKEST.

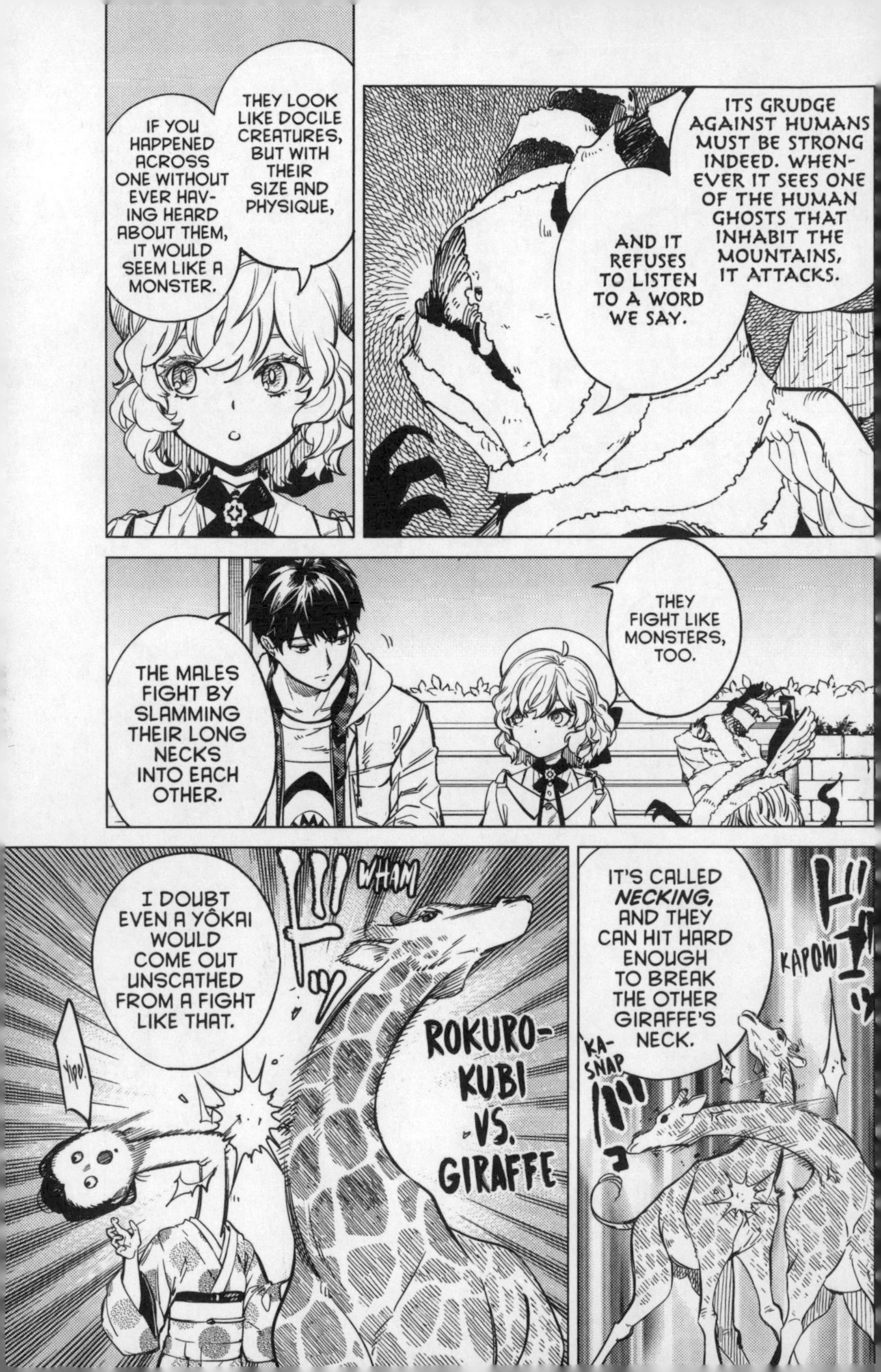
ITS GRUDGE AGAINST HUMANS MUST BE STRONG INDEED. WHEN-EVER IT SEES ONE OF THE HUMAN GHOSTS THAT INHABIT THE MOUNTAINS, IT ATTACKS.
AND IT REFUSES TO LISTEN TO A WORD WE SAY.
THEY LOOK LIKE DOCILE CREATURES, BUT WITH THEIR SIZE AND PHYSIQUE,
IF YOU HAPPENED ACROSS ONE WITHOUT EVER HAV-ING HEARD ABOUT THEM, IT WOULD SEEM LIKE A MONSTER.
THEY FIGHT LIKE MONSTERS, TOO.
THE MALES FIGHT BY SLAMMING THEIR LONG NECKS INTO EACH OTHER.
IT'S CALLED *NECKING,* AND THEY CAN HIT HARD ENOUGH TO BREAK THE OTHER GIRAFFE'S NECK.
KAPOW
KA-SNAP
I DOUBT EVEN A YÔKAI WOULD COME OUT UNSCATHED FROM A FIGHT LIKE THAT.
WHAM
ROKURO-KUBI VS. GIRAFFE
Yipe!

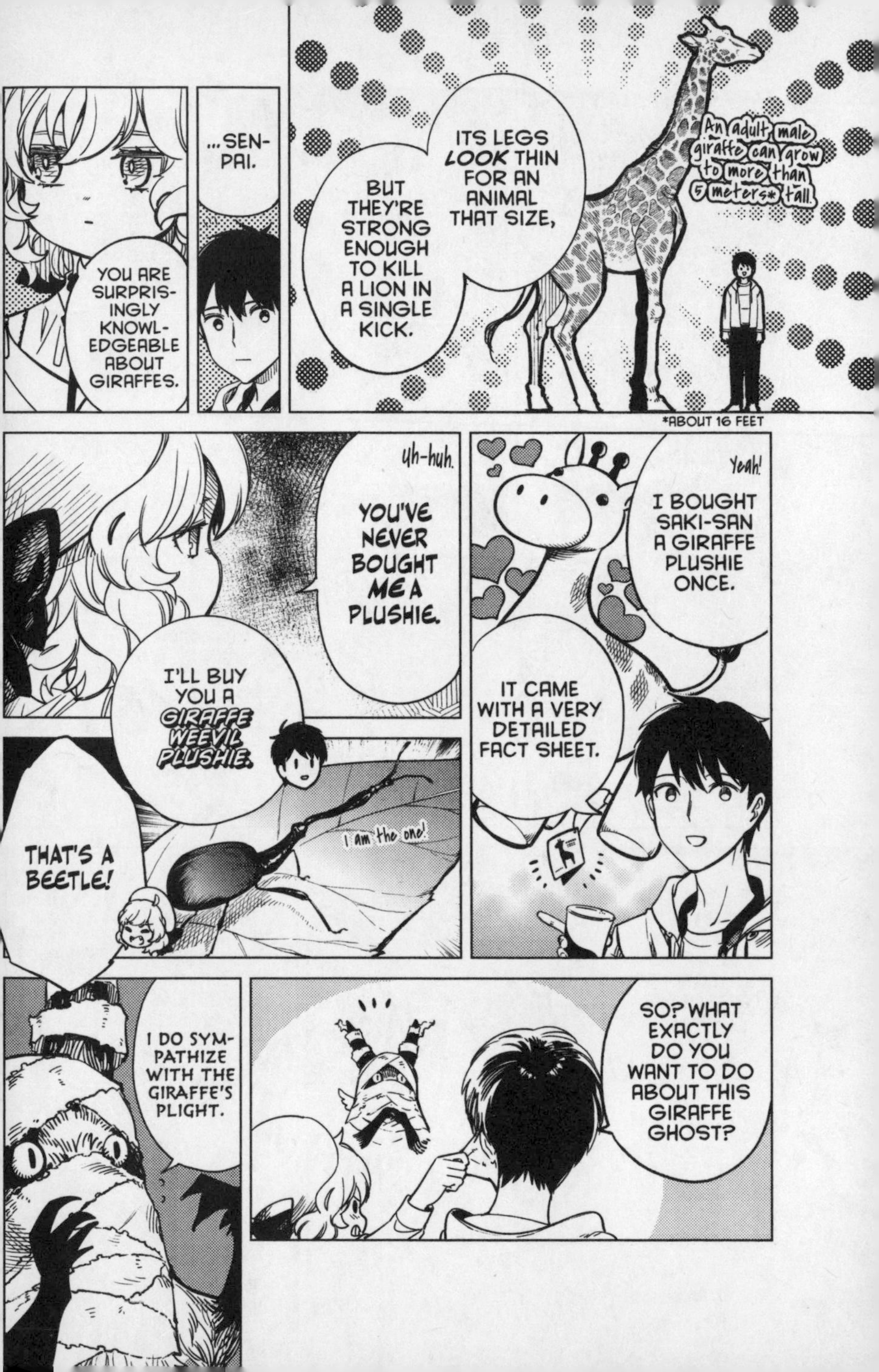
An adult male giraffe can grow to more than 5 meters* tall.
ITS LEGS LOOK THIN FOR AN ANIMAL THAT SIZE,
BUT THEY'RE STRONG ENOUGH TO KILL A LION IN A SINGLE KICK.
...SEN-PAI.
YOU ARE SURPRISINGLY KNOWLEDGEABLE ABOUT GIRAFFES.
Yeah!
I BOUGHT SAKI-SAN A GIRAFFE PLUSHIE ONCE.
IT CAME WITH A VERY DETAILED FACT SHEET.
uh-huh.
YOU'VE NEVER BOUGHT ME A PLUSHIE.
I'LL BUY YOU A GIRAFFE WEEVIL PLUSHIE.
I am the one!
THAT'S A BEETLE!
SO? WHAT EXACTLY DO YOU WANT TO DO ABOUT THIS GIRAFFE GHOST?
I DO SYMPATHIZE WITH THE GIRAFFE'S PLIGHT.
*ABOUT 16 FEET

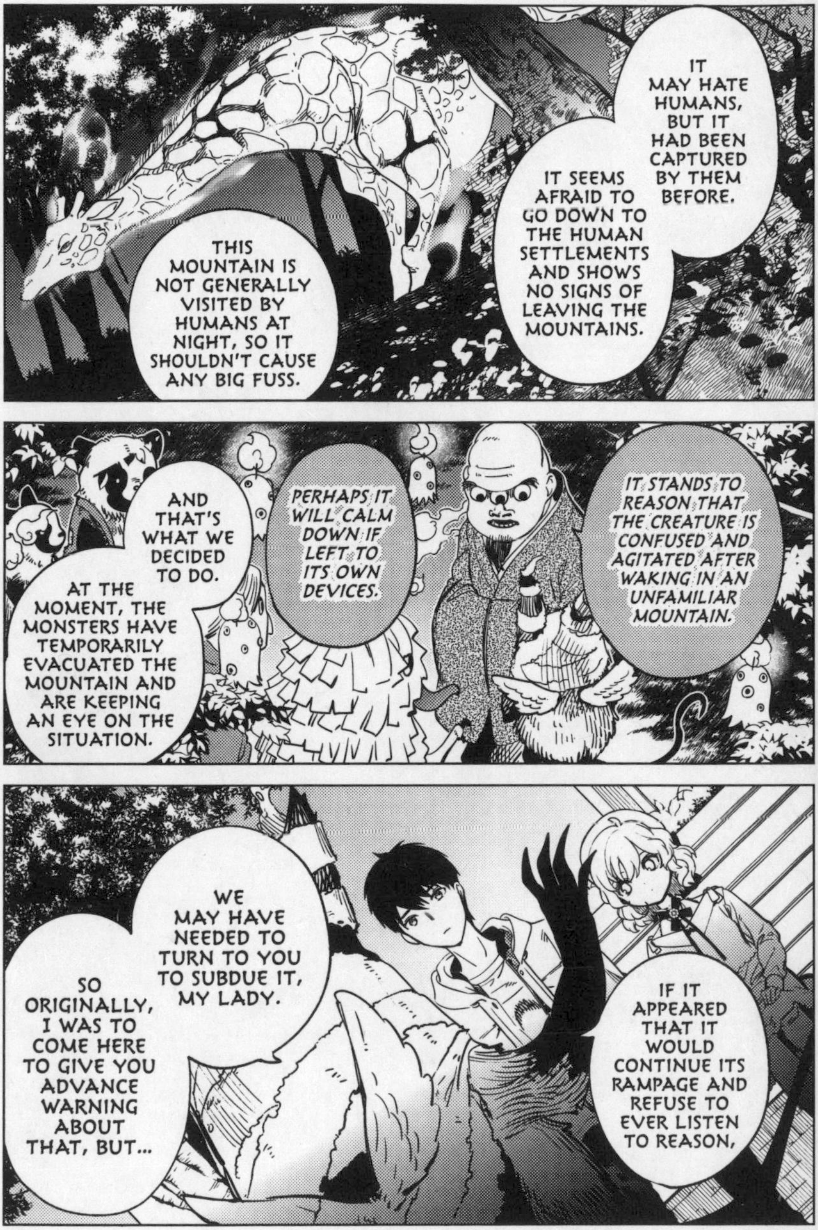
IT MAY HATE HUMANS, BUT IT HAD BEEN CAPTURED BY THEM BEFORE.
IT SEEMS AFRAID TO GO DOWN TO THE HUMAN SETTLEMENTS AND SHOWS NO SIGNS OF LEAVING THE MOUNTAINS.
THIS MOUNTAIN IS NOT GENERALLY VISITED BY HUMANS AT NIGHT, SO IT SHOULDN'T CAUSE ANY BIG FUSS.
IT STANDS TO REASON THAT THE CREATURE IS CONFUSED AND AGITATED AFTER WAKING IN AN UNFAMILIAR MOUNTAIN.
PERHAPS IT WILL CALM DOWN IF LEFT TO ITS OWN DEVICES.
AND THAT'S WHAT WE DECIDED TO DO.
AT THE MOMENT, THE MONSTERS HAVE TEMPORARILY EVACUATED THE MOUNTAIN AND ARE KEEPING AN EYE ON THE SITUATION.
IF IT APPEARED THAT IT WOULD CONTINUE ITS RAMPAGE AND REFUSE TO EVER LISTEN TO REASON,
WE MAY HAVE NEEDED TO TURN TO YOU TO SUBDUE IT, MY LADY.
SO ORIGINALLY, I WAS TO COME HERE TO GIVE YOU ADVANCE WARNING ABOUT THAT, BUT...

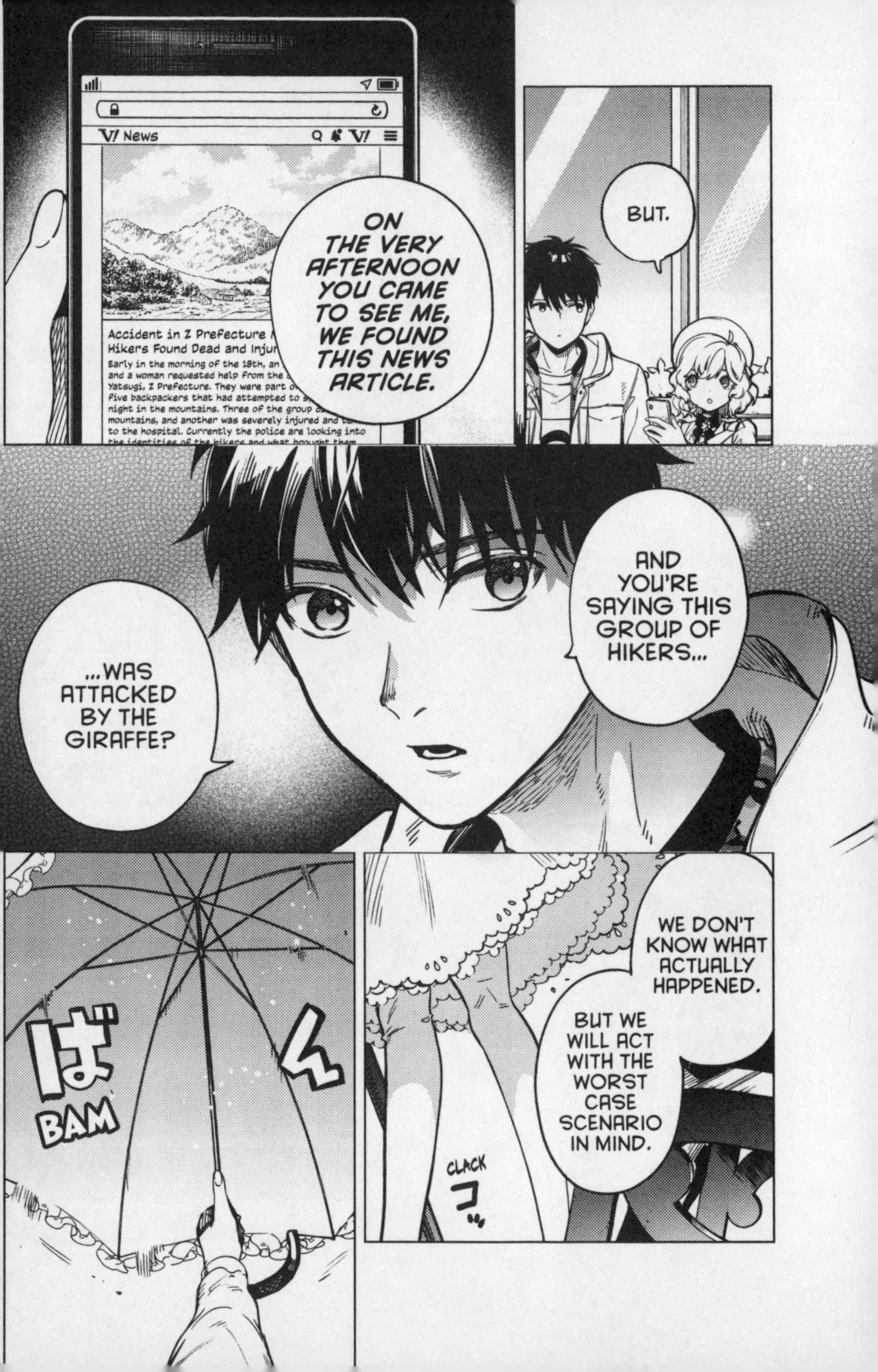

BUT.
ON THE VERY AFTERNOON YOU CAME TO SEE ME, WE FOUND THIS NEWS ARTICLE.
V! News
Accident in Z Prefecture
Hikers Found Dead and Injur
Early in the morning of the 18th, an
and a woman requested help from the
Yatsugi, Z Prefecture. They were part o
five backpackers that had attempted to s
night in the mountains. Three of the group
mountains, and another was severely injured and t
to the hospital. Currently the police are looking into
AND YOU'RE SAYING THIS GROUP OF HIKERS...
...WAS ATTACKED BY THE GIRAFFE?
WE DON'T KNOW WHAT ACTUALLY HAPPENED.
BUT WE WILL ACT WITH THE WORST CASE SCENARIO IN MIND.
CLACK
ばん
BAM

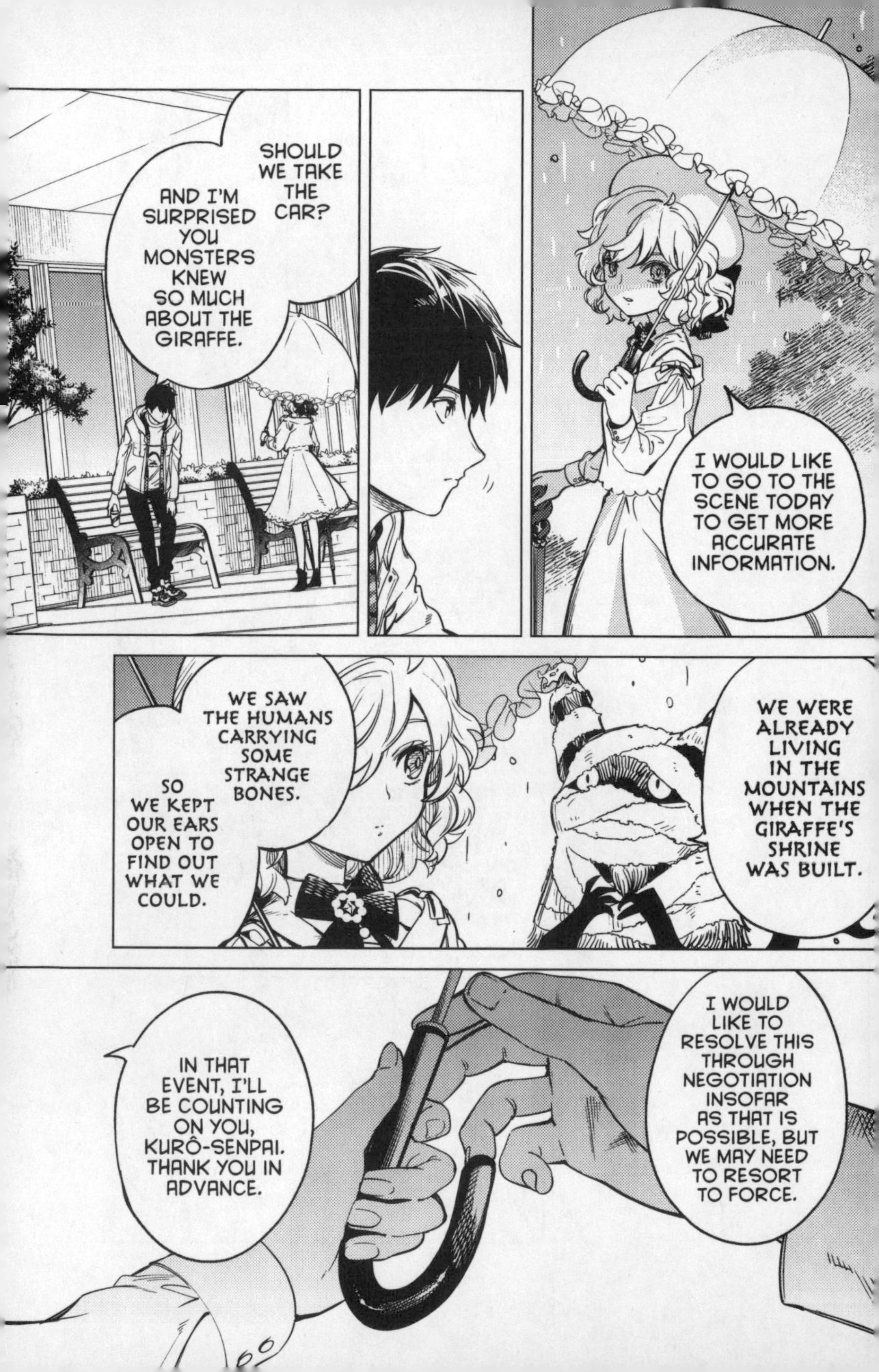
I WOULD LIKE TO GO TO THE SCENE TODAY TO GET MORE ACCURATE INFORMATION.
SHOULD WE TAKE THE CAR?
AND I'M SURPRISED YOU MONSTERS KNEW SO MUCH ABOUT THE GIRAFFE.
WE WERE ALREADY LIVING IN THE MOUNTAINS WHEN THE GIRAFFE'S SHRINE WAS BUILT.
WE SAW THE HUMANS CARRYING SOME STRANGE BONES.
SO WE KEPT OUR EARS OPEN TO FIND OUT WHAT WE COULD.
I WOULD LIKE TO RESOLVE THIS THROUGH NEGOTIATION INSOFAR AS THAT IS POSSIBLE, BUT WE MAY NEED TO RESORT TO FORCE.
IN THAT EVENT, I'LL BE COUNTING ON YOU, KURÔ-SENPAI. THANK YOU IN ADVANCE.

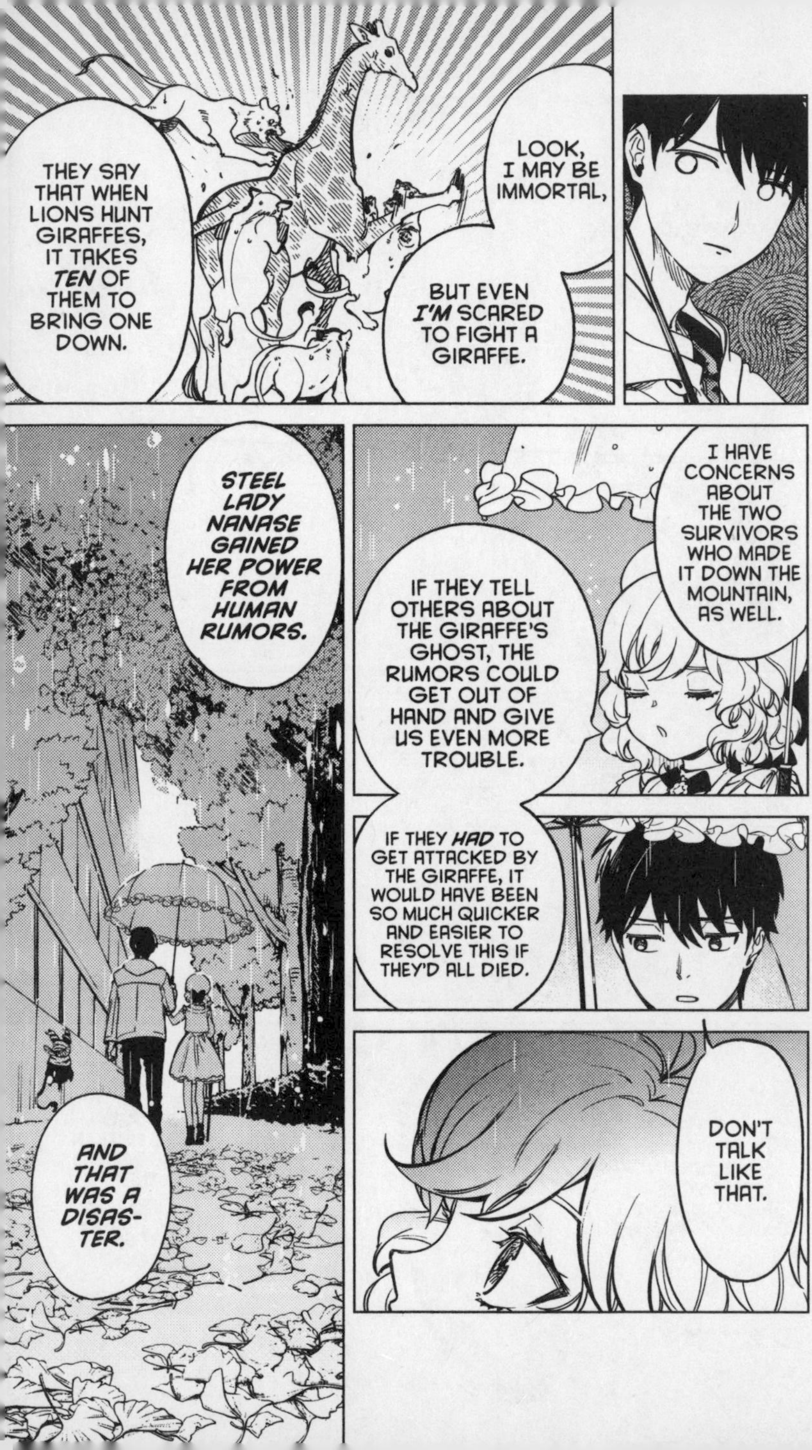
LOOK, I MAY BE IMMORTAL,
BUT EVEN *I'M* SCARED TO FIGHT A GIRAFFE.
THEY SAY THAT WHEN LIONS HUNT GIRAFFES, IT TAKES *TEN* OF THEM TO BRING ONE DOWN.
I HAVE CONCERNS ABOUT THE TWO SURVIVORS WHO MADE IT DOWN THE MOUNTAIN, AS WELL.
IF THEY TELL OTHERS ABOUT THE GIRAFFE'S GHOST, THE RUMORS COULD GET OUT OF HAND AND GIVE US EVEN MORE TROUBLE.
IF THEY *HAD* TO GET ATTACKED BY THE GIRAFFE, IT WOULD HAVE BEEN SO MUCH QUICKER AND EASIER TO RESOLVE THIS IF THEY'D ALL DIED.
DON'T TALK LIKE THAT.
STEEL LADY NANASE GAINED HER POWER FROM HUMAN RUMORS.
AND THAT WAS A DISASTER.

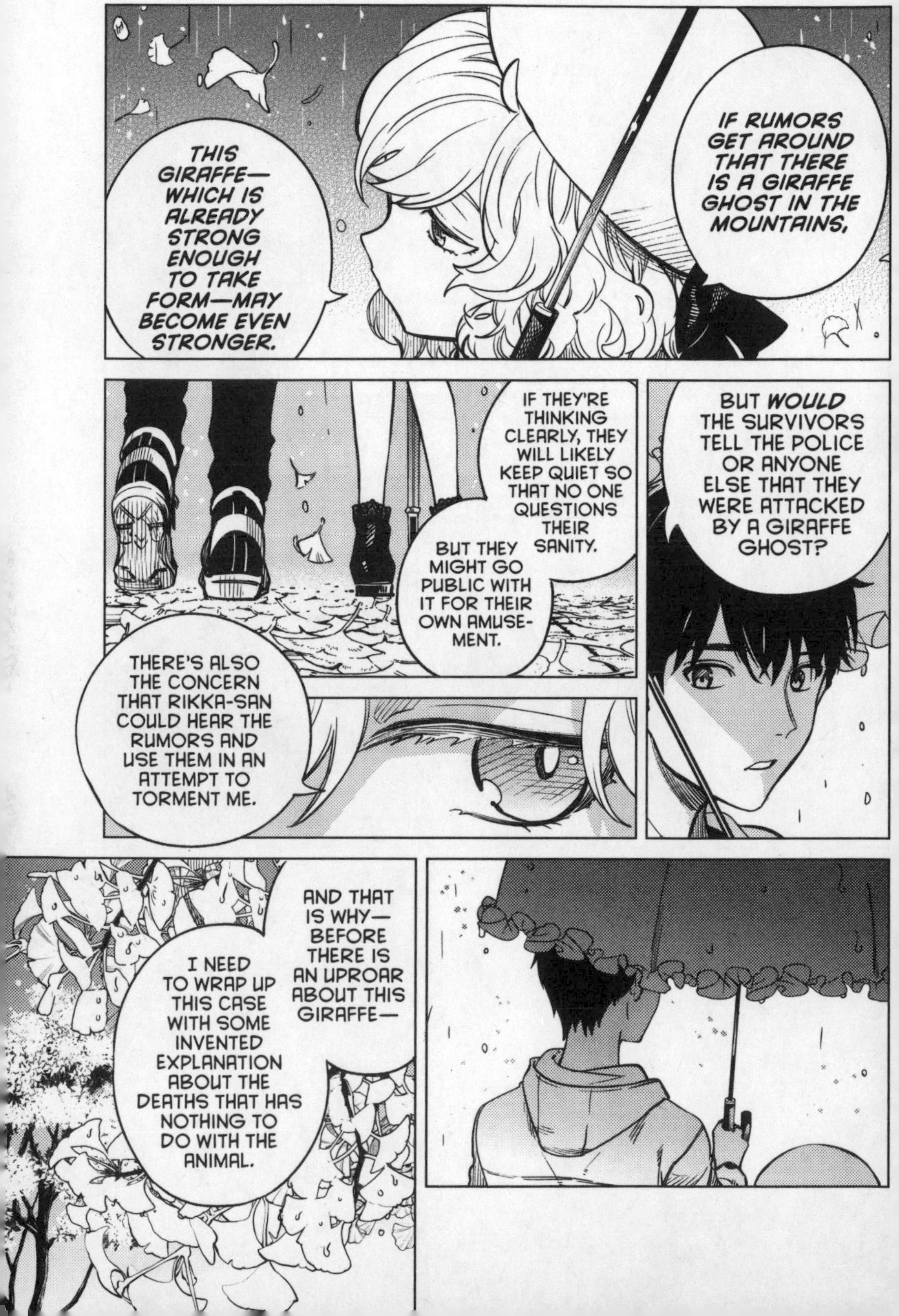
IF RUMORS GET AROUND THAT THERE IS A GIRAFFE GHOST IN THE MOUNTAINS,
THIS GIRAFFE—WHICH IS ALREADY STRONG ENOUGH TO TAKE FORM—MAY BECOME EVEN STRONGER.
BUT WOULD THE SURVIVORS TELL THE POLICE OR ANYONE ELSE THAT THEY WERE ATTACKED BY A GIRAFFE GHOST?
IF THEY'RE THINKING CLEARLY, THEY WILL LIKELY KEEP QUIET SO THAT NO ONE QUESTIONS THEIR SANITY.
BUT THEY MIGHT GO PUBLIC WITH IT FOR THEIR OWN AMUSE-MENT.
THERE'S ALSO THE CONCERN THAT RIKKA-SAN COULD HEAR THE RUMORS AND USE THEM IN AN ATTEMPT TO TORMENT ME.
AND THAT IS WHY—BEFORE THERE IS AN UPROAR ABOUT THIS GIRAFFE—
I NEED TO WRAP UP THIS CASE WITH SOME INVENTED EXPLANATION ABOUT THE DEATHS THAT HAS NOTHING TO DO WITH THE ANIMAL.

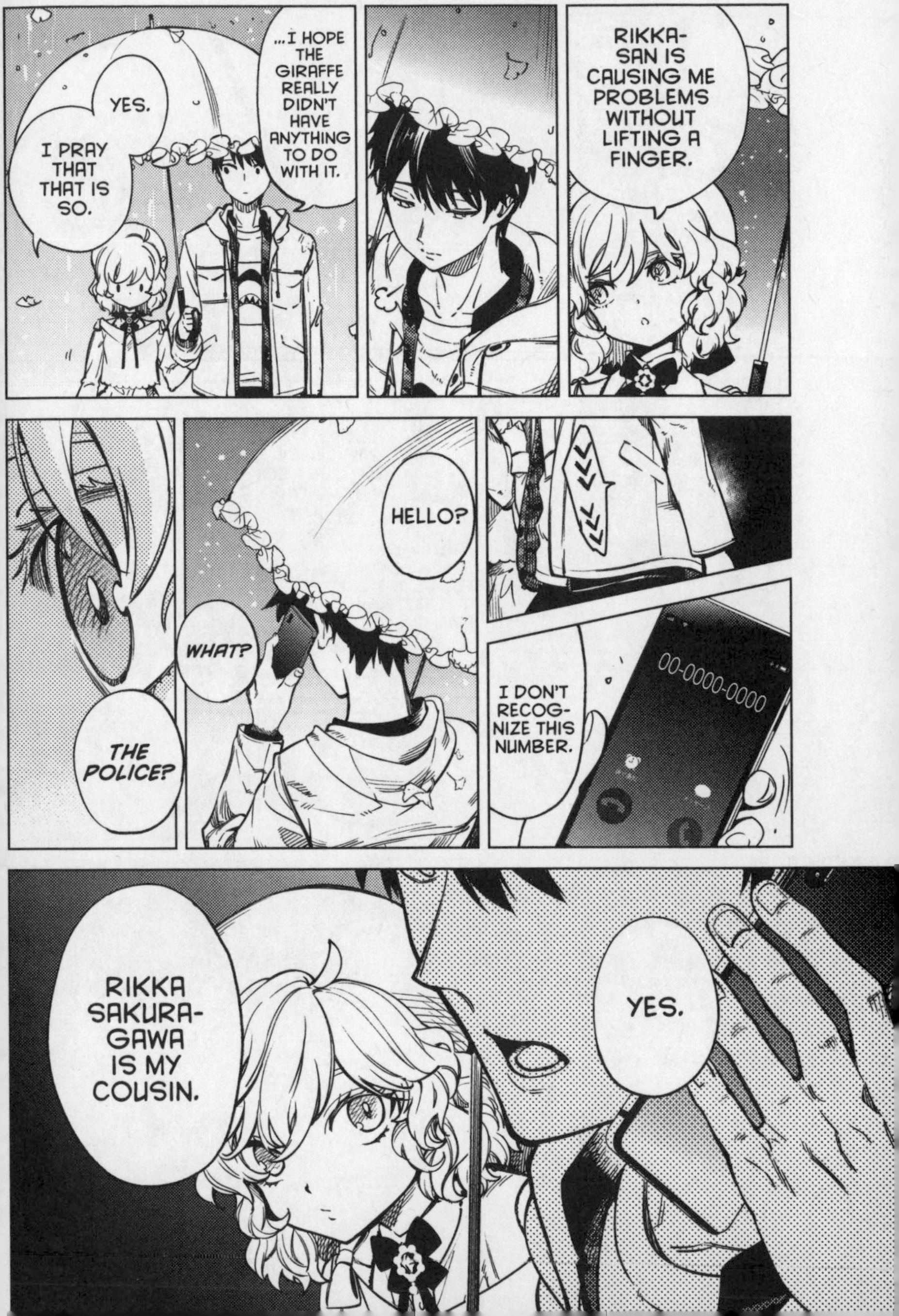
RIKKA-SAN IS CAUSING ME PROBLEMS WITHOUT LIFTING A FINGER.
...I HOPE THE GIRAFFE REALLY DIDN'T HAVE ANYTHING TO DO WITH IT.
YES.
I PRAY THAT THAT IS SO.
00-0000-0000
I DON'T RECOGNIZE THIS NUMBER.
HELLO?
WHAT?
THE POLICE?
YES.
RIKKA SAKURAGAWA IS MY COUSIN.

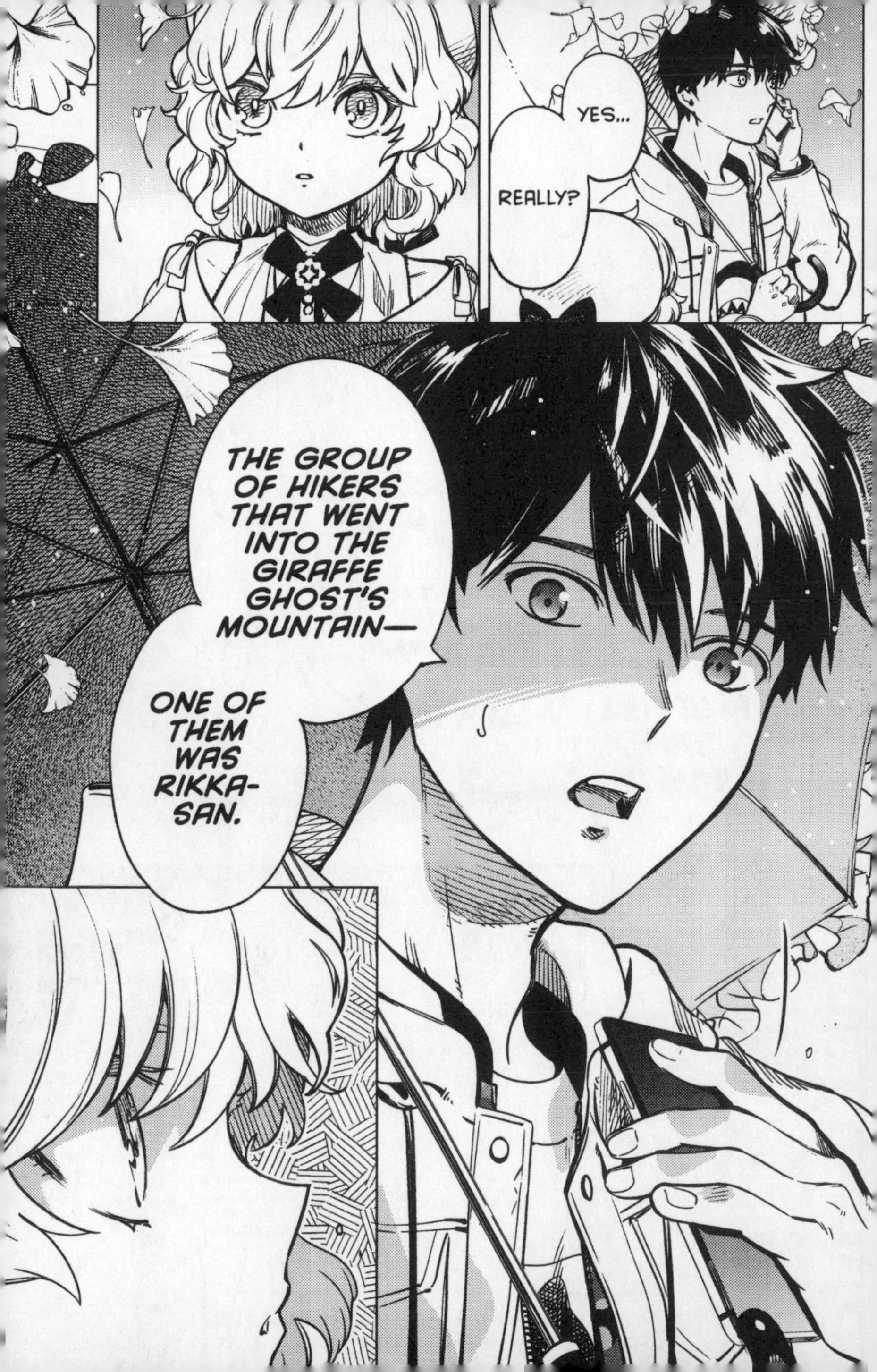
YES...
REALLY?
THE GROUP OF HIKERS THAT WENT INTO THE GIRAFFE GHOST'S MOUNTAIN—
ONE OF THEM WAS RIKKA-SAN.

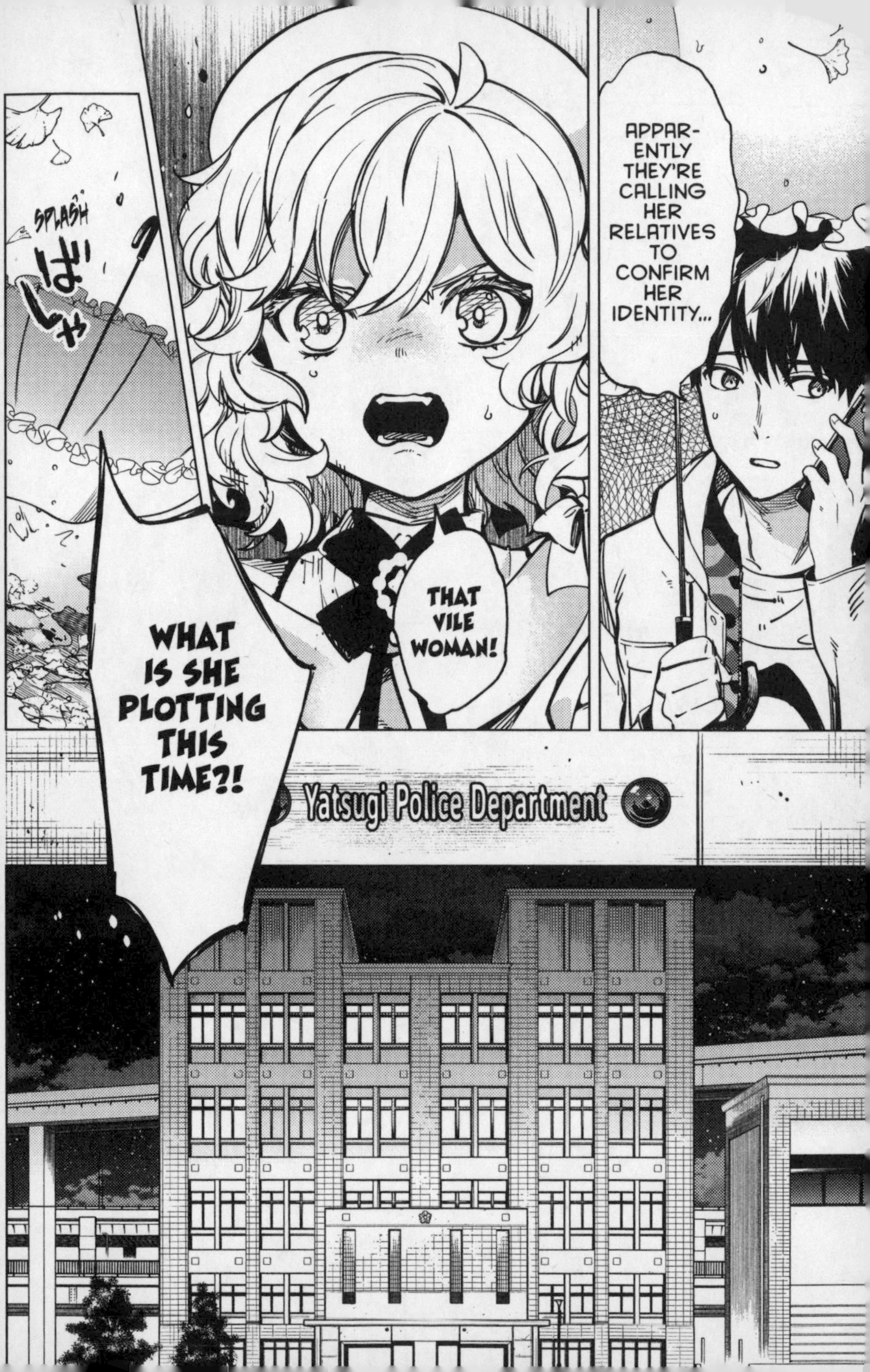
APPARENTLY THEY'RE CALLING HER RELATIVES TO CONFIRM HER IDENTITY...
THAT VILE WOMAN!
SPLASH
ばしゃ
WHAT IS SHE PLOTTING THIS TIME?!
Yatsugi Police Department

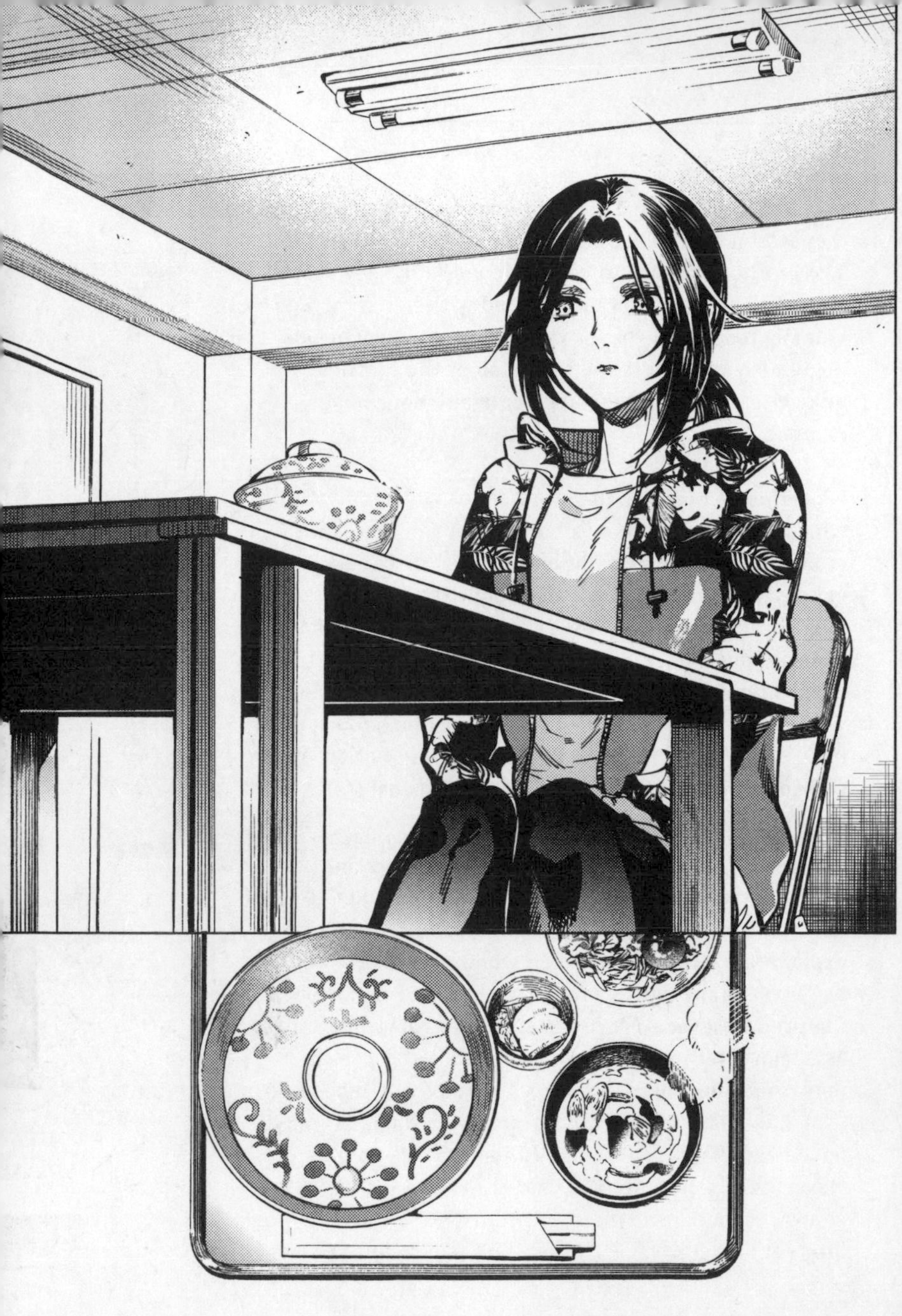

◆ TO BE CONTINUED IN VOLUME 15

About the Common Sense the Author Agonizes Over

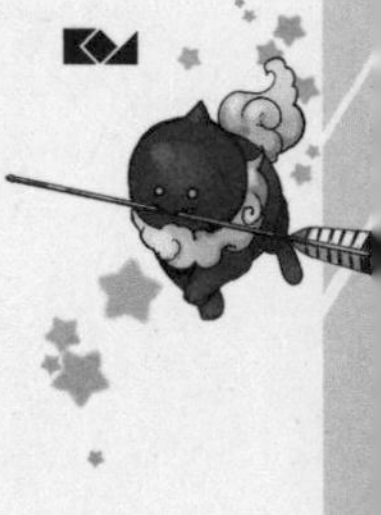

I am Kyo Shirodaira. This is volume 14. This time we focused on Rikka-san, but she doesn't truly return to the story until after the "to be continued." I'm very sorry. Iwanaga and Kurô will be reunited with her soon, and you might say that that's where the real story begins. You might also say that it seems like all of the plotting will be over by the time they see her again, so, as usual, it's complicated.

Now, this volume has the story about Ôoka judgments, which I wrote as kind of a bonus chapter. Many of the stories about him were either made up or tweaked versions of stories from other countries, so Ôoka judgments lean heavily towards fiction. Be that as it may, Ôoka Echizen-no-kami Tadanosuke really did exist, and he was popular among the common people, which is why such stories were made up about him, so you can't necessarily write them all off as complete fiction. When someone is famous, embellished stories come with the territory.

And I write that as if I'm some kind of expert, but depending on the person, Ôoka judgments and Ôoka Echizen may be familiar enough that they require no explanation, and you might be wondering why I would use up so many words on him. Ôoka Echizen has been featured in several TV dramas, and he sometimes appears as a character in novels and manga. Mystery fans may remember the short story "*Korosareta Ten'ichibô* (The Execution of Ten'ichibô)" by Shirô Hamao (I may have used that story as inspiration for this volume). Nevertheless, he's not the kind of person that will always show up in Japanese history lessons, so if you have no interest in historical TV drama and you're not familiar

with historical novels, it's possible you've never heard of the guy.
When writing stories, I end up wondering how much I need to explain.
I can imagine that something that's obvious to me may not make any
sense to the reader (depending on the reader), and in this day and age
with all the diverse interests and lifestyles, it is extremely difficult to
gauge how much background information the reader will need.

For this story, too, I think it would have been very clever to just make
sure to bring up the term "Ôoka judgment" early on, then have one
of the competitors try to win the archery challenge with the same
logic from the Ôoka Judgment without explaining the story about
the women fighting over the child. Anyone who knows about Ôoka
judgments would see what I did. And I can see where giving a specific
example ahead of time might make the story too predictable and ruin
its pacing.

But I can't deny the fact that anyone who doesn't know the story
would have a hard time understanding why it turned out that way.
So that's why I decided to include an explanation in the story, but
it's something I still agonize about. To balance it out, I also included
explanations for William Tell and Nasu no Yoichi in the novel version.
I feel like I need to explain Nasu no Yoichi, but maybe not William Tell.
I'm not quite sure. I mean, it's not entirely unthinkable that, in the
future, there won't be any giraffes in zoos, and the people of the time
will be so unfamiliar with the species that a detailed explanation about
it would be necessary.

In the next volume, Rikka-san will likely be calling the shots. How will
Iwanaga meet her defeat? Well, I hope to see you again.

Kyo Shirodaira

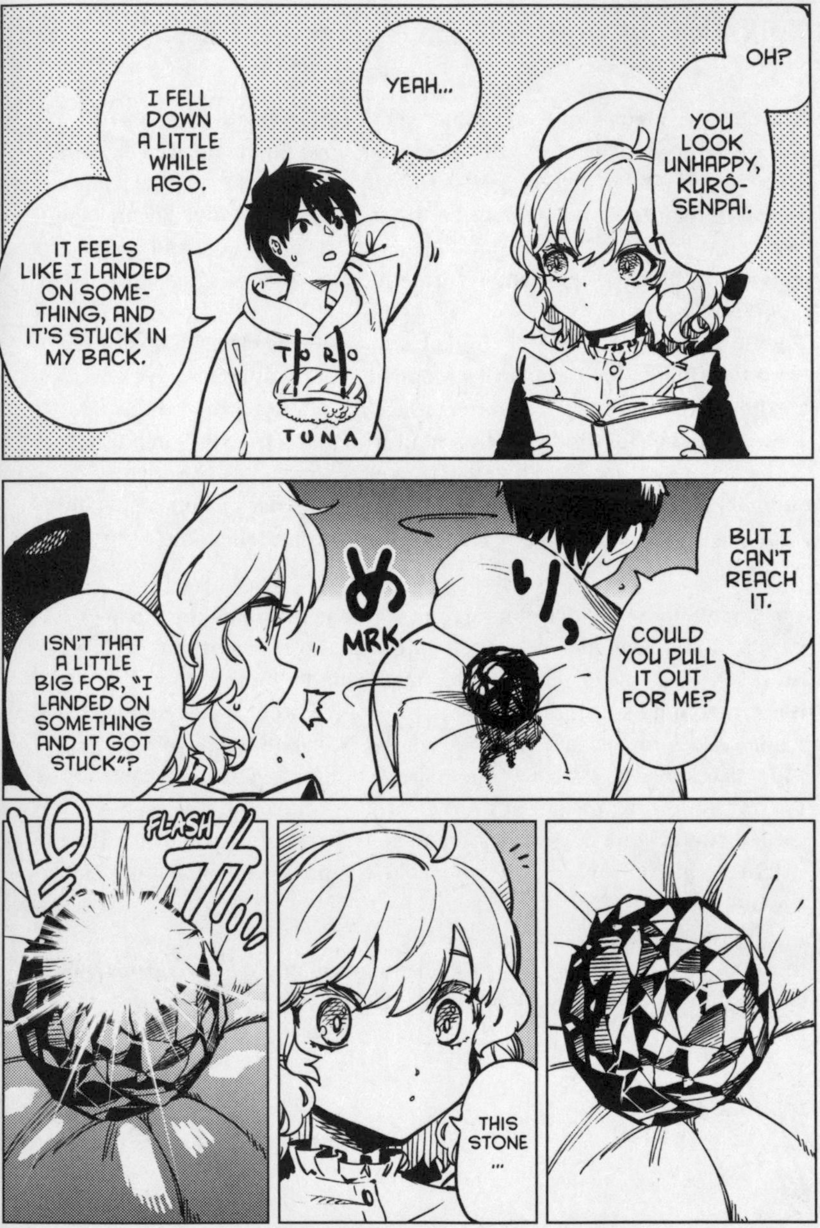
OH?
YOU LOOK UNHAPPY, KURÔ-SENPAI.
YEAH...
TO RO
TUNA
I FELL DOWN A LITTLE WHILE AGO.
IT FEELS LIKE I LANDED ON SOME-THING, AND IT'S STUCK IN MY BACK.
BUT I CAN'T REACH IT.
COULD YOU PULL IT OUT FOR ME?
MRK
ISN'T THAT A LITTLE BIG FOR, "I LANDED ON SOMETHING AND IT GOT STUCK"?
THIS STONE ...
FLASH

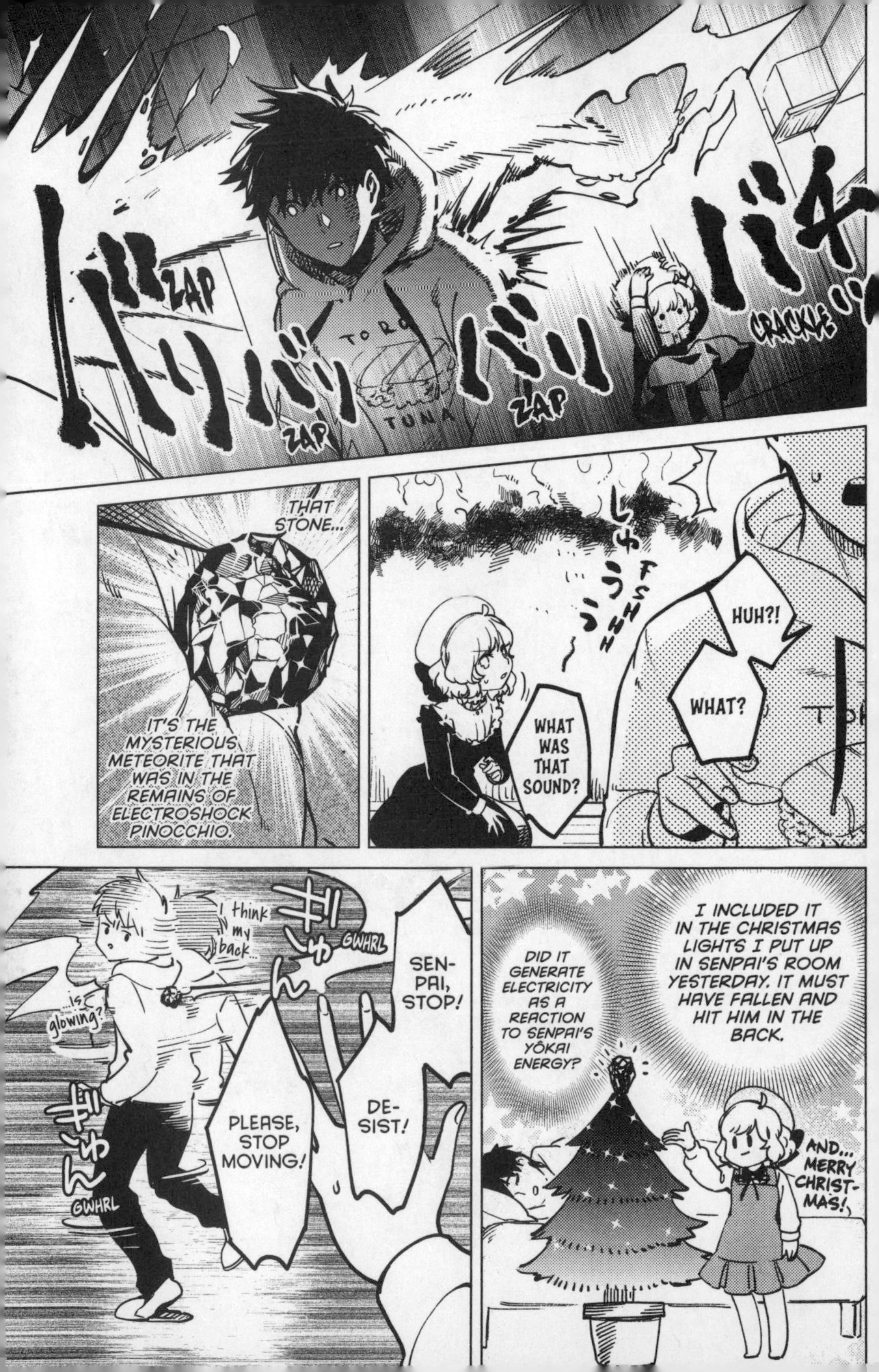
ZAP
ZAP
ZAP
CRACKLE
HUH?!
WHAT?
FSHHH
WHAT WAS THAT SOUND?
THAT STONE...
IT'S THE MYSTERIOUS METEORITE THAT WAS IN THE REMAINS OF ELECTROSHOCK PINOCCHIO.
I INCLUDED IT IN THE CHRISTMAS LIGHTS I PUT UP IN SENPAI'S ROOM YESTERDAY. IT MUST HAVE FALLEN AND HIT HIM IN THE BACK.
DID IT GENERATE ELECTRICITY AS A REACTION TO SENPAI'S YÔKAI ENERGY?
AND... MERRY CHRIST-MAS!
SEN-PAI, STOP!
GWHRL
I think my back...
...is glowing?
DE-SIST!
PLEASE, STOP MOVING!
GWHRL

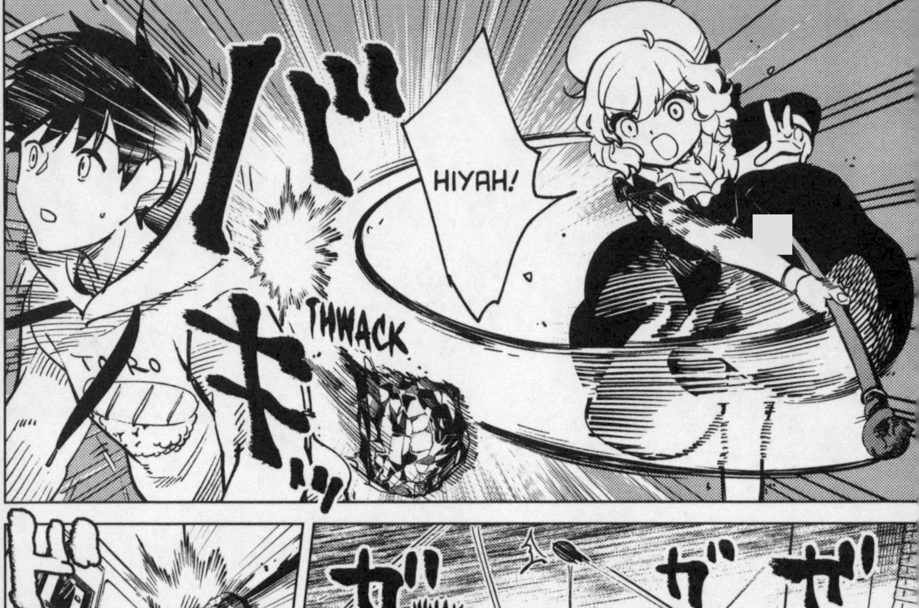
HIYAH!
THWACK
WHAK
WHAK
WHAK
WHAK
WHAK
WHAK
KAPOW
Breaker

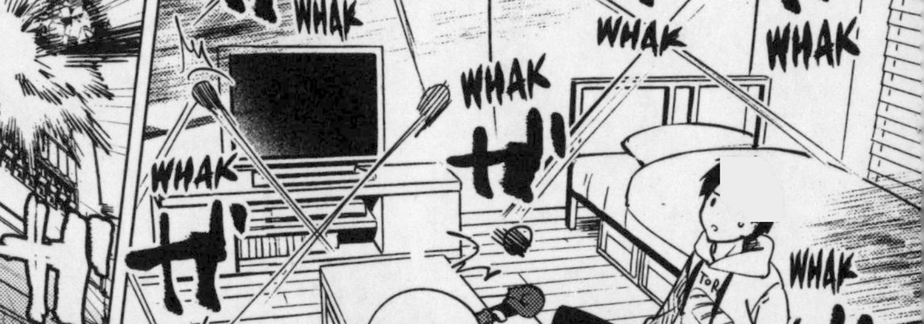
SPUTT
SPUTT
...IT STOPPED.
WHEW
AND SO DID MY APARTMENT'S POWER.
Good grief.
ZAP
FIN

Thank you for picking up volume 14! I hope you'll read the next one, too.

- Staff
Asai
Shimameguri
Gomakurô

- Editors
O-kawa
T-da

(honorifics excluded)

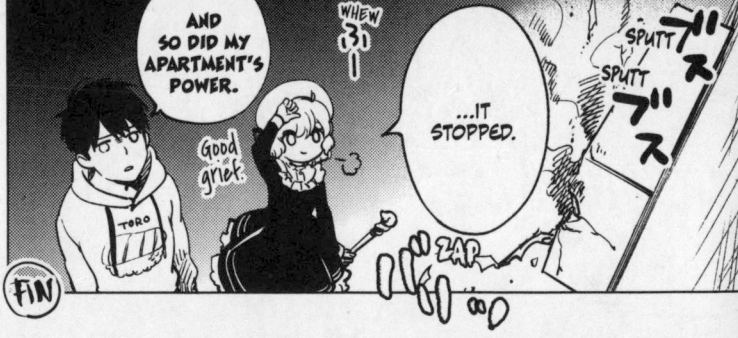

A VERY "SPECIAL" MANGA, CELEBRATING ITS NEW ANIME!

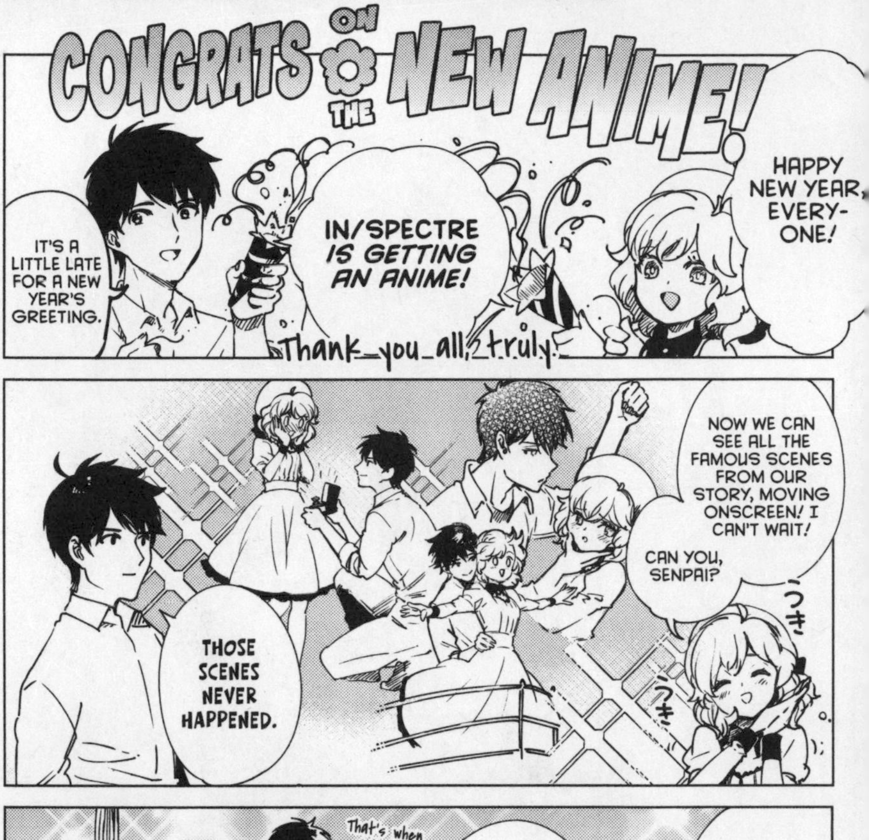
CONGRATS ON THE NEW ANIME!
HAPPY NEW YEAR, EVERY-ONE!
IN/SPECTRE IS GETTING AN ANIME!
IT'S A LITTLE LATE FOR A NEW YEAR'S GREETING.
Thank you all, truly.
NOW WE CAN SEE ALL THE FAMOUS SCENES FROM OUR STORY, MOVING ONSCREEN! I CAN'T WAIT!
CAN YOU, SENPAI?
うき
うき
THOSE SCENES NEVER HAPPENED.
BUT THEY MIGHT WANT TO CENSOR THE BEDROOM SCENES.
AND THE MANGA VERSION IS HIGHLY ACCLAIMED FOR PRESENTING ALL THE MOUNTAINS OF EXPOSITION IN THE FORM OF PILLOW TALK.
TO THINK IT WOULD BACKFIRE ON US LIKE THIS.
That's when a kappa showed up right there in front of us...
WE PRESENTED THEM IN NO SUCH WAY.

*NOTE: THIS PAGE WAS FIRST PUBLISHED IN *MAGAZINE R* ISSUE 1, PUBLISHED FEBRUARY 2019.

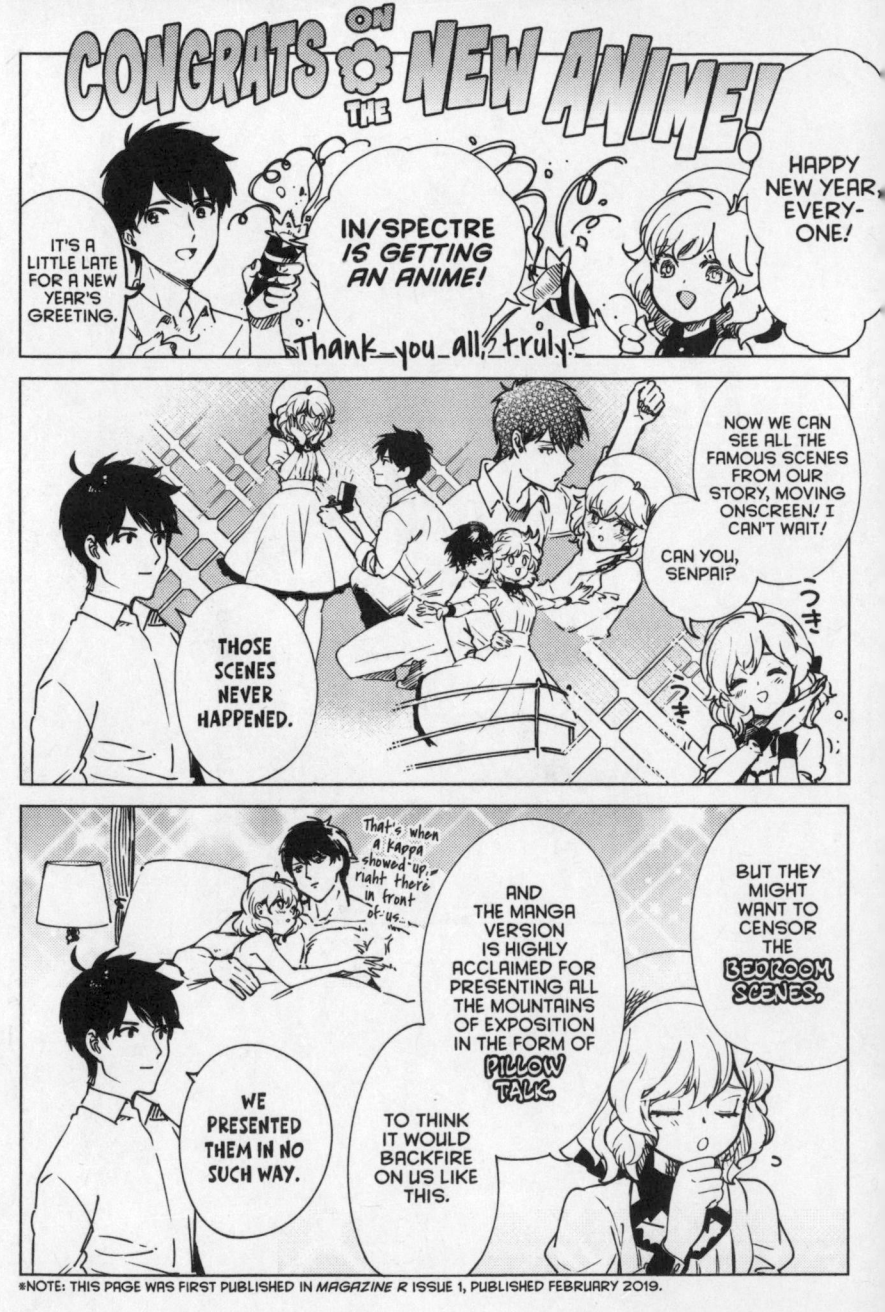

IN/SPECTRE

TRANSLATION NOTES

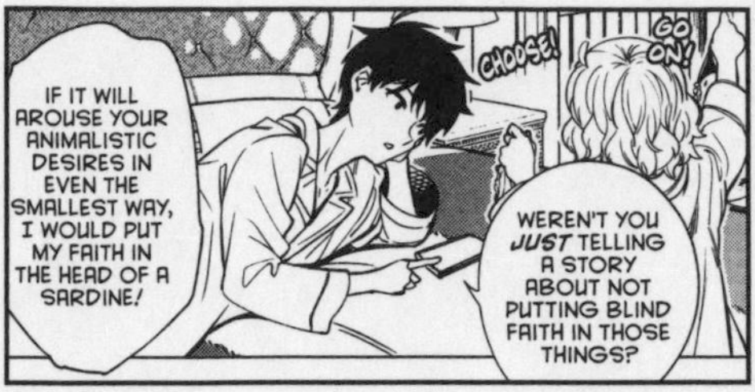
GO ON!
CHOOSE!
IF IT WILL AROUSE YOUR ANIMALISTIC DESIRES IN EVEN THE SMALLEST WAY, I WOULD PUT MY FAITH IN THE HEAD OF A SARDINE!
WEREN'T YOU *JUST* TELLING A STORY ABOUT NOT PUTTING BLIND FAITH IN THOSE THINGS?

Put my faith in the head of a sardine, page 77

Here, Kotoko refers to a Japanese saying that translates as, "People believe in the head of a sardine, after all," and means that even something as insignificant as a sardine's head can have great significance to someone who believes in it. The choice of sardine head is a reference to a tradition from the Japanese holiday of Setsubun, which celebrates the coming of spring. One of the traditions of this holiday is to make a talisman out of a sardine's head and some holly, or *hiiragi*, and pinning it to a house's entrance to ward off evil spirits.

Nasu no Yoichi and William Tell, page 83

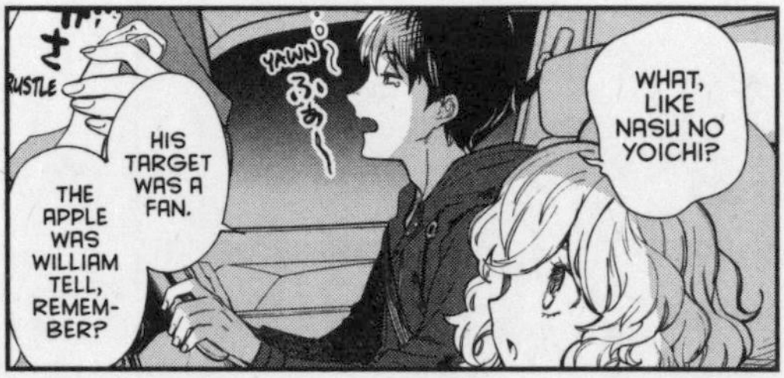
WHAT, LIKE NASU NO YOICHI?
YAWN
ふぁ〜
HIS TARGET WAS A FAN.
THE APPLE WAS WILLIAM TELL, REMEMBER?
さ
RUSTLE

During the Genpei Wars, at the Battle of Yashima, the Taira clan tied a folding fan to the mast of one of their ships and dared the Minamoto side to shoot it down from the shore. In the most famous feat of archery in Japanese history, Nasu no Yoichi rode his horse into the waves and hit the moving target with his first shot.

William Tell is a Swiss folk hero, also known for his excellent marksmanship. He offended a government official, and was sentenced to death along with his son. But the official was intrigued by tales of Tell's marksmanship, and so offered to spare Tell's life if he could shoot an apple off of his son's head in one attempt. Needless to say, he succeeded.

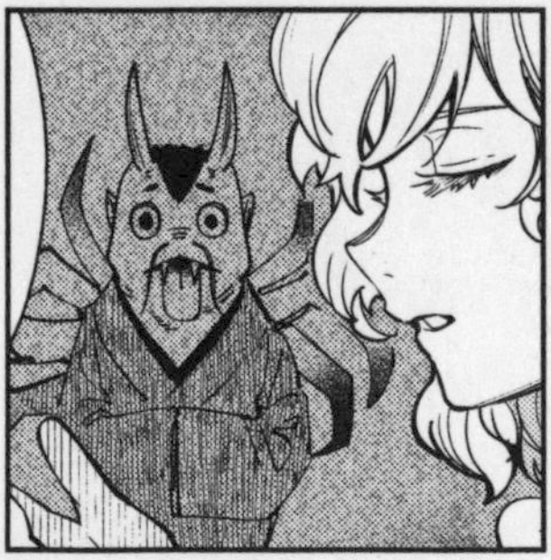

Yanari, page 105

Roughly translating to "sound made by a house," a Yanari is the yōkai that causes furniture and other household objects to shake for no discernible reason. It's basically the Japanese version of a poltergeist, which is German for "rumble ghost."

Kirin and giraffe, page 129

In Japan, the word *kirin* has been used for "giraffe" for more than 200 years. The first recorded usage was from 1799, on a diagram drawn by physician and scholar Katsuragawa Hoshû. It is believed that, when he drew his diagram, he had not actually seen a giraffe, but was instead basing it off of drawings by Polish scholar and physician John Johnston. These drawings do bear a resemblance to the *kirin* of legend depicted in the manga.

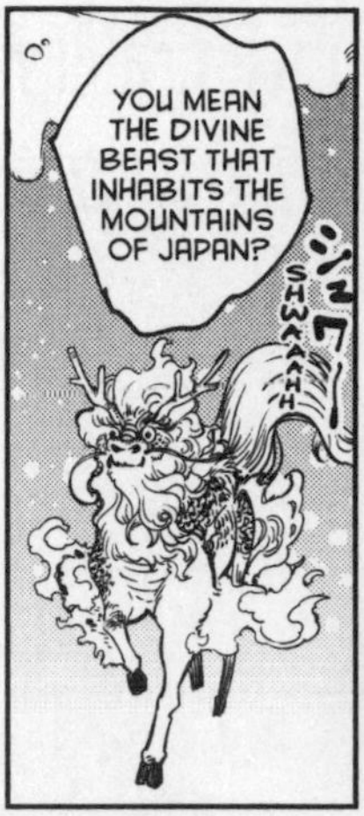
YOU MEAN THE DIVINE BEAST THAT INHABITS THE MOUNTAINS OF JAPAN?
SHWAAAHH

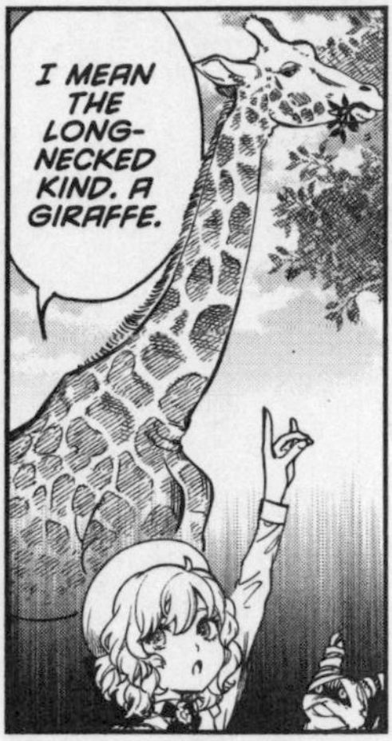
I MEAN THE LONG-NECKED KIND. A GIRAFFE.

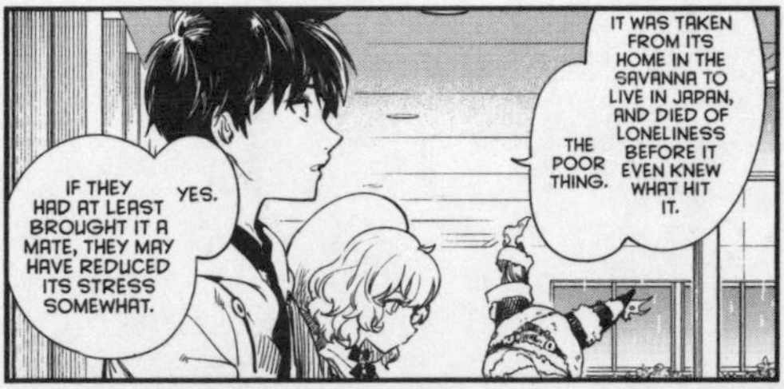
IT WAS TAKEN FROM ITS HOME IN THE SAVANNA TO LIVE IN JAPAN, AND DIED OF LONELINESS BEFORE IT EVEN KNEW WHAT HIT IT.
THE POOR THING.
YES.
IF THEY HAD AT LEAST BROUGHT IT A MATE, THEY MAY HAVE REDUCED ITS STRESS SOMEWHAT.

The giraffe's sad tale, page 131

Kotoko's story about the first live giraffe in Japan differs from the official history, but is remarkably similar. In 1907, the Ueno Zoo (a zoo that still exists to this day) imported a pair of giraffes from Germany. The giraffes were indeed very popular, and they did also die shortly after their arrival in Japan, due to troubles keeping their new enclosure sufficiently warm for the giraffes to survive winter in a colder climate.

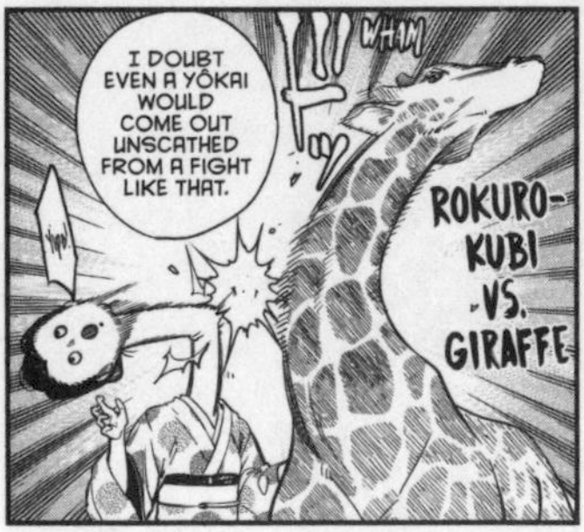
WHAM
ROKURO-KUBI -VS.- GIRAFFE
I DOUBT EVEN A YÔKAI WOULD COME OUT UNSCATHED FROM A FIGHT LIKE THAT.

Rokuro-Kubi, page 137

As the picture suggests, a Rokuro-Kubi ("Pulley Neck"), is a long-necked yôkai. These yôkai appear as normal women by day, while their necks will stretch and their heads wander by night.

Young characters and steampunk setting, like *Howl's Moving Castle* and *Battle Angel Alita*

Beyond the Clouds © 2018 Nicke / Ki-oon

A boy with a talent for machines and a mysterious girl whose wings he's fixed will take you beyond the clouds! In the tradition of the high-flying, resonant adventure stories of Studio Ghibli comes a gorgeous tale about the longing of young hearts for adventure and friendship!

The boys are back, in 400-page hardcovers that are as pretty and badass as they are!

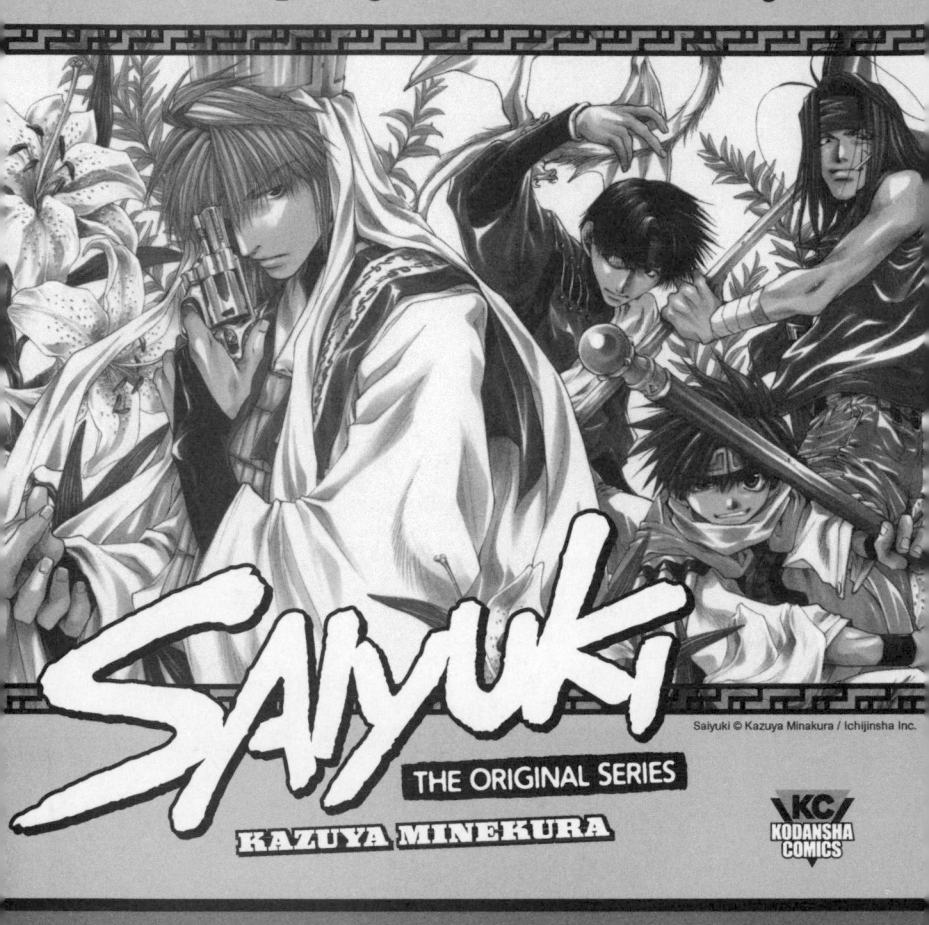

Saiyuki © Kazuya Minakura / Ichijinsha Inc.

SAIYUKI
THE ORIGINAL SERIES
KAZUYA MINEKURA

KC KODANSHA COMICS

"AN EDGY COMIC LOOK AT AN ANCIENT CHINESE TALE." —YALSA

Genjo Sanzo is a Buddhist priest in the city of Togenkyo, which is being ravaged by yokai spirits that have fallen out of balance with the natural order. His superiors send him on a journey far to the west to discover why this is happening and how to stop it. His companions are three yokai with human souls. But this is no day trip — the four will encounter many discoveries and horrors on the way.

FEATURES NEW TRANSLATION, COLOR PAGES, AND BEAUTIFUL WRAPAROUND COVER ART!

In/Spectre 14 is a work of fiction. Names, characters, places, and incidents are the products of the author's imagination or are used fictitiously. Any resemblance to actual events, locales, or persons, living or dead, is entirely coincidental.

A Kodansha Comics Trade Paperback Original
In/Spectre 14 copyright © 2020 Kyo Shirodaira/Chashiba Katase
English translation copyright © 2021 Kyo Shirodaira/Chashiba Katase

Published in the United States by Kodansha Comics, an imprint of
Kodansha USA Publishing, LLC, New York.

Publication rights for this English edition arranged through
Kodansha Ltd., Tokyo.

First published in Japan in 2020 by Kodansha Ltd., Tokyo
as *Kyokou Suiri*, volume 14.

ISBN 978-1-64651-279-9

Original cover design by Takashi Shimoyama and Mami Fukunaga (RedRooster)

Printed in the United States of America.

www.kodansha.us

9 8 7 6 5 4 3 2 1

Translation: Alethea Nibley & Athena Nibley
Lettering: Lys Blakeslee
Editing: Vanessa Tenazas
Kodansha Comics edition cover design by Phil Balsman

Publisher: Kiichiro Sugawara

Director of publishing services: Ben Applegate
Associate director of operations: Stephen Pakula
Publishing services managing editors: Alanna Ruse, Madison Salters
Production managers: Emi Lotto, Angela Zurlo